Critical Essays on
Simone de Beauvoir

Critical Essays on
World Literature

Robert Lecker, General Editor
McGill University

Critical Essays on Simone de Beauvoir

Elaine Marks

G. K. Hall & Co. • Boston, Massachusetts

Library of Congress Cataloging in Publication Data

Critical essays on Simone de Beauvoir.

  (Critical essays on world literature)
  Includes index.
  2. Beauvoir, Simone de, 1908– —Criticism and interpretation.
  I. Marks, Elaine. II. Series.
PQ2603.E362Z64 1987 848'.91409 86-33539
ISBN 0-8161-8836-X (alk. paper)

This publication is printed on permanent/durable acid-free paper
MANUFACTURED IN THE UNITED STATES OF AMERICA

To Germaine Brée

CONTENTS

PREFACE

Simone de Beauvoir — teacher, philosopher, political activist, writer, autobiographer, essayist, journalist, novelist, playwright, atheist, existentialist, and feminist — died in Paris at the age of seventy-eight on 14 April 1986. The obituaries that followed her death, both in France and in the United States, emphasized two aspects of her life and work: her relationship to Jean-Paul Sartre, who had died six years earlier — almost to the very day, as several commentators noted — and the publication in 1949 of *The Second Sex*, her two-volume inquiry into the ways in which women, particularly although not exclusively in Western culture, are constructed. In these newspaper accounts Jean-Paul Sartre was viewed as the indispensable source both of her desire to write and of the direction of her writing; *The Second Sex* was seen as her most significant work because, so the reasoning went, it was to have an impact on the women's liberation movements and on feminist theory and practice of the late 1960s and early 1970s. And in writing about women, some critics insisted, Simone de Beauvoir was at last on her own, no longer in the shadow of Jean-Paul Sartre.

It would be unwise to belabor the questionable status of some of these statements. They are, in themselves, a significant comment on the significance of Simone de Beauvoir. It would be more profitable, for our purposes, to begin by redirecting the emphasis on her contribution as a writer and activist to a more contextual perusal of the critical reception of her writings: the twenty-five books that she published between *She Came to Stay* in 1943 and *Adieux* in 1981. *Critical Essays on Simone de Beauvoir* reproduces, both as a microcosm and as a spectrum, those articles and reviews that represent significant and/or outstanding textual moments in the study of Simone de Beauvoir by critics in Canada, France, Great Britain, and the United States.

There are two areas in which *Critical Essays on Simone de Beauvoir* presents a special set of problems. The first of these is that the critical material included here predates Simone de Beauvoir's death. There is usually a noticeable shift in emphasis in critical texts written after the death of a writer, and this volume cannot record that shift. The second and perhaps more serious problem is that Simone de Beauvoir is a French writer. The question of translation has been a central one in the preparation of this volume. Because of the delicate issue of sexism in language use, I have made certain decisions, with the agreement of the individual translators, that weaken the emphasis on gender in French. I have, for example, consistently referred to the novelist or writer as "she" in order to avoid the political incorrectness of the generic he/him and the aesthetically awkward compromise of he/she or the conflation of a singular noun and verb with a plural pronoun, as in "they" or "their." The difficulty is that in certain translated texts there is now a discrepancy between the aggressive and polemical tone of the narrative voice attacking Simone de Beauvoir and the marked presence, produced by this same narrative voice, of feminine pronouns constantly linked with the word "writer." (To ease the translation problem I have included a list of Simone de Beauvoir's major texts, followed by the most widely available and accurate English translations.)

Where bibliographical research is concerned, no one works alone. There are several volumes that are indispensable to any scholarly project concerning Simone de Beauvoir, and these I have assiduously consulted. One of the most useful resources is the annotated bibliography prepared by Anne-Marie Lasocki for *A Critical Bibliography of French Literature*, vol. 6, edited by Douglas W. Alden and Richard A. Brooks (1980). Her bibliography contains material written between 1945 and 1975. Although it is not, and does not claim to be, complete, the sixteen book-length studies written about Simone de Beauvoir within that period in French and English are represented. In Anne-Marie Lasocki's own study, *Simone de Beauvoir ou l'entreprise d'écrire* (1971), she includes in her bibliography articles in English, German, Italian, Polish, and Spanish as well as in French. There is also a bibliographical inventory both of Simone de Beauvoir's own texts and of texts written about Simone de Beauvoir and her writing in Claire Cayron's *La Nature chez Simone de Beauvoir* (1973). Anne Whitmarsh, in her *Simone de Beauvoir and the Limits of Commitment* (1981), picks up where Claire Cayron leaves off and gives us a comprehensive list of articles and books on Simone de Beauvoir since 1970 as well as a list of books that contain essential background material.

Two of the most useful bibliographical studies focus on the writings of Jean-Paul Sartre and Simone de Beauvoir, respectively. There are numerous annotations concerning Simone de Beauvoir in Michel Contat and Michel Rybalka, *Les écrits de Sartre* (1970). Using a similar model, Claude Francis and Fernande Gontier published *Les écrits de Simone de Beauvoir* (1979), an indispensable volume that provides a detailed chronology of Simone de Beauvoir's life and writing including her comments on her own work, the publishing and translation history of each work, and over three hundred pages of texts that have never before been published in French. Claude Francis and Fernande Gontier are also the authors of a biography entitled *Simone de Beauvoir* and published in 1985. This biography, although repudiated by Simone de Beauvoir, relies heavily on the four volumes of her autobiography, *Memoirs of a Dutiful Daughter* (1958), *The Prime of Life* (1960), *Force of Circumstance* (1963), and *All Said and Done* (1972), as well as on her two autobiographical texts, *A Very Easy Death* (1964), an account of her mother's illness and death, and *Adieux* (1981), an account of the last ten years of Jean-Paul Sartre's life and his death. The biography also contains significant new material relating to the financial ruin of Simone de Beauvoir's maternal grandfather, Gustave Brasseur, and information and commentary culled from the 1,682 pages of an unpublished correspondence written by Simone de Beauvoir to the writer Nelson Algren between 1947 and 1960. I would also like to acknowledge the existence of the *Simone de Beauvoir Society Newsletter*, edited by Yolanda Astarita Patterson, which keeps subscribers informed about publications, conferences, and other activities relating to Simone de Beauvoir, and to the Simone de Beauvoir Institute at Concordia University in Canada.

The body of critical studies that exists in 1986 on the life and the work of Simone de Beauvoir is, as one might expect, partial and biased, partial in the sense that critics concentrate on certain works or themes to the exclusion of others and biased in the sense that critics are obsessively concerned with the differences between Simone de Beauvoir's attitudes toward religion, marriage, motherhood, death, or politics and their own. Within this corpus of critical studies I would like to acknowledge three general, introductory studies to the writings of Simone de Beauvoir: Robert Cottrell, *Simone de Beauvoir* (1975), Konrad Bieber, *Simone de Beauvoir* (1979), and Terry Keefe, *Simone de Beauvoir: A Study of Her Writings* (1983). Each of these books succeeds in covering most of Simone de Beauvoir's writings, in suggesting interesting readings of individual texts, and in raising questions of connections between texts and contexts that are essential to any preliminary investigation. The absence of extracts from these studies in this volume is a tribute to the rigorous manner in which the chapters in these three books hold together within a tightly knit structure. Of the thirty books devoted exclusively to the writings of Simone de Beauvoir since Geneviève Gennari's *Simone de Beauvoir* (1958), only one, Francis Jeanson's *Simone de Beauvoir ou l'entreprise de vivre* (1966), is represented in my selection. For reasons that also involve length, coherence, and quality, articles and essays, usually more difficult to locate than books, seemed a more appropriate choice for this collection.

And there is more to come. Deirdre Bair's authorized biography of Simone de Beauvoir will be published in the United States by Summit Books of Simon and Schuster. Future publications also include a special issue of *Yale French Studies* on Simone de Beauvoir, edited by Hélène V. Wenzel, and a collection of Lorraine Hansberry's prose to be edited by Robert Nemiroff. This collection will contain an essay by Lorraine

Hansberry entitled "Simone de Beauvoir and *The Second Sex*: An American Commentary, 1957."

To conclude, I would like to thank Yvonne Rochette Ozzello for her valuable assistance in reviewing the introduction and the translation of essays by René Etiemble and Béatrice Slama. I would like to acknowledge my dependence on Amy Scarr, research assistant extraordinaire. Her commitment to the project and her meticulous attention to detail in the preparation of this manuscript elevate bibliographical, clerical, and editorial assistance and practice to the level of an art.

INTRODUCTION

In the conclusion to her provocative study *Simone de Beauvoir: A Feminist Mandarin* (1985), Mary Evans writes:

> Given the extent of de Beauvoir's work and the attention that it has attracted, it might be expected that critics and defenders would be numerous. However, the secondary literature on de Beauvoir is both limited and curiously muted in its criticism. For feminist critics, this could be explained by an unwillingness to challenge or criticize the work of a woman who has contributed an enormous amount to the development of feminism. But others besides feminists have been equally unforthcoming in their discussion of de Beauvoir. Part of this lack of interest can be explained by the traditional sexism of many academic and literary critics: because de Beauvoir has written (although by no means exclusively) about women it is quite acceptable to dismiss her work as "merely" about women. Women, and women who write about women, are easy to dismiss as outside the consideration of a serious-minded critic.[1]

I would like to address the two major questions raised by Mary Evans: why has there been relatively little serious criticism on Simone de Beauvoir's writing, and why has there been so little critical debate? In approaching these questions, it is instructive to look also at the secondary literature that discusses the work of other women writers who belong more or less to Simone de Beauvoir's generation and to determine whether the same queries might apply to them. And indeed it is striking to note that among French women writers, Nathalie Sarraute, Marguerite Yourcenar, and Violette Leduc have also received little serious critical attention. Until quite recently the same was also true of Colette and, with the exception of several excellent readings of her novel *Moderato Cantabile*, of Marguerite Duras.

I suspect that the major reason for the dramatic difference in the quantity, if not the quality, of the secondary literature on writers who are women as compared to writers who are men is that in spite of the general success of women's studies programs and the inclusion in most literature departments of at least one course on women writers, neither the study of

French women writers nor the writing of doctoral dissertations on French women writers is encouraged in the United States. And the doctoral dissertation, frequently revised for publication as a book, furnishes an important percentage of the scholarly books on literature published in the United States. Between 1954 and 1984 there have been approximately twenty doctoral dissertations devoted exclusively or in part to Simone de Beauvoir. Of these, five have been published as books. As the figures suggest, the study of women writers is still not taken seriously by many scholars within academia, and the prestige that accrues to work done on women writers is considerably less than the prestige associated with research related to a major male writer. Another reason that may help explain the paucity of critical studies on French women writers relates to new directions in textual criticism that, since the late 1960s, have tended to dismiss or at least diminish the importance of authors and their intentions. The emphasis on textual criticism reinforces the position of the accepted canon as critics reread, in new ways, texts of well-known male authors. Consequently, introductory studies that present the writer and her work, the text and the context, the life and the times have, perhaps too hastily, perhaps temporarily, gone out of style. Finally, and this may seem paradoxical, because there has been less written about women writers there is less to write. On the other hand, the more that has been written about a particular writer or a particular work, the more there is to write. Commentary calls for and forth more commentary.

The feminist inquiry has also played its part in emphasizing women writers and at the same time making it difficult to write about them. The difficulty arises when feminist critics feel the necessity of raising the feminist question, of placing the writer and the text in relation to feminist positions. Is the writer a feminist? Does the writer make a contribution to the feminist inquiry? In order to avoid a negative response to these and related questions, the choice may be not to tangle with women writers at all.

I do not, however, agree with Mary Evans that "the secondary literature on de Beauvoir is . . . curiously muted in its criticism." At least half of the critical essays I have included in this volume are, whether discreetly or obtrusively, sarcastic. They present Simone de Beauvoir as a slightly ridiculous figure, naive in her passions, sloppy in her scholarship, inaccurate in her documentation, generally out of her depth and inferior as a writer. Indeed, the tone of superiority that many critics, of both sexes, adopt when writing about Simone de Beauvoir deserves special attention. From the beginning of her career, Simone de Beauvoir has been subject to passionate, occasionally strident critiques. Some of these critiques may be understood as responses to the controversial discourses that at different moments and in varied doses traverse and inform her texts. Her atheistic existentialism, her neo-Marxism, her oscillations between the sense of the absurd and the need for political commitment, her interest in non-

Lacanian psychoanalysis, her involvement with feminist theory and practice, and her reiterated pronouncements on the dangers that the institutions of marriage and motherhood represent for women have aroused her critics, particularly in France, to produce often scathing reviews. The most extravagant examples of these are found in the book signed by the pseudonym La Vouldie: *Madame Simone de Beauvoir and Her "Mandarins"* (1955). There are also those vituperative reviews of or comments on *The Second Sex* by such critics as François Mauriac, Pierre de Boisdeffre, Roger Nimier, Armand Hoog, and Marie-Louise Barron, which Simone de Beauvoir enumerates and analyzes in *Force of Circumstance.*[2]

One of the most constant negative critiques, repeated by critics cross-culturally, is that Simone de Beauvoir is too serious, that she and her texts lack humor. Certainly, if we were to compare the texts of Simone de Beauvoir with those of Roland Barthes, for example, we would be struck by the blatant contrast between Barthes's playfulness with and self-consciousness about words as opposed to Simone de Beauvoir's refusal of such play. But something else is at work in the charge of seriousness and the absence of humor, something that seems to be related to expectations about women's position as writers and intellectuals. If, in 1986, it is acceptable for a woman to be a writer, to have a recognizable style, and to write well, it is still not acceptable for a woman to be a thinker, to take on the world, as it were, to meditate in public on questions of life and death, to write about sexuality, religion, and relations of power. In this respect, Simone de Beauvoir is the example par excellence of the woman writer who arouses hostile reactions.

Some of the feminist critiques that have been presented at conferences and symposia since 1979,[3] the year of the thirtieth anniversary of *The Second Sex*, are also marked by hostile reaction. It is not always easy to distinguish serious critical questioning from passionate hostility. Although I would in no way charge contemporary British, Canadian, French, or United States feminists with either conscious intentions or unconscious motivations in any way similar to those of the irate French critics who read *The Second Sex* in 1949, there is, on the part of certain feminist critics, such a fundamental discrepancy between their theoretical direction and the theoretical direction of Simone de Beauvoir that hostility and debate may sometimes appear conflated. I have included in this volume texts by Juliet Mitchell on Simone de Beauvoir and psychoanalysis, by Gerda Lerner on Simone de Beauvoir and women's history, and by Mary Evans on Simone de Beauvoir and relations between women and men that elaborate on profound theoretical and methodological differences. Juliet Mitchell argues that Simone de Beauvoir either ignores or fails to understand the Freudian concept of the unconscious; Gerda Lerner argues that Simone de Beauvoir's analysis of women is fundamentally ahistorical and that women have indeed had a history and a culture; Mary Evans argues that Simone de Beauvoir rejects the "real" problems faced by women and men and fails to recognize those needs and desires that do not originate on the conscious level.

In this volume there are no examples of texts written by members of the French group *politique et psychanalyse (politics and psychoanalysis)*, a group formed in Paris following the events of May 1968 and dedicated to the working through of historical materialism and Lacanian psychoanalysis in relation to the question of woman. It is significant that no one belonging directly or peripherally to this group has ever written about Simone de Beauvoir. We cannot overlook the fact that members of this group were not initially encouraged to write, since writing itself was considered to be a phallocentric activity. But the silence that surrounds the name and the writings of Simone de Beauvoir also suggests the degree to which the members of *politique et psychanalyse* considered their work diametrically opposed to hers, considered her activities complicitous with the reigning networks of power. Because Simone de Beauvoir continued to use and to justify her use of a language that allowed rapid communication of information and ideas, her writings were dismissed by *politique et psychanalyse* as both uninteresting and dangerous. It is worthy of note that in the 1975 issue of the French journal *L'Arc* on Simone de Beauvoir and the women's struggle, Hélène Cixous's contribution, her now classic essay "The Laugh of the Medusa," never once mentions Simone de Beauvoir or any of her writing. In the seminar on "feminine writing" that Hélène Cixous has been directing for the past seven years at the University of Paris VIII (Vincennes-Saint-Denis), Simone de Beauvoir and the word "feminism" are occasionally alluded to derogatorily as examples of an out-of-date theoretical and political approach to questions of sexual difference. In the interviews between the German feminist Alice Schwarzer and Simone de Beauvoir that took place between 1972 and 1982, Simone de Beauvoir refers obliquely to the work of Hélène Cixous when she speaks disdainfully of the "new femininity."[4] For a more detailed account of Simone de Beauvoir's reactions to the post-1968 interest in sexual difference, I would refer readers to the French journals *Questions Féministes* and *Nouvelles Questions Féministes* (published in Paris) which, since 1977, have printed essays on feminist theory and practice that relentlessly oppose the influence of Lacanian psychoanalysis on the French feminist scene. Simone de Beauvoir was the official sponsor of the journal. *Feminist Issues*, published by the Feminist Forum of Berkeley, California, reproduces in English translation many of the French articles.

I would, therefore, agree with Mary Evans's assessment of the position of Simone de Beauvoir vis-à-vis her critics only insofar as sarcasm and derogatory statements do not necessarily imply serious argumentation. It may well be true that where questions of feminist theory are concerned, respect and/or hostility on the part of contemporary women theorists toward Simone de Beauvoir's positions have resulted in their silence. To my knowledge, neither Luce Irigaray nor Julia Kristeva has written about Simone de Beauvoir. Given the kinds of questions in which they are interested, this can hardly be an oversight. However, unlike Mary Evans, I have not focused exclusively on feminist critics since 1968 or on explicitly feminist issues in my investigations. Simone de Beauvoir was an "existentialist" before she was a "feminist," and if she accepted the label "feminist" in 1973, she never disowned her "existentialist" affiliation. Therefore, it is not surprising that my tentative conclusions concerning the status of the critical corpus that surrounds Simone de Beauvoir's work will, at certain points, differ from those of Mary Evans. Neither Elizabeth Hardwick, Mary McCarthy, Mary Ellmann, nor René Etiemble, for example, can be considered "muted" in their criticism.

I have not attempted in this volume to achieve inclusiveness. I have not attempted to cover all of Simone de Beauvoir's writings with critical pieces. Nor have I attempted to eliminate either the severe critics or the hagiographers. I have made my selection from among critical texts written in French and English on the basis of quality, quality with respect to a theoretical, political, historical, and stylistic contribution, even if this involved some inevitable overlapping in the texts of Simone de Beauvoir to which the critics and theorists refer. I have also tried, with the cooperation of research assistants, to sample what has been written about Simone de Beauvoir and her writings in Holland, Italy, Latin America, Poland, Spain, Scandinavia, the Soviet Union, and West Germany.[5] For Simone de Beauvoir is an international figure who is not written about exclusively in the countries represented in this volume. The other countries I have attempted in some small measure to investigate were not selected at random. I suspected that there would be considerable material, relatively speaking, about Simone de Beauvoir in countries like Poland whose interest in French language, literature, and culture, if it has sometimes wavered, has never waned. I was not mistaken. Other countries like the Soviet Union were predictable insofar as they translated texts that could be read as attacks on bourgeois capitalist consumer society, for example, *Les Belles Images* and *A Very Easy Death*.

Based on a limited sample from these countries, what stands out is the degree to which the political context determines what is translated and published, how it is read, and where it is reviewed. In the Soviet Union and particularly in Poland, considerable attention was given in the press to *The Mandarins*, published in France in 1954. Reviewers were excited by the political positions and choices of French left-wing intellectuals in the post–World War II period. In an article, "The Fate of the Existentialist Novel," published in the Soviet Union by E. Yevnina in the journal *Literary Questions*, April 1959, *The Mandarins* is compared favorably to Jean-Paul Sartre's *Roads to Freedom* and Albert Camus's *The Plague*. Simone de Beauvoir is seen as moving away from the errors of existentialism and toward a more "realistic" approach to life. The characters in *The*

Mandarins, according to the reviewer, are live people who love, who suffer, and through whom we sense the complexities of human relationships. E. Yevnina praises the anti-American stand explicit in the novel as well as the way in which Simone de Beauvoir shows the clash between the United States and the Soviet Union during the period of the cold war. E. Yevnina also praises the evolution of Simone de Beauvoir's hero, Henri Perron, who, unlike Sartre's Mathieu and Camus's Dr. Rieux, finds a way out of the dead-end in which he found himself. The conclusion to the review is that French existentialists are moving closer to the socialist camp and are rejecting individualism.

When *The Mandarins* appeared in Poland in a Polish translation, there were several reviews of the novel. In a few of them, Simone de Beauvoir was accused of not knowing Marxists and, therefore, of portraying them unrealistically. In an article in a woman's magazine, *A Woman and Life*, no. 10, 1958, signed R. H., the negative opinions of a group of readers reveal their strong ethical bias. Readers accused her novel of being immoral and the author of being profligate. They felt that the novel was devastating for young people and inappropriate for the Polish spirit. One reader insisted that Poland should not take from the West such objectionable literature. Although many Polish reviews are critical of Simone de Beauvoir's positions as she states them explicitly in her essays and her autobiography and more ambiguously through her novels, although one reviewer may claim that people are writing memoirs because they are no longer interested in politics and another may appear to be shocked by the "exhibitionism" and the "obscene details" of this "unstable lady" (Beata Lewanska, 1961), the number of reviews and articles in Poland suggests, beyond a serious interest in French literature in general and literature that deals with political questions in the post–World War II period in particular, a fascination with the way in which Simone de Beauvoir dares to raise political and sexual questions.

In other Western European countries political and ethical concerns are less apparent. In West Germany, critical interest in Simone de Beauvoir seems to have concentrated on the theme of death, its elaboration in her work and in the work of Heidegger and Sartre. For example, Erich Schmalenberg's *Das Todesverständnis bei Simone de Beauvoir: Eine Theologische Untersuchung* (Simone de Beauvoir's understanding of death: a theological study [1972]). Since the mid-1970s, the emphasis has been on questions concerning women and feminism. For an interesting analysis of *The Second Sex* and its relation to Simone de Beauvoir's novels, see Cornelia Wagner's *Simone de Beauvoir Weg Zum Feminismus* (Simone de Beauvoir's road toward feminism [1984]).

In Holland, interest in Simone de Beauvoir seems to have focused on the story of her life, her relations with Jean-Paul Sartre, and how she has negotiated the difficult situation of living close to a famous man. Simone de Beauvoir has enjoyed considerable success in the Dutch press both as a thinker and as a popular female figure about whom the public would like to know more and to gossip. In 1972, Gilbert Willens published a book entitled *Simone de Beauvoir*, a general introduction to her life and work in which he insists on her importance as a pedagogue. On 19 April 1986, five days after her death, the Dutch newspaper *Vrij Nederland* referred to Simone de Beauvoir as "the grandmother of feminism."

In Italy, a more limited bibliographical search suggests an intellectual concern in relation to Simone de Beauvoir, with questions of autobiography, psychoanalysis, and Marxism. A book by Enzio Biagini, *Simone de Beauvoir*, was published in 1982, and the journal *Communità* has reprinted interviews and articles by Alice Jardine and Dorothy McCall that have appeared in the United States in the journal *Signs*.

In Denmark, Norway, and Sweden, Simone de Beauvoir has been written about in relation to her opinions and her theoretical positions concerning women, her relationship with Jean-Paul Sartre, and her views on old age. There is an emphasis in the Scandinavian countries on social issues and on Simone de Beauvoir's place as a philosopher within the Western philosophical tradition. In 1981 Queen Margrethe of Denmark and Prince Henrik translated *All Men are Mortal* into Danish. In 1983 Simone de Beauvoir was awarded the Sonning prize by the Danish government. Several interviews and articles describing and praising Simone de Beauvoir's life and work appeared in the Danish press at that time.

Relatively little critical material on Simone de Beauvoir existed in Spain before the death of Franco. Since his death in 1975, Simone de Beauvoir's name has appeared with a certain regularity as a point of reference in books about women and feminism. In Latin America, particularly in Argentina, Brazil, Colombia, and Mexico, Simone de Beauvoir is also referred to regularly in discussions of social and historical issues relating to women. Three women writers, the Mexican writer Rosario Castellanos and the Argentinian writers Silvina Bullrich and Vitoria Ocampo, have played an important role in the diffusion of Simone de Beauvoir's theoretical directions and political positions throughout Latin America.

Although I have not used any of the critical essays that were discovered through these searches, I have gained certain insights that I think are important and should be shared with the readers at the beginning of this essay. The first of these insights deals with the fact that the world is indeed divided into cultural spheres and that in some of these spheres writing that originates in France, I am tempted to say Paris, plays a privileged role, sets standards, influences the formulation of the canon. Simone de Beauvoir clearly benefits from being a French and a Parisian writer. The second insight deals with the importance of translation and the question of timing. How long after an important text has appeared is it translated into other languages and into which languages? Time lags produce interesting phenomena in the world of criticism. For example, the translation into Polish in 1972 of *The Second Sex*, twenty-three years after the French publication in 1949, and the translation into German of several of Simone de Beauvoir's earlier texts in 1968 and in the 1970s. Many of the debates among contemporary feminists only make sense if we know what the debaters have read, when they read it, and in which translation. The third and most banal insight is that, if inclusiveness is not possible, it nevertheless seems important to give some idea of the extent to which Simone de Beauvoir is an international figure and a widely read, popular, and controversial writer. She is one of those writers who must be considered in both literary and cultural studies.

With the exception of the three opening portraits by Jean-Paul Sartre, Colette Audry, and Alice Schwarzer, I have chosen to present the reviews and the articles selected for this volume in chronological order rather than separating them by genre (reviews and articles) or separating them into categories such as articles on individual works or general works. The reviews I have included all contain reflections on the whole of Simone de Beauvoir's work, and the general essays often concentrate on specific texts. The reader will notice the prevalence of references to *The Second Sex*, *Memoirs of a Dutiful Daughter*, *A Very Easy Death*, and *Old Age*. It seems clear that during the forty-five years in which Simone de Beauvoir has been written about in newspapers, literary magazines, women's magazines, scholarly journals, and specifically feminist journals and books, the major emphasis has been on her autobiographical writings and on her substantial essays on women and on old age.

The chronological order in which I have placed reviews and essays has obvious advantages. From the opening text by the phenomenologist philosopher Maurice Merleau-Ponty on *She Came to Stay* to the closing text by Virginia Fichera on *Who Shall Die?*, readers will be able to note changes in theoretical, ideological, and stylistic modes of critical writing and to enjoy the play of difference underlined by — although not exclusively the result of — this temporal sequence. There are differences between the approaches of such United States "intellectuals" of the 1950s as Mary McCarthy and Elizabeth Hardwick and the approaches of United States "feminists" of the 1980s such as Carol Ascher and Kate Millett; differences between the French "existentialist" discourses of Maurice Merleau-Ponty and Francis Jeanson and the French "feminist" discourses of Catherine Clément and Michèle Le Doeuff; differences between the polemical and ideological rhetoric of René Etiemble and François Mauriac and the ludic seriousness of Alice Jardine and Mary Lydon; differences between the slightly ironic and patronizing tone of René Girard and the protective, almost tender tone of Colette Audry and Béatrice Slama. Differences also between British, French, and United States critics; between male and female critics; between academic critics like T. H. Adamowski, Jacques Ehrmann, and Terry Keefe and writer-journalists like Elizabeth Janeway and François Mauriac; between acerbic critics of Simone de Beauvoir like René Etiemble, Elizabeth Hardwick, and Mary McCarthy and strong, almost hagiographic supporters like Claude Roy, Francis Jeanson, and Kate Millett.

Many of these differences would be apparent whatever the order of presentation might have been, but chronology, for all its banality, allows us to see in texts the pervasive presence of changing contexts: the movement from existentialist preoccupations and the importance accorded the individual as a center of perception and consciousness to the structural questions raised by psychoanalysis; the textual questions raised by post-structuralism; the feminist questions raised by the women's liberation movements; and the decline in the number of important reviews and articles written by male critics after the 1960s. All of these changes are dramatically present in the table of contents. This volume should, therefore, have a double value, as a collection of some of the most interesting pieces that have been written about Simone de Beauvoir and as a recapitulation of significant mo(ve)ments in theory and criticism from the late 1940s to 1986.

It is not surprising that, from the quantitative point of view, Simone de Beauvoir has received greater attention in France in the number of reviews, articles, and books published about her than she has elsewhere in the world. Of the thirty or more books written about Simone de Beauvoir since 1958, sixteen have been published in France, five in the United States, four in Germany, three in Great Britain, and at least one in the Scandinavian countries and in Italy. A characteristic of all of these books, even those written during the late 1970s and the 1980s when avant-garde critical modes had relegated the author to a somewhat marginal position, is the central position accorded Simone de Beauvoir as a writer and a woman with ideas and opinions on important issues. It could be argued that because of the nature of Simone de Beauvoir's writings, because of her own preoccupation with the representation of herself and with writing, it would be difficult if not impossible for critics to write about her without emphasizing these categories. The result has been that, within the contemporary critical spectrum, Simone de Beauvoir, in the 1980s, stands almost alone as a tenacious representative of that "existentialist humanism" that has been, of late, so maligned.

Before the impact of the women's liberation movements of the late 1960s on Simone de Beauvoir and her readers, her novels, essays, memoirs, and single play tended to be written about in terms of her contributions, as a novelist and as a philosopher, to Sartrean atheistic existentialism and, as a chronicler, to the depiction of the lives of Parisian left-bank intellectuals. It was evident to many critics that, from the beginning of her writing career, Simone de Beauvoir was concerned primarily with how to live a life, how, with a heightened degree of self-consciousness, in a historical period permeated by war and atrocities, to see clearly and to choose authentically. Her obsessions with death and mortality, her emphasis on human relationships as both doomed to failure and susceptible to amelioration, the contradictions and ambiguities in her writing seem to have angered some of her critics and confused others. Those who were angered by her "messages," by her positions taken and often didactically expounded, were usually impatient with her insistence on setting down all the peripetia of the journey on which she had set out, as if no one before her had traveled a similar road.

Her supporters, her disciples, her faithful readers were of another mind. It will take at least another twenty-five years before scholars can determine the extent of the influence of Simone de Beauvoir on her many readers, not only those who wrote her regularly asking for advice, but those more reserved women, and I suspect some men, for whom her journey was indeed unique. It may seem blasphemous, or at the very least an exaggeration, to compare the nature of Simone de Beauvoir's influence on the lives of these women and men to that of figures such as Jesus Christ or, more reasonably, Jean-Jacques Rousseau. To the degree that this influence involves identification and imitation as well as transferential relations, the comparisons are not too farfetched. The conflicts and the rebellions she narrates in the four volumes of her autobiography, particularly her skirmishes with the Catholic church and with God, her encounters and negotiations with lovers and friends, her extended relationship with Jean-Paul Sartre, her political activities as a writer and as a woman, her worldwide travel have become models of what it is possible for women and men to do or to envisage doing in the course of a lifetime. To the degree that her life, as she wrote it, has become exemplary, Simone de Beauvoir has succeeded in accomplishing, through her writing, the goals she defined in *Memoirs of a Dutiful Daughter*:

> Through the heroine [Maggie Tulliver in *The Mill on the Floss*], I identified myself with the author [George Eliot]: one day other adolescents would bathe with their tears a novel in which I would tell my own sad story. . . . If at one time I had dreamed of being a teacher it was because I wanted to be a law unto myself; I now thought that literature would allow me to realize this dream. It would guarantee me an immortality which would compensate for the loss of heaven and eternity; there was no longer any God to love me, but I should have the undying love of millions of hearts. By writing a work based on my own experience I would re-create myself and justify my existence. At the same time I would be serving humanity: what more beautiful gift could I make it than the books I would write? I was interested at the same time in myself and in others; I accepted my "incarnation" but I did not wish to renounce my universal prerogative. My plan to be a writer reconciled everything; it gratified all the aspirations which had been unfolding in me during the past fifteen years.[6]

The profound impact of Simone de Beauvoir's writings, and the unexpected consequences of following in the footsteps of another are discussed in this volume in the texts by Carol Ascher, Kate Millett, and Béatrice Slama. Written within different theoretical discourses and from different feminist positions, each of these three texts represents the kind of critical response that Simone de Beauvoir hoped to elicit. A response that includes the writer as author and narrator, the reader as author and narrator, and the text in its dialectical relation to the human world.

It seems appropriate to conclude this introduction with a symbolic figure, Little Red Riding Hood, used by Simone de Beauvoir in the opening paragraph of the *Memoirs of a Dutiful Daughter*. The story of Little Red Riding Hood continues to be rewritten and retold by successive generations of writers and storytellers. Unlike Hélène Cixous, for whom the Little Red Riding Hood is a metonymy for the forbidden clitoris of the little girl, Simone de Beauvoir evokes the figure of herself "disguised as Little Red Riding Hood." She does not retell the story. Her reference to Little Red Riding Hood establishes a relationship between the structural elements in the story of Little Red Riding Hood and her own adventures. Whereas her best friend Elisabeth Mabille and her beloved cousin Jacques succumb to the wicked wiles of the Catholic bourgeoisie, the narrator, Simone, is never (b)eaten. I will, in my turn, use Little Red Riding Hood as a metaphor for the relationship between Simone de Beauvoir and her writings on one hand, and her critics on the other. The metaphor will allow me to highlight the ways in which she and her texts have been devoured by hostile critics or regurgitated whole without interpretation or analysis by the faithful. I would suggest, then, that what is needed in Simone de Beauvoir criticism is more work on close textual and contextual analyses as in the essays by Alice Jardine and Mary Lydon, more work on Simone de Beauvoir as a figure in culture studies as in the essays by Catherine Clément, Mary Evans, Virginia Fichera, and Béatrice Slama. I would place very high on a research agenda attempts to determine what the impact of Simone de Beauvoir on her varied readers around the world may have been as well as attempts to reinterpret the crucial relationship with Jean-Paul Sartre, with other male lovers, and with intimate female friends. In order to do this work successfully, it will be necessary to change figures of speech and to bring together the forbidden clitoris, the courageous little girl, the writer, and her texts.

I would suggest picking up on a word used by Béatrice Slama and replacing Little Red Riding Hood by the more mature figure of the "Pioneer," etymologically the foot soldier "who marches with or in advance of the army or regiment having spades, pick axes, etc., to dig trenches, repair roads, and perform other labors in clearing and preparing the way for the main body" (*OED*). The pioneer is an indefatigable walker, an industrious worker, "one who goes before to prepare or open up the way for others to follow . . . one who begins, or takes part in beginning, some enterprise, course of action." The pioneer engages in repairing and exploring. The pioneer is an originator, an initiator, and a forerunner.

Further exploration of the metaphor of the pioneer as it helps to elucidate the case of Simone de Beauvoir will be the task of those who elect to work on a corpus as complex and as varied as that of Simone de Beauvoir.

ELAINE MARKS

University of Wisconsin–Madison

Notes

1. Mary Evans, *Simone de Beauvoir: A Feminist Mandarin* (London: Tavistock Publications, 1985), 121.

2. Simone de Beauvoir, *Force of Circumstance*, trans. Richard Howard (Middlesex, England: Penguin Books, 1968), 195–203.

3. In particular, the *"Second Sex"* conference held at New York University in September 1979; "After the Second Sex," an international conference held at the University of Pennsylvania in April 1985; and the colloquium on Simone de Beauvoir held at the French House of Columbia University in April 1985. The special sessions on Simone de Beauvoir at the annual meetings of the Modern Language Association in 1981–85, at which mostly professors of French in the United States deliver papers, focused on thematic and textual readings that are not primarily concerned with ideological and theoretical controversy.

4. Alice Schwarzer, *After "The Second Sex": Conversations with Simone de Beauvoir*, trans. Marianne Howarth (New York: Pantheon Books, 1984), 103 and passim.

5. I would like to name and to thank the research assistants in Madison, Wisconsin, who have worked with me in these areas: Kit Belgum for Germany; Mario Ferri for Italy; Samuel Hanchett for the Soviet Union; Linda Howe for Latin America and Spain; Robyn Peterson for the Scandinavian countries; and Jola de Weerd for Holland and Poland.

6. Simone de Beauvoir, *Memoirs of a Dutiful Daughter*, trans. James Kirkup (New York: Harper Colophon Books, 1974) 140–42.

Bibliography of Works by Simone De Beauvoir

L'invitée. Paris: Gallimard, 1943. (*She Came to Stay.*)

Pyrrhus et Cinéas. Paris: Gallimard, 1944. (Pyrrhus and Cineas.)

Le sang des autres. Paris: Gallimard, 1945. (*The Blood of Others.*)

Les bouches inutiles. Paris: Gallimard, 1945. (Useless Mouths or *Who Shall Die?*.)

Tous les hommes sont mortels. Paris: Gallimard, 1946. (*All Men are Mortal.*)

Pour une morale de l'ambiguïté. Paris: Gallimard, 1947. (*The Ethics of Ambiguity*.)

L'Amérique au jour le jour. Paris: Morihien, 1948. (*America Day by Day*.)

L'existentialisme et la sagesse des nations. Paris: Nagel, 1948. (Existentialism and Ordinary Wisdom.)

Le deuxième sexe. Paris: Gallimard, 1949. (*The Second Sex*.)

Les mandarins. Paris: Gallimard, 1954. (*The Mandarins*.)

Privilèges. Paris: Gallimard, 1955. (Privileges.)

La longue marche. Paris: Gallimard, 1957. (*The Long March.*)

Mémoires d'une jeune fille rangée. Paris: Gallimard, 1958. (*Memoirs of a Dutiful Daughter.*)

La force de l'âge. Paris: Gallimard, 1960. (*The Prime of Life.*)

La force des choses. Paris: Gallimard, 1963. (*Force of Circumstance.*)

Une mort très douce. Paris: Gallimard, 1964. (*A Very Easy Death.*)

Les belles images. Paris: Gallimard, 1966. (*Les Belles Images.*)

La femme rompue. Paris: Gallimard, 1968. (*The Woman Destroyed.*)

La vieillesse. Paris: Gallimard, 1970. (Old Age, or *The Coming of Age.*)

Tout compte fait. Paris: Gallimard, 1972. (*All Said and Done.*)

Quand prime le spirituel. Paris: Gallimard, 1979. (*When Things of the Spirit Come First.*)

La cérémonie des adieux. Paris: Gallimard, 1981. (*Adieux.*)

Portraits

Sartre Talks of Beauvoir

An Interview with Madeleine Gobeil*

GOBEIL: Simone de Beauvoir has spoken about you at great length in her memoirs, but you, on the other hand, have written nothing about her. It's rather surprising.

SARTRE: It's true that I've never written anything about Castor. [Simone de Beauvoir is known to her friends as Castor, the French word for beaver.] The fact is that I've never had occasion to. I began my autobiography with *The Words*, but I don't even know whether I'll continue. I leave off at the age of ten.

When I was ten, I didn't know Castor. Besides, she was a very little girl at the time. But if she has involved me so completely in the three volumes of her memoirs, if she has, in a way, told about my life and my relationship with her, that means I'm completely in agreement with what she said about me and about our relationship. I read her books several times and made suggestions, but I never commented on what she said about me. This ought to be regarded as an absolute proof. Not only is she the person who knows me best, but I think that everything she says about the mutual importance of our relationship is quite true. The fact is, as she says, that for almost thirty years we've never gone to bed at odds with each other. I'm wrong—we once did, but I think it was for a silly reason.

We do get angry with each other, as you can imagine, but only over questions of a philosophical nature and, in general, questions that are badly formulated. As she has said—though I noticed it before she did—when we're both asked a question at the same time, we usually give the same answer. It's really quite curious. We have such a large stock of common memories that ultimately we react to a situation in the same way—I mean with the same words, words that are conditioned by the same experiences. People who live together share lots of experiences, and they eventually come to have a common memory.

GOBEIL: What do you think of Simone de Beauvoir as a woman?

*Reprinted from *Vogue*, July 1965, 72–73. Translated by Bernard Frechtman.

15

SARTRE: I think she's beautiful. I've always thought her beautiful, even though she was wearing a hideous little hat when I first met her. I was dead set on making her acquaintance because she was beautiful, because she had, and still has, the kind of face that appeals to me. The wonderful thing about Simone de Beauvoir is that she has a man's intelligence — you can see from the way I'm talking that I'm still a bit feudal — and a woman's sensitivity. That is, I've found in her everything I could possibly want. And we've never really quarrelled, except about silly things. For example, in 1939 we quarrelled in Naples about whether or not the Neapolitans should be obliged to live in the houses that were being built for them. The argument ended with my saying to her, "You're a fascist!" and with her answering, "And you, you'll never amount to anything! Never, never, never."

GOBEIL: Would you have been different if you hadn't known her?

SARTRE: It's very hard to tell what you owe someone. In a way, I owe her everything. On the other hand, I would obviously have written even if she hadn't existed, since I wanted to write. But why is it that my complete confidence in her has always given me complete security, a security which I couldn't have had if I'd been alone, unless I were puffed with pride, as many writers are and which I am not, though I may be in other areas? When I show her a manuscript, as I always do, and when she criticizes it, I get angry at first and call her all kinds of names. Then, I accept her comments, always. Not as a matter of discipline, but because I see that they're always pertinent. They're not made from the outside, but with an absolute understanding of what I want to do, and at the same time, with an objectivity that I can't quite have.

She's in perfect agreement with what I say, even though she may think that it ought not to be said at that particular time. She trusts my judgment, since I want to write that particular thing. And since I want to write it, she's completely involved in it too. She's very severe, and so am I. After reading the first version of *The Respectful Prostitute*, she exclaimed: "Oh, it's disgusting! I now see all your tricks. It hasn't a leg to stand on."

I revised the play within twenty-four hours, and she finally said it was very good. Once she gives me, as it were, the "imprimatur," I have complete confidence in her. Other people's criticism has never made me change my mind about what I've written. To some extent, it can be said that I write for her, or, to put it more accurately, I write so that she can filter what I've set down. I then feel that it's fit for the public. You know, that's a very rare feeling. A man like Camus wrote in a state of doubt. That's natural, and it's even a virtue which I recognize he had.

Montherlant doesn't write in a state of doubt. Remember what Costals says, at a certain point, in *Les Jeunes Filles*, "Costals wrote three pages and what he wrote was good." It's absolutely impossible for a writer to think that all by himself. The only thing he can say is: "I can't do any

better at the moment." Consequently, Camus's doubts, his anxiety, his stubbornness about certain matters are things which I find quite honoura-ble in a writer. It's even the writer's condition. But, thanks to Castor, it's a condition that's alien to me. I never have doubts. I merely wonder what she's going to think about what I've written, but I don't feel anxious. If she thinks it's bad, I rewrite it, and that's that. The only time I have doubts is when I write something and she's not there.

GOBEIL: But her sensibility seems to be very different from yours. She seems to have a deeper love of life.

SARTRE: She calls me a "whited sepulchre" because she really does enjoy life much more than I. I follow her, but I get a bit winded. It is only on one subject that she leaves me flat and that is politics. She doesn't give a damn about it. It's not that she actually doesn't give a damn about it, but she doesn't want to get involved in the political rat race.

GOBEIL: What do you think about Simone de Beauvoir as a writer?

SARTRE: I don't pay compliments and I say things simply. She seems to me a very good writer. She has achieved something which has manifested itself particularly since *The Mandarins*. It's apparent in the memoirs and in her book *A Very Peaceful Death*, which I consider the best thing she's written. What she has achieved is immediate communication with the public. Let's put it this way: there's a difference between her and me. I don't communicate emotionally, I communicate with people who think, who reflect, who are free in relation to me. That may or may not be a good thing. But Simone de Beauvoir communicates emotionally at once. People are always involved with her by virtue of what she says. She has a way of challenging the other person immediately, but as a friend. She never acts as if she were superior to the reader. Her way of speaking about herself is a way of speaking about others. She has a way of both accepting and criticizing herself that enables the reader to recognize himself. She's neither too severe nor too indulgent. As for me, I don't talk about myself in such a balanced way. I'm either too complacent or too severe. She has the right relationship with herself. That's what's meant by seeing oneself in perspective. It's not only a matter of literature, it's a matter of life.

If she sees things in perspective in literature, it's because she really sees them that way in life. She's a person who—how shall I put it?—who doesn't think about herself. She doesn't think about herself spontaneously. She thinks about what confronts her. It can be the desert, in which case she'll feel the desert. It can be a person, in which case she'll be concerned with the person's problems. Castor is a person whose spontaneity is, I think, untainted with alienation, the desire to appear, or to preserve, to keep. In short, her spontaneity goes out to the person because she herself is free.

When she raises questions about herself, it's not because she's narcis-sistic, but because she has a sensibility that's surprised to have an ego and that says to itself: "Indeed, I'm subjective, I too exist, what does that mean?" Her memoirs, on which she's been working for seven years, are, to some extent, a way of retrieving a sensibility that reaches out to the other person, without any detour and without any secrecy. I assure you, the soundest kind of sensibility. . . .

Portrait of the Writer as a Young Woman
Colette Audry*

When you write the portrait of a writer you met long before the publication of her first book and whose still anonymous face you knew at a time when her work was nothing but a vague project in her mind, you want to conjure up a picture as intimate as the perception that Emily Brontë might have had of her sister Charlotte as the two of them chatted while doing the housework in their father's parsonage; or something like what Musset saw of George Sand when he visited her in an attic room on the Quai Malaquais and quipped:

> George is in her garret
> Between two flower pots
> She smokes her cigarettes. . . .

But you also want to reveal how the writer perceives herself, to expose the forces and desires which root her in the world, and, finally, to make clear the purpose of her whole work. Through such a picture we would see her live as we ourselves live, and at the same time we would see her transformed into what she became. However, such a picture has not yet been seen, no one can give it a shape, much less transmit it. For it does not exist.

We had a friend. We were all young. She had started writing a book, was not pleased with it and dropped it to begin another and, brave as she was, a third one. There was no limit to her courage. She was going to be a writer, of that she was sure and so were we. But, in fact, her future work did not count more for us than her opinions, her travels. She was what counted: what she said, how she joked, loved, scorned. And one day, a few years later, in the provincial town where we lived, we received a package from the Gallimard publishing house: it was her first book. From that day on, while she continued to be herself, she would also never cease to be for us the part of her that had been transfused into the printed lines, this

*Translated by Yvonne Rochette Ozzello for this volume from *Biblio*, November 1962, 3–5. Reprinted by permission of the author.

superimposition of herself upon herself, indistinguishable from her and yet never to be confused with her.

There is no total picture, just memories. I recall a slender stranger with a very bright face, who, a long time ago, came to us in our small, old teachers' office on a peaceful, sunny first day of the Fall semester. She seemed to be excessively polite, but her good manners contrasted with her husky voice and her rapid way of speaking. More memories: her beige velvet jacket would appear as she opened the café door; her desperate face when a pudding does not turn out well; a huge busy restaurant where we speak with her while waiting for Sartre; a back room where we play pool together. Her bold laughter peals out. Hotel rooms where she literally camped; a street going down to the harbor where we stroll beside her; the May sun setting over the Seine from the terrace of a restaurant in the village of Duclair.

We stopped seeing her face. We see again places where we were together but no longer face to face. From that moment on, we only perceived the look in her eyes, inseparable from her voice, from what she said, from the preciseness of her assertions, from her naive attention when she asked questions, from her slightly awkward and pointed shyness when she confided in us. Someone with whom we would never tire of speaking and who aroused in us our most exacting attitude toward ourselves and toward the world. In fact, one of those few presences which justify our stay on this earth.

One of her first books was to be a collection of short stories which she wanted to call *When Things of the Spirit Come First* in mockery of an unfortunately already famous title. In this book she wanted to portray a series of characters busy pampering their inner life and finding exquisite intentions in their cowardice or minor crimes. I was delighted. I was getting involved in politics and trying to move away from the "inner life" and from a certain type of literature of that period. But I tended to drop the problem instead of cross-examining it. Simone de Beauvoir's presence helped me settle that very question.

In *The Prime of Life* she wrote: "I have never met anyone as gifted for happiness as I am, no one has ever pursued it so relentlessly." Indeed, it seemed that she was moving on in happiness, with her solid appetites and an exceptional eagerness for work and for play, transforming every minute into moments of happiness, happy even through her fits of despair and bitterness which were as sudden and brief as summer storms. I myself refused to see misery as a sign of "having been chosen," and I was determined not to endow it with any particular value; but after watching my new friend, I came to think that the will to happiness was one of life's essential qualities. And we did not question the very nature of happiness because it seemed evident to us that it could never rest on mediocre compromises. If we were to pick up this topic today in one of the endless conversations in which we would indulge then (as only young people can talk who have not yet found their proper occupation and who want to find it and having found it must in exchange give up leisure time), we would probably modify our beliefs of that period: in particular, we would say that it is not happiness that one must — or can — pursue in this world but rather preliminary conditions to happiness, and these are clearly different from happiness itself. However, I do not think that we would completely repudiate our past principles. At any rate, I learned from her, from her entire mode of being (and I don't believe she was aware of it), that happiness is a certain way of living, that it is not the opposite of suffering but that it helps endure suffering and that this is the way it should be.

But when I talk about her, what can I say that she has not already expressed herself? It seems to me that everything is in *Memoirs of a Dutiful Daughter* and *The Prime of Life*. Her seriousness, for instance.

"An austere and unrelenting seriousness, the reason for which I do not understand but to which I yield as to an overwhelming necessity," she wrote as an adolescent in her journal. This seriousness is one of her traits that some readers have the most trouble accepting or understanding. Why? Perhaps because it behooves one not to be serious as it behooves one to claim having been a poor student at fifteen; perhaps also because some people tend to imagine that seriousness means lack of gaiety, whereas it only means refusing frivolousness. Besides, you can easily speak of your own seriousness in your autobiography but not of your gaiety, for your own gaiety is not tellable. Her books cannot convey Simone de Beauvoir's gaiety, but they sometimes contain anecdotes with a form of dry and merciless humor which, were they part of a conversation, would end with a big burst of laughter.

"An unrelenting seriousness," harsh toward others as well as herself, and which is disturbing. Because, again, in an autobiography you can tell about your seriousness, but you cannot talk about your generosity, the warmth of your own receptiveness to others, without being complacent, even if you were able to detect in yourself such generosity and such warmth when you are so deeply serious. Thus, the written text subtly betrays its author, and the human being overflows the text.

This seriousness was certainly "a necessity," and it is easy to understand that Simone de Beauvoir had to give in to it. Let us remember where she came from and what itinerary she had to complete, moving away from a quasi-prehistorical milieu and family in order to catch up with her times and keep up her momentum. This serious little girl did not rebel, she only wanted to believe what she was told, to obey and to develop like those who looked after her. It is only through the strength and seriousness of her mind, her good will, her desire to be in tune with grown-ups that, day after day, she came to clash with the contradictions of a small world where "you condemned lying but you carefully avoided truth," and to realize that, in the last analysis, she could count on no one but herself.

Claudel writes about one of his characters:

> He was not wont to contradict but to ponder, like a good soil which receives all kinds of seeds.
> And since what is false cannot take root, it dies.

This is exactly as one can imagine her, receiving opinions and principles with good will, a faith which, in turn, would become the most corrosive of acids.

She wrote about some of her discoveries:

> I asked [my father] what a defeatist was. "A bad Frenchman who hopes that France will be defeated," he replied. I did not understand. Thoughts come and go in our heads in their own way. You don't believe what you believe on purpose. Anyway, my father's outraged tone and my mother's scandalized face convinced me that you must not rush to formulate out loud all those disquieting thoughts that you happen to be whispering under your breath.

Had she been more frivolous, she would have put up with the grown-ups' inconsistencies, she would have settled for an equally inconsistent mixture of rebelliousness and submissiveness and played at being independent without ever being able to reach freedom. Instead, she fully conquered her freedom, almost without knowing that she did, because what she was primarily looking for was not even freedom but truth in the world and in her own existence.

I used to be surprised to find so much indifference toward the position of women in the very person who would later write *The Second Sex* (but neither of us knew that at the time). There again, she was bypassing revolt. Although her relationship with Sartre was totally "egalitarian" (we used to discuss with a mixture of glee and perplexity a statement by Simone Weil who insisted that she rejected love because "it was not an egalitarian feeling"), she did not attempt to hide the important role that Sartre had played in her development. But, in a way, this role was precisely the role that her father assigned to the man in a married couple: "A wife is what a husband makes out of her." For once, she was not rejecting her family's norms because she was not in a position to have to reject them. And, having been raised with the idea that men are superior, she believed it was a fair and good thing to feel somewhat dominated, probably because she was convinced that you must pursue freedom from the position in which you are as a being molded by your own past. Such wisdom must have protected her from many skirmishes, useless efforts, and false problems; it must have allowed her to increase the possibilities of her courage through a remarkable saving of her energy.

If only I could return for a minute, a single minute, to that small, sunny, dusty teachers' office and see this unknown woman coming to shake hands! As if nothing as yet had happened. . . .

Introduction [to After "The Second Sex": Conversations with Simone de Beauvoir]

Alice Schwarzer*

I met her for the first time in 1970. It was not exactly a warm meeting—not on her part anyway. But then, we had met by chance. In fact, I was there because of Sartre. It was during the "mini-May" in Paris in 1970. For days and weeks, scandalous political trials had been taking place at the State Security Court (a para-military court which was not finally disbanded until after the socialists came to power). Those on trial were mostly French Maoists, the children of May '68, who had been concentrating their work on the factories and shanty towns. At the time, their political role was important as a catalyst for unofficial (and often violent) labour disputes and social protest. Occupying a factory and taking the boss or senior managers hostage had become more or less routine. Government reaction was swift: laws were changed (the maximum sentence for occupying a factory and taking hostages was increased to "life"), and the police machine was made even more sophisticated. Some of the militant young intellectuals who had gone into the factories and out into the suburbs were arrested or harassed. Others went underground. When the best-known of them went on trial, there were fierce public debates and violent street clashes between demonstrators and the police.

I was working as a foreign correspondent in Paris. My main interests and subject areas were the effects of May 1968, and industrial and social action in particular. One of the burning issues in France and in West Germany at the time was the question of "revolutionary violence." Does one have the right to resist, and if so, how far can "counter-violence" go?

At the time, Jean-Paul Sartre sympathised openly with the Maoists, serving them both as patron and propagandist; he was legally responsible for the Maoist publication La Cause du Peuple [People's cause], he handed out leaflets outside the Renault factory to demonstrate his support, and made a number of highly-regarded comments on the political trials, the critical tenor of which made the government uneasy. He had agreed to give me an interview on the subject of "revolutionary violence" on a day when one of these trials was in progress. So there I was in his one-room apartment on the Boulevard Raspail. He had agreed to give me a half-hour interview. As our extremely intense conversation was coming to an end, a key turned in the lock and Simone de Beauvoir came into the room. She gave me a brief irritated look, and then quickly, almost brusquely,

*Reprinted from After "The Second Sex": Conversations with Simone de Beauvoir, translated from the French by Marianne Howarth. English Translation © 1984 by Marianne Howarth. Reprinted by permission of Pantheon Books, a division of Random House, Inc., and Chatto & Windus Ltd.

reminded Sartre that they had to go to a press conference. Then she sat down at Sartre's desk at the back of the room to wait. She bristled with impatience. I could sense her annoyance at the delay and was embarrassed. It was my first experience of Simone de Beauvoir's "tête de chameau," her notoriously dismissive manner when situations or people do not suit her. Much later, I realised that she is a very uncompromising person. The other side of the coin is that once she has taken someone to her heart, it takes a lot for her to drop that person.

When the interview was over, the three of us went down in the cramped lift in Sartre's block. She curtly brushed aside my timid attempts at conversation.

It did not matter. For me to come face to face with the author of *The Second Sex* — this "beacon which Simone de Beauvoir lit to show women in the second half of this century the way," as a colleague of mine put it a few years ago — was still a truly moving encounter. In the darkness of the Fifties and Sixties, before the new women's movement dawned, *The Second Sex* was like a secret code that we emerging women used to send messages to each other. And Simone de Beauvoir herself, her life and her work, was — and is — a symbol; a symbol of the possibility, despite everything, of living one's life the way one wants to, for oneself, free from conventions and prejudices, even as a woman.

In the months following May 1970, political events came thick and fast. The first women's groups in France were founded that summer. I joined them in September, and the following spring the MLF (Mouvement de la Libération des Femmes [Women's liberation movement]) launched a sensational campaign against the ban on abortion. Three hundred and forty-three women, including some very well-known ones, stated publicly that they had had an abortion, and demanded the same right for every woman. Simone de Beauvoir was among them.

Just a few months before, the first French feminist collective publication (*L'an zéro* [Zero year]) had been at great pains to take Simone de Beauvoir to task for being "Sartre-fixated" and, worse still, for writing for a male publication (*Les Temps Modernes* [Modern Times]). Today Simone de Beauvoir still recalls that "I was very angry about that."

At the same time, though, some women in the movement did seek contact with her and asked her to join them. And she agreed, quite naturally and without reservation. For us feminists, the fact that she did so was not just a major source of support, it was also a moving gesture of affirmation and encouragement.

In all the years since then, she has never refused anything to the women she worked with politically, or in whom she confided on a personal level. Just as Sartre became a "compagnon de route" for part of the radical left, so Simone de Beauvoir played the same role for one part of the women's movement, the radical feminists. She gave her support, and indeed still does, to acts of political provocation, took part in various campaigns and contributes her important strategies (for example in 1974, when she proposed a "League for Women's Rights" — modelled on the "League for Human Rights" — of which she is still President).

From the end of 1970, I was among the women who worked with her politically. One of the many activities undertaken by the movement was to set up an illegal abortion network and to introduce the new, non-surgical, suction method into France. It was by no means clear at the time whether the Pompidou government would react in a repressive way against the feminists, as it had done against the Maoists, for example. So to cover ourselves, we performed the first abortions in the apartments of so-called "public figures" (so that if there was a scandal, it would be a real scandal!). Simone de Beauvoir did not hesitate to make her apartment available.

The storm we had unleashed with the abortion campaign, in particular, took us by surprise. The feminist movement had started out with a few dozen activists. By the autumn of 1970, the militants could be numbered in the hundreds in Paris alone. The movement rapidly emerged as a political force in 1970–71, and one to be reckoned with right across the spectrum, from the established parties to alternative groups. Three to four thousand women, Simone de Beauvoir among them, took part in the march for the right to abortion on 11 November 1971.

At the same time, we started organising a "Tribunal," to be held in February 1972 in the Paris Mutualité. It was to be called "Days of Denunciation of Crimes against Women." A handful of women, including Simone de Beauvoir, planned and organised it. Gradually, it became clear that within the MLF, an organisation representing a wide range of issues and political opinion from its inception, Simone de Beauvoir's choice of contacts was by no means haphazard. Then and now, she sought out women who started with a materialist analysis of the situation of women (and the world), and strictly rejected any belief in "the nature of women." For example, Anne Zelensky, one of the people who has been active with her in the "League for Women's Rights"; Christine Delphy, who edits the theoretical feminist publication (*Nouvelles*) *Questions Féministes* [New feminist issues]; and the group of women she worked with for many years on "le sexisme ordinaire" (everyday sexism) for *Les Temps Modernes*.

We all remember the de Beauvoir of those days very well. To begin with, we treated her with a mixture of respect and familiarity, and before long we all became extremely fond of her. She was always on time for our working meetings (unpunctuality is one of her pet aversions), and always got straight down to the matter in hand. Her contributions to discussion were distinguished by a piercing clarity and a devastating disregard for convention (nothing was too radical for her); yet at the same time, her demeanour was sometimes touchingly well brought-up.

The way she could hold her handbag on her lap. . . .

It was a period of innovation — everything seemed possible, political work was like a drug filling our entire lives. Evenings of meetings, campaigns, discussions, meals. These meals with de Beauvoir, "les bouffes," soon became a favourite routine. We took turns cooking the meals (although she never did. She hates cooking!) There were generally six or eight of us, all women. There was much eating, drinking, laughing and making of plans.

It was during one of these "bouffes" that we came up with the idea for my first interview with Simone de Beauvoir. There were two fundamental reasons behind it. On the one hand, it seemed important to me that the "conversion" of the author of *The Second Sex* to feminism should be made known to the public — after all, she had always distanced herself from feminism and had often stated her belief that the women's question would be automatically solved within a socialist framework. And on the other, quite simply, we needed the money to hire the Mutualité. The rooms cost 10,000 francs for the weekend; we had raised 8,000, and in fact we came up with the remaining 2,000 by selling the interview to the French weekly, *Le Nouvel Observateur* [New observer].

The interview made history. It appeared at the beginning of 1972, at a time when the women's movements in all the Western countries were obstinately insisting on their own identity and so coming into conflict with the left, from which many of the militant activists originally came.

"I am a feminist," Simone de Beauvoir now declared publicly, and so committed herself to the need for a separate, autonomous women's movement, while also criticising political parties in capitalist and socialist countries alike. The interview was translated into many languages, even Japanese, and a pirated edition did the rounds of several women's groups.

A year later, I made a documentary on Simone de Beauvoir for West German television — in my capacity as a foreign correspondent, I worked mainly for West German radio and television. She enjoyed the filming, despite all the bureaucracy and tedious attention to detail — she is a passionate cinema-goer. The conversation (the second in this book) in which de Beauvoir and Sartre answer questions about their relationship is taken from this broadcast. Conducted in Rome in September 1973, it is, as far as I know, the only interview in which both together answer questions about the ground rules of their relationship — a relationship which has been (and undoubtedly still is) a model for many generations of a partnership joined in love and contracted in freedom.

Those days in Rome marked the beginning of our friendship, over and above our political and journalistic work. I remember particularly the long evenings on the *terrazza*, which de Beauvoir, Sartre and I would spend putting God and the world to rights. One of the things we all three had in common was a love of gossip. . . .

It was a brief interlude in our political work, which continued back in Paris. Protest campaigns and feminist activities and initiatives . . . there was nothing we were not ready to take on. Simone de Beauvoir herself always favoured a dual strategy involving both legal and illegal work. However, she never wavered in her rejection of all existing political parties and her decision to work only outside them.

She was, and is, incorruptible. There have been numerous attempts to clip her wings and those of the women's movement, but her reaction has always been one of clear-sighted derision. For example, in our third conversation, held in 1976, her comment on "International Women's Year" was, "the next thing will be an International Year of the Sea, then an International Year of the Horse, the Dog, and so on. . . . People think of women as objects, that are not worth taking seriously for more than a year in this man's world."

She constantly reminded us of the central points of her political understanding and analysis, and warned against the new trend, discernible since the mid–1970s, to ascribe a mystic status to motherhood and to believe in the "nature of women." "Given that one can hardly tell women that washing up saucepans is their divine mission, they are told that bringing up children is their divine mission."

As has so often happened before, her pronouncements, especially those on the subject of motherhood, provoked a storm of protest. Women from all over the world even wrote to her home address in Paris, saying that she was hostile to mothers, that she was frustrated, that she should not throw the baby out with the bathwater. Those who cannot come to terms with the rigour and uncompromising nature of Simone de Beauvoir's thoughts and way of life have always been determined not to understand her.

De Beauvoir has been asked any number of times whether she is not missing something crucial as a non-mother. But has anyone ever asked Sartre whether he feels completely fulfilled as a person, despite the fact that he has never been a father? Because of this inequality, some of her statements on the subject of motherhood understandably reveal a certain irritation, but there is also genuine anger about the way women deceive themselves or are manipulated on this central issue.

What does Simone de Beauvoir say about motherhood? That motherhood is not a woman's life work. That the capacity for biological motherhood (i.e. giving birth) does not automatically mean a duty to be a social mother (i.e. bringing up the child). That motherhood is not in itself a creative act. That in current conditions, motherhood often makes slaves of women and ties them to the house and/or to their role. That we must therefore put an end to this kind of motherhood, and the division of labour along male/female lines. And finally, that the basis of this male/female division of labour is the concept of a "feminine" maternal nature, invented by men — a maternal nature that is by no means inherent in women, but imposed on them by education. Simone de Beauvoir says, "Women are exploited — and they allow themselves to be exploited — in the name of love."[1] Golden words, now as always.

The re-mystification of motherhood is at the heart of the "new femininity." In our third published conversation, held in 1976, we both thought it important to warn against the renaissance of the "eternal feminine." Once again, Simone de Beauvoir is sharply critical of any belief that women are "other," let alone "superior." "That would be the most sinister biological distortion and in total contradiction to everything I think. When men tell us just to go on being a woman, leave all the irksome things, like power, honour, careers to us, be glad that you are as you are, in tune with the earth, preoccupied with human concerns. . . . When men say that to us, it is really very dangerous."

Since then things have gone from bad to worse. Times are getting harder — and the temptation to seek refuge in the fatal illusion of the "eternal feminine" is ever greater. An international economic crisis and an equally international reassertion of maculinity are both rebounding on us women. The last conversation in this book, held in September 1982, and perhaps the most personal in content and tone, returns in a very topical way to those dangers. It shows Simone de Beauvoir once again as one of the most honest and most radical feminists of our time.

Still the most important theoretician of the new feminism, without whose contribution the new women's movements would certainly not have made as much progress as they have, she relates her observation of the situation today to her personal experience and the tradition she established; she recalls the furore — what a revelation it was — when *The Second Sex* was published in 1949, and shows how the old stereotypes persist.

On the eve of her seventieth birthday, in January 1978, we had a conversation about her own old age. Here, the author of *Old Age* — a work that I believe to be comparable to *The Second Sex* in its radical vision and depth — reveals a trait that I consider very characteristic. Simone de Beauvoir is not a particularly introspective person. The fact that she wrote this comprehensive work on old age does not mean that she has much more to say about her own old age than many other people. In her, this is presumably not just a limitation but also a defence, and it lends her moral strength a touch of ingenuousness.

In her old age Simone de Beauvoir is just the same as she always has been — passionately involved with literature and politics. She still travels a great deal and is surrounded by a small but devoted circle of friends, her "family." "I shall never be alone until the day I die," she says, and she is probably right. Although Sartre, the most important person in her life for over half a century, died in the spring of 1980, she is not at all lonely today.

The shock of Sartre's death is something she has not forgotten; but she has survived it, and reflecting on it has been a great comfort. She overcomes her grief in her latest book, *La Cérémonie des Adieux* [Adieux], and pays her life companion her final deep respects. With unsentimental accuracy and yet great tenderness, she describes Sartre's last years, and is brave enough to talk about illness and death. She has also published the wonderfully lively and unpretentious conversations about literature that they held during this period, causing another scandal as a result. Is it legitimate to portray such an eminent man in all his frailty and ill-health? Simone de Beauvoir says that one must, because it forms an integral part of his life.

Her modest yet obstinate reserve comes across throughout the book. Whenever Sartre addresses her in the dialogues or wants to talk about her, she interrupts him, "Don't let's talk about me. This is about you." But this modesty is backed up by an iron will. Simone de Beauvoir says of herself, "I have never met anyone, in the whole of my life, who was so well equipped for happiness as I was, or who laboured so stubbornly to achieve it."

Her happiness was by no means handed to her on a plate; she worked for it enormously hard and with courage. At one point in her memoirs, she describes a stay at an oasis in Algeria. It was 104°F in the shade. And what was she doing there? "I was working," she writes laconically.

But no account of her intelligence and her energy would be complete without mentioning her beauty. Of all the women I know, she is one of the very few — if not the only one — who have fought for the right to be intelligent *and* beautiful, to abound with energy *and* sensuality. One of her former pupils, Sarah Hirschmann, remembers the young teacher in Marseilles: "She was wearing a lilac silk blouse and a pleated skirt, young, her black hair swept up with combs, in contrast to her light, translucent eyes which were outlined with blue eye-shadow. For years we had been taught by stiff, ageless women with their hair in buns. Miss de Beauvoir seemed unbelievably glamorous."

Simone de Beauvoir is one of the few women philosophers of modern times, a leading theoretician and a distinguished journalist. She is recognised as a major literary figure both by the critics and by her enormous public who devour her novels and memoirs. It is a record to be proud of. Yet one important aspect is missing from this list: her life, which she has translated into action, over and above her writing and thinking. There, it seems to me, lies the real secret of her fascination and her uniqueness — the interplay and interaction of word and deed. For her, her work is her life.

She is a woman who refuses to accept her role passively, who has taken a stand, flouting all convention and opposition. She never marries — yet her love is deep and faithful. She does not have any children — yet a large part of the younger generation sees her as a model in areas of vital importance. She does not seek to conform — yet she does not evade the issue either; she takes to the battlefield and resists, both physically and intellectually, all pressure, including modish whims. She does not tie herself down, yet she has her roots: in her city, in people and ideas, which she pursues and develops with clarity and consistency, yet she is always ready to change and to radicalise.

She describes and reflects upon her life — in so far as she wants to divulge anything—in her memoirs. Sometimes, though, her novels are actually more revealing. Those which are inspired by her own experience (such as her first book, *She Came to Stay*) seem more powerful to me than those, like *The Blood of Others*, which were written to expound too highly structured an idea. In the last conversation with Sartre, de Beauvoir asks him whether he would prefer to go down in history as a philosopher or a writer, assuming he had to choose. A writer, says Sartre. I put this question indirectly to de Beauvoir and she, too, voted for literature. Comparing her work to Sartre's, she says, "I set my store by literature."

If I had to decide, I would ascribe to her more significance as a theorist (without forgetting that her theories only derive their power taken in conjunction with her life and her literary work). *The Second Sex*, her physiological, psychological, economic and historical study of the internal and external reality of women in a male-dominated world, is a pioneering work without parallel. Even today, thirty-three years after it was first published, it is still the most exhaustive and far-reaching theoretical work on the new feminism!

Of course, the new women's movements, which have very complex historical origins and which have emerged all over the Western world, would exist even without Simone de Beauvoir. But I suggest that without her they would still be on very shaky ground today, and that in theoretical terms they would still be labouring with every step across ground which the vanguard has already covered in seven-league boots.

What intellectual freedom, what confidence, what intellectual curiosity and what a lot of hard work it must have taken to produce a work like *The Second Sex*! During the war, women had taken "men's jobs," and had gained experience and self-confidence. In the years immediately after the war, they were sent back home and they submitted to the dictates of "femininity" once again. That was when Simone de Beauvoir wrote *The Second Sex*, and raised the banner of revolt. On her own.

Of course, some points in *The Second Sex* are outmoded today (such as her analysis of the historical origins of partriarchy, where the current state of knowledge then resulted in her relying too heavily on Bachofen and Engels). Yet the exhaustive exposition of her own central statement—"One is not born, but rather becomes, a woman"—is not only as valid today as it has always been, but is even more topical than ever, because of the new mystification of the feminine. Simone de Beauvoir shows us that we can and must shake ourselves out of our slave mentality, though we have been moulded by the dictates of femininity and are trapped by our oppressors, even in our beds. She embodies the existentialist demand that one change from object to subject, refuse to be passive and act in spite of everything, and thus—and at this price—become a human being.

"The majority of women resign themselves to their lot without attempting to take any action; those who have tried to change it have not wanted to be confined by the limits of their peculiarity, so causing it to triumph, but to rise above it. When they have intervened in the course of world affairs, it has been in accord with men, and from a masculine perspective," de Beauvoir says in *The Second Sex*, and she has been a living example of this all her life. The fate of being a woman has never been a vocation for her. Liberation from this role has always meant breaking out of femininity.

For de Beauvoir the existentialist, "women's destiny" must be taken as a challenge. Her particular contribution has been to link a profound analysis of the origins of our bonds with the realisation that we women can free ourselves from them, and set out on the uphill path. It is a liberty that has its price.

In the last sentence of *The Second Sex*, Simone de Beauvoir expresses the wish that one day men and women will "unequivocally affirm their brotherhood." That is undoubtedly the most daring and most noble vision of a society delivered from the pressure of sex (and other) roles, and from master-slave relationships.

For me, Simone de Beauvoir's life and work represent a challenge for men *and* women alike. Her theories may well provide women with an explanation of their condition, but never an excuse for it.

Note

1. This quote has been edited out of the French version. In the German edition it appears in the third interview (Translator's note).

Articles, Essays, and Reviews

Metaphysics and the Novel   Maurice Merleau-Ponty*

> "What surprises me is that you are touched in such a concrete way by a metaphysical situation."
> "But the situation is concrete," said Françoise, "the whole meaning of my life is at stake."
> "I'm not saying it isn't," Pierre said. "Just the same, this ability of yours to put body and soul into living an idea is exceptional."
>
> S. de Beauvoir, L'Invitée

I

The work of a great novelist always rests on two or three philosophical ideas. For Stendhal, these are the notions of the Ego and Liberty; for Balzac, the mystery of history as the appearance of a meaning in chance events; for Proust, the way the past is involved in the present and the presence of times gone by. The function of the novelist is not to state these ideas thematically but to make them exist for us in the way that things exist. Stendhal's role is not to hold forth on subjectivity; it is enough that he make it present.[1]

It is nonetheless surprising that, when writers do take a deliberate interest in philosophy, they have such difficulty in recognizing their affinities. Stendhal praises ideologists to the skies; Balzac compromises his views on the expressive relations of body and soul, economics and civilization, by couching them in the language of spiritualism. Proust sometimes translates his intuition about time into a relativistic and skeptical philosophy and at other times into hopes of immortality which distort it just as much. Valéry repudiated the philosophers who wanted at least to annex the *Introduction à la méthode de Léonard de Vinci*. For a long time it looked as if philosophy and literature not only had different ways of saying things but had different objects as well.

Since the end of the 19th century, however, the ties between them

*Reprinted from *Sense and Non-Sense*, trans. Hubert L. Dreyfus and Patricia Allen Dreyfus (originally published in French, 1948; Evanston: Northwestern University Press, 1964), 26–40. Reprinted by permission of Northwestern University Press.

have been getting closer and closer. The first sign of this reconciliation was the appearance of hybrid modes of expression having elements of the intimate diary, the philosophical treatise, and the dialogue. Péguy's work is a good example. Why should a writer from then on need to use simultaneous references to philosophy, politics, and literature in order to express himself? Because a new dimension of investigation was opened up. "Everyone has a metaphysics — explicit or implicit — or he does not exist."[2] Intellectual works had always been concerned with establishing a certain attitude toward the world, of which literature and philosophy, like politics, are just different expressions; but only now had this concern become explicit. One did not wait for the introduction of existential philosophy in France to define all life as latent metaphysics and all metaphysics as an "explicitation" of human life.

That in itself bears witness to the historical necessity and importance of this philosophy. It is the coming to consciousness of a movement older than itself whose meaning it reveals and whose rhythm it accelerates. Classical metaphysics could pass for a speciality with which literature had nothing to do because metaphysics operated on the basis of uncontested rationalism, convinced it could make the world and human life understood by an arrangement of concepts. It was less a matter of explicitating than of explaining life, or of reflecting upon it. What Plato said about "same" and "other" doubtless applies to the relations between oneself and other people; what Descartes said about God's being the identity of essence and existence pertains in a certain way to man and, in any event, pertains to that locus of subjectivity where it is impossible to distinguish the recognition of God from thought's recognition of itself. What Kant said about Consciousness concerns us even more directly. But after all, it is of "same" and "other" that Plato is speaking; it is God that Descartes is talking about in the end; it is Consciousness of which Kant speaks — not that other which exists opposite from me or that self which I am. Despite the most daring beginnings (for example: in Descartes), philosophers always ended by describing their own existence — either in a transcendental setting, or as a moment of a dialectic, or again in concepts, the way primitive peoples represent it and project it in myths. Metaphysics was superimposed in man upon a robust human nature which was governed by tested formulas and which was never questioned in the purely abstract dramas of reflection.

Everything changes when a phenomenological or existential philosophy assigns itself the task, not of explaining the world or of discovering its "conditions of possibility," but rather of formulating an experience of the world, a contact with the world which precedes all thought *about* the world. After this, whatever is metaphysical in man cannot be credited to something outside his empirical being — to God, to Consciousness. Man is metaphysical in his very being, in his loves, in his hates, in his individual and collective history. And metaphysics is no longer the occupation of a few hours per month, as Descartes said; it is present, as Pascal thought, in the heart's slightest movement.

From now on the tasks of literature and philosophy can no longer be separated. When one is concerned with giving voice to the experience of the world and showing how consciousness escapes into the world, one can no longer credit oneself with attaining a perfect transparence of expression. Philosophical expression assumes the same ambiguities as literary expression, if the world is such that it cannot be expressed except in "stories" and, as it were, pointed at. One will not only witness the appearance of hybrid modes of expression, but the novel and the theater will become thoroughly metaphysical, even if not a single word is used from the vocabulary of philosophy. Furthermore, a metaphysical literature will necessarily be amoral, in a certain sense, for there is no longer any human nature on which to rely. In every one of man's actions the invasion of metaphysics causes what was only an "old habit" to explode.

The development of a metaphysical literature, the end of a "moral" literature: this is what, for example, Simone de Beauvoir's *L'Invitée* signifies. Using this example, let us examine the phenomenon more closely, and, since the characters in the book provoked the literary critics to censure them for immorality, let us see whether there is not a "true morality" beyond the "morality" at which these characters jeer.

II

There is a perpetual uneasiness in the state of being conscious. At the moment I perceive a thing, I feel that it was there before me, outside my field of vision. There is an infinite horizon of things to grasp surrounding the small number of things which I can grasp in fact. The whistle of a locomotive in the night, the empty theater which I enter, cause to appear, for a lightning instant, those things which everywhere are ready to be perceived — shows performed without an audience, shadows crowded with creatures. Even the things which surround me exceed my comprehension, provided I interrupt my usual intercourse with them and rediscover them, outside of the human or even the living world, in their role as natural things. In the silence of a country house, once the door has been shut against the odors of the shrubbery and the sounds of the birds, an old jacket lying on a chair will be a riddle if I take it just as it offers itself to me. There it is, blind and limited; it does not know what it is; it is content to occupy that bit of space — but it does so in a way I never could. It does not run off in all directions like a consciousness; it remains solidly what it is; it is in itself. Every object can affirm its existence only by depriving me of mine, and I am always secretly aware that there are other things in the world beside me and what I see. Ordinarily, however, I retain of this knowledge only what I need to reassure myself. I observe that, after all, the thing needs me in order to exist. Only when I discover the landscape hidden until then behind a hill does it fully become a landscape; one cannot imagine what a thing would be like if it were not about to, or able to, be seen by me. It is I who bring into being this world which seemed to exist without me, to surround and surpass me. I am therefore a consciousness, immediately present to the world, and nothing can claim to exist without somehow being caught in the web of my experience. I am not this particular person or face, this finite being: I am a pure witness, placeless and ageless, equal in power to the world's infinity.

It is thus that one surmounts or, rather, sublimates the experience of the Other. We easily escape from transcendence as long as we are dealing only with things: the transcendence of other people is more resistant. If another person exists, if he too is a consciousness, then I must consent to be for him only a finite object, determinate, *visible* at a certain place in the world. If he is consciousness, I must cease to be consciousness. But how am I then to forget that intimate attestation of my existence, that contact of self with self, which is more certain than any external evidence and which is the prior condition for everything else? And so we try to subdue the disquieting existence of others. "Their thoughts are the same to me as their words and their faces: objects which exist in my own particular world," says Françoise in *L'Invitée*. I remain the center of the world. I am that nimble being who moves about the world and animates it through and through. I cannot seriously mistake myself for that appearance I offer to others. I have no body. "Françoise smiled: she was not beautiful, yet she was very fond of her face; it always gave her a pleasant surprise when she caught a glimpse of it in a mirror. Most of the time she did not think she had one." Everything that happens is only a spectacle for this indestructible, impartial, and generous spectator. Everything exists just for her. Not that she uses people and things for her private satisfaction; quite the contrary, because she has no private life: all other people and the whole world coexist in her. "Here I am, impersonal and free, right in the middle of the dance hall. I simultaneously contemplate all these lives, all these faces. And if I were to turn away from them, they would soon disintegrate like a forsaken landscape."

What strengthens Françoise' conviction is that, by an extraordinary piece of luck, even love has not made her realize her limits. Doubtless Pierre has come to be more to her than an object in her own particular world, a backdrop for her life as other men are. But for all that, he is not an Other. Françoise and Pierre have established such sincerity between them, have constructed such a machine of language, that they are together even when living apart from each other and can remain free in their union. "There was just one life and at its center one being, of which one could say neither that it was 'he' nor that it was 'I,' but only 'we.'" Every thought and every event of the day were communicated and shared, every sentiment immediately interpreted and made into a dialogue; the we-ness was sustained by all that happened to each one of them. For Françoise,

Pierre is not an opaque being who masks everything else; he is simply a mode of behavior as clear to her as to himself, in harmony with a world which is not his private domain but belongs equally to Françoise.

To tell the truth, there are cracks in this construction right from the start. Simone de Beauvoir points out some of them: the book starts with a sacrifice on the part of Françoise. "Françoise looked at his fine green eyes beneath their curling lashes, the expectant mouth: If I had wanted to. . . . Perhaps it still was not too late. But what could she want?" The consolation is convenient. I am losing nothing, Françoise tells herself, because I *am* my love for Pierre. Still, she is not at the point where she does not see Gerbert, does not consider an affair with him, nor does she tell Pierre all these first private thoughts. "Elsewhere" and "other" have not been eliminated; they have merely been repressed. Is Françoise wholly absorbed in the we-ness they have constructed? Is that common world, recreated and enlarged every day by their tireless conversations, really the world itself, or isn't it rather an artificial environment? Have they not exchanged the complacencies of the inner life for those of the life in common? Each questions himself before the other, but before whom are they questioned together? Françoise says ingenuously enough that the center of Paris is always where she is. This makes one think of children who also "have no inner life" and always believe themselves to be in the midst of the world because they project everything, including their dreams, into that world: they remain for all that no less in the midst of their subjectivity, since they do not distinguish these dreams from real things. Just as children do, Françoise always recoils before new things because they threaten to upset the environment she has constructed for herself. The real world, with all its harshness, does not permit so much precaution. If Françoise and Pierre arouse so much envy and even hatred around them, isn't it because the others feel shut out by this two-headed wonder, because they never feel accepted by them, but always betrayed by Françoise with Pierre, by Pierre with Françoise? Elisabeth and soon Xavière feel drained of their substance, receiving only strictly rationed kindnesses in return.

This eternal love of Pierre and Françoise is nonetheless temporal. Its not being threatened by Pierre's other love affairs is conditional on Pierre's telling Françoise about them, on their becoming objects of discussion, simple provinces in the world for two, and on Pierre's never really getting involved in any of them. It so happens that Pierre subscribes to these conditions of his own accord: " 'You know very well,' he said, 'that I never feel compromised by what goes on inside of me.' " For him, love means wanting to exist and to count for another. "To make her love me would be to impose myself upon her, to enter her world and to triumph there in accordance with her own values. . . . You know very well that I have an insane need of such triumphs." But do the women he "loves" ever really exist for him absolutely? His "adventures" are not his true adventure which he lives only with Françoise. His need for other love affairs is anxiety before the Other, a concern with having his mastery recognized and a quick way of verifying the universality of his life. Since Françoise does not feel free to love Gerbert, how could she leave Pierre free to love other women? No matter what she says, she does not love Pierre's *effective* liberty; she doesn't love him truly in love with another woman. She does not love him in his liberty unless it is a freedom to be indifferent, free of all involvements. Françoise, like Pierre, remains free to be loved but not to love. They are confiscated by each other, which is why Françoise draws back before an affair with Gerbert that would mean a genuine involvement and instead seeks Xavière's tenderness. The latter, so she thinks at least, will anchor her more securely in herself. "What delighted her most of all was to have annexed this sad little existence to her own life . . . ; nothing gave Françoise greater joy than this type of possession; Xavière's gestures, her face, her very life needed Françoise in order to exist." Just as the nations of Europe sensed French imperialism beneath the "universalist" policies of the National Convention, other people cannot help feeling frustrated if they are only dependencies in the world of Pierre and Françoise, and people sense beneath the generosity of these two a highly calculated enterprise. The other person is never admitted between them except warily, as a guest. Will he be satisfied with this role?

The metaphysical drama which Pierre and Françoise had succeeded in forgetting by dint of generosity is abruptly revealed by the presence of Xavière. Each in his own way has achieved the appearance of happiness and fulfillment by means of a general renunciation. " 'I for one,' said Xavière, 'was not born resigned.' " They thought they had overcome jealousy by the omnipotence of language; but when Xavière is requested to verbalize her life, she replies, " 'I don't have a public soul.' " One should make no mistake about the fact that if the silence she demands is perhaps that of equivocations and ambiguous feelings, it may also be that in which true commitment develops beyond all arguments and all motives. " 'Last night,' she said to Pierre, with an almost painful sneer, 'you seemed to be living things for once, and not just talking about them.' " Xavière challenges all the conventions by which Françoise and Pierre had thought to make their love invulnerable.

The dramatic situation of *L'Invitée* could be set forth in psychological terms: Xavière is *coquettish*, Pierre *desires* her, and Françoise is *jealous*. This would not be wrong. It would be merely superficial. What is coquetry if not the need to count for another person, combined with the fear of becoming involved? What is desire? One does not simply desire a body — one desires a being which one can occupy and rule over. Pierre's desire is mixed with his consciousness of Xavière as a valuable creature, and her value comes from her being completely what she feels, as her gestures and her face show at every moment. Finally, to say that Françoise is jealous is only another way of saying that Pierre is *turned toward*

Xavière, that he is for once living a love affair, and that no verbal communication, no loyalty to the conventions established between himself and Françoise can re-integrate that love into Françoise's universe. The drama is therefore not psychological but metaphysical: Françoise thought she could be bound to Pierre and yet leave him free; not make a distinction between herself and him; will herself by willing him, as each wills the other in the realm of Kantian ends. The appearance of Xavière not only reveals to them a being from whom their values are excluded but also reveals that each of them is shut off from the other, and from himself. Among Kantian consciousnesses harmony can always be taken for granted. What the characters in this book discover is inherent individuality, the Hegelian self which seeks the death of the other.

The pages in which Françoise witnesses the ruin of her artificial world are perhaps the most beautiful in the book. She is no longer at the heart of things as if this were a natural privilege of hers: the world has a center from which she is excluded, and it is the place where Pierre and Xavière are to meet. With the others, things retreat beyond her grasp and become the strange debris of a world to which she no longer holds the key. The future ceases to be the natural extension of the present, time is fragmented, and Françoise is no more than an anonymous being, a creature without a history, a mass of chilled flesh. She now knows there are situations which cannot be communicated and which can only be understood by living them. There was a unique pulsation which projected before her a living present, a future, a world, which animated language for her — and that pulsation has stopped.

Does one even have to say that Pierre loves Xavière? A feeling is the name conventionally given to a series of instants, but life, when considered lucidly, is reduced to this swarming of instants to which chance alone gives a common meaning. In any case, the love of Françoise and Pierre only seemed to defy time insofar as it lost its reality. One can escape the crumbling of time only by an act of faith which now seems to Françoise a voluntary illusion. All love is a verbal construction, or at best a lifeless scholasticism. They had been pleased to think they had no inner lives, that they were really living a life in common. But, in the last analysis, if it is true that Pierre does not accept complicity with anyone against Françoise, is it not at least in complicity with himself and, at each moment, is it not from his solitude where he judges her that he rushes once again into the interworld they had built? Henceforth, Françoise can no longer know herself from inner evidence alone. She can no longer doubt that, under the glance of that couple, she is truly an object, and through their eyes she sees herself from the outside for the first time. And what is she? A thirty-year-old woman, a mature woman, to whom many things are already irrevocably impossible — who, for example, will never be able to dance well. For the first time she has the feeling of being her body, when all along she had thought herself a consciousness. She has sacrificed everything to this myth.

She has grown incapable of a single act of her own, of living close to her desires, and it is for this reason that she has ceased to be precious to Pierre, as Xavière knows so well how to be. That purity, that unselfishness, that morality they used to admire become hateful to her because they were all part of the same fiction. She and Pierre thought they had gone beyond individuality; she believed she had overcome jealousy and selfishness. How was she to know? Once she has recognized in all seriousness the existence of another person and accepted the objective picture of her life which she sees in the glances of other people, how could Françoise take as indubitable her own feeling about herself? How is one to recognize an inner reality? Has Pierre stopped loving her? And Françoise, is she jealous? Does she really scorn jealousy? Isn't her very doubt of this scorn itself a construction? An alienated consciousness can no longer believe in itself. At the moment when all projects thus collapse, when even the self's hold on itself is broken, death — which one's projects had traversed without even suspecting it up to now — becomes the only reality, since it is in death that the pulverization of time and life is consummated. Life has rejected Françoise.

The illness which comes over her is a sort of temporary solution. In the clinic to which she has been brought she neither asks herself any more questions, nor does she any longer feel abandoned because she has broken with her life. For the moment, the center of the world is in that room, and the most important event of the day is being X-rayed or having her temperature taken or the first meal she is going to get. All things have mysteriously regained their value: this container of orangeade on the table, that enameled wall are interesting in themselves. Every passing moment is replete and self-sufficient, and when her friends come up from Paris, they come out of nowhere each time they appear and are as intermittent as characters in a play. The petty discussions they bring to her bedside have no reality beside her solitude, which is no longer isolation. She has withdrawn from the human world where she was suffering into the natural world where she finds a frozen peace. As ordinary language so well expresses it, she *took* sick. Or would the crisis which is now subsiding perhaps have been less violent if it had not been for fatigue and the oncoming illness? Françoise herself will never know. All life is undeniably ambiguous, and there is never any way to know the true meaning of what we do. Indeed, perhaps our actions have no *single* true meaning.

Likewise, there is no way to tell whether the decisions Françoise reaches when, with renewed strength, she resumes her place between Pierre and Xavière are more truthful in themselves or whether they merely express the well-being and optimism of recovery. Xavière and Pierre have grown closer to each other during her absence and have ended by agreeing that they love one another. This time there must be no giving in to any ambiguous suffering. And after all, perhaps the only reason Françoise feels abandoned is that she remains aloof. Perhaps she can overtake this couple already formed without her; perhaps they can all live the same life if only Françoise will also accept responsibility for the enterprise of the trio. But she now knows that there is such a thing as solitude, that everyone decides for himself, that everyone is condemned to his own actions. She has lost the illusion of unobstructed communication, of happiness taken for granted, and of purity. But what if the only obstacle had been her own refusal, if happiness could be *made*, if freedom did not consist in cutting oneself off from all earthly involvements but in accepting and so going beyond them? What if Xavière had rescued them from the scholasticism which was killing their love? "What if she were finally to decide to plunge forward with all her might, instead of standing stock still, with limp and empty arms?" "It was so simple: this love which suddenly made her heart swell with sweetness had always been within arm's reach; she had only to stretch out her hand, that shy, greedy hand."

She will, then, reach out her hand. She will succeed in sticking with Pierre in his jealous passion for Xavière, right up to the moment when he spies on Xavière through a keyhole. And the trio will fail nevertheless. Just because it is a trio? True, the enterprise is a strange one. It is essential for love to be total, since the lover loves *a person*, not just *qualities*, and the beloved wants to feel justified in his very existence. The presence of a third person, even though and, in fact, just because he too is loved, introduces a mental reservation in each one's love for the other. The trio would really exist only if one could no longer distinguish two pairs of lovers and one pair of friends, if each one loved the other two *with equal feeling*, and if the good hoped for from them in return were not just their love for him but their love for one another as well; if, finally, they really lived as a threesome, instead of living two by two in alternating complicities with a general reunion every now and then. This is impossible; but a couple is hardly less impossible, since each partner remains in complicity with himself, and the love one receives is not the same as the love one gives. The immediate lives even of two people cannot be made one; it is the common tasks and projects that make the couple. The human couple is no more a *natural* reality than the trio. The failure of the trio (like the success of a couple) cannot be credited to any natural propensity. Are Xavière's defects then to be held responsible? She is jealous of Pierre, jealous of Françoise, jealous of their affection for their friends. Perversely, she upsets all this diplomacy "just to see what will happen." She is egoistic, which is to say that she never goes beyond herself and never puts herself in another's place: "Xavière did not care about making other people happy; she took a selfish delight in the pleasure of giving pleasure." She never lends or gives herself to any project. She will not work at becoming an actress or cross Paris to see a movie. She never sacrifices the immediate, never goes beyond the present moment. She always sticks to what she feels. Thus there is a certain kind of intimacy she will always evade; one may live beside her but never with her. She remains focused on herself, locked in moods one is never sure of truly understanding, about which perhaps there is no truth to be understood. But who knows? Can we tell what Xavière would be like in *another situation*? Here as everywhere, moral judgment does not go very far. Françoise' love for Pierre succeeds in accepting Pierre's love for Xavière because it is deeper and older; and for this very reason Xavière can never accept the love between Pierre and Françoise. She senses a harmony between them which is over her head. Before meeting her they lived a whole *amour à deux* which is more essential than their predilection for her. Is it not precisely the torture of the trio that makes her incapable of loving either Pierre or Françoise in earnest?

It is not "Xavière's fault," nor Françoise', nor Pierre's; yet it is the fault of each of them. Each one is totally responsible because, if he acted differently, the others in turn would have treated him differently; and each can feel innocent because the others' freedom was invisible to him, and the face they offered to him was as fixed as fate. It is impossible to calculate each one's role in the drama, impossible to evaluate the responsibilities, to give a true version of the story, to put the events into their proper perspective. There is no Last Judgment. Not only do we not know the truth of the drama, but there is no truth — no other side of things where true and false, fair and unfair are separated out. We are inextricably and confusedly bound up with the world and with others.

Xavière sees Françoise as a forsaken, jealous woman, "armed with a bitter patience." There is not one word of this judgment, much as it rouses her indignation, which Françoise has not secretly said to herself. She has felt isolated, she has wished she might be loved as Xavière was, and she has put up with, not wished for, Pierre's love for Xavière. This does not mean that Xavière *is right*. If Françoise really had been forsaken, Xavière would not have felt so strongly how much she meant to Pierre. If Françoise had been jealous, she would not have suffered with him when he himself was jealous of Xavière: she loved Pierre in his liberty. One might answer, it is true, that Françoise' jealousy diminishes in direct proportion to the diminishing happiness of Pierre's love for Xavière. And so on, and so forth, *ad infinitum*. The truth is that our actions do not admit of any one motivation or explanation; they are "over-determined," as Freud so profoundly said. " 'You were jealous of me,' " Xavière says to Françoise, " 'because Labrousse was in love with me. You made him loathe me and took Gerbert away from me as well, to make your revenge even sweeter.' " Is this true, or is it false? Who is Françoise? Is she what she thinks of herself or what Xavière thinks of her? Françoise did not *intend* to hurt Xavière. She finally yielded to her fondness for Gerbert because she had come to understand that each of us has his own life and because she wanted to confirm her own existence after so many years of renunciation. But is the meaning of our actions to be found in our *intentions* or in the effect they have on others? And then again, are we ever completely unaware of what the consequences will be? Don't we really desire these consequences too? That secret love for Gerbert would be bound to look like revenge to Xavière—which Françoise could have guessed; and in loving Gerbert she implicitly accepted this consequence. Can one even say "implicitly"? "Strict as an order—as austere and pure as an icicle. Devoted, disdained, stuck in moral ruts. And she had said: No!" Françoise wanted to shatter the image of herself she had seen in Xavière's eyes. Is this not her way of saying that she wanted to get even with Xavière? We must not speak of the unconscious here. Xavière and the history of the trio are quite plainly at the root of the affair with Gerbert. It is simply that all of our actions have several meanings, especially as seen from the outside by others, and all these meanings are assumed in our actions because others are the permanent coordinates of our lives. Once we are aware of the existence of others, we commit ourselves to being, among other things, what they think of us, since we recognize in them the exorbitant power to *see us*. As long as Xavière exists, Françoise cannot help being what Xavière thinks she is. From this there follows the crime which, though it is no solution, since Xavière's death makes her dying image of Françoise eternal, ends the book.

Was there any solution? One might imagine a repentant or sick Xavière summoning Françoise to her side in order to confess her deceit. But Françoise would have been silly indeed to let this pacify her. There is no privilege inherent in the exaltation of repentance or of the last moments. One may very well feel that one is concluding one's life, dominating it, and solemnly handing out pardons or curses, but there is no proof that the convert or the dying man understands himself or others any better than before. We have no other resource at any moment than to act according to the judgments we have made as honestly and as intelligently as possible, as if these judgments were incontestable. But it would be dishonest and foolish ever to feel acquitted by the judgment of others. One moment of time cannot blot out another. Xavière's avowal could never obliterate her hatred, just as Pierre's return to Françoise does not annul the moments when he loved Xavière more than anything else.

III

There is no absolute innocence and—for the same reason—no absolute guilt. All action is a response to a factual situation which we have not completely chosen and for which, in this sense, we are not absolutely responsible. Is it Pierre's fault or Françoise' that they are both thirty years old and Xavière twenty? Again, is it their fault if their simple presence condemns Elisabeth to feelings of frustration and alienation? Is it their fault they were born? How can we ever feel totally accountable for any of our actions, even those we have deliberately chosen, since at least the necessity of choosing has been imposed on us from the outside and since we have been cast into the world without first being consulted? All personal

guilt is conditioned and overwhelmed by the general and original culpa-
bility with which fate burdens us by causing us to be born at a certain
time, in a certain environment, and with a certain face; and if we can
never feel justified no matter what we do, doesn't our conduct cease to
matter? The world is such that our actions change their meaning as they
issue and spread out from us. Sift through her memories as Françoise may,
the moments she spent with Gerbert in that country inn contain nothing
that is not radiant or pure. But the same love appears base to Xavière.
Since this is how it always is, since it is our inevitable fate to be seen
differently from the way we see ourselves, we have every right to feel that
accusations from the outside do not quite pertain to us. The fundamental
contingency of our lives makes us feel like *strangers* at the *trial* to which
others have brought us. All conduct will always be absurd in an absurd
world, and we can always decline responsibility for it, since in our heart of
hearts, "We are not of the world" (Rimbaud).

It is true that we are always free to accept or refuse life. By accepting
it we take the factual situations — our bodies, our faces, our way of
being — upon ourselves; we accept our responsibilities; we sign a contract
with the world and with men. But this freedom, the condition of all
morality, is equally the basis of an absolute immoralism because it remains
entire, in both myself and others, after every sin and because it makes new
beings of us at every instant. How could an invulnerable liberty prefer any
one line of conduct, any one relationship to another? Whether one
emphasizes the conditioning of our existence or, on the contrary, our
absolute liberty, our actions have no intrinsic and objective value — in the
first case, because there are no degrees of absurdity, and no conduct can
prevent us from bungling; and, in the second, because there are no degrees
of freedom, and no conduct can lead us to perdition.

The fact is that the characters in *L'Invitée* lack any "moral sense."
They do not find good and evil in things. They do not believe that human
life, by itself, makes any definite demands, or that it follows a self-
contained law as trees or bees do. They consider the world (including
society and their own bodies) as an "unfinished piece of work" — to use
Malebranche's profound phrase — which they question with curiosity and
treat in various ways.

It is not so much their actions which bring down censure on these
characters. Books, after all, are full of adultery, perversion, and crime,
and the critics have come across them before this. The smallest town has
more than one *ménage à trois*. Such a "family" is still a family. But how is
one to accept the fact that Pierre, Françoise, and Xavière are totally
ignorant of the holy natural law of the couple and that they try in all
honesty — and without, moreover, any hint of sexual complicity — to form a
trio? The sinner is always accepted, even in the strictest societies, because
he is part of the system and, as a sinner, does not question its principles.
What one finds unbearable in Pierre and Françoise is their artless

disavowal of morality, that air of candor and youth, that absolute lack of gravity, dizziness, and remorse. In brief, they think as they act and act as they think.

Are these qualities only acquired through skepticism, and do we mean that absolute immoralism is the last word in an "existential" philosophy? Not at all. There is an existentialism which leans toward skepticism, but it is certainly not that of *L'Invitée*. On the pretext that every rational or linguistic operation condenses a certain thickness of existence and is obscure for itself, one concludes that nothing can be said with certainty. On the pretext that human acts lose all their meaning when detached from their context and broken down into their component parts (like the gestures of the man I can see but do not hear through the window of a telephone booth), one concludes that all conduct is senseless. It is easy to strip language and actions of all meaning and to make them seem absurd, if only one looks at them from far enough away: this was Voltaire's technique in *Micromégas*. But that other miracle, the fact that, in an absurd world, language and behavior do have meaning for those who speak and act, remains to be understood. In the hands of French writers existentialism is always threatening to fall back into the "isolating" analysis which breaks time up into unconnected instants and reduces life to a collection of states of consciousness.[3]

As for Simone de Beauvoir, she is not vulnerable to such criticism. Her book shows existence understood between two limits: on the one hand, there is the immediate closed tightly upon itself, beyond any word and any commitment (Xavière); and, on the other, there is an absolute confidence in language and rational decision, an existence which grows empty in the effort to transcend itself (Françoise at the beginning of the book).[4] Between these fragments of time and that eternity which erroneously believes it transcends time, there is an effective existence which unfolds in patterns of behavior, is organized like a melody, and, by means of its projects, cuts across time without leaving it. There is undoubtedly no *solution* to human problems; no way, for example, to eliminate the transcendence of time, the separation of consciousness which may always reappear to threaten our commitments; no way to test the authenticity of these commitments which may always, in a moment of fatigue, seem artificial conventions to us. But between these two extremes at which existence perishes, total existence is our decision by which we enter time in order to create our life within it. All human projects are contradictory because they simultaneously attract and repel their realization. One only pursues a thing in order to possess it, and yet, if what I am looking for today must someday be found (which is to say, passed beyond), why bother to look for it? Because today is today and tomorrow, tomorrow. I can no more look at my present from the point of view of the future than I can see the earth from Sirius.[5] I would not love a person without the hope of being recognized by him, and yet this recognition does not count unless it is always free, that is, never possessed. But, after all, love does exist. Communication exists between the moments of my personal time, as between my time and that of other people, and in spite of the rivalry between them. It exists, that is, if I will it, if I do not shrink from it out of bad faith, if I am of good faith, if I plunge into the time which both separates and unites us, as the Christian plunges into God. True morality does not consist in following exterior rules or in respecting objective values: there are no ways to *be* just or to *be* saved. One would do better to pay less attention to the unusual situation of the three characters in *L'Invitée* and more to the good faith, the loyalty to promises, the respect for others, the generosity and the seriousness of the two principals. For the value is there. It consists of actively being what we are by chance, of establishing that communication with others and with ourselves for which our temporal structure gives us the opportunity and of which our liberty is only the rough outline.

Notes

1. As he does in *Le Rouge et le noir*: "Only I know what I might have done . . . , for others I am at most a 'perhaps.' " "If they had notified me of the execution this morning, at the moment when death seemed ugliest to me, the public eye would have spurred me on to glory. . . . A few perceptive people, if there are any among these provincials, could have guessed my weakness. . . . But nobody would have *seen* it."

2. Charles Péguy, *Notre Jeunesse*.

3. Sartre criticized Camus for giving way to this tendency in *L'Étranger*. (English translation by Stuart Gilbert, *The Stranger* [New York, 1954].)

4. I am keenly aware of how regrettable it is to write such a weighty commentary about a novel. But the novel has won its place in the public esteem and has nothing to lose or gain from my remarks.

5. This idea has been developed in Simone de Beauvoir's essay *Pyrrhus et Cinéas*.

Mlle. Gulliver en Amérique   Mary McCarthy*

In January, 1947, Simone de Beauvoir, the leading French *femme savante*, alighted from an airplane at LaGuardia Field for a four months' stay in the United States. In her own eyes, this trip had something fabulous about it, of a balloonist's expedition or a descent in a diving bell. Where to Frenchmen of an earlier generation, America was the incredible country of *les peaux rouges* and the novels of Fenimore Cooper, to Mlle. de Beauvoir America was, very simply, movieland—she came to verify for herself the existence of violence, drugstore stools, boy-meets-girl, that she

*Reprinted from *The Humanist in the Bathtub* (New York: New American Library, 1964), 20–27. Reprinted by permission of the author.

had seen depicted on the screen. Her impressions, which she set down in journal form for the readers of *Les Temps Modernes*, retained therefore the flavor of an eyewitness account, of confirmation of rumor, the object being not so much to assay America as to testify to its reality.

These impressions, collected into a book, made a certain stir in France; now, three years later, they are appearing in translation in Germany. The book has never been published over here; the few snatches excerpted from it in magazine articles provoked wonder and hostility.

On an American leafing through the pages of an old library copy, the book has a strange effect. It is as though an inhabitant of Lilliput or Brobdingnag, coming upon a copy of *Gulliver's Travels*, sat down to read, in a foreign tongue, of his own local customs codified by an observer of a different species: everything is at once familiar and distorted. The landmarks are there, and some of the institutions and personages—Eighth Avenue, Broadway, Hollywood, the Grand Canyon, Harvard, Yale, Vassar, literary celebrities concealed under initials; here are the drugstores and the cafeterias and the busses and the traffic lights—and yet it is all wrong, schematized, rationalized, like a scale model under glass. Peering down at himself, the American discovers that he has "no sense of *nuance*," that he is always in a good humor, that "in America the individual is nothing," that all Americans think their native town is the most beautiful town in the world, that an office girl cannot go to work in the same dress two days running, that in hotels "illicit" couples are made to swear that they are married, that it almost never happens here that a professor is also a writer, that the majority of American novelists have never been to college, that the middle class has no hold on the country's economic life and very little influence on its political destiny, that the good American citizen is never sick, that racism and reaction grow more menacing every day, that "the appearance, even, of democracy is vanishing from day to day," and that the country is witnessing "the birth of fascism."

From these pages, he discovers, in short, that his country has become, in the eyes of Existentialists, a future which is, so to speak, already a past, a gelid eternity of drugstores, juke boxes, smiles, refrigerators, and "fascism," and that he himself is no longer an individual but a sort of Mars man, a projection of science fiction, the man of 1984. Such a futuristic vision of America was already in Mlle. de Beauvoir's head when she descended from the plane as from a space ship, wearing metaphorical goggles: eager as a little girl to taste the rock-candy delights of this materialistic moon civilization (the orange juice, the ice creams, the jazz, the whiskeys, the martinis, and the lobster). She knows already, nevertheless, that this world is not "real," but only a half-frightening fantasy daydreamed by the Americans.

She has preserved enough of Marxism to be warned that the spun-sugar façade is a device of the "Pullman class" to mask its exploitation and cruelty: while the soda fountains spout, Truman and Marshall prepare an anti-Communist crusade that brings back memories of the Nazis, and Congress plots the ruin of the trade unions. "The collective future is in the hands of a privileged class, the Pullman class, to which are reserved the joys of large-scale enterprise and creation; the others are just wheels in a big steel world; they lack the power to conceive an individual future for themselves; they have no plan or passion, hope or nostalgia, that carries them beyond the present; they know only the unending repetition of the cycle of seasons and hours."

This image of a people from Oz or out of an expressionist ballet, a robot people obedient to a generalization, corresponds, of course, with no reality, either in the United States or anywhere else; it is the petrifaction of a fear very common in Europe today—a fear of the future. Where, in a more hopeful era, America embodied for Europe a certain millennial promise, now in the Atomic Age it embodies an evil presentiment of a millennium just at hand. To Mlle. de Beauvoir, obsessed with memories of Jules Verne, America is a symbol of a mechanical progress once dreamed of and now repudiated with horror; it is a Judgment on itself and on Europe. No friendly experience with Americans can dispel this deep-lying dread. She does not wish to know America but only to ascertain that it is there, just as she had imagined it. She shrinks from involvement in this "big steel world" and makes no attempt to see factories, workers, or political leaders. She prefers the abstraction of "Wall Street."

This recoil from American actuality has the result that might be expected, a result, in fact, so predictable that one might say she willed it. Her book is consistently misinformed in small matters as well as large. She has a gift for visual description which she uses very successfully to evoke certain American phenomena: Hollywood, the Grand Canyon, the Bronx, Chinatown, women's dresses, the stockyards, the Bowery, Golden Gate, auto camps, Hawaiian dinners, etc. In so far as the U.S. is a vast tourist camp, a vacationland, a Stop-in Serv-Urself, she has caught its essence. But in so far as the United States is something more than a caricature of itself conceived by the mind of an ad man or a Western Chamber of Commerce, she has a disinclination to view it. She cannot, for example, take in the names of American writers even when she has their books by her elbow: she speaks repeatedly of James Algee (Agee), of Farrel (Farrell), O'Neil (O'Neill), and of Max Twain—a strange form of compliment to authors whom she professes to like. In the same way, Greenwich Village, which she loves, she speaks of throughout as "Greeniwich," even when she comes to live there.

There are minor distortions. What is more pathetic is her credulity, which amounts to a kind of superstition. She is so eager to appear well informed that she believes anything anybody tells her, especially if it is anti-American and pretends to reveal the inner workings of the capitalist mechanism. The Fifth Avenue shops, she tells us, are "reserved for the capitalist international," and no investigative instinct tempts her to cross the barricade and see for herself. Had she done so, she might have found suburban housewives, file clerks, and stenographers swarming about the racks of Peck & Peck or Best's or Franklin Simon's, and colored girls mingling with white girls at the counters of Saks Fifth Avenue. A Spanish painter assures her that in America you have to hire a press agent to get your paintings shown. An author tells her that in America literary magazines print only favorable reviews. A student tells her that in America private colleges pay better salaries than state universities, so that the best education falls to the privileged classes, who do not want it, and so on. At Vassar, she relates, students are selected "according to their intellectual capacities, family, and fortune." Every item in this catalogue is false. (Private colleges do not pay better salaries—on the contrary, with a few exceptions, they pay notoriously worse; family plays no part in the selection of students at Vassar, and fortune only to the extent that the tuition has to be paid by someone—friend, parent, or scholarship donor; you do not have to hire a press agent; some literary magazines make a positive specialty of printing unfavorable reviews.)

Yet Mlle. de Beauvoir, unsuspecting, continues volubly to pass on "the low-down" to her European readers: there is no friendship between the sexes in America; American whites are "stiff" and "cold"; American society has lost its mobility; capital is in "certain hands," and the worker's task is "carefully laid out." "True, a few accidental successes give the myth of the self-made man a certain support, but they are illusory and tangential. . . ."

The picture of an America that consists of a small ruling class and a vast inert, regimented mass beneath it is elaborated at every opportunity. She sees the dispersion of goods on counters but draws no conclusion from it as to the structure of the economy. The American worker, to her, is invariably the French worker, a consecrated symbol of oppression. She talks a great deal of American conformity but fails to recognize a thing that Tocqueville saw long ago; that this conformity is the expression of a predominantly middle-class society; it is the price paid (as yet) for the spread of plenty. Whether the diffusion of television sets is, in itself, a good is another question; the fact is, however, that they *are* diffused; the "Pullman class," for weal or woe, does not have a corner on them, or on the levers of political power.

The outrage of the upper-class minority at the spectacle of television aerials on the shabby houses of Poverty Row, at the thought of the Frigidaires and washing machines in farmhouse and working-class kitchens, at the new cars parked in ranks outside the factories, at the very thought of installment buying, unemployment compensation, social security, trade-union benefits, veterans' housing, at General Vaughan, above all at Truman the haberdasher, the symbol of this cocky equality—their outrage is perhaps the most striking phenomenon in American life today.

Yet Mlle. de Beauvoir remained unaware of it, and unaware also, for all her journal tells us, of income taxes and inheritance taxes, of the expense account and how it has affected buying habits and given a peculiar rashness and transiency to the daily experience of consumption. It can be argued that certain angry elements in American business do not know their own interests, which lie in the consumers' economy; even so, this ignorance and anger are an immense political fact in America.

The society characterized by Mlle. de Beauvoir as "rigid," "frozen," "closed" is in the process of great change. The mansions are torn down and the real-estate "development" takes their place: serried rows of ranch-type houses, painted in pastel colors, each with its picture window and its garden, each equipped with deep-freeze, oil furnace, and automatic washer, spring up in the wilderness. Class barriers disappear or become porous; the factory worker is an economic aristocrat in comparison to the middle-class clerk; even segregation is diminishing; consumption replaces acquisition as an incentive. The America invoked by Mlle. de Beauvoir as a country of vast inequalities and dramatic contrasts is rapidly ceasing to exist.

One can guess that it is the new America, rather than the imaginary America of economic royalism, that creates in Mlle. de Beauvoir a feeling of mixed attraction and repulsion. In one half of her sensibility, she is greatly excited by the United States and precisely by its material side. She is fascinated by drugstore displays of soap and dentifrices, by the uniformly regulated traffic, by the "good citizenship" of Americans, by the anonymous camaraderie of the big cities, by jazz and expensive record players and huge collections of records, and above all — to speak frankly — by the orange juice, the martinis, and the whiskey. She speaks elatedly of "my" America, "my" New York; she has a child's greedy possessiveness toward this place which she is in the act of discovering.

Toward the end of the book, as she revises certain early judgments, she finds that she has become "an American." What she means is that she has become somewhat critical of the carnival aspects of American life which at first bewitched her; she is able to make discriminations between different kinds of jazz, different hotels, different night clubs. Very tentatively, she pushes beyond appearance and perceives that the American is not his possessions, that the American character is not fleshly but abstract. Yet at bottom she remains disturbed by what she has seen and felt, even marginally, of the American problem. This is not one of inequity, as she would prefer to believe, but of its opposite. The problem posed by the United States is, as Tocqueville saw, the problem of equality, its consequences, and what price shall be paid for it. How is wealth to be spread without the spread of uniformity? How create a cushion of plenty without stupefaction of the soul and the senses? It is a dilemma that glares from every picture window and whistles through every breezeway.

If Americans, as Mlle. de Beauvoir thinks, are apathetic politically, it is because they can take neither side with any great conviction—how can one be *against* the abolition of poverty? And how, on the other hand, can one champion a leveling of extremes? For Europeans of egalitarian sympathies, America *is* this dilemma, relentlessly marching toward them, a future which "works," and which for that very reason they have no wish to face. Hence the desire, so very evident in Mlle. de Beauvoir's impressions and in much journalism of the European left, not to know what America is really like, to identify it with "fascism" or "reaction," not to admit, in short, that it has realized, to a considerable extent, the economic and social goals of President Franklin D. Roosevelt and of progressive thought in general.

January, 1952

The Subjection of Women   Elizabeth Hardwick*

Vassal, slave, inferior, other, thing, victim, dependent, parasite, prisoner—oh, bitter, raped, child-swollen flesh doomed to immanence! Sisyphean goddess of the dust pile! Demeter, Xantippe, Ninon de Lenclos, Marie Bashkirtsev, and "a friend of mine. . . ." From cave to café, boudoir to microscope, from the knitting needles to the short story: they are all here in a potency of pages, a foreshortened and exaggerated, a mysterious and too clear relief, an eloquent lament and governessy scolding, a poem and a doctoral thesis. I suppose there is bound to be a little laughter in the wings at the mere thought of this madly sensible and brilliantly obscure tome on women by Simone de Beauvoir, *The Second Sex.*

Still the more one sinks into this very long book, turning page after page, the more clearly it seems to lack a subject with reasonable limitations and concreteness, a subject on which offered illustrations may wear some air of finality and conviction. The theme of the work is that women are not simply "women," but are, like men, in the fullest sense human beings. Yet one cannot easily write the history of people! This point may appear trivial; nevertheless, to take on this glorious and fantastic book is not like reading at all—from the first to the last sentence one has the sensation of playing some breathlessly exciting and finally exhausting game. You gasp and strain and remember; you point out and deny and agree, trying always to find some way of taking hold, of confining, defining, and understanding. What is so unbearably whirling is that the author too goes through this effort to include nearly every woman and

*Reprinted from *A View of My Own.* © 1962 by Elizabeth Hardwick. Reprinted by permission of Farrar, Straus & Giroux, Inc.

attitude that has ever existed. There is no difference of opinion, unless it be based upon a fact of which she may be ignorant, she has not thought of also. She makes her own points and all one's objections too, often in the same sentence. The effort required for this work must have been killing. No discredit to the donkey-load undertaking is meant when one imagines Simone de Beauvoir at the end may have felt like George Eliot when she said she began *Romola* as a young woman and finished it an old one. (This touching remark did not refer to the time spent in composition, but to the wrinkling weight of the task.)

I quote a sentence about the *promises* the Soviet Union made to women: ". . . pregnancy leaves were to be paid for by the State, which would assume charge of the children, signifying not that they would be *taken away* from their parents, but that they would not be *abandoned* to them." There is majesty here and the consolations of philosophy, perhaps also, in this instance, a bit of willful obfuscation; but that kind of strangeness occurs endlessly, showing, for purposes of argument at least, an oversensitivity to difficulties. A devastating dialogue goes on at this author's desk. After she has written, "the State, which would assume charge of the children," there is a comma pause. In that briefest of grammatical rests, voices assault her intelligence saying, "But suppose people don't want their children taken away by the State?" If all these disputing voices are admitted, one on top of the other, you are soon lost in incoherence and fantasy. Another instance: "It is understandable, in this perspective, that women take exception to masculine logic. Not only is it inapplicable to her experience, but in his hands, as she knows, masculine reasoning becomes an underhanded form of force." A few pages on: "One can bank on her credulity. Woman takes an attitude of respect and faith toward the masculine universe. . . ."

I take up the bewildering inclusiveness of this book, because there is hardly a thing I would want to say contrary to her thesis that Simone de Beauvoir has not said herself, including the fact, mentioned in the preface, that problems peculiar to women are not particularly pressing at the moment and that, by and large, "we have won." These acknowledgments would seem of tremendous importance, but they are a mere batting of the eye in this eternity of "oppression."

In spite of all positions being taken simultaneously, there is an unmistakable *drift* to the book. Like woman's life, *The Second Sex* is extremely repetitious and some things are repeated more often than others, although nearly every idea is repeated more than once. One is justified, then, in assuming what is repeated most often is most profoundly felt. The diction alone is startling and stabs the heart with its vigor in finding phrases of abjection and debasement. It is as though one had lived forever in that intense, shady, wretched world of *Wozzeck*, where the humor draws tears, the gaiety is fearful and children skip rope neither knowing nor caring their mother has been murdered. "Conjugal slavery, annihilation, servant, devaluation, tyranny, passive, forbidden, doomed, abused, trapped, prey, domineer, helpless, imprisoned," and so on. This immediately suggests a masochistic view of life, reinforced by the fact that for the male quite an opposite vocabulary has dug into this mind like a tick: "free, busy, active, proud, arrogant, master, existent, liberty, adventure, daring, strength, courage. . . ."

Things being as they are, it is only fair to say that Simone de Beauvoir, in spite of her absorbing turn of phrase, miraculously does *not* give to me, at least, the impression of being a masochist, a Lesbian, a termagant, or a man-hater, and that this book is not "the self-pitying cry of one who resents being born a woman," as one American housewife-reviewer said. There is a nervous, fluent, rare aliveness on every page and the writer's more "earnest" qualities, her discipline, learning and doggedness, amount not only to themselves, that is, qualities which certainly help one to write long books, but to a kind of "charm" that ought to impress the most contented woman. This book is an accomplishment; on the other hand, if one is expecting something truly splendid and unique like *The Origins of Totalitarianism* by Hannah Arendt, to mention another woman, he will be disappointed.

The Second Sex begins with biological material showing that in nature there are not always two sexes and reproduction may take place asexually. I have noticed in the past that many books strongly presenting feminine claims begin in this manner, as if under a compulsion to veil the whole ideal of sexual differentiation with a buzzing, watery mist of insect habits and unicellular forms of life. This is dramaturgy, meant to put one, after a heavy meal, in a receptive frame of mind. It is the dissonant, ambiguous music as the curtain rises on the all too familiar scene of the man at the hunt and the woman at the steaming pot; the scene looks clear enough, but the music suggests things may not be as they appear. That woman may not have to carry those screaming brats in her womb, after all, but will, if you don't watch out, simply "divide"! And the man: it is possible in the atomic age that a pin prick may fertilize the egg and then where will he be? This material is followed by curiosities from anthropology: some primitive societies thought the woman did it all alone and the man was no more important than a dish of herbs or a draft of beet juice.

These biological and anthropological matters are of enormous fascination, but often, and a bit in this present work too, a false and dramatic use is made of them: they carry a weight of mystification and intensity quite unjustified when the subject is the modern woman. They would seem to want to throw doubt upon what is not yet doubtful: the bisexual nature of human reproduction. We are relieved when the dividing amoebas and budding sponges swim out of view.

The claim of *The Second Sex* is that what we call the feminine character is an illusion and so is feminine "psychology," both in its loose meaning and in the psychoanalytical view. None of these female traits is "given" — the qualities and incapacities women have shown rather consistently in human history are simply the result of their "situation." This situation is largely the work of men, the male sex which has sought its own convenience with undeviating purpose throughout history. The female situation does not derive, at least not sufficiently to explain it, from women's natural physical and psychological difference, but has much of its origin in economics. When man developed the idea of private property, woman's destiny was "sealed." At this time women were cut off from the more adventurous activities of war, forays, explorations, to stay at home to *protect* and *maintain* what men had achieved by their far-reaching pursuits. The woman was reduced to a state of *immanence*: stagnation, the doing of repetitive tasks, concerned with the given, with maintaining, keeping, mere functioning. Man, however, is a free being, an *existent* who makes choices, decisions, has projects which are not confined to securing the present but point to the unknown future; he dares, fails, wanders, grabs, insists. By means of his activities he *transcends* his mere animal nature. What a man gives, the woman accepts; she decides nothing, changes nothing; she polishes, mends, cleans what he has invented and shaped. The man risks life, the woman merely produces it as an unavoidable function. "That is why superiority has been accorded in humanity not to the sex that brings forth but that which kills." The man imagines, discovers religions; the women worship. He has changed the earth; she arises each morning to an expectation of stove, nursing, scrubbing which has remained nearly as fixed as the course of our planets. Women continue in immanence not out of desire, but from "complicity." Having been robbed of economic independence, experience, substance, she clings unhappily because she has not been "allowed" to prepare for a different life.

Naturally, it is clear many women do not fit this theory and those who may be said to do so would not describe it in the words of Simone de Beauvoir. These persons' claims are admitted quite fully throughout the book, but always with the suggestion that the women who seem to be "existents" really aren't and those who insist they find fulfillment in the inferior role are guilty of "bad faith."

That is as it may be, but what, one asks at the beginning, about the man who, almost without exception in this work, is a creature of the greatest imagination, love of liberty, devotion to projects; ambitious, potent and disciplined, he scorns a life of mere "love," refuses to imprison himself in another's being, but looks toward the world, seeks to transcend himself, change the course of history. This is an exaggeration of course. For every Ophelia one remembers not only Cleopatra but poor Swann, unable, for all his taste and enthusiasm, to write his book on Vermeer, drowning his talent in the pursuit of pure pleasure which can only be given by the "other," Odette; for every excited Medea who gave up herself, her place, to follow the fickle man you remember not only Joan of Arc but that being of perfect, blowsy immanence, the Duke of Windsor, who abandoned the glories of a complex project for the sweet, repetitive, futureless domesticity of ocean liners and resorts. And Sartre has written a whole book on Baudelaire, a fascinating and immensely belligerent one, that claims Baudelaire resented responsibility for his own destiny, refused his possibilities of transcendence, would not make decisions, define himself, but flowed along on a tepid river of dependence, futility, refusal — like women, fond of scents and costumes, nostalgic, procrastinating, wishful.

It would seem then that men, even some "heroic" ones, often allow themselves to be what women are forced to be. But, of course, with the greatest will in the world a man cannot allow himself to be that most extremely doomed and chained being — the mother who must bear and raise children and whose figure naturally hangs over such a work as *The Second Sex* like Spanish moss. Simone de Beauvoir's opinion of the division of labor established in the Garden of Eden, if not as some believe earlier, is very striking: "giving birth and suckling are not *activities*, they are natural functions; no projects are involved; and that is why woman found in them no reason for a lofty affirmation of her existence — she submitted passively to her biologic fate. The domestic cares of maternity imprisoned her in repetition and immanence; they were repeated from day to day in an identical form, which was perpetuated almost without change from century to century; they produced nothing new."

But what difference does it make that childbearing is not an activity, not perhaps an instinct; it is a necessity.

The Second Sex is so briskly Utopian it fills one with a kind of shame and sadness, like coming upon old manifestoes and committee programs in the attic. It is bursting with an almost melancholy desire for women to take their possibilities *seriously*, to reject the given, the easy, the traditional. I do not, as most reviewers seem to, think the picture offered here of a woman's life is entirely false — a lifetime of chores is bad luck. But housework, child rearing, cleaning, keeping, nourishing, looking after — these must be done by someone, or worse by millions of someones day in and day out. In the home at least it would seem "custom" has not been so much capricious as observant in finding that women are fairly well adapted to this necessary routine. And they must keep at it whether they like it or not.

George Orwell says somewhere that reformers hate to admit nobody will do the tedious, dirty work of the world except under "some form of coercion." Mopping, ironing, peeling, feeding — it is not absurd to call this unvarying routine *slavery*, Simone de Beauvoir's word. But its necessity does not vanish by listing the tropical proliferation of open and concealed forms of coercion that may be necessary to make women do it. Bachelors are notoriously finicky, we have all observed. The dust pile is revoltingly real.

Most men, also, are doomed to work of brutalizing monotony. Hardly any intellectuals are willing to undertake a bit of this dreadful work their fellow beings must do, no matter what salary, what working conditions, what degree of "socialist dignity" might be attached to it. If artists could save a man from a lifetime of digging coal by digging it themselves one hour a week, most would refuse. Some would commit suicide. "It's not the time, it's the anticipation! It ruins the whole week! I can't even read, much less write!"

Childbearing and housekeeping may be repetitive and even intellectually stunting. Yet nothing so fills one with despair as those products of misplaced transcendent hope, those millions of stupid books, lunatic pamphlets, absurd editorials, dead canvases and popular songs which have clogged up the sewers and ashcans of the modern world, representing more wretched labor, dreaming, madness, vanity and waste of effort than one can bear to think of. There is an annihilating nothingness in these undertakings by comparison with which the production of one stupid, lazy, lying child is an event of some importance. Activity, transcendence, project — this is an optimistic, exhilarating vocabulary. Yet Sartre had to disown the horde of "existents" who fell to like farm hands at the table, but were not themselves able to produce so much as a carrot.

Are women "the equal" of men? This is an embarrassing subject.

Women are certainly physically inferior to men and if this were not the case the whole history of the world would be different. No comradely socialist legislation on woman's behalf could accomplish a millionth of what a bit more muscle tissue, gratuitously offered by nature, might do for this "second" being: "On the average she is shorter than the male and lighter, her skeleton is more delicate . . . muscular strength is much less in women . . . she has less respiratory capacity, the lungs and trachea being smaller. . . . The specific gravity of the blood is lower . . . and there is less hemoglobin; women are therefore less robust and more disposed to anemia than are males. Their pulse is more rapid, the vascular system less stable. . . . Instability is strikingly characteristic of woman's organization in general. . . . In comparison with her the male seems infinitely favored." There is a kind of poetry in this description which might move a flighty person to tears. But it goes on: "These biological considerations are extremely important. . . . But I deny that they establish for her a fixed and inevitable destiny. They are insufficient for setting up a hierarchy of the sexes . . . they do not condemn her to remain in a subordinate role forever."

Why doesn't this "condemn her to remain in a subordinate role forever"? In my view this poor endowment would seem to be all the answer one needs to why women don't sail the seven seas, build bridges, conquer foreign lands, lay international cables and trudge up Mount Everest. But forgetting these daring activities, a woman's physical inferiority to a man is a limiting reality every moment of her life. Because of it women are "doomed" to situations that promise reasonable safety against the more hazardous possibilities of nature which they are too weak and easily fatigued to endure and against the stronger man. Any woman who has ever had her wrist twisted by a man recognizes a fact of nature as humbling as a cyclone to a frail tree branch. How can *anything* be more important than this? The prodigious ramifications could occupy one for an eternity. For instance: "At eighteen T. E. Lawrence took a long bicycle tour through France by himself; no young girl would be allowed to engage in any escapade, still less to adventure on foot in a half-desert and dangerous country, as Lawrence did a year later."

Simone de Beauvoir's use of "allow" is inaccurate; she stresses "permission" where so often it is really "capacity" that is involved. For a woman a solitary bicycle tour of France would be dangerous, but not impossible; Lawrence's adventure in Arabia would be suicidal and so a woman is nearly unimaginable as the author of *The Seven Pillars of Wisdom*. First of all the Arabs would rape this unfortunate female soldier or, if they had some religious or practical reason for resisting temptation, they would certainly have to leave her behind on the march, like yesterday's garbage, as the inevitable fatigue arrived. To say that physical weakness doesn't, in a tremendous number of activities, "condemn her to a subordinate role" is a mere assertion, not very convincing to the unmuscled, light breathing, nervously unstable, blushing feminine reality.

Arabian warfare is indeed an extreme situation. But what about solitary walks through the town after midnight? It is true that a woman's freedom to enjoy this simple pleasure would be greatly increased if men had no aggressive sexual feelings toward her. Like a stray dog, also weaker than men, she might roam the world at will, arousing no more notice than a few pats on the head or an irritable kick now and then. Whether such a change is possible in the interest of the weaker sex is very doubtful.

There is the notion in *The Second Sex*, and in other radical books on the subject, that if it were not for the tyranny of custom, women's sexual life would be characterized by the same aggressiveness, greed and command as that of the male. This is by no means certain: so much seems to lead right back where we've always been. Society must, it seems, inhibit to some extent the sexuality of all human beings. It has succeeded in restraining men much less than women. Brothels, which have existed from the earliest times, are to say the least a rarity for the use of women. And yet women will patronize opium dens and are frequently alcoholic, activities wildly destructive to their home life, beauty, manners and status and far more painful and time-consuming than having children. Apparently a lot of women are dying for dope and cocktails; nearly all are somewhat thrifty, cautious and a little lazy about hunting sex. Is it

necessarily an error that many people think licentious women are incapable of experiencing the slightest degree of sexual pleasure and are driven
to their behavior by an encyclopedic curiosity to know if such a thing
exists? A wreck of a man, tracking down girls in his Chevrolet, at least can
do *that!* Prostitutes are famously cold; pimps, who must also suffer
professional boredom, are not automatically felt to be impotent. Homosexual women, who have rebelled against their "conditioning" in the most
crucial way, do not appear to "cruise" with that truly astonishing, ageless
zest of male homosexuals. A pair seems to find each other sufficient.
Drunken women who pick up a strange man look less interested in a sexual
partner than in a companion for a drink the next morning. There is a
staggering amount of evidence that points to the idea that women set a
price of one kind or another on sexual intercourse; they are so often not in
the mood.

This is not to say women aren't interested in sex *at all*. They clearly
want a lot of it, but in the end the men of the world seem to want still
more. It is only the quantity, the capacity in that sense, in which the sexes
appear to differ. Women, in the language of sociology books, "fight very
hard" to get the amount of sexual satisfaction they want — and even harder
to keep men from forcing a superabundance their way. It is difficult to see
how anyone can be sure that it is only man's voracious appetite for
conquest which has created, as its contrary, this reluctant, passive being
who has to be wooed, raped, bribed, begged, threatened, married,
supported. Perhaps she really has to be. After she has been conquered she
has to "pay" the man to restrain his appetite, which he is so likely to reveal
at cocktail parties, and in his pitifully longing glance at the secretary — she
pays with ironed shirts, free meals, the pleasant living room, a son.

And what about the arts — those womanish activities which are, in
our day, mostly "done at home." For those who desire this form of
transcendence, the other liberating activities of mankind, the office, the
factory, the world of commerce, public affairs, are horrible pits where the
extraordinary man is basely and casually slain.

Women have excelled in the performance arts: acting, dancing and
singing — for some reason Simone de Beauvoir treats these accomplishments as if they were usually an extension of prostitution. Women have
contributed very little to the art of painting and they are clearly weak in
the gift for musical composition. (Still whole nations seem without this
latter gift, which may be inherited. Perhaps even nations inherit it, the
male members at least. Like baldness, women may transmit the gift of
musical composition but they seldom ever suffer from it.)

Literature is the art in which women have had the greatest success.
But a woman needs only to think of this activity to feel her bones rattling
with violent distress. Who is to say that *Remembrance of Things Past* is
"better" than the marvelous *Emma?* *War and Peace* better than *Middle-*

march? *Moby Dick* superior to *La Princesse de Clèves?* But everybody says so! It is only the whimsical, cantankerous, the eccentric critic, or those who refuse the occasion for such distinctions, who would say that any literary work by a woman, marvelous as these may be, is on a level with the very greatest accomplishments of men. Of course the *best* literature by women is superior to *most* of the work done by men and anyone who values literature at all will approach all excellence with equal enthusiasm.

The Second Sex is not whimsical about women's writing, but here again perhaps too much is made of the position in which women have been "trapped" and not enough of how "natural" and inevitable their literary limitations are. Nevertheless, the remarks on artistic women are among the most brilliant in this book. Narcissism and feelings of inferiority are, according to Simone de Beauvoir, the demons of literary women. Women want to please, "but the writer of originality, unless dead, is always shocking, scandalous; novelty disturbs and repels." Flattered to be in the world of art at all, the woman is "on her best behavior; she is afraid to disarrange, to investigate, to explode. . . ." Women are timid and fall back on "ancient houses, sheepfolds, kitchen gardens, picturesque old folks, roguish children . . ." and even the best are conservative. "There are women who are mad and there are women of sound method; none has that madness in her method that we call genius."

If women's writing seems somewhat limited, I don't think it is only due to these psychological failings. Women have much less experience of life than a man, as everyone knows. But in the end are they suited to the kind of experiences men have? *Ulysses* is not just a work of genius, it is Dublin pubs, gross depravity, obscenity, brawls. Stendhal as a soldier in Napoleon's army, Tolstoy on his Cossack campaigns, Dosotevsky before the firing squad, Proust's obviously first-hand knowledge of vice, Conrad and Melville as sailors, Michelangelo's tortures on the scaffolding in the Sistine chapel, Ben Jonson's drinking bouts, dueling, his ear burnt by the authorities because of a political indiscretion in a play — these horrors and the capacity to endure them are *experience*. Experience is something more than going to law school or having the nerve to say honestly what you think in a drawing room filled with men; it is the privilege as well to endure brutality, physical torture, unimaginable sordidness, and even the privilege *to want*, like Boswell, to grab a miserable tart under Westminster Bridge. Syphilis and epilepsy — even these seem to be tragic afflictions a male writer can endure more easily than a woman. I should imagine a woman would be more depleted by epilepsy than Dostoevsky seems to have been, more ravaged by syphilis than Flaubert, more weakened by deprivation than Villon. Women live longer, safer lives than men and a man may, if he wishes, choose that life; it is hard to believe a woman could choose, like Rimbaud, to sleep in the streets of Paris at seventeen.

If you remove the physical and sexual experiences many men have made literature out of, you have carved away a great hunk of masterpieces. There is a lot left: James, Balzac, Dickens; the material in these books, perhaps not always in Balzac, is a part of women's lives too or might be "worked up"—legal practices and prison conditions in Dickens, commerce in Balzac, etc.

But the special *vigor* of James, Balzac, Dickens or Racine, the queer, remaining strength to produce masterpiece after masterpiece—that is belittling! The careers of women of prodigious productivity, like George Sand, are marked by a great amount of failure and waste, indicating that though time was spent at the desk perhaps the supreme effort was not regularly made. Who can help but feel that *some* of James's vigor is sturdily rooted in his masculine flesh and that this repeatedly successful creativity is less likely with the "weaker sex" even in the socialist millennium. It is not suggested that muscles write books, but there is a certain sense in which, talent and experience being equal, they may be considered a bit of an advantage. In the end, it is in the matter of experience that women's disadvantage is catastrophic. It is very difficult to know how this may be extraordinarily altered.

Coquettes, mothers, prostitutes and "minor" writers—one sees these faces, defiant or resigned, still standing at the Last Judgment. They are all a little sad, like the Chinese lyric:

> Why do I heave deep sighs?
> It is natural, a matter of course, all
> creatures have their laws.

Simone de Beauvoir, the Concrete Mandarin
René Etiemble*

In the days of the warlords and the Kuo-min-tang, how easy leftists and even Stalinists found it to write appropriately about China![1] You took a trip there; you described quite simply what you saw in China at the time of the Sino-Japanese *incident* or what could be observed just about everywhere during those happy years when the banking families to which Tchang Kaicheck was to become allied considered that the area "bounded by the four seas"—China, in other words—was their private domain just as the five hundred million Chinese were their slaves. Out of this era came Andrée Viollis's *Shanghai* and Egon Erwin Kisch's *Secret China*, two books which twenty years later one can still read without having to revive the first favorable opinion they inspired at their publication. At most,

*Translated by Germaine Brée for this volume from *Hygiène des Lettres III* (Paris: Gallimard, 1958), 76–113. © 1958 by Editions Gallimard. Reprinted by permission of Editions Gallimard.

there might be some minor rectifications here and there. When discussing the Chinese opera which we applauded in Paris a year ago, Egon Erwin Kisch criticizes Mei Lan-fang for wanting to reform a desperately aristocratic and feudal art ("it's as if one wanted to adapt oratorios for a jazz orchestra"). I am far, today, from agreeing with him. He criticizes the falsetto voice of the singers, the way the actors walk, placing their heels on the ground with the tip of the foot raised (as if "terrestrial women" ever walked that way). One might as well fault Papageno for singing Mozart as no "terrestrial men" ever spoke. But children dying of hunger and tuberculosis in front of "child-size" machines made specially for them, the very machines used one hundred years ago in Lancashire factories; but the *poluski gels*, the *poruski girls*, in other words the Shanghai prostitutes, those, for instance, of the Tumble-Inn, "the most exquisite and best groomed in the whole city" (weekly medical visit, Dr. R. Holper, M.D.), but the insane asylum in comparison with which our asylums take on a cosy, generous, and philanthropic air; but the life of the coolies, the misery and debauchery; the practice of infanticide organized for the sole benefit of ever fatter paunches for a few Chinese landowners and European traffickers; the China of the concessions and the Christian generals: yes, that was China. That was the so-called "new life" that had been promised to the entire population.

Since, over there, Mao Tse-tung became President Mao, how is it that when our Stalinists go off on pilgrimages to the T'ien-ngan man, the lucidity which previously helped them to judge ancient China so well has suddenly deserted them when they have to speak of present-day China? Why must that fellow traveler, Pierre Gascar, illustrating his *Open China*, write (or tolerate that someone else write in his place), the legend that accompanies a photograph facing page 48, the photograph of a grandmother holding a baby: "Two faces of China: the one marked by ancestral lassitude; the other round, filled with the energy of a young life which the clenched fists assert." What I saw in the face of the grandmother, rather than the stigmata of an age-old weariness, were the wrinkles one expects at her age. And I'd like to know in what corner of the world babies of that age don't keep their little fists closed? *Little fists, babies*, if I resort to such inane words, it is only to show to what extent the use of a certain vocabulary can intentionally add revolutionary meaning to a perfectly banal photograph.

In defense of these travelers, one might say that, whether or not they are Stalinist, they know not a word of Chinese and are at the mercy of their informants. But neither Andrée Viollis nor Egon Erwin Kisch spoke that language. If at least these recent tourists abstained from peddling around their ideas concerning Chinese characters! They wouldn't think of it! For M. Adalbert de Segonzac, Chinese is the "only language which does not allow one to grasp the general sense of a conversation; because of the intonations, it is impossible, if one has not understood, to distinguish where a sentence ends, or recognize the interrogative mode" (*Visa to Peking*). He concludes that a language so perverse should be romanized. M. Gascar draws a subtle inference from that surprising power: "It is a language which, phonetically, often calls to mind the discourse of uncertainty, a halting language in which affirmative forms are absent; for the traveler arriving in Peking in 1954, that is rather reassuring." Can obsequiousness be carried further? Could anyone familiar with the iron laws imposed on the Chinese in 1955 and the pervasive dogmatism that permitted only certainty and enthusiastic compliance ("at that time we were animals, robots," a scholar confessed to me, one who could breathe at last two years later), could anyone accept M. Gascar's statement? A statement all the more suspect because it had been arrived at via an error as to the nature of Chinese.

If only these progressists' ignorance of Chinese had counseled some slight caution! Make no mistake! One of them offers you his *Keys to China*, the other proposes to explain everything and everybody.

Like everyone else today, I have just come back from Peking, Shanghai, Lo-yang, Lan-tcheou, and other such, enough to dazzle you outright. Although for some 28 years I had been preparing for this journey that I desired but without great hope of accomplishing; although I took just about all the courses in Chinese language and civilization available in Paris; although, at the time, I had even deposited a thesis topic on Taoist thought — when I measure the gaps in my knowledge of China, I wonder how I have the nerve to intervene in this debate. Alas, since the sinologues speak only to their peers and abandon the field to the loquacious — true, Laloy has given us his *Mirror of China*, but most of the scholars are silent — it is perhaps appropriate that those of us speak who, far from considering themselves erudite, can at least speak from grounds other than mere presumption.

By tens of thousands the French today have discovered China through M. Claude Roy (and I know what several cultivated Chinese think of him); by tens of thousands they will read *The Long March* since that weighty tome is signed by a Goncourt prize winner who is also the author of *The Second Sex*. Since those two connivers won't double-cross each other; since Mme de Beauvoir makes no mention of anything which in *Keys to China* contradicts what she herself asserts; since, in return, he declares himself to be "enchanted by," better still, "enlightened by" the "intelligent insights," the "novel observations" his dear friend has generously ladled out (*Liberation*, June 19, 1957) — this even though those "intelligent insights" cancel out all he described — forgetful readers won't realize that our two accomplices are laughing at them, and, reconciled in the face of Stalin's anti-Semitism, have pledged themselves to keep a fraternal silence. Finally, if Claude Roy feels empowered to teach us that those arrant reactionaries, the Confucians, have buried China under a leaden mantle which Mao will lift; and if he is right in supposing that the good, inoffensive fisherman in

China infallibly professes Taoism, then Simone de Beauvoir, to a lesser or greater degree, must be wrong, who informs us that the Chinese counter-revolutionaries often like to build their organizations around Taoist groups and that today's China asks its faithful to revere Confucius. If, rightly and for good reasons, Claude Roy despises our alphabetical languages, so colorless with their weak *a*, their pitiable *b*, their ineffectual *c*, and dogmatically argues that Chinese patriotism will first be linguistic and so set out to save the Chinese characters, on what grounds does Mme de Beauvoir assume the right to exonerate him, she who holds the opinion that anyone who defends those characters must be a cross between a fascist and a vainglorious mandarin, quite incapable of recognizing a concept, in other words, a chap like me.

Are we dealing with *inner contradictions*, as they are called of late in the jargon of our scholastics, which are esteemed beneficial, or rather with *external* ones, which would be quite different? When he left for China, M. Claude Roy had been dabbling in a recent sympathy for the rationalist and progressist Confucius. He was soon enlightened. Confucius was not popular at the time. Thence his *Keys to China* where, repudiating what he had learned, this strong personality suddenly discovered the unsuspected depth of his sympathy for those same Taoists he had, until then, condemned without in the least understanding them.

Three years later, Our Lady of Beauvoir set out on her pilgrimage. Confucius had become respectable again. What a good opportunity to set Claude Roy straight! Not at all! Only a good occasion to take me to task for my bad faith. Had I not said that the Chinese communists did not set much store by Confucius? So that's where the ethics of ambiguity, so dear to our lovely lady have led! It would have been easy to observe, nonetheless, that the China of February 1, 1951, the China of Claude Roy was not following the same directives as the China of 1955 through which Jean-Paul Sartre and Simone de Beauvoir were traveling. And both, too, were quite different from the China I saw in May–June 1957. That China was busy wondering what the *hundred flowers* was about and the *hundred philosophers*; a China so intoxicated by its young freedoms and, frankly, so immoderate about it that I am hardly surprised that the rainy month of August — during which, the press tells us, the floods destroyed such quantities of rice or wheat — also drowned out the *hundred flowers* and 99% of the philosophers.

By a curious effect of ballistics, of which I'd like to find the law, the mud slung by *The Long March* splatters only those who have never compromised, who never will compromise with tyrannies, whatever the favors these hold out to them.

By the way, what is exactly *The Long March? China from day to day?* A travelogue? A journalistic report? Come now! "Reporters explore a stable present whose more or less contingent elements serve as keys to one another." You can see that an existentialist thinker, who accepts herself as such even though as a result she is a little boring, could not, without losing prestige, limit herself to an exploration of the unstable present of a China every component of which acquires the status of indispensability. Having thus defined the grounds for her modesty, Mme de Beauvoir gives herself the task to *illuminate, in the light of the China of yesterday*, all the *knowledge* she has been able to acquire on the spot. So, rather than an impossible metaphysical report, what she presents to us is an *essay on China*.

We must hail her courage; for, in Mme de Beauvoir's terms, the Chinese past only hesitantly ventures beyond the three Manchu centuries and those Mings who, toward the end of the fifteenth century, succeeded the Mongol conquerors. In the course of her travels, she did not, to my knowledge, scrutinize the neolithic sites, examine the engraved bones of Ngan Yang, visit the Han tombs, or handle objects from the Warring Kingdoms. What little she has written on the T'ang and Song dynasties can only distress those cultivated Chinese who, on the strength of her reputation, will try to read her.

In brief, the position taken by our neo-sinologue is the following: as an existentialist thinker I know nothing of the future of China, so I shall explain it to you through the Chinese past of which, as Simone de Beauvoir, I am entirely ignorant. See, for example, page 387, where she speaks of the frescoes of Touenhouang: "the artistic value of these frescoes is not exceptional; but every phase of civilization has left its mark on them." Here, in a single sentence, are two monumental errors. The first is a matter of factual judgment; the second a value judgment (ah, yes! we, too, can marshal scraps of jargon). It is far from true that all the phases of Chinese civilization have left their mark on Touen-houang. The first grottoes go back to the Souei, to the end of the sixth century; the last, the tantric paintings, date from the Mongol dynasty (fourteenth or fifteenth century). Mme de Beauvoir considers as null and void the fifteen or twenty centuries of Chinese civilization which preceded the Souei. What interest can she find in the Chang bronzes, the Han sculptures? Formalistic, all of them, mere feudal art; good for mandarins. Furthermore, it is also far from true that "the artistic value" of these frescoes is not exceptional. In order to pass judgment on the Touen-houang paintings, should one not have looked at them rather closely? But Mme de Beauvoir informs us that she had been unable to get to Ts'ien Fo Tong, to the grottoes of the Thousand Buddhas. According to her, she would have had to travel several days by caravan starting from Lang Tcheou (by which she means Lan-tcheou, the capital of Kan-Sou). Three hours in a plane and nine in a jeep would have saved her from so hazardous a judgment; hazardous but indispensable, like everything that concerns the present state of today's China. Before condemning Touen-houang, might she not at least have studied the black and white reproductions published by Pelliot? What?

Pelliot? How dare I mention that "capitalist spy"? that "bourgeois objectivist" who looted Touen-houang? In brief, the most erudite of our sinologues at the beginning of the twentieth century. All in all, Mme de Beauvoir cast a contingent eye on the gouache copies which were being exhibited during her stay in Peking. She saw *asparas* swirling around the ceilings (she means *apsara* [nymphs] in the Chinese of the fei-t'ien) and a few scenes of ploughing. She has heard of the "Western paradise." Enough to come to a quick conclusion: that after "a short creative period there followed long drawn out boring centuries"; and that it is high time that the school of Guerassimov-Fougeron should at long last teach the Chinese the art or painting in oils and without recourse to calligraphy. The landscapes of the Song period did not, either, live up to the expectations of our expert. Those of you who see in those silk scrolls one of the five or six most moving forms which nature assumed in the mind of an artist, learn now that the decadent mandarins who painted them in those days of feudal oppression erred to the point of "expressing through them the metaphysics of the time," thus disqualifying themselves. Neither Sartre in his novels nor Simone de Beauvoir in her really *Useless Mouths* ever committed so serious an error. They both take great care not to fabricate novels or plays that speak of existentialism. . . . Whereas, those deplorable Song painters place people "in the bosom of a nature that surpasses them," "insignificant" men, "broken down," in a word, "solitary" men. Instead of drawing wheat fields or potters' kilns, they combine — ingeniously, arealistically, asocially, thereby antisociolistically — mountains and lakes whose shapes harmonize, calm the viewer, and look beautiful. Simone de Beauvoir detests nature. To cultivate one's garden is the ethic of an anticommunist (a word which, in her case, is not just a key word but a master key). I do not in the least question her right to prefer to the fragrance of the garrigue[2] and of reseda, the smell of hotel rooms; and the flowers on their painted wallpaper to mountains of Mi Fei (those at least which have been attributed to Mi Fei). I am suggesting, on the other hand, that what she has written about Touen-houang and the Song painters should preclude her from claiming that she will explain, in the light of an ancient China about which she is almost entirely ignorant and understands nothing at all, a present-day China whose language she does not know and which, like everybody else, she visited, performed her three little pirouettes, and left.[3]

A compulsive workaholic, and a most intelligent woman when she doesn't choose to play the fool, Simone de Beauvoir did not forget to read a dozen or so books at the Bibliothèque nationale and to supplement her files by working a little at the Institute of Advanced Chinese Studies. From the notes she compiled one can reconstitute her bibliography. For instance, I know where she found the information concerning A-lo-pen, presented as the transcription of the Syriac *rabban* and her interpretation of Ta Ts'in in the Si-ngan-fou stele. However, I must add that the commentary on A-lo-pen has long since been discredited (by Pelliot himself, which should give food for thought) and that Ta Ts'in is a very hard name to translate. Roman Empire? Occidental? Christian? or Nestorian Patriarchy? Roman Empire or Nestorian Patriarchy: one must confess those two notions don't always coincide. Of what concern is this to Mme de Beauvoir whose modest proposal is only to explain the China of the year 2000 by the China of the year 2000?

She read fast and badly. It takes more than six months to form—let's not say a sinologue—but a simile Sino-specialist. A drudge though we know her to be, capable of knocking off six hundred important pages on any topic whatsoever within eight or ten months, on occasion she may stumble. The five or six pages where she summarizes the past history of Chinese agriculture in terms of her theory begin with the second millenium before the Christian era and end with the Mongols. What an atrocious condition at all times and everywhere was that of the Chinese countryside! One can wager Mme de Beauvoir forgot to read Marco Polo and what he tells us about Mangi and Cathay. One could swear that she scorned the accounts of the missionaries who, between the sixteenth and eighteenth centuries, made the prosperity of China known to the West. One suspects finally that she overlooked Mencius and all that has been written about the typically Chinese system of the rights of tenure, the *t'sing*. Eight families cultivated eight plots of land in rotation, while a ninth was cultivated in common, the product of which went to the prince. Even if mythical, the *t'sing* has played too great a part in Chinese speculation to allow Mme de Beauvoir to conjure it away. The dialectic of infra and super structures (as one says, I believe, if schooled in that jargon) would make it imperative for her to explain the *t'sing* and in what ways it prepared and justified collective farms. Not a word. Elsewhere in the book, we learn that Wang Ngan-Che himself sought only to increase the state revenues and how his fiscal policies merely aggravated peasant misery. This was aimed at making clear to my brand of *anticommunism* that no one in China before Mao Tse-tung had ever done anything for the peasants. So she proves two and two make five! The Jesuit Amiot did, after all, make an engraving of Confucius distributing to the people, in a year of great famine, the sacks of grain piled up in the state granaries, precisely in view of just such a peril; so for my part I tend to think, fascistically, that this corresponds, in the eighteenth century, to the Chinese idea of good government. And since the history manuals printed for the pioneers accord Wang Ngan-Che a major role—he has the right to a portrait—the mandarin I am alleged to be is strongly inclined to doubt that it is because the wicked Wang starved the peasantry.

Simone de Beauvoir, miscast mandarin that she is, has no luck. Whether she speaks of Yue Fei, "one of the great figures of Chinese history," or of Yong-lo, of Koubilai Khan, or of Ts'in Che Houang-ti, the only prince before Mao Tse-tung to "decisively influence Chinese history" or when she refers to what she grotesquely calls the tridemism of Sun Yat-sen (i.e., the *san min tchou-yi: the three popular or democratic principles*), she infallibly displays her ignorance. More Stalinist than Stalin, she has to admire Ts'in Che Houang-ti, the man communist China began by repudiating and who is only now beginning to be partially rehabilitated. As for her good friend Yue Fei, she has no inkling that he broke a peasant revolt by force of arms and that many a Chinese wonders today whether he deserves the temple and the cult ascribed to him, etc. Simply to enumerate the lacunae and paralogisms in her pretentious essay would require at least another twenty pages.

I would, however, shortchange her if I did not discuss the value of the chapter she wrote on the reform of Chinese writing. Only on that day when, liberated from its painting, its architecture, its poetry, its calligraphy, all those vestiges of feudal times, China at long last abandons itself to the delights of Zhdanovism, will Beauvoir feel able to assume her second sex completely, to prepare without delay for that ultimate revolution she feels is for her mandatory. Intelligent as she is, she understands perfectly well that Margoulies, whom she has not read, is right and that China, bereft of its characters, would in truth lose its own specific character. So she has decided that Chinese socialism would be achieved only in barbarity and with a stroke of her well-informed pen — a single stroke — she does away with all the Chinese characters. Whoever refuses to romanize them is a fool, a fascist. The choice, in fact, has already been made and that cad Etiemble will be thoroughly disgruntled.

"The choice has already been made." Really? If Mme de Beauvoir had only taken the trouble to read the *Jen min je pao* of May 21, 1957, she would have seen that, the day before, the commission for the reform of Chinese writing had heard Kao Ming-k'ai and Tchou Tsou maintain that Chinese ideograms should be romanized. Yuan Man-ts'ing, a chemist, spoke in his turn: "If one were not afraid to wound our national pride, one could speak of the obsolete nature of the characters, difficult as they are to read, to write, to print." In his official jargon Mr. Yuan accused those who refuse to romanize Chinese of "subjectivism" (i.e., more or less of egocentrism). Now we know that today one accuses anybody one wants to get rid of of *subjectivism*, of *dogmatism*, or of *bureaucratism*, those components of the *san hai*, the three scourges of China so roundly criticized by Mao Tse-tung. Mr. Yuan himself attacked the commission, guilty in his eyes of "supporting the diffusion of the traditional language, limiting themselves to simplifying the characters, for lack of the courage to come out with an overall plan for their romanization." The dean of the University of Pei-ta, Mr. Yang Houei, then explained the commission's reasons for planning to defend the characters. He was seconded by Mr. Li Tch'ang-che, a professor at the Normal School of Peking, and by a geologist, Mr. Wong Wen-hao. Not content with condemning all plans for romanization, Mr. Wong Wen-hao called even the reform of the characters into question. Quoting several distressing examples of the confusion caused by the reform, he argued that the teaching of the exact sciences could only suffer from the simplification of the characters, and asked them to reconsider, better still, to restore to their old form, those that had been mutilated.

As Mme de Beauvoir states it: *the choice has already been made.* Only the Hong Kong mandarins and the accomplice Etiemble dare today to speak in defense of classical Chinese.

A conversation I had five days later in Peking with two ministers, one of whom was the minister of education, made it quite clear that the commission's set task was indeed to reform without romanizing. That obviously fascist minister from Hong Kong, the Chinese minister of public education, declared that he opposed romanization, and his colleague asked me to send him my articles on that topic. "We'll have them translated into Chinese," he said with a laugh. To clear away all my doubts, I asked to meet with the secretary of the commission for the reform of Chinese writing. Former professor of Chinese at the School for Oriental Studies, Vadime Elisseeff knew the ropes. After a long conversation, in the course of which we discussed the reform from the technical point of view, it became clear to me that, far from sharing the strong convictions of our mandarin, the commission had never envisaged the abolition of the characters. "That's what you are saying today, a tactical retreat perhaps." The answer was categorical: "The *han tseu* (Chinese characters) are eternal." We then asked our interlocutors if we could communicate to the press news so serious and joyous for the lover of Chinese. "Of course."

The news agency France-Presse soon after diffused a communiqué in which Mr. Locquin explained very precisely what the reform of the characters would and would not entail. The text did not have the good luck to please our ultras. *Liberation* added a few words: "We remind you, also, that a monthly review, entitled *Pinjin* and printed in roman characters, is now being published in Peking as an experiment" (June 28, 1957). The correspondent of the bureau in Peking, meanwhile, was commended for having so perfectly explained the statement: "The *han tseu* are eternal." As a Russian biochemist I was lucky to meet in Paris put it: "Nature, sometimes, is less progressist than our comrades."

As for progressism, Mme de Beauvoir has no rivals. Judge for yourself:

> The mandarins of Hong Kong protest: it took a long time to learn calligraphy, the nationalist papers argue; but, in itself, calligraphy constituted a complete artistic education; with its disappearance precious values will be lost. Etiemble, who mistakes himself for a mandarin, chimes in: "Deprived of its characters, China will lose its own specific character." With this weak pun he proves that, for him, China is limited to a few old books. In truth, if the reform inspires a strong

resistance among the anticommunists, it is because its purpose is to democratize culture concretely and multiply the elites. When they defend the characters, yesterday's elites are pleading in favor of their privileges.

Honest as I know Mme de Beauvoir to be, she will certainly hasten to correct all her howlers and, in the next edition of *The Long March*, will, of course, wish to inform her numerous readers that the fascist she judges me to be is in perfect agreement with the Chinese minister of national education and the Chinese secretary of the commission for the reform of writing. To make honesty less costly, I'm willing to pass on to her a quotation which will allow her to extricate herself from embarrassment without losing her mandarin dignity. A specialist in calligraphy once wrote that the discipline "is considered in China as a beneficial exercise, like skating, golf, tennis. Not only does it involve the fingers, the wrist, and the arm, but when the text is of consequence, the whole body. That is why we practice calligraphy in the morning, when the body is alert. And not without results: many of our calligraphers have reached extreme old age." You see? Since calligraphy can develop the muscles of the future soldiers, those progressists who are most devoted to Stalinist peace — of the kind that thrives in Budapest — might put up with it. It would thus become concretely civilizing.

Varied though the lacunae in her knowledge are which motivate Mme de Beauvoir's contempt for Chinese culture and her hopeful anticipation of a land soon to be populated by illiterates without a country and which only geographers could still designate as China, she occasionally blunders into opinions with which I agree. Although I question her argument that "any regime" in the situation of the communists "would do exactly what they are doing." For instance Tchang Kai-chek, who governed China until 1949, developed a quite different style. Along with many others, rather better informed than is Mme de Beauvoir, I think that today things in Asia being what they are, the communists are alone in wanting to pull China out of the filth and debasement in which the Western imperialisms were at pains to keep it plunged for the sole benefit of a banking dynasty. No, of course, "China is no paradise; it needs to become wealthier and more liberal; but if we consider with impartiality where it is coming from and toward what it is moving," we can hardly refute the argument that, for the masses at least, the present dictatorship is by far the least harmful of those, military, civilian, or Manchu, under whose rule it has suffered in the past. There is another page in *The Long March* which I can applaud:

> What irritates me most is the favorable disposition of some travelers who are ready a priori to admire those achievements the meaning of which one can only understand within their historical evolution. It is not true that villages are wealthier and more comfortable in China than in

France: what is remarkable is how they have improved in comparison with the past. It is not true that *the* Chinese woman is, in general, the most emancipated woman in the world. It is naive to marvel at the fact that the Peking archbishop openly supports the regime: if he opposed it, he would no longer be archbishop. Such an enthusiasm shocks me, not only because it creates many errors of interpretation, but because China deserves to be known for what it truly is; to refuse to acknowledge its difficulties is to underestimate its efforts. I fear that the propaganda of such zealots might turn against them when people understand that they saw China with preconceived views. It's too bad.

Yes, indeed; and too bad that Mme de Beauvoir voices such stereotyped though correct opinions, irreproachable though badly formulated, only to fall herself, immediately, into the errors she castigates.

After she has described, in rustic, Edenic terms the pleasure gardens that the old imperial park furnished the people of Peking — the pioneers, boaters, and picnickers — why must she add: "In France there is nothing more depressing than a public garden"? Whether socialist or capitalist, a tavern is a tavern, a picnic is a picnic, and a village fair, a village fair. At the tomb of that imperialistic emperor, that political noddle Yong-lo who inspired our mandarin to write a few idiocies, the bistros, popular jingles, cars, and dust was certainly not progressist.

Zealotry, too, and less excusable, when Mme de Beauvoir inveighs against the homosexuality that tarnished feudal China. So as to hew to what she takes to be the right line, she strikes out against and condemns pell-mell eunuchs, dwarf shrubs, Chinese women's mutilated feet, and the altogether too silky tails of the fishes which seem to her monstrous. The Chinese are wary of so extravagant a puritanism. They are proud to show the carefully bred fishes in their tubs, protected by screens, and for whose benefit the vermin on which the fish thrive is carefully cultivated. Red China does not blush for shame over its red, i.e., goldfishes. So that she can condemn "the infantile and bizarre eroticism depicted in China's ancient novels, the vogue of homosexuality," Simone de Beauvoir has to detect in it a mental flaw. The refinements of Chinese eroticism then appear to be a poor camouflage for "the monotony of a civilization of immanence." Fine words these, to dazzle small brains. Instead of referring vaguely to ancient novels which she can't have read in extenso, unexpurgated (so far as I know, none exists in a language accessible to her), I wish she had consulted serious studies that deal with the topic. I also should like to understand why it is that the famous author of the pages in *The Second Sex* that glorify Lesbos and of the article *Sade* in the dictionary of *Famous Writers* suddenly assumes the role of a conformist. Out of philosophic scruples? Was it because she had discovered in Sade, with delectation, what Jean-Paul Sartre discovered in Genet, a man finally who, "freely assuming" the given, "avoids *being* bad by *making himself so.*" In final analysis, a man "engaged himself totally" in the "problem" that "haunts" us: "the real relationship of man to man"? If she studied Chinese eroticism, however skimpily, she would find out that it is no less thought out, no less "assumed," as she puts it in her patois, than that of the divine marquis. Without priding myself on knowing much about it, I can't ignore the fact that Taoism and Tantrism, from which Chinese eroticism is derived, constitute life-systems that bear comparison with *Philosophy in the Boudoir*. Should I refer our zealot to the *Pao p'o-tseu*, to Maspero's article on the sexual practices of the Taoist sages (*Asiatic Diary*, 1937) to van Gulik's *Erotic Color Prints of the Ming Period, with an Essay on Chinese Sex Life from the Han to the Ch'ing Dynasty* (published in New Delhi)? It could be asking too much of her. She should be content with the few introductory pages given to *Esculape* in October 1956 by the honorary dean of the Faculty of Medicine of Hanoi, Professor Huard: "Sexual Hygiene and the Chinese Treatises on the Bedroom." The article was reproduced in his *Structure of Chinese Medicine*.[4] Simone de Beauvoir would glimpse the fact that Chinese eroticism, which does indeed treat sapphism and pederasty with wise indulgence, practices neither sadism nor masochism. But, faithful to the philosophic logic of the *yin-yang* system, it feels no aversion toward certain maneuvers of the feminine sex which can result in death. I see nothing "infantile" about that. If Mme de Beauvoir insists on considering as "infantile" the practice of compressing the spermatic canal so familiar to the Taoists anxious to preserve their *yang* principle entire, I can assure her that our adolescents are no less "infantile." In order to defend socialism, why denigrate Chinese erotics, condemn what is pompously called *antiphysis* (i.e., antinature), and at fifty adopt the garb of a communist prude?

Zealotry again, and here intolerable, to write that Peking "offers a perfect image of the classless society. Impossible to distinguish an intellectual from a worker, a poor housewife from a female capitalist." I willingly concede that at the time when she was traveling in China, everyone was clad in "the classical suit of blue cotton," and that in 1957 when I was in Peking or elsewhere, uniformity was giving way to fantasy everywhere. Nonetheless, the quality of the material, its shade of blue, the cut of the jacket, and crease in the trouser leg gave me immediate and exact information concerning the wearers. It may be that because I have frequented dressmakers, milleners, and furriers more than is customary, I am a little too sensitive to elegance. But many of my acquaintances who did not spend their childhood inhaling the odor of Revillon furs reacted as I did. True, I never saw in Peking anyone as refined in their costume as the Chinese diplomats who greeted us at the embassy in Berne. The Peking streets, it is true, do not show that variety which, so curiously, survives in Shanghai. But to assert that a poor housewife cannot be distinguished from a female capitalist can mean only that one has accepted, once and for all, to deal in pious lies.

Zealotry borders on the despicable when Mme de Beauvoir dares to say that

> generally speaking, the richest Chinese live as simply as the poor ones. First, they would not dare display their wealth for fear of severe criticism and also because many of them are not inclined to such ostentation. Then, there are today few privileges that money can buy. Cars are strictly for work. There is no night-life. The bare minimum of luxury is available: going frequently to theaters and restaurants, wearing beautiful silk garments at home, and buying furniture, paintings, and art objects. Moreover, the inequalities intrinsic to capitalism will soon disappear, and the advantages which come with high salaries have their drawbacks: the best paid officials are those who are expected to produce the greatest effort; their time and their energies are so stringently mobilized that they don't have the slightest opportunity to live a life of pleasure.

I called on Kouo Mo-jo in his private residence; on Pa Kin in his large house surrounded by a well-tended garden; on Fong Yeou-lan in the villa ascribed to him by the University of Pei-ta; and on another academic, a communist official, an old militant who for years had lived in clandestinity and showed us with delight — how I understand him — the richly furnished rooms, the "modern" comfort which at long last he could enjoy. The house allotted to him was the equivalent of that of an American dean or full professor. I readily admit that these men deserve to live and work in something other than a mud hut or the model apartment of a working-class family. But none of them, whether Kouo Mo-jo, with his luminous face; or Pa Kin, independent in his judgments as I know him to be; or Fong Yeou-lan, who knows by heart the chapter of the Li Ki on the conduct befitting scholars; or the brave old militant I have just mentioned, ever suggested to me that he was living "almost as simply as the poor." I have always judged my privileges as such, not merely when the Chinese served up fifteen- or twenty-course banquets, or when eating lacquered duck, but even when partaking of ordinary meals which always comprised a more than sufficient number of rich and savory dishes; and I have sometimes suffered from being privileged. It is not the fault of the regime if, at present and for a long time to come, the masses can be allowed only a bowl of rice, steamed bread, noodles boiled in water, with a few rare vegetables, small portions of fish from time to time; or at other times, a few scraps of meat. Even if one parceled out to the 600 million Chinese the 150 lacquered ducks sold in Peking's specialized restaurant every Sunday; or between them all the pork, chickens, fish, bear's paws, and shark's lips which are the share of the rich, the daily fare of the poor would not be greatly improved. But, in truth, nowhere except in Egypt have I had the sense of a more unjust inequality between, let's say, *my* lot — not to mention that of the really wealthy — and the lot of the destitute. With my apartment, my cook, my car, and able as I was to afford all the "palace hotels" and night clubs, it pained me to be brushing up against a misery which Cocteau could qualify as "sumptuous," but which I felt I was insulting every day. I admit that a day came, however, when I realized I was not suffering enough any longer: it was high time to leave. For Mme de Beauvoir, six weeks proved enough to allow her to prevail upon herself not to see the atrocious condition which, the government recognizes it daily, is the lot of the Chinese people. As long as the leaders have not resolved the problem of natality through draconian means, I do not see how they can feed the humble. Consequently, I am careful not to blame them for what cannot be avoided, but I feel justified in regretting that what Mme de Beauvoir reveals, beneath her humanistic and progressist jargon, is a disconcerting lack of feeling and imagination. So, to eat one's fill of delicate dishes; to go often to the most refined restaurants; to collect works of art among the rarest; to dress at home in the most expensive silk brocades: all this in China turns out to be "living a simple life," almost as simple as that of the 550 million poor. What servility there is in claiming that these survivals of a rather less simple life are vestiges of capitalism! I met no capitalist. Managers, or rather, officials, artists, writers. And I had the same feeling as in Moscow in 1934 and 1947. Whatever the regime, be it even Stalinist or allegedly communist, a privileged class will appear or be reconstituted and if the word class not being Marxist enough, pains you, we can substitute "layer." The life of those who belong to that "layer," either in Peking or Moscow, has nothing in common with the life of the working class. I am not sure that this scandal can be avoided. Should I camouflage it, for the none too glorious purpose of preserving my self-righteous conscience, by declaring that when I live like the bourgeoisie in capitalist countries, my life is "almost as simple as the life of the poor"? Even at the cost of passing as a fascist mandarin in the eyes of our fair lady, a man who refuses to assume his mandarinate, I admit that the meaning of words such as "poor" and "destitute" remains painful for me.

I observed with pleasure that the responsible ministers frankly contradict our assumer of fantasies. Mr. Li, for instance, the minister of public health, published in the *Jen min je pao* of March 8, 1957, the speech he had given the day before at the national convention of the party. He estimated that of 3,213 working-class families in one section of Peking, 643, that is, 20%, had produced four children. "The average income of these families is 80 yuan a month (1,200 francs at the time). This means that each individual, adults included, disposes of 13 yuan per month. In families with five children, the individual's budget falls to 10 yuan a month; and to less than 5 yuan for really large families."

Undernourishment then causes grave illnesses. Tchao, for instance, is employed by the postal services. He earns 70 yuan a month. At 28 his wife has already given birth to six children. Many of them suffer from rickets. One of them, a girl, is crippled. His wife is pregnant again. Souen works in a butcher's shop, earns 40 yuan a month (60 francs). His wife, who is mentally ill, has already given birth to nine children (one of whom she has given away). This year again she had a miscarriage. Mme de Beauvoir carefully avoids details of this kind since her ideology requires that, in China, indigents and millionaires lead the same kind of life. She might have wondered at least how it happened that a socialist government would abandon to their miserable fate all those families burdened by offspring. Would it not have sufficed, to save these children from rickets, to give their parents premiums for high natality as we do in France? Well no, that would be impossible. The Chinese are too given to procreation. When in misery, they proliferate; give them premiums, they'll swarm. At the present rhythm, the Chinese, who can't avoid foreseeing they will be a billion within a quarter of a century, will be ten billion in a hundred years or so. As is natural and wise, the communist leaders have reinvented the doctrine Bergson developed in *The Two Sources of Ethics and Religion*: they severely punish families that become too large. How better make the people understand how fatal is their error than to let them die of hunger? However dazzling may be your arguments concerning immanence and transcendence, my answer is, in accord with the Chinese ministers, that China is poor, desperately poor, and to continue to proliferate would be catastrophic.

Mme de Beauvoir speaks mostly of Peking, but let us consider the countryside. According to the report of the minister of public health, "the average yearly income there of an adult worker in good health is 40 or 50 yuan." An official of the Cultural Association told me that, in many regions, peasants still live as they did in the days of the Han. Since that doesn't mean much to our specialist, I respectfully advise her to read the article of Henri Maspero on "Private Life in China during the Han Period." The rich, who, at the time, had few slaves, had trouble keeping their houses in order, especially because the law forbade them to employ more than thirty serfs. But, luckily, they could hire paid workers: "not only do we find a class of poor people whose job it is to rent themselves out as servants, but a number of people of diverse origins have been led to do so temporarily because of extreme poverty." Even today the government advises the rich to keep their servants. All it requires of them is that the servants be paid the set tariff. Modest as they are—30 yuan a month is a maximum—the wages of a servant, to a peasant, are heaven on earth.

It is true that Mme de Beauvoir has a way all her own to "confront," as she puts it, salaries and the cost of living. She "confronts" them "concretely," meaning at random. "Per month a worker earns 40 to 80 yens: 40 if he is unskilled, 80 if he is qualified. As an interpreter, Tsai earns 70 yens. A university professor gets about 140 yens. Some famous actors and directors get 240 yens." You will conclude that the range of salaries in China is rather narrow and that, on the average, people are paid 60 yuan a month. Wrong. The 500 million Chinese who work the Chinese soil earn,

on the average, according to official statistics, *40 to 50 yuan a year.*
Besides, the range is broader, a lot broader, than what our neo-sinologue
claims. A high school teacher may earn 140 yuan; a university professor
200 and more; a museum curator at Touen-houang, counting his premium
for remoteness from Peking may earn 340; a Shanghai radiologist and
faculty professor, 400, not counting the indemnity for perilous posts, a car,
and chauffeur. Some opera actors get as much as 1,500 yuan, and popular
writers may earn tens of thousands of our francs. Finally, most of the
wealthy will soon own cars. I know several thrifty types who are already
counting on buying theirs. In some shops I noticed Zeiss cameras selling at
3,000 yuan apiece (4,500 francs), and people buy them. For me, who does
not "concretely confront" salaries and prices and who wanders about, nose
in the air, content to look at the shops, the homes of the poor, the menu of
those who eat in the street, I say simply, Confucian-style, that wealth is
wealth, poverty, poverty. And that whoever lives in a six-room house,
served by three servants, who eats meat every day and enjoys central
heating, leads a life in no way comparable to that of the Chinese who,
without paid vacations, with no vacations at all, work from dawn to dusk
in rice paddies which gnaw away at their bodies. Nor is it even comparable
to the life of specially privileged workers to whom two rooms for five
people can be allotted, with a water outlet in the kitchen. With a great to-
do over "concrete examples," "concrete experiences," and "concrete objectives," not forgetting the "concrete reasons" that condition the "concrete
unity" or at least the "concrete possibility" of the "concrete unity" of
"concrete reality," Mme de Beauvoir "concretely demonstrates" that, for
"lack of a concrete hold over the countryside" and of "concrete possibilities" of "concrete emancipation" for the women, the freedom of marriage
is not yet "concretely acquired." Happily, the class which "incarnated the
central authority concretely" has already been replaced by a party which,
by practicing a "concretely prudent and moderate repression," offers the
Chinese worker the "concrete possibility" of raising the level of his
technical know-how. In rural society it sometimes happens that remnants
of feudalism become "concretely allied to modern directives." "Concretely,
however," the concretization of all these assumptions of immanence,
transcendence, and "transimmanendanse"[5] have turned Mme de Beauvoir
into a *concrete mandarin.*

In the derogatory sense of the word, he alone merits the name of
mandarin who prefers his own interest or the prince's to the interests of the
people and who, rather than truth seeks profit or glory. To avoid the
accusation of mandarinism it is not enough not to know Chinese; one
should, besides, not be afraid to displease. It is from the Confucians
Simone de Beauvoir execrates, in proportion to her ignorance concerning
them, that I learned, once and for all, the true code of conduct of the man
of letters: "Does someone try to circumvent a man of letters by gifts,

wealth? Or tempt him through pleasure and love? Even the sight of those desirable things can not shake his virtue. Does the crowd do him violence, do soldiers come to arrest him? They will not make him alter his comportment. The man of letters lives among the men of his time and meditates on the ancients. He acts according to his century. It is up to the centuries to come to imitate him. He may displease his contemporaries; his superiors may not promote him; his inferiors may not praise him; while flatterers and slanderers may unite to destroy him. They may take his life; they will be unable to tear out his will. Even when, in action or abstention, he exposes himself to danger, he stubbornly persists, to the very end, in his purpose. In his purpose, he does not forget the suffering of the people." Well! In *The Long March* Mme de Beauvoir never ceases to forget the suffering of the people and to betray truth. How she must despise the Chinese to think they are duped by such impertinent praise. I can prove that they are not, by citing two or three examples. Agreeing here with Claude Roy, she declares that Fong Yeou-lan, the erudite historian of Chinese philosophy, finally "adhered to Marxism." I admire Mr. Fong's knowledge. Last year, in Geneva, I saw a great deal of him. This year I saw him again in Peking. I shall bring to the French his latest work on Chinese thought. Yet I have always told my friends that Mr. Fong was not at all Marxist. When Tcheou Yang, the member of the Central Committee in charge of propaganda, wanted me to understand the extent to which the policy of the *hundred flowers* was extolling liberalism, this is what he said: "Fong Yeou-lan is an idealist; we know it. Just the same he teaches at Pei-ta." First point. According to our mandarin, "the intellectuals (in China) today are in positions of the first rank; this is one of the outstanding characteristics of new China." But as soon as the campaign of rectification permitted people to say a little of what they thought, it became evident that people in China were treated somewhat as in Russia: like valets. This year many articles have come out accusing the communists of treating scholars and writers with scant respect. In China, one wit said, intellectuals "are bedroom objects; used when needed at night; discarded during the day." Yet it was in 1955 that Mme de Beauvoir became acquainted with Chinese intellectuals, at the very time of their oppression. Second point. Finally (so to speak, for her book does not rate a third chronicle), according to her, Tibet will soon be "concretely attached to China," and the Tibetans are so enthusiastic about the new roads linking them to the socialist world that they have named them "the golden bridge" and "the miraculous rainbow." Mme de Beauvoir will surely be delighted to learn that, in the sixth paragraph of his latest report, Mao Tse-tung says exactly the opposite:

> Conditions in Tibet are not yet ripe enough for us to introduce democratic reforms. In accord with the seven-part agreements signed by the Central Government of China and the local government of Tibet, it will be necessary, sooner or later, to reform its social structures. But we

must beware of impatience. We shall be able to carry out our plans only when those reforms seem acceptable to the large majority of the inhabitants as well as to their more important leaders. We have just now made the decision to attempt no democratic reform during the second five-year plan. It is only in the light of what the situation will be at the start of the third plan that we can decide what we can do for the Tibetans.

Third point, etc. So much for that.

Based on ignorance and arrogance, stuffed with as many errors as zealous lies, *The Long March* is worthless. One last example. We are told that "the Western powers have filled their museums with Chinese art treasures." That is no simple question. I have discussed it with more than one expert. But the only country which can cynically exhibit fragments torn around 1920 from the frescoes of Touen-houang is not France—certainly not. Nor indeed the United States. Our mandarin should go to Leningrad and visit the Hermitage Museum. A final example: "2,800 Houei families in Peking practice the Muslim religion." Fantastic! Houei in Chinese means Muslim. So translate: "2,800 Muslim families in Peking practice the Muslim faith."

If only our concrete mandarin respected style abstractly in her writing. For our misfortune, her interest in it is concrete. We are served all the clichés of vulgar journalism; "philosophicating"[6] jargon, improprieties, hiatuses, and cacophony. When she is not mistakenly using "legislature" for "legislation," she is pedantically underscoring "the dualist idiosyncrasy of the bourgeoisie." When one is not "aiming" at "concrete results," one gives "imperative orders" or discourses on "contraceptual politics," even on "disanalphabetization." Mme de Beauvoir can't manage to think without the help of at least three words in "-tion" per sentence. Here come: "the accelera*tion* of the socializa*tion*"; "should collectiviza*tion* be accompanied by mechaniza*tion* or precede it? Without hesita*tion* the second solu*tion* prevailed." Glory then to the metaphor thanks to which Mme de Beauvoir illustrates her understanding of socialist realism: "To develop on a *large scale* a light industry can only be carried out on the *basis* of the modest peasant economy: it presupposes a *large-scale* economy." You could argue that our author won a Goncourt prize so that, inevitably, her writing shows traces of the kind of style such an award requires. That may be so. But when Mme de Beauvoir writes badly in a style worse than she comes by naturally, Mme de Beauvoir also wishes, wishes most especially, to pay homage to the Stalinists.

That is that. I have said only a small part of what I had to say. *The Long March* will go on selling for many years because "a narrative inspired by the most crass ignorance is as apt to stir passions as one historically exact," to quote from the dictionary of Pierre Bayle, which, alas, we no longer read.

P.S. Since I wrote this chronicle I had dinner with someone who, ten hours a day for the past ten years, has studied the politics and economy of China. You should hear what he had to say about the book of our mandarin! It is easy to forgive an error, a failure of memory, at least so it seems to me; but a hundred, five hundred errors? I happened to criticize Simone de Beauvoir for making an erroneous reference. Because there was no library in the place where I was writing, I had resorted to memory. It played me a trick. Though Simone de Beauvoir may not have noticed this inadvertence. I'm happy to point it out to her, in compensation. When I republish my essay that appeared in the journal *La Nef*, I'll delete those three or four words and my article won't lose a thing. Relieved of its errors, what will remain of the pretentious "essay" of our specialist?

Notes

1. This essay was originally published in the journal *Evidences*, September–October and November 1957.

2. Translator's note: *garrigue*: dry limestone lands in Languedoc rich in fragrant herbs.

3. Translator's note: allusion to a French nursery rhyme about puppets.

4. Lectures at the Palace of Discovery, ser. D, no. 49, pp. 82–88.

5. Translator's note: word invented by Etiemble.

6. Translator's note: word invented by Etiemble.

27 October 1958   François Mauriac*

The *Memoirs of a Dutiful Daughter* by Simone de Beauvoir. How inappropriate the irony of this title is to the seriousness of the book! It is hard to read for a Christian because the real subject is the loss of faith of a person blessed with a fine mind. And certainly, the family group that is described could be held responsible. However, I, too, was raised in a similar bourgeois atmosphere (in spite of considerable differences, but it would take too long to tell my story), and I have remained a believer.

Simone de Beauvoir, as a child and an adolescent, did not come into contact only with mediocre or ignorant Catholics. Several of her teachers were neither mediocre nor ignorant. At the Sorbonne, before she met Sartre, her dearest friends were Catholic students who did not give her a low opinion of religion. The truth is that she wanted to lose her faith. In the past I had thought about writing a treatise on the role of the will in believing and, therefore, on the role of the will in the loss of faith.

Even before she was aware of it, this prodigiously gifted adolescent

*Translated by Elaine Marks for this volume from *Le Nouveau Bloc-Notes (1958–1960)* (Paris: Flammarion, 1961), 120–21. Reprinted by permission of Editions Flammarion.

was looking for a way out of the bourgeois milieu in which she was suffocating — but this would come to nothing — a way out of this universe in which an implacable Providence gazes at her intently with his eternal eye. The day on which she finally escapes from this eye, when she emerges into the emptiness of a world without God, the child whose chains have fallen cries for joy: it is a backwards illumination; but she alone chose it. As for me at the same age, with what passion, on the contrary, did I defend myself against objections (which were related less to philosophy than to history: it was the period of modernism and Loisy encouraged us to do critical readings of texts). "And you, too, you want to leave me?" This question asked of his disciples by Christ, under conditions in which many had moved away from him, is a question all young intellectual Christians hear at a certain moment; they see others around them moving away from the faith. And a handful of young Christian students remains close to the Lord. . . .

If there were only the story of this terrible little girl, it would be sufficient to hold our attention. But Simone de Beauvoir behaves in relation to all those who cross her path in life in a way that Sartre does not allow the novelist to behave with his characters: she knows them from the inside. These creatures who have really lived are shown to us from within, as if Simone de Beauvoir had created them; whereas, in reality, she but knew them and loved them, she but suffered because of them. Unforgettable Zaza whose fate serves so well this hatred of Catholicism, this veiled resentment against everything that is Christian. . . .

One day at the Sorbonne Simone de Beauvoir met Simone Weil: their lofty styles did not mix. Of the two Simones, the one who was born Jewish, who did not like the Roman church, who died without baptism, she is the one to whom Christ, one day, revealed himself (she tells us this explicitly), and she lived sustained by Him and for Him until her death. And the other Simone, the pious student of the Desire School, who took communion three times a week, became this implacable and scornful adversary whom it is nonetheless impossible for us not to admire and love. I can daydream indefinitely about that.

Simone de Beauvoir   Claude Roy*

Great strategists know that, in warfare, the most difficult of arts is to stage a retreat. Good writers know that of the literary arts, autobiography is the most difficult. Knowledgeable readers do not condone those who go

*Translated by Germaine Brée for this volume from *L'homme en question: Descriptions critiques* (Paris: Gallimard, 1960), 3:254–63. © 1960 by Editions Gallimard. Reprinted by permission of Editions Gallimard.

around repeating "I don't read novels anymore, or poems or plays; none of these interest me, only memoirs." There are many memoirs, but few of them are good. Almost no one has the nerve to write his life story for the sole purpose of personal elucidation. There are a few brilliant examples, from the *Confessions* of Saint Augustine to those of Rousseau. But, on the whole, writers, statesmen, generals are willing to step on stage only when cast in a flattering role. They depict themselves only in the interest of self-justification and self-defense or for their own gratification. An undistinguished author will find it easier to write a passable novel than passable memoirs: because fictional characters, even when the novelist, as the saying goes, "has passed on to them a lot of himself," need not be justified, defended, saved. All they need is a modicum of life. But as soon as the detestable and delicious "I" takes center stage, everything changes. An historic account turns into a plea in self-defense; sympathy becomes complacency; scrupulous attention to detail becomes weakness; and omission, cowardice. One is almost tempted to think that, so far as the art of autobiography is concerned, autobiographers have found only one way of seemingly avoiding the "see what an admirable person I am," and that is to conjugate the verb "show how ignoble I am." Passion for truth then turns into the art of highlighting one's weaknesses and vices. One tells the truth because one tells everything; one tells everything because one has told the worst. This may well be just another way of casting oneself in the grand role: the role of a cad, of a cruel, cowardly, or vain man: a role, nonetheless, outstanding, consequent, exciting. A fine role, yes. From Gide to Maurice Sachs this technique of self-abasement has been brilliantly exemplified. When reading some of those modern confessions, one sometimes wonders whether the writer did not pile it on out of fear of leaving something out. Consequently, there are autobiographies of self-flagellation just as there are autobiographies of self-congratulation and others that purr contentedly along as the writer plays and plays over again the record of his memories in order to bathe in emotion:

> Tell me what you have done
> You who are here
> Weeping all the time
> Tell me what have you done
> With your youth? . . .

To speak of oneself is the easiest of things. To speak of oneself equitably is the most difficult. An "I" one doesn't detest enough soon becomes detestable, and an "I" one detests too much becomes improbable.

It seems to me that in her novels and essays Simone de Beauvoir dealt with one theme only: relations between human beings. Such a statement seems trite: is there any other topic? Yet when I think of other great works, a personality comes forth, a face, silhouette, detached from all others, and one might say, sufficient unto themselves emerging out of an apparent solitude. In contrast, what I remember of Simone de Beauvoir's books are not essentially characters, types, or personalities. The world she describes is a universe of relations. The scenes of her novels which remain etched in my memory almost never present a close-up of some character, isolated, but rather a decor inhabited by many actors whose relations with each other are described or suggested with remarkable precision. What has fascinated her from *She Came to Stay* to *The Mandarins* is not so much what goes on inside people but what is going on between them. She makes sure, at least, that nothing happens inside them that does not happen between them. "Every conscience desires the death of the other"; this famous Hegelian statement, which she used as the epigraph for her first book, has as a corollary an idea which underlies all Simone de Beauvoir's work: namely, that life resides only in and through one's consciousness of others. Simone de Beauvoir is not of the race of Kipling's famous cat, the Cat Who Walked By Itself.

What makes Simone de Beauvoir's *Memoirs of a Dutiful Daughter* exceptionally fine reading is the discovery that Simone de Beauvoir has established the most equitable of relationships with herself. She indulges in no complacency nor anger. She doesn't see herself as the center of the world, but never forgets that she is the center of her world. She is not overly fond of herself, but she does not disparage herself too systematically. She obviously prefers to value herself highly and to live so that she can do so. She takes immense pride in what she requires of herself and observes herself with an extreme modesty. One might anticipate that her childhood memories of herself and her world could become the story of Simone told by Beauvoir. "I" would then turn into another, and that other could be used systematically to illlustrate the points of view developed in *The Ethics of Ambiguity*, *Pyrrhus and Cinéas*, and *The Second Sex*. The small Simone who went to school at the Institution Désir (Désir Institution), who played with her sister, who felt cosily warm and comfortable in a well-ordered world, under the eye of God, discovered that grown-ups could quarrel and be inconsistent, and consequently were not infallible. The child Simone who lost her faith and for the benefit of her little friend Zaza reinvented perfect love, the child Simone who was beginning to turn into the older Simone and decided to realize herself through writing, who defined herself little by little in friendship and disillusions, that young Simone ran the risk of becoming a particular example to illustrate the doctrine which Mme de Beauvoir was later to develop. She ran the risk of being transformed into a subject for self-dissection to serve in the defense and illustration of the mature points of view that the adult who looks back at the little girl had cultivated later on.

There is at least one fictional character about whom no novelist can say she got away from her, disobeyed, turned into another, of whom the novelist cannot claim she doesn't know what that character will do in the following pages, at the next turning point—that is the novelist herself, when she takes herself as subject-object. Moreover, when the writer is as rigorously intelligent as Simone de Beauvoir, one might feel a little apprehensive. I confess I did. I wondered whether this exemplary young woman might not have been so energetically kept in hand that she could only emerge from the control of those hands more dead than alive. I have never found that Simone de Beauvoir conceived of her fictional characters as heroes in thesis novels. It sometimes happens that they are people who uphold a thesis, which is quite a different thing. They have the passion for proving or disproving which is the hallmark of intelligence, but they do not make me feel that they were invented in order to prove or illustrate a general idea or that they are ventriloquized toy soldiers in a philosophical *Kriegspiel*. But before I read the *Memoirs of a Dutiful Daughter*, I was afraid that Simone de Beauvoir would find in Simone de Beauvoir the first of her thesis-novel-heroes: herself. I am pleased to note that my fears were unwarranted. In this thick volume little Simone proves only Mme de Beauvoir's high quality and intelligence. For those who admire her, the book will be doubly precious. Beauvoir has not summoned Simone to subject her to a third degree trial of identity. It is rather little Simone who has things to tell us about that adult and great writer called Beauvoir. What she has to say is beautiful.

For instance, some characters in Simone de Beauvoir's novels are moved by the passion of love. In the second volume of *The Second Sex* there is a wonderful analysis of the personality of *L'Amoureuse* (the female lover). But to my mind, Simone de Beauvoir never wrote anything simpler, purer about love than the two pages in her autobiography in which she tells how she discovered that she loves her school friend Elisabeth, known as Zaza. The discovery begins with a vague, undefinable discomfort, for no specific reason, soon followed by a lightning revelation: the child's discovery at the source of that melancholy of the place Zaza occupies in her heart. "I did not require Zaza to have such definite feelings about me: it was enough to be her best friend. The admiration I felt for her did not diminish me in my own eyes. Love is not envy. I could think of nothing better in the world than being myself, and loving Zaza."

If I were a lycée professor, I should surely be in trouble with the "Inspecteur général" for giving my students as the topic for an essay "Compare Montaigne's friendship for La Boétie and Simone de Beauvoir's for Zaza." The inspector would quite certainly be wrong; that comparison is mandatory.

The child Simone de Beauvoir has lived through the so-called "belle époque," the Great War, the post- and interwar years in the forty-centuries-old Paris out of which, in the last forty years, came the world of today and which now looks down at us with some surprise from the pinnacles of memory. As she writes her memoirs, we cannot expect her to recall for us—unless it be indirectly—the color of the days, the atmosphere of the times in which she lived. This does not mean that Simone de Beauvoir is a writer for whom the outside world does not exist. After all, human beings, too, are a part of the outside world, they who alone exist in her eyes. She seems to be indifferent to settings, landscapes, objects, details, to all the little things that serve to recall an atmosphere. She sees only faces, only souls awaken her curiosity, and she takes interest only in the interpersonal relations between people. At least essentially so. She has deliberately eliminated from her book anything picturesque, any sensuous appeal to the eye. She grew up in the Paris of "horizon blue" (uniforms), of cubism, of the transition from horse and carriage to cars, from Russian ballet to the theater of the Cartel without ever giving the slightest attention to the spectacle of life around her. It seems that if the world of nature ever existed for her, it was in her early childhood and briefly. Her memory has retained no landscapes, furnishings, dresses, no traits that characterize a period, speak of a social climate—nothing except looks exchanged, people loved, and those dialogues of minds through which a girl becomes herself. Her *Memoirs* are not the novelist's novel of her own life. They are the work of a moralist. One feels that Simone de Beauvoir chose to forget everything except those she loved and the little girl, later the adolescent who lived and loved.

Moving between the Beauvoir apartment and the Désir Institution, which hardly deserved its name, the author of *The Second Sex* lived the life of a carefully brought up school girl, the child of worthy parents, a good daughter, a good student, a good sister, a good sort, firmly set in her solid, structured world: God was in heaven, Papa and Mama at home, the poor in their place, the rich in theirs. The chorus of grown-ups went gravely repeating that life is not gay and set up for its successors a preestablished schedule: "To bear children who, in their turn, would bear children in an endless reiteration of that same boring old litany."

The first part of her story, no doubt also the most difficult to reconstitute, shows an already ardent and intrepid young Simone who, bit by bit, breaks down and disrupts the prescribed constraints of that reassuring world. Adults didn't live in the state of divine harmony they tried to impose on others. They sometimes held different opinions on vital topics. "Truth, even, was no longer guaranteed." One day, the pinnacle of the entire edifice, God, disappeared. Young Simone then feels herself metamorphosed by a single stroke of the magic cogito. The little girl, certified model 1914–20, makes way for one of those creatures who haunt the pages of *Being and Nothingness* and *The Mandarins*. That creature is 9 or 10 years old. Simone considers her with sympathy. "I was alone. Alone: without a witness, without an interlocutor, without recourse." A few days later this small existentialist, before existentialism, declares that she is "condemned to death." Little by little she becomes conscious of what she is choosing to be. She will assure her salvation through writing, through the achievement of some major work. A great life is the realization in one's mature years of the thought of one's youth. Simone de Beauvoir realized all her youthful dreams.

"Without an interlocutor, without recourse." That is true in the main. Yet *Memoirs* contains a hymn of gratitude addressed to interlocutors and to the recourse of friendship. Simone de Beauvoir's entire childhood and adolescence are illuminated by a passionate friendship of which the writer speaks with admirable tact and warmth. The child, Elisabeth Mabille, known as Zaza, was to die young, destroyed by the conformism of a family which systematically repressed her sensibilities and played havoc with her fate. Simone de Beauvoir has described the evolution of her friendship for Zaza with flawless acumen. When Zaza disappears from her horizon, though other friendships were already, so to speak, relaying that one, Zaza's departure will leave a never filled void in the young woman's heart. From the last episodes in that story a group of brilliant and iconoclastic young men emerge, described by the memorialist with much grace: Paul Nizan, Herbaud, and a young denizen of the rue d'Ulm Normal School who at twenty, comparing the men of his generation and their predecessors, had declared "We are less happy but more likable"—a rather comic statement at first hearing but quite true when reread, given the fact that the author of that declaration was called Jean-Paul Sartre.

Memoirs is one of those books of which one has the feeling that it did its author good to write and that many others will find it good to read. The story is told thoughtfully, with much humor; it is tragic and gay, one of those great undertakings of self-and-world evaluation which help those who engage in them and those who travel along to become stronger, more lucid, and happier. Simone de Beauvoir considers herself without complacency, but with no regrets nor weakness. Rather than telling us her story, Simone de Beauvoir is calling herself to account. Her enterprise will thus serve everyone. Dutiful? In the trivial sense of the word, she may have been so at first. But at the point of arrival when with the last period the autobiography breaks off with her adolescence, Simone de Beauvoir does not seem "dutiful," but rather in good form.

Where love and friendship are not contagious, they are merely trivial. Elisabeth Mabille died many years ago on the threshold of adolescence. By now she might be only a small, colorless phantom, one of those whose light murmur is submerged by the winds of memory, whose words can no longer be heard. But through the miracle of friendship, Simone de Beauvoir has succeeded in keeping Zaza alive, intact, has made us love Zaza as she loved her. And, step by step, taking her friend by the hand, leading her slowly out of the past, she makes us hear her laughter, her voice, and her plaint. We feel, too, that she has made us understand something essential about herself.

Psychoanalysis has accustomed us to ferret out from behind motifs and texts other hidden motifs and buried secrets. There is no great work that does not originate in some passion: the key that opens up its deep chambers is to know from what the creator was seeking deliverance, or vengeance, what it was she wished to overcome or to achieve.

The Second Sex was not the first treatise on the "feminine condition" that we had read. Why then, when we read it, did it seem so unlike any other? It was a huge piece of work, put together with the care and erudition which, in a thesis, we usually find both dazzling and a little painful. It was more than obvious that Simone de Beauvoir was unusually intelligent, unusually cultivated. But this did not account for the strange force of those two large, rather ponderous and slow volumes, for the dynamism behind their patient and plodding gait. Behind the edifice itself there were thousands of index cards, thousands of texts, years of reflection and experience. There was much more: passion. Among scientific works, some call to mind a barge or launch, clumsy, loaded to capacity, without grace. Others evoke Noah's ark, built in response to some pressing injunction, in order to escape from a precise danger. *The Second Sex* is one of these. We now know what injunction Simone de Beauvoir was heeding, whom she wished to save. It wasn't herself because she had already saved herself. If her vast and weighty book was alive, it is because it was dedicated to a small dead girl whose disappearance had persisted in the heart of her friend as an irreparable scandal. Skimpy works are those that settle mean accounts. But there are also generous balance sheets. We now know what balance sheet Simone de Beauvoir has never ceased to draw up. The question she has never stopped asking is: Why did Zaza die?

"For many years I thought her death had been the price paid for my freedom." Those are the last words of *Memoirs*, all through which there flits a young girl, full of laughter, fantasy, and tenderness, whose name is Zaza. Zaza does not die by chance at the end of the story. Her disappearance is due to a ritual murder to which she herself painfully acquiesces. Zaza's Christian faith sustains in her the certitude that she must obey her parents; they decide to marry her off according to their views, not to her heart. Since she cannot both live and obey, Zaza, it seems, chooses to die. When she is on the threshold of death, her parents are ready to concede all that they had previously denied her. To a sobbing Mme Mabille, M. Mabille says, "We have only been instruments in the hands of God."

Memoirs is a fearless, passionate book, the story of a girl who decided with total determination to wrench herself free from what M. Mabille had called "the hands of God." Yet, one constantly encounters in the book a sense that one is almost tempted to call Christian a human feeling to which Christianity has given one of its deepest and most daring expressions, through the belief in the communion of saints and the reversibility of merits. During her adolescence Simone de Beauvoir witnessed the defeat and destruction of two people who were very close to her. Zaza is destroyed, and the first man with whom she herself was in love, her cousin, slowly stagnates because he refuses both to choose himself and just to choose, sinking into indolence, alcoholism, general decline, and finally death. One can surmise that Simone de Beauvoir thinks that in some way it was for her that those two beings died and that their failure might take on meaning if only she were able to transform it into a victory or counter it with a victory. Obscurely, deeply, the unbeliever she is seems to believe that there are lives she must redeem. Obscurely, deeply, unbeliever though she be, her liberated mind is not liberated from the certainty that the dead little girl in her past died *for* her. "Her death was the price paid for my freedom." Transcending Hegel's dictum that every conscience seeks the death of the other, Simone de Beauvoir's is one of those consciences that (also) desire that others live.

Memoirs of a Dutiful Existentialist
René Girard*

Mme de Beauvoir's existence has always been governed not by Heideggerian *Angst*, as orthodoxy demands and as earlier writings seemed to indicate, but by a relentless drive to *happiness*. Those Americans who still regard French existentialism as a school of idleness and Buddhist-like indifference to things mundane should read *Les Mémoires d'une jeune fille rangée* (*Memoirs of a Dutiful Daughter*) and *La Force de l'âge*. If these two volumes do not correct their misconceptions, nothing ever will. Mme de Beauvoir gives us the key to her whole life, in a sentence which would have delighted the sociologist Max Weber: "In my case the idea of salvation had survived the disappearance of God, and my strongest conviction was that each person must see to his own salvation." This is an excellent definition of that modern spirit, competitive and puritanical, which erects philosophical systems as well as industrial empires. It is no small pleasure to sit down in a comfortable chair and to watch Mme de Beauvoir save herself — through hundreds of pages of lively prose and a few decades of feverish activity. As a little child, she had formed the project of visiting even the tiniest corners of the globe, down to the last ditch and to the smallest clump of trees. During her many travels, she is haunted by the fear of missing *something*, and she leafs frantically through, she *compulse frénétiquement* her various guidebooks. When she is in Marseilles, she goes on solitary excursions and she walks longer, faster, and farther than anybody else. She reads everything, from *Was ist Metaphysik* to *Fantomas* and *Chéri-Bibi*; she sees all the plays, she goes to all the exhibitions; she studies music, painting, sculpture, geography and physiology, besides philosophy. She gives courses and she writes a great number of books. She

*Reprinted by permission from *Yale French Studies* 27 (Spring–Summer 1961):41–46.

practices winter sports and she learns how to ride a bicycle. Her capacity for absorbing what she calls "happiness" is truly frightening. And the salvation she pursues is typical of our age, insofar as it is a strictly individual one; she must build her happiness all alone, *toute seule, sans secours*. Even anti-capitalism is approached with typical capitalistic avidity. Mme de Beauvoir is too intelligent, of course, not to perceive the dark dialectical implications of this voracious appetite.

How can we save ourselves, concretely, in the absence of God, if not by surpassing our fellow human beings in all sorts of worldly endeavors? Early in life, Mlle de Beauvoir was one of those little female prodigies who win all the prizes in school and get the *mentions très bien*, thus poisoning the lives of their more relaxed brothers and cousins. These female prodigies are one of the truly national institutions of France. Academic achievements of children are a major field of competition between families of the middle class. The girls are usually ahead of the boys because they are more eager to please their fathers. Immediately after the *baccalauréat*, however, they are expected to abandon all intellectual pursuits in order to become wives and mothers. Competition is suddenly shifted to other fields. Little geniuses with their heads full of trigonometry and Kantian philosophy are often seen never to open another book for the rest of their lives.

Being a particularly brilliant subject, Mme de Beauvoir could not stand the thought of forsaking the *mentions très bien*, and she simply refused to be reconverted to home life, thus manifesting for the first time that spirit of rebellion which made her famous and which is still alive in her. However much we admire this valorous feat, we must not exaggerate the scope of the revolution. Mme de Beauvoir rejected only the moribund aspects of French bourgeois morality, and for the sole purpose, besides, of upholding more vigorously its one essential tenet which demands that everything be turned into a competitive examination and that everybody try to run away with the first prize. Mme de Beauvoir, as we all know, has been running away with first prizes ever since that initial exploit. To such a woman, existentialism and marxism were two more academic subjects which she mastered as easily as the others and which exerted considerably more influence on her than trigonometry and Kantian philosophy would have, had she agreed to become an ordinary housewife and mother. The dutiful daughter became a dutiful existentialist. Mme de Beauvoir is probably less a revolutionist than she thinks, but she is a good writer and a brilliant Left Bank intellectual. It is only in France, perhaps, that such a person could become the spokesman for the growing class of progressive and intelligent career women. Mme de Beauvoir is the voice of all the other feminine first prize winners. She reinterprets the traditional culture of France from the perspective of the career woman; she expresses a viewpoint entirely novel to the French social set-up in a language worthy of a long intellectual past.

Mme de Beauvoir perceives and formulates some of the conflicts inherent to the situation of a career woman but she denies the existence of others, and these unsolved conflicts add fuel to the fire of righteous indignation which burns high and bright, in the heart of this remarkable woman, each time *alienation* seems to threaten her precious freedom. Mme de Beauvoir and Jean-Paul Sartre never married because they were afraid of *alienating* each other. *Alienation* lurks again when Mme de Beauvoir feels overwhelmed by undifferentiated sex desire. Can a woman remain free to choose her lovers with her head rather than with her senses? Can she remain faithful to the chosen one within the precisely defined limits of a sexual lend-lease program? Strait is the gate between *alienation* to society and *alienation* to instinct. But Mme de Beauvoir, like a Cornelian heroine, wins all her battles; she can experience the ecstasy of dark passion while remaining perfectly dignified and independent: ["The joy of loving should be as inevitable and unexpected as the heavy swell of the sea, like the blossoming of a sin."] She goes into a frenzy of self-surrender while keeping a watchful eye over her Adversary, the little devil *Alienation*. This, undoubtedly, is the neatest trick of the past two or three thousand years. Sartre, among others, has devoted several hundreds of pages to proving that love cannot be like the blooming of the peach tree. But Sartre, obviously, is far behind Mme de Beauvoir in the pursuit of happiness.

Mme de Beauvoir's free, happy and spontaneous love does not come from Sartre but from Rousseau, from Mme de Staël and Lamartine, as well as from George Sand and the first Alfred de Musset (the Musset who had not yet encountered George Sand). The modern career woman is really a romantic in disguise. At times, it is true, she sounds more like M. Jules Romains than like Lamartine. But M. Jules Romains, too, is a romantic in disguise. We keep reading the name of Jean-Paul Sartre, in *La Force de l'âge*, but all we hear is *Jallez*, or perhaps *Jerphanion*. There already was a faint flavor of *bonne volonté* in the less pessimistic passages of *Les Chemins de la liberté*. Perhaps all existentialists from *Normale supérieure* must sound like M. Jules Romains when they turn from negative to positive thinking.

Mme de Beauvoir really succumbs, in parts of *La Force de l'âge*, to the old myth of romantic spontaneity. The myth is not absent from the Sartrian notion of freedom but it is Sartre's greatness that he tried desperately to chain this uncontrollable dragon, and he gave it as limited a place as he could in his philosophy. He could not destroy the myth, however, and this explains, perhaps, why it can wage such a powerful counter-offensive in the recent books of Mme de Beauvoir. Since *Les Mandarins*, the myth has successfully reoccupied all the positions from which Sartre had painfully extirpated it; it proliferates luxuriantly; it blooms everywhere like the flower of the peach tree. With Sartre's waning influence, Mme de Beauvoir is reverting to a much more naïve, more elemental and often quite charming form of romantic individualism.

As a curious consequence of this evolution, the heroic years of *La Nausée* turn, under the pen of Mme de Beauvoir, into the exact antithesis of this famous book. Unlike Roquentin who believes that "adventure" is "bunk" and that traveling is a bore, Mme de Beauvoir and her companion meet the unexpected at every turn and embrace it passionately. The Sartre we have all imagined brooding somberly about *la contingence* was really drinking manzanilla to the sound of the guitar, in the side-walk cafés of old Madrid; he was eagerly exploring Barcelona's picturesque Barrio Chino; he was greedily snapping mental pictures of bullfights and tricorned gendarmes. It is difficult to assess how much irony entered into the creation of this *anti-nausée*.

Let us follow the two happy tourists into the Prado museum. Before meeting Mme de Beauvoir, the unfortunate Jerphanion—pardon me, Jean-Paul Sartre, was afflicted with a decidedly middle-brow outlook on the art of painting. He paid more attention to the "story" of a picture than to its style; he commented glibly upon the sentiments expressed by the characters, and he fell into a deplorable silence when it came to shapes and colors. He even presumed to like a painter as contemptible, in the modern scale of values, as far "out," we might say, as Guido Reni. *Horresco referens.* Mme de Beauvoir, needless to say, put a quick end to that heretical nonsense. She taught her friend true spontaneity and he became so well trained that he automatically exclaimed: "C'est de l'O-péra" whenever confronted by a figurative painting. Having rid himself of his ignorance, he embraced the rigid faith of a neophyte, thus providing an even nicer background for Mme de Beauvoir's delicate nuances of taste. One of these fine points is the author's fondness for Titian, a master widely suspected of operatic tendencies. This subversive inclination reveals a great indifference to established values; it fits in nicely, too, with Mme de Beauvoir's role as the extoller of "happiness" and "life," versus Sartre's intellectualism.

Are the "monsters, demons and cripples" of Hieronymus Bosch preferable to the "cruelty" of Goya's portraits, and to the "black madness" of his later work? So many enchanting beauties make it difficult to exercise the faculty of judgment, and the Mme de Beauvoir of 1929 decided that Bosch was supreme; the Mme de Beauvoir of 1959 rectifies this gross error and puts Goya first. Both preferences are spontaneous, of course, since the only sentiments Mme de Beauvoir is willing to entertain are those which are "spontaneously provoked by their object." It must be noted, however, that Mme de Beauvoir was all for Bosch when the dominant esthetic was surrealism and that she shifted her allegiance to Goya when everybody looked at this painter through the eyes of André Malraux. Like so many women writers addicted to spontaneity, Mme de Beauvoir gives us the impression that whatever is fashionable today will remain fashionable forever. As a matter of fact, she almost convinces us that there is no such thing as fashion. Her severe criticism of her own pre-existentialist period contributes enormously to that feeling of eternity. Humanity was still at the groping stage in 1929; even its elite had not yet reached the definitive answers on every subject. Mme de Beauvoir constantly points out how much *idealism*, in that antediluvian period, how much of the bourgeois was still present in her revolt against the bourgeoisie. We never quite manage to understand when and how the author finally rid herself of the disease but we know that the cure must have been successful and complete, because the opinions of the present are not submitted to the same searching criticism as the opinions of the past. There is nothing relative, nothing *historically* or *socially* conditioned about Mme de Beauvoir's latest word on marriage, happiness, Guido Reni, Hieronymus Bosch, the Barrio Chino and *Was ist Metaphysik*. What will happen the day *Was ist Metaphysik* is toppled from its present eminence? What will happen the day Guido Reni is exalted again? It is to be feared that the force of one age will turn into the weakness of another, and that many pages of Mme de Beauvoir's memoirs will sound more and more, with the passing of time, the way M. Jules Romains began to sound after the opening of the Second World War.

But other pages will remain. As the war approaches, historical events take precedence over the search for happiness. The 1940–44 period is the best part of the book. There is less tourism, less surface exploration and more progress in depth. It is impossible not to admire the Mme de Beauvoir of the occupation years, and not to sympathize with much of what she writes and does. She never loses her sense of values and she never abandons hope. She never allows her revulsion for the mad and chauvinistic world of the early forties to turn into the paralyzed fascination evidenced by so many works of art of the period. *La Force de l'âge*, at its best, is a hymn to individual freedom and to the life of the intellect; at its worst, it is a *summa* of the French intelligentsia during the *entre-deux guerres* and the Second World War; it is a description of its way of life and a répertoire of its opinions and intellectual fads; it is, at any rate, a priceless document for future historians of taste. It also contains an enormous amount of information on the genesis of Sartrian ideas and of Sartrian literature — even though Roquentin is constantly, and perhaps significantly, misspelled as *Roquantin*.

Mme de Beauvoir, anyway, is not thinking of posterity; she is thinking of the present, and the present is hers, whatever criteria we may choose in order to decide the matter. *La Force de l'âge* is a charming book and its success is well deserved. Once again, the first lady of existentialism is running away with the first prize.

Simone de Beauvoir and the Related Destinies of Woman and Intellectual

Jacques Ehrmann*

"Freedom must project itself toward its own reality via a content whose value is founded on freedom itself." — S. de Beauvoir, *Pour une morale de l'ambiguïté*

Two themes may be distinguished, in Simone de Beauvoir's writings, that receive particular attention and to some extent account for the specific quality of her work. These are *womanhood* and *the role of the intellectual*. While there are other aspects to her thinking, it is permissible to regard these two as the poles around which all else revolves.

Throughout her life Simone de Beauvoir has sought to demonstrate that she is not simply *a* woman but *this* woman. She has always striven to become the woman she actually is, whose "existence, although not yet ended . . . has a significance the future is unlikely to modify." Such is her assertion, now that she has turned fifty.

In her *Memoirs of a Dutiful Daughter* she reveals how she became what she is. From the outset, and while still a child, she accepted her lot as a woman much as one accepts the data of a problem. "I had no regrets about being a girl," she writes. "As I said before, I wasted no time in vain regrets, and cheerfully accepted what had been given me." And elsewhere: "I stoutly rebelled against my childhood, but never against my woman-hood" — "In my games and musings and projects I never changed myself into a man, my imagination was entirely taken up with anticipating my destiny as a woman."

In other words, she accepted herself as she was. That does not at all amount to saying that she agreed to become what other people demanded of her. Yes, she was a woman, but she had no thought of imprisoning herself therein as in a *nature*. While this was her condition, she refused to assume it as a *fatality*. "One is not born a woman, one becomes a woman," that is the thesis she maintains throughout her voluminous *The Second Sex*.

Who was this woman she strove to become? As a child, Simone de Beauvoir already enjoyed her studies and was eager to read and to learn. But study, as she saw it, had teaching as a necessary concomitant — what had been given her could be truly her own, it seemed, only if she passed it on to others. "Teaching my dolls could not satisfy me, I had no interest in mimicking actions, I wanted really to pass on what I knew. By teaching reading, writing and arithmetic to my sister, I experienced at the age of six the pride of effective action. . . . By transforming ignorance into knowl-

*Reprinted by permission from *Yale French Studies* 27 (Spring–Summer 1961):26–32.

edge, by implanting truths in a virgin intelligence, I was creating something real."[1]

She tells us, too, how the pride her father took in such a brilliant, industrious little girl gives way to mixed feelings not far removed from consternation when he sees her grow into a "jeune fille" so devoted to her studies that practically no time is left for the conventional interests of girls of her class. In bourgeois society, during this century's first fifty years, it was quite unfitting for a woman to be an "intellectual." She scandalized· her father, proud though he was of his own love of literature, by looking forward to a career in teaching. "You will lose caste," he told her.

Her father erred, obviously, by treating as subordinate what was the essential thing in his daughter's makeup, her taste for intellectual endeavor. What he regarded as essential for a woman (the acceptance of a traditionally approved life style involving husband, children, kitchen and feminine finery) was, for her, a side issue.

The girl, consequently, in order to win her freedom as a woman, her freedom to be human, had to vanquish her milieu and its traditional outlook. She had to convince others (her parents, first of all, then her friends, and finally her public) that she *could* be different from what is usually demanded of a woman. Thus it is as a woman that she will venture on what traditionally is a male preserve. Yet when Simone de Beauvoir compared herself with her "more feminine" friends, she could see nothing to envy. And with a clear vision of the destiny she was aiming at, she told herself: "I flattered myself that a woman's heart was combined in me with a man's brain. I discovered myself to be Unique."

She knew that writing was her vocation. At the age of fifteen, in reply to the question " 'What do you want to do when you are grown up?' I gave the prompt answer, 'I want to be a famous author!' " And she comments: ". . . the most famous of my sisters had won renown in literature." Another remark reveals the adolescent girl even more strikingly: "Besides, I had a taste for communication." Does not this bias explain why the child of six passed on her learning to her sister?

Everything about her was placed at the service of this generous goal. "My life must be useful! The whole of my life must be useful! . . . every bit of me was needed." Literature would never be for her, as it had been for her father, a means of "avenging oneself on reality by enslaving it to fiction."

It can be seen that the significance she attributed to her vocation at once placed her at a far remove from what is customarily expected of the woman writer who, as a "femme-artiste," is admired above all for her delicate sensibility, her subtle analysis of emotion and her fragile dream castles. Simone de Beauvoir wants none of this. There is about her nothing of a Colette and her cajoleries, to take but one example. Even as a writer she will not be like other women.[2] "I could do nothing with the marvelous," she writes. By this she means, I take it, all the extravaganzas of imagination and revery. Perhaps that is why her novels have so little of the novel in them. They always retain some features of a line of argument, of a rational demonstration.[3] The transposition or interpretation of reality is, one senses, not for her. She probably looks on imagination with suspicion as the father of lies. She aims at a literature that will lie as little as possible, at works that are not exercises in falsehood. Neither as woman nor as writer (if the two can be dissociated) does Simone de Beauvoir tolerate the least touch of coquetry. To write a book is not to exploit a gift or exhibit one's charms, it is to do a piece of work.

She had decided to be useful. Yet nothing about her evokes one who tends the sick with ready compassion and unbounded devotion. To be useful is not to give way to pity. It means to observe, to bear witness, to explain. One might with some measure of justification regard her as a woman doctor. She herself encourages us to do this, and it is no accident that she depicts herself as follows, in *The Mandarins*: "I looked at people through a doctor's eyes, and that made it hard for me to have ordinary human contacts with them." Thus what counts, for her, is to remain cool and to record the symptoms, to analyze and prescribe. She must maintain her distance, her self-control and an entire lucidity.

With this we arrive at the second aspect of Simone de Beauvoir's work mentioned in the opening paragraph. My feeling is that the "personal" part of *The Mandarins* is not so satisfactory, with its account of the affair between Anne, the heroine, and the American writer, Lewis. Their relationship and their passions fail to touch us because the author makes insufficient use of the techniques of the novel. But when politics comes to the fore, when Simone de Beauvoir presents to us the central questions debated by French intellectuals in the post-war years, the book takes on conviction right away. Why is this? Because the author is no longer obliged to handle emotions but judgments, because political, unlike amorous, passions exist in an intellectual context that lets logic function. *The Mandarins*, then, is less the novel it claims to be than a chronicle, an eye-witness account of the problems faced by the French Left after the Liberation. As a document, too — in view of the situation that confronted France in the immediate past — it has again come to possess a certain actuality.[4]

At a time when many French intellectuals have taken a more and more categorical attitude concerning the Algerian war, signing manifestos calling for such drastic action that they are unprecedented in the political annals of recent years, and establishing networks of resistance against the prolongation of colonial warfare — at a moment when agitation in France was reaching a climax, when the threat of open conflict, with the danger of actual bloodshed, was setting Right against Left — a rereading of Simone de Beauvoir's book inevitably gives rise to the reflection that this recent political fever is but the resurgence of the enthusiasms, the anguish and disappointments experienced by intellectuals in the years following the end of the war.

The problems they faced were, indeed, once again to become crucial. *The Mandarins* pondered over (and one must still ponder) the inevitable overlapping of politics and literature, and contained a full-dress debate of the question (which Sartre's *What is Literature?* had examined in the domain of literary criticism) of the intellectuals' personal commitment.

By showing us such men at odds with each other — these writers and journalists who are among the most impressive of those now living — by letting us see what attitudes they adopt toward the gravest political problems and what solutions they propose, Simone de Beauvoir enables us to realize clearly something of inestimable importance, if we would understand current French intellectual history. Namely, that commitment has no precise meaning until it is placed in its historical and political context. No doubt, the tradition of a literature wedded to the expression of ideas and of "humanitarian" ideals has thoroughly impregnated French literature for centuries past. But what marks off the intellectuals of *The Mandarins* from their forerunners is that the men of previous generations were not directly involved in politics, whereas their successors are acutely aware (if for some it is a distasteful awareness) that there can be no question of abstaining. For the earlier writers "politics" had purely moral connotations which today's writers are trying to shake off.[5]

To read *The Mandarins* is to reach the unshakable conviction that denunciations of torture, of war and of concentration camp can no longer be restricted to exclusively moral preoccupations, of idealist and ahistorical concerns and scruples; that it no longer ties in with some abstract notion of a universal Good that will establish the concord of all mankind but is indissolubly bound up with particular social and historical circumstances. And nothing is changed by the reluctance of some persons to admit that this is so.

Since the intellectual is unavoidably involved in politics the moment he sets out to examine the general problems of his day, his position as a witness (that is, as expressing his individual conscience) is called into question. What can he do to safeguard liberties and ward off injustice if all his warnings, appeals, and menaces remain hidden on the book-laden shelves of his study, or in the obscure pages of a review read only by initiates?

More than ever conscious of his powerlessness, if the voice of the masses fails to reëcho his own, he feels the need to gather around him a vast audience, to sense a direct connection with a public whose leader he would be. He needs a widely read newspaper, and the crowds at political rallies.[6] Simone de Beauvoir tells of all this, of the hope that her fellow combatants entertained, and of the disappointment that followed their defeat. The collapse of the movement that Sartre had initiated was due, in actual fact, to the lack of a sufficiently large audience among the generality of Frenchmen.

Disappointing as the outcome may be, by the light of recent events (I am thinking of the attention aroused by the "Manifesto of the 121" concerning the right to insubordination in an unjust war) some possibility of optimism still remains. Is it not strange that at the very moment when the morale of the French Left is at its lowest, when the slough of despond appears to stretch in all directions — see, in this connection, Sartre's preface to Paul Nizan's *Aden-Arabie* — that a sudden upwelling of effective political action occurs, with a small group of intellectuals in the forefront? It becomes clear, at such moments of acute crisis as that experienced by France toward the close of 1960, that public opinion may be significantly affected by the stand taken by men it has never hailed as its political leaders but in whom it recognizes, almost instinctively, its most clear-headed masters in the practice of thinking.

The reader is entitled to ask, at this point, what relationship can be found between the two themes apparently so far apart that have occupied us here. I would reply that, in one as in the other, human freedom is at stake. Simone de Beauvoir is indeed speaking of herself, when she offers us the example of a woman who has rejected the conventional paths trodden by womanhood, but this individual example may acquire the force of a principle. It is a principle which she submits to ceaseless examination, not only in her life but in her books also. And when she defends the "second sex," she speaks of all women to all women. She speaks to them of a woman's rights, of her right to choose her own life, to assume responsibility for her own destiny and to refuse what society would thrust upon her.

And a like responsibility is involved — this time on the political plane — when she portrays the French "mandarins" of the post-war years. Just as a woman can no longer be satisfied to be attractive and nothing more, similarly the intellectual cannot continue to play the seer, enveloping himself in a timeless purity and timeless irresponsibility.

If men do indeed possess some measure of liberty, it is only by assuming it with complete awareness that they can invent and bring to fruition values by which they have chosen to guide their lives.

Notes

1. It will later become plain to what extent these remarks hold for Mme de Beauvoir as a writer.

2. I have just come across this commentary by a woman writer interviewed for a weekly paper: "Women write skilfully. In psychology they are unexcelled. But they lose themselves in detail, they fail to rise above the immediate occasion. With the sole exception of Simone de Beauvoir, women simply do not have the necessary stamina."

3. This weakness constitutes the strength of her essays, as in the "political" part of *The Mandarins*, to be discussed later.

4. I am convinced that historians will make use of it. And without trespassing on the future, may we not say that some professors in American universities utilize *The Mandarins* as a document, when they recommend it to students in their courses on contemporary French politics?

5. One need but consult 18th-century dictionaries to realize this. Voltaire, for example, writes in his *Dictionnaire philosophique*: "Politics, a species of morality of a particular and superior kind, with which the principles of ordinary morality can sometimes be made to harmonize only by the exercise of much subtlety."

6. This is yet another element that distinguishes the commitment of a Sartre from that of a Voltaire. Voltaire did not have to consider how he could attract the attention of a party audience.

The Dutiful Simone de Beauvoir   Mary Ellmann*

Simone de Beauvoir is distinguished by her consistency; on everything she writes, her identity is stamped indelibly. Her temperament is fused with her unwavering conviction, and both assist her in affirming moral right and upbraiding moral wrong. As Henri Perron says in her novel, *The Mandarins*, "There is so much to love and to hate solidly." But Beauvoir's solidity, her urgency, her unleavened purposefulness bear down upon their varied subjects with inconsiderate weight. By contrast, Sartre's performance in his autobiography is buoyant and volatile, agitated by metaphor. Curiously, it is this levity, ascribed by Sartre (in a characteristic leap) to his having been fatherless, that seems to separate the teacher from his best pupil.

Nonetheless, the stable incorporation of temperament and conviction has enabled Mlle. de Beauvoir to be productive, to earn rightly a reputation for courageous effort, prodigious research, and straightforward habits of thought; it has prompted her to shun timidity and to enjoy emphasis. She most values her honesty: "But I repeat that I have never intentionally distorted the truth." Her stance is that of the perceptive yet uncompromising mind. Reality is to be informed, in an almost divine sense, by the human intellect. The character, Françoise, in the first chapter of Beauvoir's first novel, *She Came to Stay*, initiates this activity: "The red of the carpet gleamed through the darkness like a timid night-light. She exercised that power: her presence snatched things from their unconsciousness; she gave them their color, their smell." The same standard of the person "as the eye-that-looks, as subject, consciousness, freedom," controls Beauvoir's new book *Force of Circumstance*[1] now, twenty years later. The objects of interest to this enduring consciousness have been those interrelations of people which occur, if not always in public, in clear

*Reprinted from *Commentary* 40 (August 1965):59–62, by permission; all rights reserved.

and open sight: the confrontation of postwar intellectuals and politics
(*The Mandarins*), of generic woman and generic man (*The Second Sex*), of
human beings and their environs (*America Day by Day* and the study of
China, *The Long March*). Beauvoir's belief is that the person who writes,
or the person written about, may enter upon a kind of universality, the
freedom of becoming comprehensible to others. This belief tempted her to
the verge of biography in her study of the Marquis de Sade (*Must We Burn
Sade?*). What attracts her, as Genet's work attracts Sartre, is Sade's effort
"to make of his psychophysical destiny an ethical choice." This he
accomplished (in prison, like Genet) through writing, and writing in
general, for Beauvoir, makes possible such transmogrification. And the
more clearly each man presents himself for judgment by others, the sooner
idiosyncrasy is exchanged for ethic, the better social and political frater-
nity all men may form.

Therefore, in much of Beauvoir's writing, one cannot properly expect
to find verbal designs which delay rather than push, intrigue rather than
direct. The meaning of her words is at once adequately clear: the reader
can rush ahead with the writer, through the problem, its causes, its
effects, its proposed solution — to action! But what of the times when the
only discernible purpose in writing at all is to convey inactive, amoral,
even ecstatic sensations?

> I listened to his even breathing; he was sleeping, and I didn't have the
> heart to awaken him. It's touching to see a man asleep: so innocent a
> sight.

> It was human, teeming, real, a city of the earth in which I, a flesh-and-
> blood I, was walking. How beautiful it was under its silvery brocade! I
> looked at it wide-eyed, and something stirred timidly in my heart. We
> think that it is love that gives the world all its brilliance, but the world,
> too, swells love with its riches. Love was dead, yet the earth was still
> there, intact, with its secret songs, its smells, its tenderness.

> I remembered how I used to breathe in the pureness of the night, how it
> would go to my head, fill my whole being with joy, and I would say to
> myself that if such moments didn't exist living would hardly be worth
> the effort. Would they ever be reborn?

Not in *The Mandarins*. Summoned in these terms, memories — socially
inconsequential, personally vital — refuse to budge.

In the end, this is perhaps the first difficulty in Mlle. de Beauvoir's
effort to explore herself, the total person, incompletely prefigured in such
fictional heroines as Françoise (*She Came to Stay*) and Anne Dubreuilh
(*The Mandarins*). Now that her autobiography seems to be complete — the
Memoirs of a Dutiful Daughter (1959) and *The Prime of Life* (1962) being
joined by *Force of Circumstance* — the rules by which this self-accounting
is played, and the issues with which it copes, become clearer. One premise
has been Sartre's, that it is desirable in writing to "restore to time its actual

course." Quite logically, then, many pages (1,499) have been needed to retrace many years. A second principle is to be faithful to contingency, the uncontrollable, accidental proliferation of circumstances by which the person is surrounded. So all details, at all levels of experience, enjoy a perfect democracy. Whatever is seen is represented, just as in police photography the snapshot of the corpse is immediately followed by a snapshot of the half-empty glass of ginger ale making a ring on the bedside table. "Elegance," by which Beauvoir evidently means deliberate selection of detail, is eschewed; it is rather through loyalty to *all* of the actual that her life is to be made flesh: "I have always had the secret fantasy that my life was being recorded, down to the tiniest detail, on some giant tape recorder, and that the day would come when I should play back the whole of my past." But the tape recorder often distorts sound. The pledge of allegiance to detail alone cannot restore to circumstance, as it flung itself at Beauvoir, what Sartre calls "its brutal freshness, its ambiguity, its unforeseeability." Some involuntary selection is self-evident: the one person, especially the one vehement person, tends to see the same things everywhere. Others would notice what she missed. And, of course, the detail comes before the reader only as it is shaped in the writer's words. Elegance in the record may be objectionable, but its alternative, though it may be inelegance, cannot be reality.

The impossibility of ever giving independent life again to what had independent life before it disappeared beneath the surface of a mind, is if anything, more marked in Beauvoir than in other writers. Her opinions, her interpretations, are extraordinarily intrusive. Her convictions, like her hands, are always clenched. Such traits, advantages perhaps to the politician or social worker, are less lucky in the writer, particularly the writer bent on recreating the unpredictability of actual life. The surprise of experience is less evident than the monotony of fixed responses to it.

The *Memoirs of a Dutiful Daughter* is the best book of the autobiography, partly because it is the first, instead of the second or the third, statement of this absolute personality. It is also the most frightening. For all Beauvoir's attachment to disparate details now, the *Memoirs* is not constructed by that standard. Its materials are coherent, its single, all-pervasive aim gives it the unity of obsession. On one level, it examines the development, in her first twenty years, of the temperament and conviction by which we recognize the adult Simone de Beauvoir. She herself sees the book as a document of her escape from the shibboleths of French Catholic middle-class life. But on a second level, the book grows into an impersonal exemplum: it propounds the ravenous nature of human beginnings, each birth the creation of a new and separate appetite, a mouth stretched open. The mouth bites, the jaws chew, the throat gulps down. Presented circumstances are devoured (if they are agreeable) or spat out (if they are not). Beauvoir wanted to say, and does say, that in defiance of set persuasions and prohibitions, a person can realize his freedom. But the book unwittingly traces in the mind the outlines of absent images, the dun virtues that may lie in the acceptance of restraints.

Still, the search for food is absorbing, and finding it is always a kind of triumph. That sequence grants the *Memoirs*, like *Robinson Crusoe*, a genuine impetus. *Force of Circumstance* is, in contrast, sluggish, sated. In the *Memoirs* temperament wriggles toward its proper conviction with an almost protozoan intent; now the two have grown tired together. The early longing to write, to be published, to be recognized, has diminished to the rancors and grudges that circle within the circle of the recognized. The French middle class, that old palpable villain, is formless now. Beauvoir still hates it, but by rote, and the epithet "bourgeois idealism" has become just a rattling noise. In fact, the avid seizure of new experience in the earlier books is often now a joyless, obligatory reiteration. Human beings, the new book indicates, must endlessly repeat themselves. Not only is each person a sealed container, held for life within his own skin, but the number of things he can do, even in Paris, is cruelly limited. And the more often they are done, the less apparent reason for doing them, the less energy for doing them again.

Energy has drained away through several new ditches. The exhilaration and hope which marked the simultaneous endings of the Second World War and of *The Prime of Life*, were mauled in the political riot of postwar France, in the debasement of the Algerian war, in the discarding of liberty with which Beauvoir equates de Gaulle's return to power. Alienation from her own people through these angers coincides with an alienation from herself, a loathing of "decrepitude." Beauvoir's experiences, held together before by strength, end in a miscellany as tiring to her as to the reader.

This enervation is pronounced in what has been a recurrent subject for her, travel. As a child, spending her summers in the country, Beauvoir formed the conception that the world lay waiting for her, unconscious, uncomprehended. As a young woman, she was free at last to undertake its systematic awakening—in the course of walking tours that seem more penitential than explorative, inflicted upon the walkers and the ground itself. (Sartre paused in these exercises only to adjust his rucksack and to ponder the philosophical implications of tourism.) Every step, then, every glance, was a claim—"And the countryside was something much more than just a setting: they were conquering it bit by bit, by main force" (*The Mandarins*).

In the new book, places (Spain, Italy, Yugoslavia, Africa, Cuba, Brazil) are still digested, but the peristaltic rhythm is that of a mature constitution, settled in its diet. In the rich quarters, richness is deplored; in the poor quarters, poverty is deplored. Museums and native rites are surveyed, the masses are mingled with. (Acutely conscious of separation from others, Beauvoir enjoys being swirled about in a crowd.) The local dishes are tasted, the local intellectuals pass or fail, a few folk artifacts are purchased. Since the stock of the never-seen-before is running low, the better places are revisited and pressed into lyrical service. Rome, as always, is the favorite for alien apostrophes.

A kind of global contact has served as an approach to the problem of personal isolation. As a child, Mlle. de Beauvoir overheard her parents' aloof analysis of her and of her sister. Mother asked Father which he preferred. He was a connoisseur: "Simone is more serious-minded, but Poupette is so affectionate. . . ." (In Beauvoir's novel *All Men Are Mortal*, a father's first answer to the same question is made somewhat more palatable: "I don't know. I like both of them equally." But then, *this* father proves to be lying, he likes neither child. Later, Beauvoir herself totes up sums of emotion: "I didn't really know how much he meant to me: a little, a lot, or even more?") The two children are separate, both are separate from their parents; the city, the country, the world are multiplications of solitary units, sometimes grazing each other. Animals are a bore (their failure to *think* about the pain and death they feel, erases ambiguity from their lives), but the separate human units are fascinating. They always rouse curiosity, perhaps most when they are not known. Then they can be observed, and overheard, with detachment. France has lent itself particularly well to this study, since the same people return, for periods of time, to the same cafés: "We still took a keen interest in those stunning or seductive creatures who came to the Flore in search of a future: we watched their gambits and speculated on their past lives and weighed up their chances. Public and national disasters had not diminished the interest we took in individual human beings." But this diversion was an adult scratching of what had by then formed a scar. In the *Memoirs* the gradual realization that a full consciousness, a "rational awareness" like one's own, existed within each person, was appalling, "as shocking and unacceptable a fact as death." Beauvoir's solution was to achieve a superior, even a pre-eminent consciousness, and with it a freedom from all lesser ones. By twenty, she had succeeded in building the illusion, as she mocks it later, of being the "One and Only."

The second and third books of her autobiography are essentially the history of her losing this illusion. And, in fact, the molting of illusion is a repeated experience. Yet the sensation of disillusionment, commonly felt to be painful if salubrious, and, felt too often, accreting for many into bitterness, is in Beauvoir natural and almost blithe. She found it regrettable in Camus that, unlike her, he could not muster "the strength to rid himself of his old dreams"; this weakness turned him, Sartre said, into "the empty affirmation of an ideal." Beauvoir's own history is a parade of good riddances. (Once she regrets a concomitant lessening of her "pride and intransigence," but their diminution is not yet really conspicuous.) She will usually say, that was our mistake in that period. For its time, it wasn't an unintelligent or altogether ignoble way of thinking. It was happiness to be exuberantly wrong in the 30's, but it is just as much happiness now to be judiciously right. Worn-out notions are not missed; they mean very little once they are gone: "Yet I did not regret those days of peace and ignorance. I was too enamored of truth ever to mourn lost illusions, and such insipid ones at that."

Truth is naturally a source of gratification. But error is useful since in time it furnishes the material of metamorphosis into truth. This is looking backward, though — what if one is living in present error? No reason to panic: the brave and the brusque realize that this year's error changes into next year's truth, like the ingenuous lamb into the sagacious sheep.

Her original concept of the efficacy of writing is replaced for Beauvoir, as for Sartre, by the acceptance of inefficacy. Sartre had once looked upon writing as a second religion ("the penman appeared, an *ersatz* of the Christian that I was unable to be"). Beauvoir once thought of it as a means of saving others. The expression of herself was to help the less articulate, just as, beginning to teach, she looked down on "forty adolescent girls in whose minds I had to try to establish my own methods of thinking." Writing narrowed during the Occupation to a means of French self-preservation, "the most important possible activity imaginable." But in the course of opposing the Algerian war and the revenant de Gaulle, the stubbornness of the audience was felt more and more as an inhibitive force. There began to seem, too, less reason, or less right, to publish while "two-thirds of mankind are hungry." Though Beauvoir has, obviously, continued to write, it is partly now in order to explain how futile it is to write. The old ambition to "help others" has come to seem another of those lost egoistic illusions; the final view of writing as the satisfaction of nothing more (as she seems to put it) than creative impulse, rises to egoistic honesty.

But to be forced, as a result, to say as she does now, that only her emotions have furnished "the experience of fulfillment" is to divide herself into categories, another wry turn. For Beauvoir, to be "enamored of truth" has been to be enamored of wholeness: the two have been interwoven principles. She has been dedicated to the reunion of things which tend to break apart: her first word of rebuke is "Manichaean" (her second, "narcissistic"). An early piece of writing employed a reliable solution: it was "a long dialogue between two voices, both of which were mine." Another "contrived to set down that split between two halves of the self which is the very essence of dishonesty." Philosophy seemed a way "to seize the essence, the root, the *totality* of things." The Marquis de Sade was welcome not as author or as sexual aberrant, but "by virtue of the *relationship* which he created between these two aspects of himself." Beauvoir's fictions, as her bony exegesis of their themes makes clear, have also been efforts to encircle vagrant points of view. But less satisfactory than philosophy, since fiction in turn creates subdivisions. In the novel,

Beauvoir recognizes in theory the importance of being undecided: her essays convey her "intellectual certitudes" but in her novels, she reports, "I set great store by nuances and ambiguities." (These are filed under Fiction, Ingredients of.) Beginning work on *The Mandarins*, she hoped in defiance of the innate partiality of the novel to "tell all." But that intention had to be postponed until the autobiography. Again she had been frustrated by the necessity of narrative *form*, which divides reality into parts, ignoring some, magnifying others: "In an autobiography, on the other hand, events retain all the complications that marked their original occurrence; this fidelity to real life conveys better than even the most skillful transposition how things really happen to people." Imaginative forms are based upon an infidelity to the true, the whole, and the real — or rather, upon an abuse of them. "Fiction is built only by *pulverizing*" its sources. Real things, falling into the trap of the novel, are "refracted, diluted, hammered thin, blown up, mixed, transposed, twisted, sometimes completely reversed, and in every case re-created." After such carnage, it is hard to think quickly again in terms of creation or re-creation. And, in fact, Beauvoir finds this violent mutation between historical circumstance and fable, distasteful. As she tries to write it, she defends a literature (merging with total recall) which manipulates as little as possible the interplay and occasional union of human beings and things. Dos Passos was therefore a joy after Mallarmé, Gide, Proust. But Nathalie Sarraute is a sorrow: she prefers "interiority" to the meeting with all external reality, and so is a "schizophrenic" novelist. When, in her preface to *Force of Circumstance*, Beauvoir calls the book "my life" and declines (with what seems at the moment a puzzling ill-temper) the term "work of art," she is arguing again that artful choice is a disruptive and divisive agent.

As a child, she had similar trouble, as Sartre did, in accepting the division between words and what they stood for. Even with adult rational acceptance of the separation between the thing and its symbol, the related trouble remained of either receiving sensation or taking action except by route of word. Until an attitude toward a thing can be stated, the thing does not quite exist. Beauvoir and Sartre stand in front of the Greek temples at Paestum. They have not seen Greek temples before, and neither knows what to say. So the sensation they think these temples might provide, is suspended. Only when, with more temples, comments frame themselves for utterance, can pleasure fall. Living for Beauvoir is almost indistinguishable from its written record. Reactions to objects or to places are completed by being printed: the publication of the impressions she drew from two trips to this country, in *America Day by Day*, seems to fix them, like mounted insects, as permanent judgments.

But action, taken through words, is less definitive than reaction. Each crisis in society or politics is met by written statement. The responsibility of the citizen in these exertions is virtuous, but it involves a risk to the writer. The more closely action is merged with words, the less consideration is given the words in themselves and the more exorbitant the demand made upon them. The best words might not have won the suit, far less than the best have lost it: the writer turns on her mode of action. The words seem suspect, treacherous. They sicken their owner, like a car that stalls on the race to the hospital. Beauvoir is tempted not to read or to write anymore; she complains of a "tetanus of the imagination," and employs music for a time as therapy. But the habit is too strong: she continues to write, to make use of the unfaithful but accustomed object.

Finding a deplorable situation, she joins words into structures of offensive action, like tanks rolling across the hedges of the enemy. "I demolished certain sophistries." "I am not interested in making appeals to people's better natures when I think I've got truth on my side." But apart from forensic or practical causes, writing has to make such an appeal, not to "better" natures, but to that facet of human nature which is reached and held by talent. Even when Sartre states his disenchantment with language, his sentences exist as sentences. But certitudes alone do not sustain Mlle. de Beauvoir. Once again, her rather gallant but crude attempt to force a union is thwarted. The words, dissatisfied, secede from government by sheer insistence.

Notes

1. Putnam, 658 pp.

"Autobiographism," "Narcissism," and Images of the Self

Francis Jeanson*

If I have chosen to give to the few following pages so deliberately aggressive a title, it is because I feel I must take into account some of the criticisms addressed to Simone de Beauvoir insofar as her work has invited them by its very ambiguity, by the obvious contradiction which from start to finish furnishes its most vital dynamism.

I'll admit it at the outset. Here is a writer who has almost never undertaken, in different guises, anything other than to *speak herself*, to describe herself, to tell us the story of her life, to relate to her own person all the human problems she encountered in the world. Almost all her books can be seen as autobiographical; and among them, those which are explicitly so are sometimes disappointing from that point of view for a variety of reasons.

*Translated by Germaine Brée for this volume from *Simone de Beauvoir ou l'enterprise de vivre* (Paris: Editions du Seuil, 1966), 195–206. © 1966 by Editions du Seuil. Reprinted by permission of Georges Borchardt, Inc.

For it is after all true, first, that her novelistic world (however she may have transposed, on occasion, episodes and characters) is directly inspired by her real life. This is so true that she herself seems to have been surprised by it: "I have reread *She Came to Stay* from start to finish, and noted down what I thought of it. I recognized almost word for word things I say in my *Memoirs* and others which reappeared in *The Mandarins*. Yes—not that it's discouraging. We never write anything but *our* books."[1]

Fine. This is a classical theme which criticism, itself fairly traditionalist, has no difficulty accepting. But if we now consider autobiography as such, shall we not find it *rather flatly chronological* and deplore the kind of naive objectivism which insists on mentioning everything that took place, as if the author's preoccupation with telling prevailed over her desire to understand, as if truth might be a mere attribute of facts, developing directly out of their accumulation? The position might perhaps be acceptable if at least the readers were sure it gave them a full right of observation of the writer's private life: but this is not so. "I must warn them that I have no intention of telling them *everything*. I described my childhood and adolescence without any omissions. But if I have managed to tell the story of my past life without embarrassment or indiscreetness, I do not feel the same kind of detachment in relation to my mature years, nor do I enjoy a similar freedom when discussing them. . . . There are many things I will leave unsaid"—"In Paris, Le Havre, or Rouen, we talked mainly about the people we knew. They took up so much of our time that by refusing to talk about their lives, I flatten the image I am drawing of ours: there are obvious reasons for my silence"—"It is impossible to tell *everything*. . . ."[2]

Very well (so perhaps that well-known benevolence may concede which, in principle, lives drowsily at the heart of our most critical notions); for we are not voyeurs, and we can, if need be, admit that a writer obviously less liberated than ourselves may go as far as to conceal from us some point or other in her life. But may not such omissions retroactively make us more ready to find fault with an attitude which, based mainly on the constant minuteness of a pitiless memory, seems unable to justify itself on the whole otherwise than through the radical exhaustiveness of the accounting? If truth is a question of facts, will it not eventually be seriously mutilated by the omission of a certain number of them (which are not, it seems, among the most insignificant)? On the other hand, should we not show a modicum of skepticism in regard to so unusual an aptitude to preserve and recover the past? "*Without omitting anything* . . . ," we are told: but in the long run, as so many precise reminiscences come raining down, may we not be tempted to suspect a troublesome aptitude for *reconstruction*?

As for me, I'll try to express the convictions nourished in me by probably the most attentive rereading to which Simone de Beauvoir's work has ever been submitted.

Beginning with the last question raised, I shall situate myself in opposition to the critical stance from which it derives and which seems untenable, and that, in its very principle. For we are placed here in front of a quite rigorous alternative. Either Simone de Beauvoir re-created her life in the telling or else she actually remembered it from beginning to end. Any third hypothesis must be excluded out of hand. One cannot both invent and remember with so much precision, with such an abundance of details, without condemning oneself very soon and visibly to the worst sort of incoherence. In the abstract, then, one remains free to conceive of our author as the most remarkable of the century, or as a woman who bravely undertook to speak herself. Concretely, you have no other choice: it is a fact that, on the one hand, she consulted numerous documents (her diary, all sorts of letters exchanged with her closest friends), and that, on the other hand, we dispose of enough objective, public, irrefutable proofs to confirm, in terms of the coherence of her life, the exactness of her self-description. Let us then admit it: the story offered (whatever the confusions of detail which here and there occur, the voluntary or involuntary lacunae) is essentially truthful; the facts mentioned are real.

In relation to the deliberate lacunae, I must now confess that our author's favorite explanation seems to me insufficient. She herself, on occasion, has proposed another, based not on her concern for discretion in regard to living persons but on the question of her own relation to herself. *"Why are there some things I want to say and others I want to bury? Because they are too precious (sacred perhaps) to be transformed into literature. As if death alone, only oblivion, were equal to certain realities."*[3] Let us note then that if literature was first for Simone de Beauvoir "sacred," she later became capable of detecting within it a bent toward profanation in relation to certain realities which were for her *still more* sacred.

Of this, I believe, it is important to remain conscious when we try to understand the immense need she felt to "speak herself." "I wanted to speak of myself," "I always wanted to put in all of myself," she said of her first temptation to write a book on her own childhood: *"the early desire to tell my first memories."* But it is when she describes to us how she started at long last on the enterprise and, even more, when she gives us the notes dated from that period that she no doubt makes us enter most deeply into the kind of interest that she takes in the story of her life itself.

> *I have always imagined secretly that my life was being recorded, down to the most minute detail, on some giant tape recorder and that one day I would play back my entire past. . . . At the age of fifteen, I wanted people to read my autobiography and be touched and aroused by it*; all my ambitions to become a "well-known author" were directed to this goal. *Since that time, I have often thought of writing it myself.* I am very far removed from the exaltation this dream once aroused in me; *but the desire to make it come true has always remained in my heart. . . .*[4]

She explains this, moreover, by her desire to resurrect in her own eyes the little girl she was, to "draw her out of the void": but she is now mature enough to know that that is out of the question, that she cannot succeed. In fact, it is still the "old project" that is in question ("my desire to tell my story"): what she wants to do is to *accede to the status of being by existing under the eyes of others.*" The emotional tonality (whether more or less exalted, more or less calm), according to which at that point in her life she persists in so doing, is of little importance. Later correcting the proofs of the *Dutiful Daughter*, as she decides to write a sequel to that autobiography, she notes: "*At this time, everything inclines me to narcissism.*"[5]

Will I be given time to clarify my statement if I declare that, all things considered, I decidedly do not believe that the slightest narcissism still lives in her? I have sometimes really thought so. . . . But this was because I had mistaken her rigorous attentiveness to her own existence, past and present, with a *self-complacency* any trace of which it would be hard to detect in the whole of her work. Note, for instance, how at the very time she attributes that attitude to herself, her real modes of behavior invalidate the allegation. One of the signs she puts forward of her alleged narcissism is the vivid interest she takes in the intimate diary of a young American named Joan. And this is what she had just written about it a week earlier in her own diary: "*Generally, diaries fascinate me . . . , one really plunges into another life, another frame of reference and in a sense this is the most acute of contestations: while I read her, it is she who is the absolute subject, not I.*" Unless I am mistaken, narcissism, in any conscience, does not consist of passionately involving oneself in the narcissism of someone else. And how can one deem it possible that Simone de Beauvoir indulged in such an aberration when it is so obvious that her need to "speak herself" (her need to *be* because read) was always counterbalanced by the need to have enough *value* (so that she would have anything of value whatsoever to say of herself)? Referring again to "Joan's extraordinary diary" in which we see her plunged and mired, she confesses she was touched by the warmth and intelligence with which the young woman, after reading her, alternately criticizes her or takes her defense; but she quickly adds that the pleasure it gives her is mingled with anxiety: "I should write other books, better ones, *deserve anew, really deserve to exist in this way for someone else.*"

There, it seems to me, we hold the real key to her "autobiographism": inasmuch as the look of the other can indubitably open our way to a certain form of *being*, but only on condition that we succeed in *existing* for him or her. Rather than cast suspicion on Simone de Beauvoir's literary stance by designating it as narcissistic, why not acknowledge that her way of putting herself into question, of laying herself open to our most stringent contestations, defines *her real emergence into adulthood*: this, by decisively outstripping an adolescent pose (fairly typical of the "petite bourgeoisie") manifested by extreme reticence toward her close friends and by the complete secrecy in which she wraps her own dialogue with herself. Thus, when she broaches her first private diary, she writes: "If someone, whoever it may be, reads these pages, I will never forgive that person. It would be a base and vile act. Please respect this warning in spite of its ridiculous seriousness."[6]

One might perhaps suggest, however, that she overcame her narcissism only to plunge into exhibitionism; and I myself somewhat irreverently (in the first part of this essay) proposed the fleeting image of the Castor as the stripper. . . . Well, alright, I still stand by it: it is true that the woman has chosen to strip herself naked under our eyes, more so than any "stripteaser" will ever do; that is the reason why she deserves our greatest esteem, our truest gratitude.

There are only two days of writing (whether well or badly is of no consequence, another problem only). Either one attempts to aim at the "object" itself (at the outer world in the absence of the subject, or the subject in its pure interiority); or one undertakes to disclose the world by disclosing oneself within it, that is to say, one presents to the reader a certain experience of the world, at once subjective and objective (of course), an experience conscious of its inevitable ambiguity. If you want to "spell out the world" while trying to give it meaning, you will have to agree to speak *your own self*; and if it is your good pleasure to speak of yourself, it is only by speaking *of the world* that you really manage that. That is why all real writers are necessarily exhibitionists and clowns; that is why, too, the exhibitionism and clowning of the writer, for better for worse, are *one of the forms of generosity*. When they step up to the platform, exhibit themselves under the eyes of an audience to which they abandon themselves, the man or the woman who has chosen to write is most certainly pursuing a personal illusion, but it is only at the cost of giving the world to their readers, of communicating a vision of the world that, from time to time, they'll have some chance of obtaining some recognition. Whoever has not desired simultaneously to communicate with the other (willed the endless work entailed) and the recognition of his own being will never become *a writer*—except perhaps in the eyes of a small minority, pitifully attached to the cultural myths (aestheticism, psychologism, absurdism) of a bourgeoisie on the defensive, imprisoned in its own inertia. This means, in consequence, that, all things considered, the writer does not point her work either toward the world or herself, but to a *specific truth inherent in his own presence to the world*—and that his most essential ambition is to communicate it to us, to the point of sharing it with us if possible.

Many critics still reason as if one could condemn a work for its offense against public proprieties (perhaps its sense of decency?), as if it were inevitably obscene to speak of oneself when addressing others. The actual facts, maybe, all too often justify them. But, they are wrong as to the principle. For each one of us must wish for the capacity to understand everything that is human — the realization, by others, of our common potentialities. The *obscene* is only that which we cannot manage to integrate, to which we cannot give meaning. One of the most fundamental social functions of the writer is surely to incite us to diminish, in our consciences and hearts, the "Devil's share" (the dark fringes we call Evil) by trying to give meaning to what seemed to us obscene. This requires, after all, some slight effort, too, on our part. As for me, I would much rather see a few adults "scandalized" by the "flaunting" of certain problems, for they'll recover after all, than to see *even today* so many young consciences succumb to the most devastating surprises life can produce simply because those who could have provided some preparation were too scared of themselves (and their fellow human beings) to dare speak in concrete terms. How can those who speak the truth be more dangerous than the errors because of which we are dying day by day without knowing it?

There is in any case one quality we can never refuse the writer we are here discussing; this is that in her eyes the most demanding concern for truth was the single sanction for her undertaking. Simone de Beauvoir also naturally wished to *express in sentences* the events in her life, to salvage her experience *through words*. But one never observes her involved in attempts to cheat, to seduce, or to don some disguise to enhance her work, to increase her chances of salvation. She writes to be known as she is, and so invests that reality, without cease, as closely as she can. So much the worse if, in consequence, a certain number of consciences choose to look chastely elsewhere. Hers is the same need, the same "tyrannic and extravagant project" to "portray oneself from life" which, four hundred years ago, one had encountered in the man who had wanted to be himself "the substance" of his book, forewarning the reader in these words: "In whatever guise I make myself known, so long as I make myself known as I am, I've reached my goal." After Montaigne, listen to the Castor: "I wanted to be respected; but what I needed essentially was to be accepted in all my truth."[7]

When she embarks on the second volume of her autobiography, our "narcissist" notes: "For another month I will have to continue dragging *material* out of my head and stockpiling it. *Then, when I return* to Paris, I can use it to revive *a little interest in myself*, a little enthusiasm." And our "exhibitionist" remarks that during those years, *it seemed to her arrogant to speak so much of herself.*[8] For the difficulty of writing, reinforced here and there by the "difficulty of being," is enough to imbue with some measure of relativity the double temptation of becoming passionately involved with oneself and imagining oneself to be passionately interesting to others. We must not forget that she chose to write because it was reading which first saved her from boredom, then so as to escape from the world of repetition by creating something new, unique, and irreplaceable, to create herself anew so as to justify her existence, to become her own first cause and end, and as a remedy to her solitude, her "exile," to burn "in a million hearts," and to "serve humanity." We should not forget that by the time she was thirteen she already felt an ardent need to *save from silence and oblivion* all that it had been given her each day to see, to feel, and to love: "I've always had a penchant for communication"; "I was interested both in myself and others." We should not forget that she very soon conceived of her "mission," her "mandate" in two guises: "I was enjoined to lend my conscience to the *multiple splendor of life* and I had to *write in order to wrench it out of time and nothingness.*" And so she comes to distinguish between Sartre's case (he "lived in order to write") and her own case: "as for me, I attributed a supreme value to Life . . ."—a stance corroborated by a quotation from her diary, written when she was twenty-one or twenty-two years old: "I'll never be primarily a writer, like Sartre."[9] And it is true that her joy in living, during the two years of their first "contract," was completely to stifle in her the need to express herself, to appear in literary guise. "*A book, in one sense or another, is an appeal*: to whom then did I need to appeal, and from what? *I was fully satisfied. . . . To write is, in any case, to offer a world to be looked at.* As far as I was concerned, its brute presence annihilated me, and I saw nothing of it: *I had nothing to show.*"[10]

It would be an endless task to contrast those pages in which she extols speech, writing, the Verb (as well as the necessity, the beauty of that imaginary world which the work of art is in essence), and those which clearly give preference to love, happiness, the beauty of the real world, to the problems of humanity or the misfortunes of history. . . . Suffice it to recall here the two texts which surely most forcefully illustrate the tension which the author never ceased to confront between her existence itself and her desire to give it expression.

—In 1939, she tells us, "History seized hold of me never again to let go; concurrently I committed myself fully and forever to literature." We should not consider this as merely a secondary dramatization, due to circumstances, of her basic problem: "As for me, my undertaking was my life itself. . . . My life could only satisfy me if I gave literature its place." It so happened that in the ten preceding years she had written a great deal and published nothing. So she wonders when, with *She Came to Stay*, she became "publishable." The two reasons she then gives seem to me equally significant: "*Writing is a craft one learns by writing*"; "*literature is something that emerges when life is disrupted.*" In other words, writing is work, and we write only when we have something to say. "In order to write . . . the first condition is that reality ceases to be *taken for granted*; *only then are we capable of seeing that reality and giving it to be seen.*"[11]

—As for the second text, it tends to further specify that we only have something to say insofar as we have to solve some problem of existence. That is how she comes to justify the end of *She Came to Stay* (Françoise's murder of Xavière), which, in her eyes, is not justifiable as literature:

"Insofar as literature is a living activity, I found it indispensable to adopt that denouement: *for me its value was cathartic.*"[12]

This writer is indeed a living woman. A woman who, through her writing, has been able to *exorcise* her quasi-daemonic passion for autonomy, that is, for absolute sovereignty. She is a woman who single-mindedly has desired to *deserve* living in freedom and with the possibility of expressing herself freely. She did not appeal to the judgement of God, or of an abstract posterity, but to her contemporaries in her search for her own "salvation." To them, at her risk and peril, she never stopped offering the fruits of real work on herself (on her thought as well as her life): "I desired to be read in my lifetime by many people, to be esteemed to be loved"; "I am happy to see in the flesh and blood, the readers who are fond of me"; "notoriety has given me what I desired: *that my books should be loved and I myself thanks to them*; that I be listened to by them *and be of use to them by showing them the world as I saw it.*"[13]

True, her consciousness made her more and more sensitive to the "extraordinary power of the Verb" ("perhaps it is also my deepest desire that people repeat silently some of the words that I linked each with the other").[14] But, at the same time, she felt the need to get to know the world better and better ("in more detail, more exactly, and especially in a more vivid way") and through real encounters with her fellow human beings. And, in the last analysis, it is her perpetual concern to remain in everything and for all things *as true as possible*, which makes her work irreplaceable in the eyes of many readers at the same time as it condemns it to the scornful disdain of a handful of aesthetes for whom the power of the Verb is relegated to the status of fireworks and prestidigitation.

"*The fact is that I am a writer,*" she proudly proclaims. "A woman writer . . . , someone whose whole life is dominated by writing." If I were a literary critic, I would take pleasure in showing how, from *She Came to Stay* to *A Very Easy Death*, that claim seems to me warranted. It is with even greater pleasure, in fact, with real joy—unwilling to go beyond the boundaries of my project—I note in counterpoint that other profession of faith which so sumptuously complements the first: "*I am an intellectual, I recognize the value of words and of truth.*" One need only, furthermore, read through the last two volumes of her autobiography to appraise the acuteness with which our Castor put to herself "the knotty problem of literary sincerity," and how intensely she wished to address her readers more and more directly and truthfully.

Does she, finally, hold a certain *image of herself*? The answer seems to me simple: if she had one, we would know it. Her talent merely would have long since enabled her to propose it to us, with the proviso that she could then touch it up indefinitely. Instead, we see her careful to organize her *Memoirs* along chronological lines, even though she knows full well that human experience is not "a set of facts." This is because she has understood that "writers do not have the means to present at the same time the facts of a life and also its meaning." More exactly, when they claim they are giving its meaning to a life, their own, for instance, they cheat and only offer the reader images of themselves. For the alleged meaning as such does not exist. *"A life is a curious object"* which in the course of years is constantly being totalized and detotalized. If you want to show "how things really happen to human beings," it can only be by showing in turn[15] "ambiguous, discontinuous, separate truths" — whose only conceivable totalization could be, possibly, their inscription "within the unicity of an imaginary object" (a novel, for instance). That is why Simone de Beauvoir felt she could not be content with writing novels, and that is why her novels seem themselves more loaded with human truth than at the time they were published.

Notes

1. *Force of Circumstance*, p. 439. The word "our" is underlined by the author.

2. *The Prime of Life*, pp. 10, 130; *Force of Circumstance*, p. 8. In the first quote as in the third, the word "everything" is underlined by the author. — Speaking, too, of the pact she had agreed on with Sartre (concerning the freedom given the two partners to engage in "contingent love affairs," not merely passing sexual fancies), Simone de Beauvoir insists on a point they had then "carelessly evaded," the question of the third persons and how those third persons would adapt their own requirements to this arrangement. On that point, she adds, "an inevitable discretion compromised the exactitude of the picture painted in *The Prime of Life* . . ." (*Force of Circumstance*, p. 140).

3. *Force of Circumstance*, p. 453.

4. *Ibid.*, p. 393. The entire text here is underlined by the author. — To Madeleine Chapsal (*Writers in Person*, Julliard 1960) Simone de Beauvoir declared: "I'd like to have an immense documentation on my life. I'd find it terribly exciting."

5. *Force of Circumstance*, p. 435.

6. *Memoirs of a Dutiful Daughter*, p. 187.

7. *Memoirs of a Dutiful Daughter*, p. 42. Or, "I wrote these memoirs in great part to reaffirm the truth" (*Force of Circumstance*, p. 677); and, in Montaigne: "I am eager to make myself known. I am mortally afraid I'll be misrepresented by those who happen to know my name."

8. *Force of Circumstance*, pp. 452 and 486.

9. Cf. also: *"I was primarily attached to life in its immediate presence*, and Sartre first and foremost to writing" (*The Prime of Life*, p. 151).

10. *Ibid.*, p. 64. The words "to offer [a world] to be looked at" are underlined by the author.

11. *The Prime of Life*, pp. 368–374. The words "to be taken for granted," in the last quotation, are underlined by the author.

12. *Ibid.*, p. 348.

13. *Memoirs of a Dutiful Daughter*, pp. 58, 499, 677–678.

14. *Ibid.*, p. 679.

15. That is, she further notes, "one of the basic functions of literature" (*Force of Circumstance*, p. 282).

Death, Old Age, and Femininity:
Simone de Beauvoir and the
Politics of *La Vieillesse*   T. H. Adamowski*

In 1949, in *Le Deuxième Sexe*, Simone de Beauvoir was one of the early spokesmen (-women) of the most recent upsurge of feminism. Her argument then was that in the course of human history woman's role has been that of ["object"] and only rarely that of ["subject"]. As did Engels, Simone de Beauvoir recognized how closely tied into questions of political economy was the problem of the rights of the second sex in the world of the Others, the men. At the same time she refused to be intimidated by the so-called "givens" of biology. For her, anatomy and physiology were not destiny, and to argue that the womb, the menstrual cycle, and the menopause were the ineluctable limitations on woman's freedom to be ["subject"] was for Mme. de Beauvoir one more species of ["bad faith"]. No less than man was woman ["for-herself"], freedom.

Since the appearance of *Le Deuxième Sexe*, in such works as *Les Mandarins*, *La Force des Choses*, and *Une Mort très Douce*, her readers have seen Mme. de Beauvoir increasingly concerned with another "destiny." Now, in her latest work, *La Vieillesse*,[1] she has kept a promise made in *La Force des Choses* and given us a work on a topic that some of her readers have considered to be her particular obsession. Even more than in her book on women, Simone de Beauvoir is concerned in *La Vieillesse* with the political economy of her problem. Perhaps this book will also come to be seen as the tocsin of some new liberation movement, this time of the old. But *La Vieillesse* bears the stamp of the deepened interest in limitations that has characterized French Existentialism since the early 1950s. One finds this concern in a book dedicated to Mme. de Beauvoir in 1960 ["To the Beaver"], Sartre's [*Critique of Dialectical Reason*], a work that some critics have seen as an admission of the failure of Existentialism. *La Vieillesse* has certainly been influenced by the *Critique*'s Marxism, but in both works there is still a good deal of [*Being and Nothingness*]. The givens and limitations of old age, however, are much more compelling and depressing than those of femininity, and in *La Vieillesse* Mme. de Beauvoir is given a tougher run for her money: wrinkles, senility, physical decay and — most important of all — the gradual disappearance for the aged of the future that had made sense of the existentialist ["project"], all serve to mock the freedom of the aged ["for-itself"]. In this respect *La Vieillesse* reveals a new dimension of that concern of Phenomenology and Existentialism with the human body. It treats a feature of the body not found in the work of Sartre and Merleau-Ponty: the body in decline.

Simone de Beauvoir does not wish to be accused of having slighted the

*Reprinted by permission from *Dalhousie Review* 50, no. 3 (Autumn 1970):394–401.

facts of old age, and much of her book bears witness to a wide reading in the literature of science, medicine, anthropology, and history on the topic of aging. An assessment of her understanding of their interpretation of the subject must come, of course, from the relevant specialists. Certainly she does not make light of their gloomy picture, and it is clear that in so far as this book is concerned the anti-scientific tone that some readers have detected in Existentialism is nowhere in evidence. If such a "new" respect for science does exist in *La Vieillesse* it may well represent the fifteen-years debate in France between adherents of Sartrean Existentialism and those of the Structuralism associated with Claude Lévi-Strauss.

By comparison with old age, death is something ["very gentle"]. ["And in effect,"] says Mme. de Beauvoir, ["it's old age rather than death that should be opposed to life. Old age is the parody of life"] (565). She will have nothing to do with the banalities that make of old age the golden time of life, that period when one can contemplate from afar the vanities of the young. Too overwhelming is the evidence that she finds in the lives of the old, of Goethe, of Tolstoy, of Pétain and others, that in old age vanity merely finds new forms. She cites the literary evidence that sees (in the few times it looks at the aged) the foolish desires for those joys that the treason of the body now denies to the old: power and sex. Physical decline has stolen much of both, and the author supplies interesting commentary on the sexuality of the old. The flesh may be weak, but the urge is still there — as, for example, Goethe found to his dismay when he met Mme. Szymanowska. The sadness of sexuality for the aged, in the author's opinion, is a function of the meaning of sexuality in general: [". . . it is ordinarily an adventure in which each partner realises his existence and that of the other in a singular fashion; in desire consciousness loses its translucidity and makes itself body in order to attain the other as body so as to fascinate and possess the other . . ."] (338).[2] This recalls, of course, the Sartrean account of sexuality from *L'Etre et le Néant*, and we see how the old come to their condition by reference to the young; for sexuality is the means by which the person's ["virile or feminine qualities are affirmed and recognized: the person feels as if she had some value"] (338). But with the coming of what the author calls the involutions of old age, it becomes much more difficult to continue in this "projet" of fascinating the Other's body with one's own. Age shockingly transforms the body, and mutual fascination increasingly gives way to mutual shame. For the old person there is now a double burden as physical decline is coupled with memory: ["The elderly often desire to desire because they keep a nostalgia for irreplaceable experiences, because they remain tied to the erotic world that they built in their youth and maturity: it is through desire that they will restore to their memories the colours now gone pale"] (339).

This reading of the lived experience of the old is part of the second section of *La Vieillesse*, called ["Being-in-the-World"]. In the first part of the book, however, Mme. de Beauvoir deals with the phenomenology of old age but with the problems from the vantage point of what she calls "l'extériorité." Many of the problems posed *for* this admirable book come from the thoroughness with which she treats her subject from the outside. The evidence of biology, of anthropology, and of history reveal why there is the conspiracy of silence that Simone de Beauvoir finds around the problem of growing old. No matter whether one looks to societies with or without history (the "hot" and "cold" societies of Lévi-Strauss), the depressing signs of old age create a supreme difficulty for those who bear them. Mme. de Beauvoir is at pains to tell us that if history shows us societies that starve, ritualistically kill, or confine to nursing homes their aged, it also shows us societies that treat the aged with dignity. But she will not build optimism on special cases, since in all societies the decline of the body makes of the person who declines an object for the Others, the young. In all cases the aged are a special kind of problem, and it becomes more and more difficult for them to remain "sujet."

Nor is the author sentimental about the aged themselves. Indeed, it is often their own callousness towards the children they have raised — to cite an example from certain extremely poor societies — that turns the adult offspring against the now useless mouths of their aged parents. But even here the problem of callous treatment of the young is often a result of the collective's anxiety before ["scarcity"]. It is the physical weakness of old age that makes useless mouths. In other societies it is the decline of vitality coupled with the lifelong fear of one day "being without" that makes the old impose on these societies the heavy hand of gerontocracy. The aged population limits the young in so far as it is itself limited by the involution and sclerosis of body and mind. We seem to circle forever around the flame of political economy.

Involution and sclerosis. Hardening of the arteries and of the mind, these are what array themselves against ["the moralizing optimism of Plato and Cicero, against the claim that those who are old are wise . . ."] (170). Mme. de Beauvoir is careful, however, not to forget those moralists "dans les sociétés historiques" who did not turn away from the harshness of old age with platitudes on their lips: ["I admire how Montaigne, throwing overboard the soothing traditional clichés, refuses to take any mutilation for progress and to hold the mere accumulation of years for enrichment"] (172). In her comments on Montaigne she faces one of the paradoxes that give her the small hope that men are not doomed only to mutilation: "It is at the moment when he feels himself diminished that he is greatest. But doubtless he would not have attained this grandeur without the harshness that he brings to bear against himself"] (172). (One finds this paradox elsewhere — in Gide's diaries, for example, or in the old age of Renoir or of Goya.) Mme. de Beauvoir also offers a theory to explain why writers seem to find it difficult to be creative in old age — not only the weakening of the libido but also the conflict the author claims that writers live between their imaginary selves and the real world, finally resolved, after a fashion, in old age, make literary creation difficult for the old. I find it an unconvincing argument, since the decline in what Flaubert calls "l'alacrité" comes to us all; and one might argue that we all live a tension between the imaginary that we seek to realize and the reality that works to de-realize the visionary. But her case here rests to a great extent on the techniques of writing and the differences that exist between writing and other professions, e.g., politics or painting.

Beautiful old age comes to no one. But buoyed as she is by the example of a Montaigne or a Gide, the dismal view from exteriority does not lead Simone de Beauvoir to despair. One's being-in-the-world can still be what one chooses it to be, she argues, if certain conditions are fulfilled. An obstinate inertia is not one of them. Certain of the aged become caricatures of themselves while leading others to believe, falsely, that they have come successfully to grips with "la vieillesse": ["They began by willing with a certain end in view. Now they will because they have willed. In general among these people, habits, automatisms, and scleroses serve as substitutes for inventions"] (566). The "projet" is a form of activity, and mere submission to old age is not activity. Such passivity is one result of the contraction of the future that comes to the old:

> ["The elderly know that they have completed their lives and that they shall not live them over again. The future is no longer alive with promises, but it shrinks now to the dimensions of that completed being who has to live it. Indeed, human reality is burdened with a double finitude; one aspect is contingent and belongs to facticity: existence has a limit that comes from outside. The other is an ontological structure of the *pour soi*. In the last years both reveal themselves at the same time and by means of each other."] (399)

There is, Mme. de Beauvoir believes, another solution, that of continuing to pursue ["goals that give a meaning to life: devotion to individuals, to groups, to causes, social, political, intellectual or creative work"] (567). One day death will come and with it our life will become our destiny, but in the meantime the first condition for victory over old age is to remain engaged in the world. In view of the evidence she cites of the many burdens of old age one might well argue in response to Simone de Beauvoir that she has shown only too well the progressive transfiguration of ["for-itself"] into ["in-itself"] to make her concluding optimism very compelling. Perhaps such a reply is a form of bad faith. Perhaps it is only a tribute to that proclivity in Existentialism to make facticity and the limits of the situation seem more real than the freedom it celebrates.

Mme. de Beauvoir has placed her other condition for victory over old age within a context almost equally forbidding. She realizes that the possibilities for pursuing real ends are accorded to ["a handful of privileged people"]. In the entirety of La Vieillesse there is no example of a project towards such ends among the un-privileged, the poor. Certain statesmen, scientists, painters, and writers may have surmounted the barriers raised by time, but for the rest Mme. Beauvoir sees only misery (not only of poverty), solitude, and ["a generalized anxiety"]. The evidence she cites seems to reinforce her claim: in societies with history the worst ravages of old age are notoriously reserved for deprived classes (in societies without history, most often it is among those peoples who suffer from deprivation that old age is most degrading). The mass of men have always lived lives made desperate by meaningless activity. Old age is merely a form of *imprimatur* that stamps the nightmare of alienation with an official seal:

> ["When retirement frees a man from the constraints of his occupation all he perceives around him is a desert. It was never given to him to engage himself in projects which would have peopled the world with ends, with values, with *raisons-d'être*.
> "There lies the crime of our society. Its 'old-age' policy is a scandal. But more scandalous still is the treatment that it inflicts on the majority of men in their youth and maturity. It pre-fabricates the mutilated and wretched condition which is their lot in their final years."] (568)

How to make men of the aged? ["The answer is simple; they must have always been treated as men."] One must make society over, for if man had not been atomised from childhood, ["enclosed and isolated among other atoms"], he would not be exiled finally into old age. Like Sartre, Simone de Beauvoir is oppressed by that terrible creator of bourgeois solitude, possessive individualism: ["Old age exposes the failure of our entire civilization."]

The extraordinary difficulty of this final "projet," the re-making of civilization, haunts the analysis of how one cures the exiled of old age, and much of *La Vieillesse* is itself concerned with the all-too-well-known facts of the place of exile in our world, the old-age home. And yet much of this book also reveals, at the level of one ["lived experience"], that of Simone de Beauvoir, how the difficulty of growing old can come to haunt one of the privileged. For *La Vieillesse* allows us to glimpse how she has lived her own growing old—the sense of "déjà vu," the deaths of friends ["the funereal monuments that are my landmarks"].

They were wrong, those who saw in Existentialism only a modern form of despair. They had ignored the incredible optimism that found in the project a means for attaining real values in a world bounded by "nonsens." Although it is written in the glum style characteristic of Simone de Beauvoir, *La Vieillesse* maintains much of the spirit of that optimism. But in old age one Existentialist, at least, has found a tougher opponent than in other forms of determinism, and the horns of optimism have been drawn in ever so slightly: ["At sixty-five you are not only twenty years older than at forty-five. You have exchanged an indefinite future . . . for a definite one"] (400). The force of the biological "données" is not itself weakened by a vision of a new society. No matter what the society, at the level of the personal, of the existential, time brings together the contraction of the future and the decline of the body.

If her success in describing old age from the vantage points offered by exteriority and being-in-the-world seems to weaken Mme. de Beauvoir's suggested cures for this malady that comes of long life, this is not to deny her humane refusal to accept the old only as the objects that their age would seem to make of them. She is even willing to grant to optimistic and blind moralists of the past a certain measure of worth, in so far as their wishful and false perceptions of old age derived from a valid vision of the "ought," if not of the "is." In the ideal society of Simone de Beauvoir, old age would disappear *as a malady* (it recalls Marx's vision of the disappearance, in communist society, of the division of labour):

> ["As it happens now in certain privileged cases, an individual, secretly weakened by age, but not yet diminished in appearance, would one day be overcome by an illness which he could not fight off. He would die without having undergone degradation. The final years of life would then truly conform to the definition given by certain bourgeois ideologues: a moment in existence different from both youth and maturity but possessing a balance of its own, while leaving open to the individual a wide range of possibilities."] (569)

If Mme. de Beauvoir is correct in her diagnosis of ["old age"], then it would seem that the vision of health she offers in place of the illness may have to wait that time when "society regulates the general production and thus makes it possible for me to do one thing today and another tomorrow, to hunt in the morning, fish in the afternoon, rear cattle in the evening, criticize after dinner, just as I have a mind, without ever becoming hunter, fisherman, shepherd, or critic".[3]

Notes

1. *La Vieillesse.* By Simone de Beauvoir. Paris: Gallimard, 1970. Pp. 640.
2. Cf. Sartre, *L'Etre et le Néant* (Paris: Gallimard, 1943), pp. 456ff.
3. Karl Marx and Friedrich Engels, *The German Ideology* (New York, 1947), 22.

See *Le Nouvel Observateur,* Spring, 1970, for an interview in which Mme. de Beauvoir discusses some of the problems raised in her book.

Provide, Provide!   Elizabeth Janeway*

Simone de Beauvoir's study of old age was published in France as *La Vieillesse,* and in England under an exact translation: *Old Age.* How

*Reprinted from the *Atlantic* 229, no. 6 (June 1972):94–98, by permission of the author.

amused Mlle. de Beauvoir must be to find her suspicions of America's hypocritical readers confirmed by the name bestowed on her book here: *The Coming of Age!* As far as the title goes, her five hundred and seventy-two pages (plus index) might be addressed to those members of the younger generation who face, or have recently passed, their twenty-first birthday. The change neatly underlines her point: no one, not even the aged themselves, *really* wants to hear or think about the grim last days of life, narrowing down to the grave; when, as Robert Frost reminded us in the poem whose title I have borrowed, the "beauty Abishag, the picture pride of Hollywood," has become the withered hag who comes with rag and pail to wash the steps.

It is one of Mlle. de Beauvoir's strengths that she does not wince away from the unpleasant. Nor—another strength—does she wallow in it. She is, above all else, a just judge of the great issues of life, at once compassionate and objective. Her sympathies are engaged by the old, but so is her mind, and it is a powerful mind; best, I have always thought, when grappling with issues of a profound moral nature. Here she is discussing the treatment and the image, including the self-image, of the old imposed by society; but the purpose of her book is to examine society as it is revealed by treatment and image, not simply to describe and deplore the valuation set on the aged.

So this is (as was *The Second Sex*) a book about power; for any examination of how society works must come down to Lenin's question, Who does what to whom? (How one regrets the succinct Russian, "*Kto kovo?*" which fits so well into Mlle. de Beauvoir's opposing categories of "subject" and "object.") What society does to the old is to label them "objects." They lose their freedom of action and with it, their dignity. In her introduction, Mlle. de Beauvoir quotes Grimm's chilling tale about the peasant who makes his old father eat out of a small wooden trough, apart from the rest of the family. One day he finds his son fitting little boards together. "It's for you when you're old," says the child.

The tension between generations has always existed. The young challenge the old, the old fear the young's attack. But when we say this, we are blurring an important distinction. To the young, the older generations blend together: "Don't trust anyone over thirty." But the grandfathers differ from the fathers, the really aged from the mature who hold the power of action and control. When we talk of old age we are almost always talking of those who have passed beyond the wielding of power. But, as Mlle. de Beauvoir makes clear, citing examples from anthropology and from history, the attitudes of younger adults toward the aged have always been founded earlier. The memory of past power provokes a present urge of revenge or mockery. The adult generation remembers the power of its fathers and so, as that power wanes, the adults react. Treatment of the aged by adults reflects the treatment of yesterday's children by yesterday's parents.

Such treatment is deeply affected by economic possibilities and by social norms. "I have come across only one [ethnological example]," writes Mlle. de Beauvoir, "in which happy children turn into adults who are cruel to their fathers and mothers—the Ojibway. Whereas the Yakut and the Ainu, who are badly treated as children, neglect the old most brutally, the Yaghan and Aleut, who live in almost the same conditions but among whom the child is king, honor their old people. Yet the aged," she pauses to remind us, "are often the victims of a vicious circle: extreme poverty obliges the adults to feed their children badly and to neglect them." How much freedom and respect the powerful can allow the weak, then, is dependent on what is available for all. We need not be surprised to discover that the most hard-pressed communities practice both infanticide and the abandonment of the old. One provides for the future or remembers the past only after one has eaten today.

Against such threats, of course, the old have their weapons. The first is memory. In a stable society, experience increases useful knowledge. The old know the patterns of the weather, the movements of animals, and the skills of husbandry. Besides, stable societies tend to respect traditions and these the old know too and can expound. Another weapon is magic. Tradition often blends into "knowledge" of how to control the supernatural. But, more than that, the old can be seen as prenatal ghosts. If death is no more than a rite of passage and the reborn old man returns to haunt his former home, it will be *his* turn to take revenge on those who mistreated him. Certainly rites for the dead around the world emphasize the need to propitiate the ghost, to feed him well and speed him on his way, lest he linger close at hand, for if he lingers, it will only be with malicious intent. Who listens for a loving ghost?

Which literacy appears, memory loses much of its value. Fear of the supernatural comes and goes. But the third weapon of the old has never lost its weight: property. Die early and avoid the fate of the ruined beauty, Abishag, Frost advises his readers,

> Or if predestined to die late,
> Make up your mind to die in state.
>
> Make the whole stock exchange your own!
> If need be occupy a throne. . . .

In short, since this is a question of power, hold on to what you have of it. "Boughten friendship" will not save you from mockery and hate, but it will protect you from their effects, at least from their immediate effects.

The powerful, stubborn, hardfisted old, the frustrated, ambitious, resentful young—this confrontation has passed into the deepest reaches of our social awareness. These figures are part of the furniture of our minds: Fedor Karamazov, Lyndon Johnson, Chaucer's old January with his bought bride, May, Pétain challenged by De Gaulle, who later suffered a similar challenge, the old generals of the First War and the young poets in the trenches, the marching students of Paris in May, 1968, the impudent lovers of Congreve and Molière who conspire against their miserly parents, we know them all. They speak to us with a double authority, that of fact and that of myth. Hostility between generations confirms the prophecy each angry child makes to himself of the revenge he will take when his time comes. And then—

And then, even for the powerful, power passes again. What does it feel like inside, to be old when one was young, weak when one was strong? The second part of Mlle. de Beauvoir's book explores the interior world whose existence the first part has documented. Like the very rich, in Fitzgerald's well-known aperçu, the old are different from you and, maybe, me. How? and how do they perceive this difference?

In the external world, old people become objects instead of agents. Heretofore I have spoken of the wielders of power, but really this is a very small percentage of adult human beings. The poor and subordinate have always been objects, moved about by economic forces and social demands. But because they have participated in the work of the world, most of them have had the illusion that they have some control over their actions. They imagine a future; though, as psychologists have shown, the ability to plan for a future is closely tied to economic and sexual status. Women, subordinates, and the poor tend to live in the present. The coming of old age closes off the future to all. For the powerful, this is a stunning and disheartening shock. For the powerless, says Mlle. de Beauvoir, it is an equally stunning revelation of betrayal. Is this all? they are left to ask of their past lives, their *whole* lives. In today's industrial society, their hard-won skills are useless, their memories are irrelevant, ties with home and kin have withered or broken, customs have changed or vanished, ahead lie isolation, disregard, and a death among strangers. Was it for this they lived out the busy years? The devalued present calls the past into question, and the answer is mocking.

In the interior world inside each graying head there is an equally unsettling confrontation. One's old identity is somehow no longer acceptable on public exchange. One may feel nineteen or thirty-one or no age at all, but those out there get up and offer a seat on the bus, listen for a moment, laugh and go on talking, or don't listen at all. One is faced with the task—if one wants to keep in touch with reality—of remaking one's sense of oneself; and remaking it downwards, to incorporate that unflattering figure seen in the eyes of those others, the young and the powerful. One lives between lies—the inner feeling of youth, the outer judgment of age, which is true? To accept the outer judgment, one must be false to oneself; falseness, then, can spread to all one feels or knows. "Old age," writes Mlle. de Beauvoir, "is life's parody." Again, her documentation of this bitter conclusion has compelling weight.

I must speak of one omission which is understandable, though, I think, mistaken. But first I want to praise the insight, the candor, the subtle vision, and the unflinching objectivity of this whole enterprise. Reading this book took on the aspect of conducting an interior orchestra. I found myself leaping up again and again to leaf through Yeats, or Susanne Langer's analysis of the comic and tragic modes of drama in *Feeling and Form*, to reread Erik Erikson's vision of the last crisis of life as one moves from maturity to age, or Victor Turner's brilliant analysis of rites of passage in *The Ritual Process*, to recall a dozen more examples of my own touchstones of validity in human experience. Far from being depressing, *The Coming of Age* is a life-giving book. Published passages devoted to the sexual activities of the old are almost vulgarly misleading: in the book they illuminate the connection between vitality, creativity, and libido with considerable force, and indicate the effect on personal life of societal status, roles, and role-reversals. One can't abstract from a book like this without diminishing what is selected, for, by so doing, one cuts connections. Any whole is greater than the sum of its parts, and this is a noble whole. The life of the poor, the life of the mind, the triumphs and the failures of statesmen, the trials of artists, writers, and composers, myth, legend, and drama, absurdity, despair, dedication, and joy are woven together so that the many vivid examples and quotations that Mlle. de Beauvoir uses light up the conclusions she draws and keep them from seeming doctrinaire or insistent. Pedantic? Well, yes. She's a little pedantic. In her, it becomes a virtue. She supplies a baker's dozen of facts, she provides exhaustive analyses. Astonishingly, they are always interesting.

Then, what is missing? Something I would not have looked for myself until, toward the end of the book, I began to be aware, from a sentence or two of Mlle. de Beauvoir's, that she had excluded it from consideration: religion. Perhaps she is right, for considering religion without debating it as sacred truth may be more disruptive of reasoned argument than not considering it at all. But I would like to suggest that what religion *does* (leaving aside what it *is* — that is, true or not true) is posit an alternative reality to that figured forth in our daily lives. She speaks of the deadening effect on the old of having the *idea* of a future removed, of there being no more room in which to project plans or imagine action. Again, she remarks on the way in which the reality of old age shows up the assumed reality of earlier life and reveals it as a cheat. "The promises have been kept," she quotes herself from an earlier book, *La force des choses*, and ends, "I have been swindled."

Now, what religion tells us is that everyday reality is indeed untrue and invalid — a swindle — unless it is invaded and transfigured by the sacred. Can we believe this ambivalent statement? Such a question can only be argued, never decided. It will and has been *used*, taken as a directive to put up with everyday life and its horrors because they are false and will be wiped away in a better world. Alas, that does not dispose of the proposition that there may be a better world. And if one is caught in falsity, as the old are caught between "self" and "image," faith in another reality offers an alternative framework of value to which the self may be attached. But how can one ask questions like these without their seeming to be pious banalities inviting a like response? Can one ask them at all unless one asks sincerely (that is, without judging), and does this not imply one's own belief? The anthropologist can question believers in other faiths on the psychological aspects of their systems, for he is a stranger. Can a fellow member of Western society approach believers in the same way? Will his presence not, in itself, disturb the experimental equilibrium? At any rate, understandably, they are not asked.

But the problem is heightened by the fact that those old who seem to manage best (as cited here) often appear to make a connection with a reality outside that of ordinary life. Religion is not always a comfort. Victor Hugo kept his faith to the end, along with an abiding interest in young girls. To a friend he said, "I am old; I am going to die. I shall see God. . . . Talk to him! What a tremendous event! What shall I say to him?" He never wondered, Mlle. de Beauvoir notes acerbly, what God might say to *him*. Michelangelo, retaining his faith and losing his skill with advanced age, felt that God was reproving him for wasting his time on art instead of worship. Other artists have been sustained by joy in their continuing power to create: their connection, that is, with the "other reality" of art, Yeats's "artifice of eternity." Mlle. de Beauvoir's own advice is "to go on pursuing ends that give our existence a meaning," which she then sums up rather anticlimactically as "devotion to individuals, to groups or to causes, social, political, intellectual or creative work."

In the end, I suppose, one can only accept that other being, the aged image in another's eyes, as oneself if there is somehow room in one's self to take the creature in. Of all the teeming examples in this bountiful book of such a confrontation, the most useful for our shaken and frightened age seems to me an anecdote about the aged Goya, who had lived through terror, revolution, invasion, and counterterror, had painted the protagonists of all these systems, and then retired from life. Or so it seemed. But when he was eighty, he drew a self-portrait, "an ancient man propped on two sticks, with a great mass of white hair and beard all over his face, and the inscription 'I am still learning.'" Goya," writes Mlle. de Beauvoir, "was making fun of himself and his eagerness for everything new." No doubt. But what an unexpected, toe-of-the-Christmas-stocking gift to find as one's best provision for survival—the eagerness to know: "I am still learning." There's a thing to say to God!

Simone de Beauvoir: Freud and the Second Sex

Juliet Mitchell*

An entire system has been built up in this perspective, which I do not intend to criticize as a whole, merely examining its contribution to the study of woman. It is not an easy matter to discuss psychoanalysis *per se*. Like all religions — Christianity and Marxism, for example — it displays an embarrassing flexibility on a basis of rigid concepts.[1]

Not being a philosopher, Freud has refused to justify his system philosophically; and his disciples maintain that on this account he is exempt from all metaphysical attack. There are metaphysical assumptions behind all his dicta, however, and to use his language is to adopt a philosophy.[2]

Simone de Beauvoir's *The Second Sex*, strictly speaking, is not a part of the second feminist movement. Its publication in 1949 predates by almost twenty years the florescence of the political movement, and its translation into English in 1953 by exactly ten years the next major work to be written on the subject; Betty Friedan's *The Feminine Mystique*. Furthermore, it is explicitly not a feminist statement.[3] But *The Second Sex* undoubtedly had a profound influence on the first generation of new feminists and for this reason an inclusion of de Beauvoir's interpretation of Freud and Freudianism is mandatory.

The most striking feature of de Beauvoir's critique of psychoanalysis is its psychological perspective. What she likes about it is the fact of its psychology; what she dislikes is the nature of this psychology:

The tremendous advance accomplished by psychoanalysis over psychophysiology lies in the view that no factor becomes involved in the psychic life without having taken on human significance; it is not the body-object described by biologists that actually exists, but the body as lived in by the subject. Woman is a female to the extent that she feels herself as such. . . . It is not nature that defines woman; it is she who defines herself by dealing with nature on her own account in her emotional life.[4]

Psychoanalysis purports not to be a philosophy,[5] yet to de Beauvoir, it has philosophical implications. It is with these she takes issue — a task she admits to finding difficult in the face of Freud's repudiation of them. Difficult, but compulsory: for what de Beauvoir is setting up is a counter-psychological philosophy. I shall summarize here what seem to me to be the main elements of her interpretation of Freud, ranged against her

*Reprinted from *Psychoanalysis and Feminism.* © 1974 by Juliet Mitchell. Reprinted by permission of Pantheon Books, a division of Random House, Inc., and Penguin Books Ltd.

alternative propositions. We shall, I think, see that the nature of de Beauvoir's psycho-philosophical intention determines her philosophical reading of Freud.

Put crudely, the core of de Beauvoir's existentialism is the notion that the human being takes on the meaning of his or her existence in the actions and the projects formed. Each consciousness defines itself as subject, by opposing other consciousnesses and defining them as objects. Every consciousness is a transcendence which accomplishes its freedom in a perpetual surmounting of itself towards other freedoms. If any human refuses to exercise this freedom, he falls back into a state of immanence, and his freedom is degraded into facticity. If another person blocks and refuses the freedom of others, that constitutes oppression. Woman is the supreme Other, against which Man defines himself as subject, not in reciprocity, which would mean that he in turn was object for the woman's subjecthood, but in an act of psychic oppression. Woman is the archetype of the oppressed consciousness: the second sex. Her biological characteristics have been exploited so that she has become the receptacle for the alienation all men must feel; she *contains* man's otherness, and in doing so is denied her own humanity. Man, in a definition of his humanity, flings himself towards a freely chosen future. Within the animal species, the female may be superior precisely on account of her reproductive powers; but humanity is distinguished from the animals by the fact that it constantly transcends itself. Animals repeat and maintain; man creates and invents. All that is specific to humanity is concentrated in man, all that is common to mankind and the animals is concentrated in woman.

> [Man] aspires in contradictory fashion both to life and to repose, to existence and to merely being; he knows full well that "trouble of spirit" is the price of development, that his distance from the object is the price of his nearness to himself; but he dreams of quiet in disquiet and of an opaque plenitude that nevertheless would be endowed with consciousness. This dream incarnated is precisely woman; she is the wished-for intermediary between nature, the stranger to man, and the fellow being who is too closely identical.[6]

Woman is the most universal and absolute specification of alterity. She is mystery, essence (the soul). No one is born a woman: a woman is created from man's needs. She is obscure, mysterious, complete, outside the tensions and struggles of existence. For the woman, the man must become all; he is all meaning, the justification and definition of her existence, whereas for him she is a pleasure, an extra, somehow inessential. The language of reciprocity and equality is meaningless in this world divided into subjects and objects. The demand that man abandon his right to alienate himself in another, no longer to root his *natural* being in the woman (an act by which he frees himself to explore his *human* existence), is no light request: "the evolution now in progress threatens more than feminine charm alone: in beginning to exist for herself, woman will relinquish the function as double and mediator to which she owes her privileged place in the masculine universe; to man, caught between the silence of nature and the demanding presence of other free beings, a creature who is at once his like and a passive thing seems a great treasure."[7] Woman's total oppression, in de Beauvoir's scheme of things, is the economic and social exploitation of this *original psychological abuse: the creation of the second sex with its Other Realm.*

The main concepts and the main values that de Beauvoir deploys for her presentation of how it happened, what is going on and what is to be done are manifest even in this brief account. They are "choice," "freedom," "projects" on the one hand, versus "determinism," "immanence," "alienation" and "alterity" on the other. Confronted with a series of options, man chooses the dangerous future and thus becomes himself: life is the chosen struggle for freedom, death is sitting back content with the given. It is with these values and with this psychological-philosophical explanation that de Beauvoir confronts psychoanalysis. Though appreciative of its insights, she does not like what she finds there.

De Beauvoir summarizes Freud's notions of the girl's development: the polymorphous sexuality of both sexes in infancy as they pass through the oral and anal stages to become differentiated with the onset of genital sexuality. The girl has her two-tier genital development of, first, infantile clitoral sensitivity (this stage is analogous to the boy's concentration on his penis), then she makes a necessary transition at puberty to the vagina as the organ of her womanly sexuality. It is not this notorious latter notion with which de Beauvoir takes issue, but with the in-built masculinity of the model. For Freud, according to de Beauvoir, the norm is the boy, and the girl a deviation from it. This is largely true of Freud's first models, as he later self-critically acknowledged. It became a problem to which Freud made repeated reference, with increasing concern.

De Beauvoir's objection, however, to what may be termed Freud's "masculine bias" has more to do with the values elicited by this than with the fact that it could constitute a scientific flaw. For what she is contending is that Freud's thesis assumes that there is an original superiority in the male whereas to her this is only socially induced: "The little girl's covetousness [of the penis], when it exists, results from a previous evaluation of virility. Freud takes this for granted, when it should be accounted for."[8]

The sovereignty of the father is a fact of social origin, which Freud fails to account for. . . .[9]

Having dissociated compulsions and prohibitions from the free choice of the existent, Freud fails to give us an explanation of their origin — he takes them for granted. He endeavoured to replace the idea of value with that of authority; but he admits in *Moses and Monotheism* that he has no way of accounting for this authority. Incest, for example, is forbidden because the father has forbidden it — but why did he forbid it? It is a mystery.[10]

> The fact is that a true human privilege is based upon the anatomical privilege only in virtue of the total situation. Psychoanalysis can establish its truths only in the historical context.[11]

Finding that Freud fails to account for the high valuation placed on the penis and male sovereignty, de Beauvoir endeavours to make good this failure by placing the insights of psychoanalysis in a historical and philosophical context. She accepts many of the observations Freud makes, but proceeds to ask the question why.

Any account of original motivation must make certain assumptions, and de Beauvoir is no exception: her project for her whole book is, interestingly enough, most succinctly stated in the section where she assesses psychoanalysis: "I shall pose the problem of feminine destiny quite otherwise [than it is proposed by psychoanalysis]: I shall place woman in a world of values and give her behaviour a dimension of liberty. I believe that she has the power to choose between the assertion of her transcendence and her alienation as object; she is not the plaything of contradictory drives; she devises solutions of diverse values in the ethical scale."[12]

Given this presupposition of the existent's free choice in its quest of becoming, it follows that a mixed psychosocial explanation of value must be forthcoming. Quite simply, in the light of this all-prevailing "choice," what de Beauvoir sees as the Freudian stress on the significance of anatomy and the notion of drives *must* seem crudely deterministic. In de Beauvoir's version, Freud's baby comes into the world with a number of given urges (sexual ones) and a body with a fixed meaning (male or female); all the major events of infantile life follow therefrom. Whereas de Beauvoir's baby comes free of predetermined characteristics into a world of pressures and problems against which it must act or around which it must navigate in a voluntary assertion of its liberty. De Beauvoir's baby looks forward, her version of Freud's looks backwards: in psychoanalysis, she complains, "the individual is always explained through ties with his past and not in respect to a future towards which he projects his aims."[13] "The psychoanalyst describes the female child, the young girl, as incited to identification with the mother and the father, torn between 'viriloid' and 'feminine' tendencies; whereas I conceive her as hesitating between the role of *object*, *Other* which is offered to her, and the assertion of her liberty."[14]

De Beauvoir's philosophy (her existentialism) determines her rejection of Freud in two different ways. In one way, as we have seen, she posits an alternative psychology: the human aspiration to be a subject and express one's alienation in another thus making that other the object; in another way, she justifies this premise by explanations of social interaction. So we have a system which presupposes a set of values (and in this it is precisely a morality), which then proceeds to account for them in social terms (this forms the "explanation," the "account" for the absence of which she is always berating Freud). It seems from this that de Beauvoir would have found it easier if Freud had had an explicit philosophy with which her alternative proposition could contend, and in the absence of one she reads it back from the nature of his observations: she gives him a value system which she confesses to have found hard to discover in his work. Thus the terminology of psychoanalysis becomes philosophy-loaded. The child that *identifies* with a parent is *alienating itself* in a foreign image instead of spontaneously manifesting its own existence: "Interiorizing the uncon-scious and the whole psychic life, the very language of psychoanalysis suggests that the drama of the individual unfolds within him — such words as *complex, tendency*, and so on make that implication. But a life is a relation to the world, and the individual defines himself by making his own choices through the world about him."[15] In other words, concerned to assert a philosophy, de Beauvoir has had to find the source of her rejection of psychoanalysis in its implications alone.

What exactly does she see as these implications? They can, in fact, be summed up quite simply in one overall concept: determinism. I am only concerned here with the distortions of Freud's analysis that I think result from this assumption. Freud and de Beauvoir mean something different by the term, so that by and large, de Beauvoir is correcting something that is really not there; and in doing so she makes a number of quite specific errors.

The errors in interpretation arise, then, out of this charge of philo-sophical determinism, but they are compounded by de Beauvoir's stress on Freud's masculine model: "Freud never showed much concern with the destiny of woman; it is clear that he simply adapted his account from that of the destiny of man, with slight modifications."[16] This inaccuracy (Freud was greatly concerned but also greatly unsure on this question) directs de Beauvoir to more serious misreadings: "Freud at first described the little girl's history in a completely corresponding fashion [to the boy's], later calling the feminine form of the process the Electra complex; but it is clear that he defined it less in itself than upon the basis of his masculine pattern."[17] Let us hear Freud: "We have already learned, too, that there is yet another difference between the sexes, which relates to the Oedipus complex. We have an impression here that what we have said about the Oedipus complex applies with complete strictness to the male child only and that we are right in rejecting the term 'Electra complex' which seeks to emphasize the analogy between the attitude of the two sexes."[18] And: "I do not see any advance or gain in the introduction of the term 'Electra complex,' and do not advocate its use."[19]

Ironically, what has happened to de Beauvoir's version of Freud's little girl growing up is that the distinctions between the sexes have become *more* rigid and the whole process more rigidly determined than one can ever find it in Freud's original writings. Thus she reiterates Freud's early notions of an oral, an anal and a genital stage as though they were distinct steps on the march of life, whereas Freud was, in his later works, at pains to point out their constant overlap and commingling. So, too, she ignores the permeation throughout Freud's work of the notion of bisexuality: the presence in both sexes of the inclinations of the opposite sex. The dividing line between men and women is absolute in her schema in a way that it never is in Freud's. Some of Freud's musings on problems have become dicta, and what he himself rejected as an inadequate explanation has been taken as his dogmatism. Freud, bothered by the relation between activity and passivity in the two sexes, and by the difference between the aims of sexual drives and their objects, is berated by de Beauvoir for proposing for women a "passive libido," a notion Freud himself found equally absurd.

Part of the trouble comes from taking all psychoanalysts as Freud. To some extent this is understandable where we are dealing with Freudian analysts; but it is surely illegitimate in cases where there was an explicit break between Freud and these other thinkers? But de Beauvoir accords, without comment, the same status to the theories of Adler and Stekel as she does to those of Freud. Both broke with Freud, and neither they nor their followers regard themselves as psychoanalysts. The fact that the break came over precisely such questions as the nature and role of sexuality makes de Beauvoir's elision the more serious. Furthermore her heavy reliance on the findings of Helene Deutsch, who sees herself as working within the Freudian tradition, is more justifiable, but, as we have seen, is bound to present problems. At the very least, even seeing the amalgamation from de Beauvoir's viewpoint, it does make her perspective seem strangely partial. She omits, for instance, analysts such as Karen Horney, whose sociological stress would agree with her own position. Indeed over questions of penis-envy Horney's views coincide to a great degree with de Beauvoir's. Either we are looking at what Freud said, or at what a number of different analysts said, or at what a number of analysts and psychologists contend; if our intention is either of the latter, then surely there must be some rationale for the selection made? But I think the fusion de Beauvoir makes is genuine confusion. For not only does she donate terms that are Jung's or Adler's (the Electra complex, and "masculine protest") to Freud,[20] but also credits Freud with the very conception with which Jung took his departure from Freud and from psychoanalysis: the collective unconscious. This attribution would seem to me to be the distinguishing error in her assessment of psychoanalysis. It bears the brunt of the philosophy that she seeks to discover in Freud's works: "It is [the] concept of choice, indeed, that psychoanalysis most vehemently rejects in the name of determinism and the 'collective unconscious'; and it is this unconscious that is supposed to supply man with prefabricated imagery and a universal symbolism. Thus it would explain the observed analogies of dreams, of purposeless actions, of visions of delirium, of allegories, and of human destinies."[21]

But Freud never used the term the "collective unconscious"; indeed his repudiation of the concept has much in common with de Beauvoir's: "It is not easy for us to carry over the concepts of individual psychology into group psychology; and I do not think we gain anything by introducing the concept of a 'collective' unconscious."[22]

It would seem that de Beauvoir has conflated Jung's notion of a "collective unconscious" with Freud's rare but very different hypotheses of a "collective mind." In fact, Freud's concept here bears a very strong resemblance to the contentions of de Beauvoir and is as far away from the Jungian belief as anyone could wish. His only elaborations of this notion come in his inquiries outside what could strictly be regarded as psychoanalysis, in his speculations on anthropological history and the origins of religions, culture and morality—*Totem and Taboo* and *Moses and Monotheism*. I shall quote at some length, because I believe this to be a key misunderstanding of Freud's work. Freud's first venture into a reconstruction of man's history proposed an original murder of the father by a group of brothers and the subsequent guilt they experienced (see p. 403). *Totem and Taboo* is his first essay in tying up the crucial importance of the individual child's entry into human culture expressed in our society in his relationship with his parents at the moment of the Oedipus complex with a similar event in the generic history of mankind. Freud acknowledges his difficulties.

> Before I bring my remarks to a close, however, I must find room to point out that, though my arguments have led to a high degree of convergence upon a single comprehensive nexus of ideas, this fact cannot blind us to the uncertainties of my premises or the difficulties involved in my conclusions. I will only mention two of the latter which may have forced themselves on the notice of a number of my readers.
>
> No one can have failed to observe . . . that I have taken as the basis of my whole position the existence of a collective mind, in which mental processes occur just as they do in the mind of an individual. In particular, I have supposed that the sense of guilt for an action has persisted for many thousands of years and has remained operative in generations which can have had no knowledge of that action. I have supposed that an emotional process, such as might have developed in generations of sons who were ill-treated by their father, has extended to new generations which were exempt from such treatment for the very reason that their father had been eliminated. It must be admitted that these are grave difficulties; and any explanation that could avoid presumptions of such a kind would seem to be preferable.
>
> Further reflection, however, will show that I am not alone in the responsibility for this bold procedure. Without the assumption of a collective mind, which makes it possible to neglect the interruptions of

mental acts caused by the extinction of the individual, social psychology in general cannot exist. Unless psychical processes were continued from one generation to another, if each generation were obliged to acquire its attitude to life anew, there would be no progress in this field and next to no development.[23]

The unconscious is everyman's heritage of how mankind lives. As Freud says, each separate individual cannot start the process of human history anew, on his own; he must acquire it. Some common event, which may well be only a psychical event, can be hypothesized and a "scientific myth" created which would offer the sort of mythological explanation needed to account for this shared understanding and generic heritage of customs, morals and so on. Referring to the same sort of hypothesis some twenty-five years later, Freud wrote:

> We must finally make up our minds to adopt the hypothesis that the psychical precipitates of the primeval period became inherited property which, in each fresh generation, called not for acquisition but only for awakening. In this we have in mind the example of what is certainly the "innate" symbolism which derives from the period of the development of speech, which is familiar to all children without their being instructed, and which is the same among all peoples despite their different languages. . . . We find that in a number of important relations our children react, not in a manner corresponding to their own experience, but instinctively, like the animals, in a manner that is only explicable as phylogenetic acquisition.[24]

Freud is certainly not referring here to what de Beauvoir calls "prefabricated imagery and a universal symbolism." (Nor is he saying that man has animal instincts — as he remarks elsewhere, this is at best a very inadequate analogy. The "inheritance" referred to here is that of human culture.) Freud is trying to establish that the individual's psychology cannot be transferred in a complete or simple way to a collective/social situation, nor vice versa, but that the two must share common features, and these can be analysed and the mode of their interrelationship considered. The particularly human idea of the instinct that the person brings with him would seem to come in part from the accumulation of the historical experience of mankind. No more than de Beauvoir, does Freud consider (as she charges) that symbolism comes "down from heaven or rises up from subterranean depths." That is Jung. Freud and de Beauvoir agree that it is shared history that makes for shared perceptions and common symbols. Furthermore, de Beauvoir castigates psychoanalysis for positing a "mysterious unconscious" as the source of explanation; the contrary is true: psychoanalysis undertakes the elucidation of the laws of the unconscious, it precisely exists to repudiate this notional "mysteriousness." Jung's hermeneutics claimed to read the revelations of the mysterious unconscious: Freud sought merely to find therein normal thought that had undergone repression and been transformed thereby.

I have spent some time on this question, because it is the focal point of de Beauvoir's philosophical attack — after this she challenges only empirical propositions. Her own thesis underlies her criticism and certainly it is a thesis from which — put like that — Freud would have dissented, though the terms of his dissent would have been opposite to those de Beauvoir attributes to him. De Beauvoir believes in "human unity," so that although her objections to Freud are made on behalf of social reality, this philosophical notion of "wholeness," is in fact at their base. This preoccupation is manifest as her deeply held faith in her explanations of human behaviour and in her criticism of psychoanalysis as a methodology:

> . . . the concept of a simple association of elements is unacceptable, for the psychic life is not a mosaic, it is a single whole in every one of its aspects and we must respect that unity. This is possible only by our recovering through the disparate facts the original purposiveness of existence. If we do not go back to this source, man appears to be the battleground of compulsions and prohibitions that alike are devoid of meaning and incidental.[25]

It is, however, from this premise of life's unity that, from the point of view of the psychology of women, de Beauvoir's most significant objection to Freud takes place. It is the same objection that all the most important dissidents finally focused on: an objection to the prominence given to sexuality.[26] De Beauvoir believes that the sexual impulse is one among others, and by no means necessarily the most important: "In girls as in boys the body is first of all the radiation of a subjectivity, the instrument that makes possible the comprehension of the world: it is through the eyes, the hands, that children apprehend the universe, and not through the sexual parts."[27] Freud, whose theory never ignores hands or eyes, would have commented sarcastically, as he did of Jung, on how much pleasanter this version makes the whole issue, how much more acceptable a suggestion it is. De Beauvoir objects to the vagueness of the notion "sexual," and it is true that Freud's declared intention was to generalize it beyond the genital; it was by means of this extension (as he points out in the *Three Essays on Sexuality*) that he was able to revolutionize sexology by introducing infantile sexuality and seeing that this and "perverted" sex were on a continuum with so-called normal adult sexuality. His motivation for this was obviously not simply so as to set himself up in opposition to the prevalent concepts of childhood innocence and the public moral outrage at perversions, but to establish a fundamental concept: that the earliest inquiries of children, their drive for knowledge, come with the first sexual questions — which are, roughly speaking, "Where do babies come from?" and "What is the difference between the sexes?" Freud does not, as de Beauvoir suggests, generalize the concept of sexuality into vagueness — but into complexity.

De Beauvoir, then, takes issue with Freud for failing to appreciate the fundamental existential situation of alienation, the price the individual pays for separation from the whole; for placing a totally inadequate stress on social factors: it is, to her, the patriarchal culture that endows the girl with an awareness of her real *social* inferiority and the boy with his superiority; and finally Freud is guilty of endorsing the status of the second sex, by always using a masculine model. Many of the specific points she makes about the social influences on sexual differentiation are excellent — Freud would not have disagreed — but in her repudiation of the primacy of complex sexuality and her concept of an all-important original human unity and her implicit denial of the unconscious, there is a substantial difference of opinion. Existentialism is here a philosophic system of belief, whereas psychoanalysis purports to be a scientific method of investigation. They thus claim to exist on different planes, but in order to compare and contrast them and favour one above the other de Beauvoir has had to ensure that they meet on the same terrain; to do this she has infused Freudian psychoanalysis with Jungian metaphysics — this latter is more suitable for confrontation by existentialism, for — unlike Marxism or psychoanalysis — it too is a philosophy or a system of belief.

Notes

1. Simone de Beauvoir, *The Second Sex*, Jonathan Cape, 1960, p. 65.

2. ibid., p. 66.

3. Recently, in an interview in *Nouvel Observateur*, Simone de Beauvoir has announced that she has changed her position, and that now, in contradistinction to her earlier theses, she counts herself politically a feminist.

4. *The Second Sex*, op. cit., p. 65.

5. Freud stated: "Even when I have moved away from observation, I have carefully avoided any contact with philosophy proper. This avoidance has been greatly facilitated by constitutional incapacity." "An Autobiographical Study," 1925 (1924), S.E., Vol. XX, p. 59.

6. *The Second Sex*, op. cit., p. 160.

7. ibid., p. 685.

8. ibid., p. 68.

9. ibid., p. 69.

10. ibid., p. 71.

11. ibid., p. 75.

12. ibid., p. 76. De Beauvoir constantly objects (as do later feminists) to what she sees as the "determinism" inherent in psychoanalysis. But Freud's science uses the concept of overdetermination (indeed it is a term Freud invented). This is a complex notion of "multiple causation" in which the numerous factors can reinforce, overlap, cancel each other out, or contradict one another — a very different proposition from that suggested by simple determinism.

13. ibid., p. 76.

14. ibid., p. 77.

15. ibid., p. 75. It is interesting to note that though Freud certainly used the term "complex," its widespread introduction probably owes most to Bleuler, Jung and the Zurich group. The term has become a catchword in popular usage; it was never a major concept of

Freud's and was often rather loosely used to mean the totality of ideas relating to a particularly coloured emotional event; Freud's later use of it always included the notion of *repressed* ideas and hence, strictly speaking, it was only applied to the Oedipus and the castration complexes. "Tendency" quite simply is not a Freudian concept.

16. ibid., p. 66.

17. ibid., p. 67.

18. Freud, "Female Sexuality," op. cit., pp. 228–9.

19. Freud, "The Psychogenesis of a Case of Homosexuality in a Woman," 1920, S.E., Vol. XVIII, p. 155, n. 1.

20. We have seen what Freud had to say about the Electra complex; he was only slightly more tolerant of "masculine protest." Denouncing Adler's theories, Freud wrote: "Adler is so consistent in this that he positively considers that the strongest motive force in the sexual act is the man's intention of showing himself master of the woman — of being 'on top.' I do not know if he has expressed these monstrous notions in his writings" ("On the History of the Psycho-Analytic Movement," 1914, S.E., Vol. XIV, pp. 52–3); Freud's thesis assumes on the contrary that the little boy, observing sexual intercourse, imagines himself in *both* the position of the man *and* the woman. "Between them these two impulses exhaust the pleasurable possibilities of the situation. The first alone can come under the head of the masculine protest, if that concept is to retain any meaning at all . . ." (ibid., pp. 54–5). (De Beauvoir does initially attribute "masculine protest" to Adler.) It seems likely that Freud wrote his extremely important paper "On Narcissism" in part to combat Jung's notions of non-sexual libido and Adler's "masculine protest"; here he acknowledges that the "masculine protest" may, along with many other things, be an aspect of narcissism, but if it is to play a part in neurosis then the concept is simply the same as "the castration complex." A few years after the split between Adler and Freud and then Jung and Freud, Adler called his theories "Individual Psychology" and Jung adopted the term "Analytical Psychology." Freud retained "Psychoanalysis" and it is only to his work and that of his followers that the term can be correctly applied.

21. *The Second Sex*, op. cit., p. 72.

22. Freud, *Moses and Monotheism*, Part III, 1939 (1934–8), S.E., Vol. XXIII, p. 132. The term is, at best, a tautology: the unconscious *is* by definition collective, as Octave Mannoni points out in *Freud*, op. cit.

23. Freud, *Totem and Taboo*, 1913 (1912–13), S.E., Vol. XIII, pp. 157–8.

24. Freud, *Moses and Monotheism*, op. cit., pp. 132–3.

25. *The Second Sex*, op. cit., p. 71.

26. Obviously at first glance it seems a bit strange to include Reich in this charge. But we have seen how Reich too first reduced sexuality to genitality and then moved off in another direction and ended up equating it with all-inclusive life-energy.

27. *The Second Sex*, op. cit., p. 273.

Psychiatry in the Postwar Fiction of Simone de Beauvoir
Terry Keefe*

In a review recently published in *Literature and Psychology*, Dr. Simon Grolnick reminded us of some of the complexities of Jean-Paul Sartre's

*Reprinted by permission from *Literature and Psychology* 29, no. 3 (1979):123–33.

attitude towards psychoanalysis.[1] As one of the contributors to the reviewed volume points out, "One day the history of Sartre's thirty-year-long relationship with psychoanalysis, an ambiguous mixture of *equally* deep attraction and repulsion, will have to be written."[2] An interesting side-light is already thrown upon aspects of that history, however, by the postwar fiction of Sartre's life-long companion, Simone de Beauvoir. In this matter as in certain others, Beauvoir's writings, fascinating and valuable in their own right, constitute a most useful complement to those of Sartre, for whilst he has published no novels since the third volume of his wartime series, *The Roads to Freedom*, three fictional works by Beauvoir appeared in the fifties and sixties, each in part giving imaginative expression to her own intense and lasting interest in modern psychiatry.

Since the Second World War Beauvoir has written one long novel, *The Mandarins* (published and awarded the Prix Goncourt in 1954), a shorter novel, *Les Belles Images* (1966), and a collection of three stories, *The Woman Destroyed* (1967).[3] The narrative of *The Mandarins* alternates systematically between the viewpoints of Henri Perron, a journalist and author, and Anne Dubreuilh, a successful psychiatrist. Through Anne, in one half of the book the profession of psychiatry regularly comes under scrutiny from the inside, and serious questions and doubts are raised about the underlying principles of all psychotherapy. One of the principal characters linking the two halves of the narrative, moreover, has a breakdown in the course of the story and undergoes a psychoanalytical "cure." On the other hand, whilst the central figure of *Les Belles Images* has a long and continuing history of mental disturbance, the climax of the story is her firm decision to take her favorite daughter *out of* the care of a psychiatrist. In *The Woman Destroyed*, the main character and narrator of the second tale ("Monologue") is beyond any doubt a psychopathological case; and the heroine of the long third story (which gives its name to the collection) is driven to a psychiatrist by the breakdown of her marriage. In other words, in only one of the five separate stories she has published since the war (namely, "The Age of Discretion") does Beauvoir fail to bring mental illness and psychiatry quite prominently into the plot in one form or another. And this, of course, takes no account of numerous passing references to psychiatry and psychoanalytical methods in the books, or of the fact that Beauvoir's broad view of the development of the individual and of family life has very obviously been much influenced by psychoanalytical theory and modern psychiatry in general.

Early on in *The Mandarins* we learn that Anne Dubreuilh became a psychiatrist because she wished to help people to rid themselves of the obstacles they place in the way of their happiness. Her Marxist husband, Robert, had never accepted the unfavourable Communist-Party line on psychiatry and fired her with enthusiasm at the prospect of re-thinking classical psychoanalysis in the light of Marxism (73). She has always acknowledged that it is possible to question the worth of any one person's equilibrium within an essentially unjust society, but has responded to the challenge of finding an answer in each individual case, believing that to relieve patients of their personal nightmares is to enable them to face up to the real problems of the world (92). The central purpose of the novel as a whole, however, is to depict the dilemmas experienced by French left-wing intellectuals after the war, and when the story opens (Christmas 1944) it is clear that the experiences of the Occupation have marked Anne profoundly and have already changed in certain respects the nature of her relationship with her patients. Personally, she feels that to allow herself to forget the worst incidents of the war would somehow be to betray those who suffered and died, and yet her professional life is now dominated by the task of encouraging others to set aside the horrors of the past and to adjust to the present and the future.

Anne, therefore, begins to entertain rather far-reaching doubts about the nature of her work as a psychiatrist. She wonders whether, at least in these circumstances, there is not something intrinsically wrong with an attempt to assist people to forget the past. Is she right, for instance, to try to drive out of the mind of one of her child patients (Fernand) the memory of his father, who died two years earlier in Dachau (92)? It is certain that nothing she may do to "help" will bring the dead back to life or efface past evils, but above all she now lacks the faith in the future that formerly enabled her to believe it appropriate to aid patients to "neutralize" their past: her pre-war assumption that "every sane man had a role to play in a history that was leading mankind on towards happiness" is one that she can no longer accept. Yet in that case, looking only to the present, since the future is in doubt, what difference does it make whether little Fernand becomes cheerful and carefree like other children (92)?

Since Anne's professional life continues as before in spite of her acknowledgement that, if this is what she really believes, she ought to stop treating certain patients or even give up her work altogether, we may reasonably assume that the doubts assailing her do not yet amount to complete conviction that psychiatry is an unjustified activity. And indeed, although she periodically experiences great frustration and fatigue in dealing with people who cope reasonably well as adults but virtually revert to being children in her consulting-room (104), she regains some of her earlier faith in her profession when the first war-deportees begin returning to France. These "ghosts" bring back more horrifying stories of the war years than ever and they can gain no rest from their past. They are represented by one of Anne's patients in particular, a young woman whose hair is completely white. Faced with cases like this, Anne feels ashamed at not having suffered enough herself and temporarily loses some of her earlier doubts about the value of therapy: "the questions that I had asked myself now seemed quite idle ones; whatever the future might hold, these men and women had to be helped to forget, had to be cured" (266). She throws herself wholeheartedly into her work once more and enjoys a certain limited success, not just with children like Fernand, but even with patients like the young white-haired woman: "the equilibrium she had achieved wasn't marvelous, but at least she was sleeping well" (279). Before long, however, some of her doubts seem to return, for she is soon saying to Henri Perron that she finds it rather futile to be treating individual states of mind in the prevailing circumstances. Once more she claims that she no longer has enough faith in the future to believe that every life can have a purpose (319).

As far as we are able to tell, this is more or less where things stand when Anne goes to America at the beginning of the second part of the novel. Her reputation as a "brilliant doctor" is apparently already established, though she admits that she has a great deal to learn about the latest developments in American psychoanalysis. In fact, other matters (outstandingly, a lengthy love-affair with an American writer, Lewis Brogan) preoccupy her much more than her work in the second half of the book. Yet if we now learn less about her relations with her own patients, we gain a new kind of insight into her attitude towards psychoanalytical "cures" as she observes at close quarters the breakdown and treatment of her friend Paule. Anne is clear that the ethics of her profession preclude the possibility of treating Paule herself (II, 197), but although this makes matters somewhat awkward for her as Paule actually goes into decline, its effect is to allow Anne to follow in great detail the impact of psychoanalysis upon someone that she knows very well indeed. That is, she is not involved in the usual doctor-patient relationship here but is, as a result of her professional expertise and her intimate knowledge of Paule, in a privileged position from which to judge the case.

It is Anne who takes Paule to the eminent analyst, Mardrus, yet from the first we find her wondering exactly what Paule will be cured of, and what she will be like afterwards (II, 219). And in a stance paralleling her attitude towards suffering in general earlier in the book we also see her initially reacting to Paule's cure by suggesting that it has somehow cancelled out Paule's earlier pain and rendered it pointless (II, 349). She seems sympathetic to Paule's own view that her "madness" was associated with a richness of perception and a sensitivity that are now lost, but in any case she explicitly claims that there is an element of inauthenticity in Paule's new personality: "for the rest of her life she would probably play the part of a normal woman, but it was a task that scarcely inclined her towards sincerity" (II, 351). Paule, she says, seems more alien to her now than when she was mad. More significant still is Anne's view of the explanation of Paule's troubles that Mardrus has persuaded his patient to accept (that she felt guilt over her infantile jealousy of her brother, who died at the age of fifteen months, and had therefore become masochistic in her long love-affair with Henri, who was a kind of brother-substitute): "I kept quiet. I was very familiar with explanations of the kind that Mardrus had used. I, too, made use of them on occasion and I appreciated them for what they were worth. Yes, in order to cure Paule, one had to reach back into the past to destroy her love. But I could not help thinking of the sort of microbe that can be killed only by destroying the organism that it is feeding on" (II, 353).

Anne, who admitted early on that she had always been aware that "to cure is often to mutilate," finds the destruction of Paule's past increasingly difficult to accept: "I wanted to weep with her over the love that for ten years had been the pride and meaning of her whole life, and which had now been transformed into a shameful ulcer" (II, 356). She sees that many of the concerns with which Paule has replaced her love for Henri are foolish, and she cannot avoid relating all of this to her own case, refusing to believe that her feelings are ailments. She would rather go on suffering than have her past scattered to the winds, and when her affair with Brogan breaks up painfully she draws some consolation from the fact that it will continue to live in her memory (II, 424). She is so saddened by Paule's resignation to her new state, moreover, that she becomes disgusted with her own work as a psychiatrist and wants to tell her patients: " 'Don't try to get better. We always get better soon enough' " (II, 375). All of her earlier doubts are now intensified: "I could no longer understand why it is a good thing that people should sleep well at nights, make love easily, be capable of acting, choosing, forgetting, living" (II, 376). Although she is still having successes with some difficult cases, she is now going through the motions more than anything else; she becomes more and more like her own patients, with their misfortunes and obsessions, and she can see no urgent need to "cure" them. At the end of the novel, however, Anne is portrayed as being in the depths of an intense personal crisis which affects the way in which she sees *everything*, so that it is not clear how complete and permanent we should regard her disillusionment with psychiatry as being.

More important for present purposes is the fact that in the course of *The Mandarins* Beauvoir has used Anne's profession as a way of raising many points about the philosophical and moral implications of psycho-therapy that have a particular modern ring. In the way in which the nature of Anne's work (and thereby her own reactions to it) changes with the precise political and historical circumstances in the immediate postwar years, we see Beauvoir's sharp awareness of how psychiatry is related to the state of the society within which it is operating. And the point, of course, is taken one stage further than this when Anne is made to question the validity of helping the patient to adjust to a life of "normality" when the norms themselves may be anything but admirable. Beauvoir stops a little short of suggesting, as R.D. Laing was subsequently to do, that the schizophrenic is a kind of prophet in whose hands the salvation of society may ultimately lie, but she must surely, in 1954, have been among the first to express in memorable fictional terms doubts about the psychiatric concept of normality in the context of modern society. Furthermore, the way in which Anne's approach to her work is shown to be intimately linked with her personal life and circumstances is also very much in line with recent emphasis on the nature of the psychiatrist's own experience with his patient and the phenomenon of counter-transference. In general, the broad aims and the narrative sweep of a novel like *The Mandarins* provide an excellent context for the airing of fundamental and vital questions about mental illness and its treatment, since the interaction between individual and society which lies at the heart of the matter can be explored so tellingly in fiction. It is also quite clear that Beauvoir, at this stage, has mixed feelings about psychiatry, and the novel-form undoubtedly gives her rather more scope for expressing her hesitations and doubts than would the philosophical essay.

The ambiguity in her attitude is equally discernible in her subsequent works of fiction, where no major character is a psychiatrist, but where we see that Paule was simply the first in a line of case-studies in which Beauvoir continues to explore major aspects of the theory and practice of psychotherapy. The case of Monique in "The Woman Destroyed," in fact, runs quite closely parallel to that of Paule. Monique, too, (though in different circumstances and in an entirely different way from Paule) has allowed herself to become over-dependent upon her man and eventually needs psychiatric help when it becomes clear that he is going to leave her after twenty-two years of marriage. We do not observe her crisis through the eyes of another as we do with Paule, however, for the story is narrated from her own viewpoint. Hence we notice that she records in her diary various physical symptoms that suggest the onset of some kind of breakdown—loss of weight, fainting, mid-cycle bleeding—and we see both a friend and then her husband suggesting that she should see a psychiatrist. The friend claims that Monique needs only minor help rather than a full analysis but Monique cannot at first see what a psychiatrist could possibly do to help her (233), and she resists very strong pressure to consult one from her husband, who is himself a doctor (236–7). Yet she has to admit that she may be making herself ill "with the unacknowledged intention of moving him to pity" (237) and, perhaps mainly because she is afraid of the continuous bleeding, she soon gives way. As she ironically notes, she begins to pay a psychiatrist to listen to her (239).

From this point onwards, most of the parallels with Paule's case fall away: the respects in which Monique's situation is different come more to the fore and, in any case, it is suggested that Monique is in no danger of becoming deranged (239). But precisely because her case is a less extreme one, the whole question of what effect psychiatric treatment has upon her is more difficult to resolve—a difficulty only compounded by the fact that we never see Monique from the outside and have to read between the lines of her own comments. Taking at face value the totality of her remarks about the efforts of her psychiatrist, Dr. Marquet, we could easily believe that he does nothing at all for her: she soon abandons the work she has taken up on his advice ("What a joke their ergotherapy is! I've given up that idiotic job"; 241); at one point she suspects him of being in league with Maurice; she is often scathing about his analyses; and her last reference to her treatment in the diary implies that Marquet may only have made matters worse (242). Yet a careful reading of the story indicates that the picture is a more complicated one than this. At least the hemorrhage stops and Monique begins eating again within three days of her first consultation (239), and she does take up her diary once more on Marquet's advice. In a number of instances, moreover, the accuracy of his comments about Monique is confirmed by what we already know of her *in spite of herself*. Monique is blind to certain things about her own life and is an arch self-deceiver,[4] so that we are perfectly ready to accept the psychiatrist's view that her intelligence has been stultified by her obsessions and that she must be prepared to consider her own responsibility for the situation as well as that of Maurice and his mistress (239).

In principle, of course, Monique's psychiatrist is trying to do with her much the same as Mardrus did with Paule: to ease her away from preoccupations with one man and to restore her sense of individual identity. Yet in the context of the story as a whole his attempt is presented in a far more sympathetic light than is that of Mardrus. Monique overtly belittles what he is doing ("Then he began to muddle me with talk of a lost and regained personality, of distance to be adopted, of returning to myself. Claptrap"; 242), but she admits that she wants to collaborate, wants to try to find herself again (240). Moreover, when Marquet approaches the matter "from the other end" from Monique and wants to talk not about her husband and mistress but about Monique's mother and father and her father's death, the attentive reader already has reason to suppose that this is appropriate, since many earlier references buried in her diary suggest that much of her current difficulty with her husband stems from her attempt to make him conform to an ideal that her father, himself a doctor, embodied for her.[5] In other words, the psychiatrist's deep analysis of Monique's problem has a great deal of plausibility for us and is not made to appear out of the blue as a kind of *deus ex machina* as does Mardrus's explanation of Paule's state. Yet having said all of this, we cannot be absolutely sure to what extent psychiatry is effective in Monique's case. The consultations certainly *appear* to help her, contrary to her own expectations and claims, but she is still in a very bad state at the end of the story and, in any case, we have no means of knowing how well she would have coped without such help.

Much of the emphasis that Beauvoir placed, in *The Mandarins*, on the psychiatrist-patient relationship and on the nature and implications of psychiatric treatment as such comes to fall, in all of her subsequent stories, on the way in which the structure and quality of the original family situation lies at the roots of mental disturbance. Indeed, Beauvoir acknowledged in *All Said and Done*: "I am much more concerned than I used to be with the problems of childhood."[6] In some respects, therefore, the reported comments of Monique's younger daughter, Lucienne, near the end of "The Woman Destroyed," may well express the author's own views: "According to her, what counts in childhood is the psychoanalytical situation as it exists without the parents' knowledge, almost in spite of them. Education, in so far as it is conscious and deliberate, is quite secondary" (250). It is unlikely, however, that Beauvoir would wholly subscribe to Lucienne's inference that someone like her mother accordingly bears no responsibility at all for the development of her children. In fact, part of the point of the preceding story in the collection, "Monologue," is to show how, in spite of all her protestations that she was a perfect mother, Murielle actually *drove* her daughter to suicide.

In any case, Murielle is in every respect a fascinating case from the psychiatric point of view. In spite of the fact that, again, no point of view other than the heroine's own is adopted anywhere in the story, there is no shadow of doubt that she is mentally sick, and seriously so. Beauvoir herself has referred to Murielle's "distortion of reality" and claimed that she can scarcely envisage any future for her except madness or suicide.[7] And technical concepts seem far more appropriate here than is usually the case with characters in fiction: Beauvoir talks of "paraphrenia,"[8] for instance, and it is almost impossible to describe Murielle without using the term "paranoia." Indeed, irrespective of any comment by the author, Murielle's obsessions are plain for any reader to see: she not only has a persecution complex, but is also (despite her denials) preoccupied with sex in the most unhealthy way, as well as with the theme of purity and filth. It is also apparent that most or all of those around her consider her deranged, which is not in the least surprising in view of the type of conduct she engages in. Furthermore, her mental disturbance manifests itself in both real physical symptoms and an excessive concern with her own state of health; and we know that when she had to visit the doctor about serious loss of weight after her daughter's suicide, her illness was described as "psychosomatic" (113).

Yet as far as we can tell, the nearest that Murielle has come to receiving psychiatric help is in a clinic following this psychosomatic disorder. In "Monologue," that is, Beauvoir goes still further than she does in "The Woman Destroyed" in dropping her earlier emphasis on psychiatric treatment as such and stressing the family origins, or at least the family context, of mental illness. According to Murielle's account of her childhood, whilst her father loved and cherished her, her mother much preferred and favoured her brother, Nanard, thereby ruining Murielle's upbringing and her whole life. The evidence of Murielle's intense hatred of her mother is quite plain in the text and if the mother is guilty of only a small proportion of the misdeeds that Murielle charges her with, then it is certainly not without foundation. The difficulty is, of course, that it is impossible to know how much objective "truth" we must take to lie behind

Murielle's version of the past. But in certain respects the question is an unimportant one, since the link *in Murielle's mind* between her present parlous state and her early family life is a vital one. As R.D. Laing has pointed out, real patterns of relationship within the family have to be "internalized" by each member and this can bring into being a "family as a fantasy structure" which is at least as influential as the objective situation.[9] The most interesting feature of "Monologue" for present purposes is the sensitivity that Beauvoir shows to considerations of just this kind and the great skill with which she enables, or even forces, the reader to enter into Murielle's fantasy world. Moreover, the character's own level of awareness of the forces at work and of what we saw Lucienne describe as "the psychoanalytical situation as it exists without the parents' knowledge" adds yet another dimension to the complex picture and to the fascination of the story. Murielle claims (though doubtless with distorting hindsight) that although her own jealousy of her brother was normal ("all the books say so"), she had the exceptional merit of being prepared to acknowledge it (90). And although she perverts them for her own ends, she displays certain other items of psychoanalytical knowledge in referring to her own daughter ("She was at the age when young girls detest their mother. They call it ambivalence, but it is hatred"; 94), and in insisting that the children of broken marriages develop complexes (115). In short, adopting Murielle's own voice, the author in various detailed and subtle ways makes us see her character in psychiatric terms, yet offers no positive suggestion at all that any form of psychotherapy might help her. In its own manner, "Monologue" again reveals at one and the same time Beauvoir's dependence upon, and reservations about, the general discipline of psychiatry.

But it is, in fact, in *Les Belles Images*, published the year before, that we see most distinctly that whilst Beauvoir's indebtedness to psychoanalytical theory had undoubtedly increased by the mid-sixties, her doubts about psychiatric practice were at least as strong as in *The Mandarins*. Like Murielle, Laurence, the central figure and "narrator" of the story, provides more than enough material for a complex psychiatric case-study. Piecing together fragmentary comments, we learn not only that she experienced some kind of severe disturbance at the age of eleven, but also that there is a certain cyclical pattern to her depressions and that she underwent a crisis five years before the events of the book take place, as well as a near-crisis only three years before. More than this, as we watch Laurence in the story she is having serious difficulties in relating to those around her, feeling alienated from everything and everyone except her children and being unable to experience the emotions that she believes she ought to. Events build up to a new major crisis — this time concerning her elder daughter, Catherine — which constitutes the climax of the book. This particular crisis, like the earlier ones, is portrayed as relating in certain ways to the state of modern Western society. (Laurence believes that just as there were "reasons" for being disturbed in 1945, so there are in 1965, in abundance; she is therefore much more sympathetic to her daughter's anxieties about the world than are her husband and parents.) In this respect *Les Belles Images* takes up and develops the theme already broached in connection with the different historical and political circumstances described in *The Mandarins*, that mental illness and its treatment are intimately bound up with the social context in which they are set: if society itself is "sick," how can mental health consist in successfully adapting to it? But Laurence's main preoccupations in the story and the extremes to which she is driven by them are shown, above all, as stemming once more from her own upbringing, from the "psychoanalytical situation as it exists without the parents' knowledge."

While our situation as readers of *Les Belles Images* is basically similar to that in "Monologue" — we have only Laurence's views to base our judgements upon — here we do in fact see her with both her father and mother and, most important of all, we watch her eventually lose faith in her apparently crucial relationship with her father. Laurence is one of a surprisingly high number of characters in Beauvoir's later fiction who are said or seen to have an unresolved Oedipus complex. It is hinted in the story that this is at the root of any difficulties in her relations with her husband and other men (22; 44), but in any case her breakdown at the end of the book comes after a trip to Greece with her father (they actually visit the crossroads where Oedipus is said to have killed Laius), when Laurence fails to make the kind of spiritual contact with him that she desires. More specifically, her final crisis (which like those of Murielle and Monique expresses itself in severe physical symptoms, notably anorexia and vomiting) is precipitated by the surprise announcement that her father and mother are to begin living together again after a lengthy separation and Laurence's consequent acknowledgement that she has become *disillusioned* with her father (179). Equally important to the story is the fact that in her attitude towards the particular issue that provides the point of focus for the conflict at the end of the book — how Laurence's daughter Catherine should be handled — Laurence is reacting strongly against the way in which she herself was brought up by her dominant mother. Like Murielle, she claims with regret that although she was closer to her father, it was her mother who "formed" her (33), and she is quite determined by the end that Catherine shall not be forced to toe the line in the way that she was (180–1).

What is particularly intriguing about the ending of *Les Belles Images*, however, is that the particular form taken by Laurence's reaction against a childhood that we are encouraged to see in psychoanalytical terms directly brings into the picture the other main strand of Beauvoir's views on psychiatry, that is her reservations about certain aspects of psychiatric *treatment*. Laurence, despite her claim at one point that she does not know what to think about psychoanalysis (99), is shown as having firm opinions about psychiatry in general. She is instantly opposed to her husband's suggestion that Catherine be taken to see a "psychologist" and, although we probably sense that there is some truth in his retort that "parents are immediately jealous of psychologists who deal with their children" (Laurence later admits as much; 171), her rational justification of her distrust is one already familiar to us from *The Mandarins*: " 'Isn't as it should be': what does that mean? In my opinion, things aren't altogether 'as they should be' with the people you consider normal" (131–2). Like Monique, however, she eventually gives way and allows Catherine to begin going to a psychiatrist, Mme Frossard, before she goes off to Greece with her father. But even during that trip Laurence expresses doubts about her decision. Again, ideas already present in *The Mandarins*, like that of "mutilation" in psychiatric treatment, are right to the fore: "On the pretext of curing Catherine of the 'sentimentality' that bothered Jean-Charles, they were going to mutilate her" (159). When Laurence returns from Greece she at first appears willing to accept Mme Frossard's analysis and the advice that Catherine needs to be gently separated from her best friend, Brigitte (171). Yet she soon begins to resist and in the end, to her husband's great surprise, makes an issue of the matter, insisting that Catherine shall not be "mutilated," shall not be deprived of the friend that she, Laurence, never had, and shall stop seeing the psychiatrist (181).

It might be argued that Laurence's attitude towards psychiatry at the end of *Les Belles Images* is, like Anne's at the end of *The Mandarins*, something of a special case, in that she is in a very singular, disturbed state of mind and that her central preoccupation with the welfare of her daughter has little to do with psychiatry as such. But it is important to recognize that Laurence's resistance to psychotherapy is not confined to the case of Catherine or to the end of the novel. If we study her comments on her own past problems we learn that she is really rather proud of having tackled her difficulties without professional aid: "Naturally, her depression had deeper causes, but she did not need to be psychoanalysed to come out of it; she took a job that interested her; she recovered" (43). This does not, of course, prevent us from having doubts whether she is a good advertisement for the brand of self-help that she is implicitly advocating, even though her commendable stand at the end seems to be the result of a deliberate process of self-analysis ("I have drawn the curtains and, lying down with my eyes closed, I shall go over the trip again, image by image, word by word"; 153). More important here, however, is the point that, like Murielle, Laurence is portrayed as having assimilated certain Freudian insights, so that anything that she manages to do for herself is undoubtedly already dependent upon psychoanalytical theory and method: "I am aware of the real reasons behind my crisis and I have put them behind me: I brought out into the open the conflict between my feelings for Jean-Charles and those for my father and it no longer tears me apart" (44). Yet altogether much of her thinking about herself takes psychoanalytical concepts like the Oedipus complex as a starting-point, something — presumably her distrust of how psychiatrists actually treat their patients — makes her oddly wary of accepting the full implications of the type of explanation involved: "I am simply jealous. An unresolved Oedipus complex, with my mother remaining my rival. Electra, Agammemnon: is that why I found Mycenae so moving? No. No. Nonsense. Mycenae was beautiful; it was its beauty that moved me . . . I am jealous, but above all, above all . . ." (179). In other words, through the hesitations and contradictions of her heroine, Beauvoir can once more be seen to adopt in *Les Belles Images* the ambiguous, uneasy stance towards psychiatry that we have detected in other stories. She invokes theories of mental illness with varying degrees of conviction, but resists, for the most part, the notion that psychiatric treatment as it is profession- ally conceived is a desirable or appropriate procedure for dealing with it.

Although examination of further detailed evidence from the stories considered would produce nothing to modify this general account,[10] we do, of course, need to bear in mind the existence of Beauvoir's many essays and autobiographical works. Scrutiny of these would undoubtedly refine our understanding of her attitude towards psychoanalytical theory,[11] but it would not be likely to add to our knowledge of her reservations about psychotherapeutic practices, since she has said little about the latter in her non-fictional writings. Indeed, one of the tangible advantages of specifi- cally studying the fictional expressions of Beauvoir's views is that it brings out the importance of this distinction and enables us to see the whole matter in a broader perspective.

When Sartre describes himself as a "critical fellow-traveller" to psychoanalysis, he uses a description that fits Beauvoir just as well as himself, and it is in the very ambivalence implied that the importance of their continuing dialogue with Freudian theory resides. The interest of Sartre's attempt to assimilate psychoanalysis into his own philosophy at the different stages of his career has long been apparent,[12] but those of Beauvoir's fictional works written when Sartre was producing no novels can now be seen to give the topic an additional density or resonance at two levels. Both in the author's own process of creating her characters and in the struggles of particular individuals in the stories to understand them- selves and those around them, we see the vacillations and unease that result from using certain psychoanalytical concepts and methods without a wholehearted belief in, or commitment to them. And, perhaps above all, we see very closely linked with this a distrust of therapeutic practices as employed by professional psychiatrists which varies in strength and even in nature but never quite disappears. In all of these respects Beauvoir's stance in her fiction is very much in line with (and may well, via Laing and others, have actually *influenced*) recent attitudes towards psychiatry. Her stories themselves never go beyond a broad identification of psychiatry with psychoanalysis proper, but it is quite clear from them that her sympathies lie with modern attempts to break wholly new ground in both the theory and practice of psychiatry. In the latest volume of her autobiography Simone de Beauvoir reveals that she has read with great attention the works of Szasz, Cooper, Laing and others:[13] it is interesting to speculate what fictional embodiments of "anti-psychiatry" this may yet produce from her pen.

Notes

1. "Sartre and Psychoanalysis: A Current View. A review of *Between Existentialism and Marxism*," *Literature and Psychology* XXVII, No. 3, 1977, pp. 122–8.

2. J.-B. Pontalis: "reply to Sartre" in *Between Existentialism and Marxism* (transl. J. Matthews), NLB, 1974.

3. *Les Mandarins*, Gallimard, 1954 (*The Mandarins*, transl. L. M. Friedman, World Publishing, Cleveland and New York, 1955).
Les Belles Images, Gallimard, 1966 (*Les Belles Images*, transl. P. O'Brian, G. P. Putnam's, 1968).
La Femme rompue, Gallimard, 1967 (*The Woman Destroyed*, transl. P. O'Brian, G. P. Putnam's, 1969).
Page-references in the body of the article are to the later and easily available Gallimard "Folio" editions of these works (*Les Mandarins* is in two volumes); the translations of quotations are all my own.

4. On the theme of self-deception in all three of the stories of *The Woman Destroyed*, see my "Simone de Beauvoir's *La Femme rompue*: Studies in Self-Deception," *Essays in French Literature*, No. 13 (Nov. 1976), pp. 77–97.

5. At one point Monique explicitly refers to "the old ideal that my father had embodied and which is still alive in me" (138). Cf. p. 195 and p. 211.

6. *Tout compte fait (All Said and Done)*, Gallimard, 1972, p. 163.

7. *Tout compte fait*, p. 143.

8. *Tout compte fait*, p. 142.

9. R. D. Laing: *The Politics of the Family*, CBC Publications, Canada, 1969.

10. For example, whilst the numerous passing references to psychoanalysis in conversations in Beauvoir's fiction are almost invariably scornful, characters' reflections on themselves and their relations with others are, as we have seen, not infrequently couched in psychoanalytical terms. It would certainly be interesting to make a systematic examination of the extent of Beauvoir's debt to Freud in this respect.

11. One major source here would obviously be the second chapter of *The Second Sex* ("The Psychoanalytical Point of View"), where she argues that the psychoanalytic view of women is inadequate because of its failure to take account of historical and social factors.

12. As early as 1943 (in Part IV, Ch. 2 of *Being and Nothingness*) Sartre was explaining the principles of *existential* psychoanalysis, and his essays, *Baudelaire* and *Saint Genet, Actor and Martyr*, as well as the autobiographical *Words*, all constitute applications of that theory.
Later he was to argue in Ch. 2 of *Search for a Method* (the separately published introduction to *Critique de la raison dialectique*, 1960) that psychoanalysis has a legitimate place as a "privileged mediation" within Marxism. His massive *Flaubert* is an illustration of the implications of that view.

13. *Tout compte fait*, p. 163.

Operative Philosophy: Simone de Beauvoir and Existentialism

Michèle Le Doeuff*

I have been rereading the Introduction to *The Second Sex*. Incisive, forceful and wonderfully clear, such a text scarcely calls for the pretensions of an exegesis. "To be read, and reread" would seem to be the only possible commentary. Instead what I would like to do is to explicate certain impressions prompted by reading it, and first of all therefore simply to give voice to these impressions, the signs no doubt of a mute reworking of the text by a reading which progressively rewrites it. I have sought to elucidate my own, contradictory responses to Beauvoir's discourse—and this wish has embarked me on a series of considerations which are more complicated than I might have liked.

For a feminist reader, that is to say for an *interested* reading by one principally concerned to find elements of reflection which might underpin a possible practice, this book has today the appearance of a curious mixture. And thus I feel tempted to try and separate out the elements in it which I evaluate now as "positive." Very empirically, it seems to me that one finds in this work a host of observations, descriptions and analyses which I for my part can only endorse. When Simone de Beauvoir describes the repetitive nature of housework, when she analyses the censorious treatment of aggressiveness in little girls, when she sets out Stekel's notions on frigidity, when she examines the prevailing conception of women's wages as *salaire d'appoint* supplementing the husband's earnings, to my mind she provides essential elements of a *detailed* and *precise* consciousness of women's oppression. And it is certainly this detailed quality of the book that gives it its greatest utility, since oppression always also exists at points where it is least expected and where there is the danger that it will not even be noticed.

And yet, along with these highly valuable analyses of the feminine condition, one also finds in *The Second Sex* a whole conceptual apparatus which is now a trifle obsolete. What is one to make of this, for instance: "Every individual preoccupied with justifying his existence experiences this existence as an indefinite need for self-transcendence. Now what marks the specificity of woman's situation is that, while being, like every human being, an autonomous freedom, she discovers and chooses herself in a world where men force her to assume herself as the Other: they claim to fix her as an object and to vow her to immanence, since her transcendence is itself to be perpetually transcended by an other, essential and sovereign consciousness." Indeed. . . ! Is it really necessary to have recourse to such concepts as these in order to reveal the nature of women's

*Reprinted from *Ideology and Consciousness*, no. 6 (Autumn 1979):47–57. Translated from the French by Colin Gordon. Originally published in *Magazine Littéraire*, no. 145 (February 1979):18–21. © 1979 by *Magazine Littéraire*. Reprinted by permission.

oppression? Supposing one were unwilling to concede any sense to these categories? Isn't it taking a strategic risk to tie the study of oppression to considerations of this order?

The senescence of a philosophy fashionable in 1949 and out of favour today, the confused perception of the dangers involved in utilising such a perspective — for me these are two reasons for the temptation to read this feminist *Summa* in a selective manner, skipping the passages excessively marked by this philosophy. But it is more instructive if one confronts the malaise directly and tries to articulate these two sides of Beauvoir's work, as a means towards posing a question which is of some moment for us (1): in what respect, if any, is the choice of this or that philosophical reference-point a decisive factor in feminist studies? Over the last few years we have been witnessing a certain philosophist inflation in the domain of theoretical productions. Thus, Luce Irigaray's books insist on the idea that, since it is philosophical discourse that lays down the law for all other discourses, the discourse of philosophy is the one that has first of all to be overthrown and disrupted. At a stroke, the main enemy comes to be idealist logic and the metaphysical *logos*. Simone de Beauvoir's book leaves me with the contrary impression, since, within a problematic as metaphysical as any, she is still able to reach conclusions about which the least one can say is that they have dynamised women's movements in Europe and America over the last thirty years.

My object here will be to show how the ethic of authenticity functions as a pertinent theoretical lever, an operative viewpoint for exposing the character of women's oppression. Consequently one cannot, as I confess I am in the habit of doing, dissociate the philosophical substratum of Simone de Beauvoir's work from that more empirical dimension which I see as more relevant today than the conceptual grid via which this feminist investigation is executed. But even if they cannot be divorced, there is none the less no pre-established harmony between this philosophical position and the results to which it leads in *The Second Sex*. As I shall show, *Being and Nothingness*, where the same problematic of authenticity leads to entirely opposite consequences, offers proof of this. In a word, Beauvoir's text cannot be totalised except dialectically.

Let us first give a summary characterisation of the conceptual grid employed by Simone de Beauvoir. It is a dualist one; the notions function in pairs: immanence/transcendence, in-itself/for-itself, authentic/inauthentic, responsibility/bad faith, subject-project/object. It is an ethical ontology: the individual *is* subject, and when he affirms himself as such he assumes his freedom and transcendence and is in a state of authenticity. But he may also feel the "temptation to flee his freedom and constitute himself as a thing," thus evading "the anguish of existence authentically assumed." Thereupon the for-itself is degraded into an in-itself and freedom into facticity, in short there is bad faith. Lastly, this is a problematic of consciousness: "the subject only posits itself by opposing itself. It claims to affirm itself as essential and to constitute the other as the inessential."

On this basis the fundamental thesis of the book comes to be that every woman is from the start constituted as inessential: dominated, she has been obliged to submit herself to this alien point of view on her. Hence the description of an oppression which derives from a relation of force and yet is capable of producing the same effect as moral error: "Each time that transcendence collapses back into immanence, there is the degradation of existence into an "in-itself." . . . This collapse is a moral fault if it is consented to by the subject. If it is inflicted on the subject . . . it is an oppression." The analogy between error and oppression seems to have the effect of dramatising oppression: what is grasped here as oppression is what would under other circumstances be moral error. The reference to ethics remains in either case central.

The ethic in question is not hard to identify since Beauvoir herself says that her point of view is that of existentialist morality. Without laying any but the lightest stress on it, one may recall the fact that *The Second Sex* is also a labour of love and that Beauvoir brings as one of her morganatic wedding-presents a singular confirmation of the validity of the Sartrian philosophy — your thought makes it possible to think the feminine condition, your philosophy sets me on the path of my emancipation, your truth will make me free.

No doubt at the relational level this gesture is a matter of course; one has here a stereotype of philosophical liaisons. But it is less of a matter of course from a theoretical point of view. To confirm this it is enough to single out two aspects of Sartrianism as of 1943 (2): no oppression can be thematised as such in the existentialist system, women's oppression no more than any other; at the same time, the terrifying relation of men with women's bodies expressed in this system grounds an ontological-carnal hierarchy of "the masculine" and "the feminine." Hence Beauvoir's utilisation of this viewpoint emerges as a tour de force deserving of recognition.

THE BAD FAITH OF THE OPPRESSED

The ethic of authenticity denies the efficacy of social or historical determinations in favour of a classical form of voluntarism. "Constraint can have no possible hold on a freedom." Bad faith consists in the refusal to recognise oneself as a free subject and the pretence of being determined by external circumstances. Such a position carries a certain number of piquant consequences.

1. "It is senseless to dream of complaining, since nothing alien to us has decided for us what we feel, what we live, what we are. . . . Isn't it myself who decides the coefficient of the adversity of things?" "Everything that happens to us may be considered as good fortune," that is, as a means of realising that being which is in question in our being.

2. Revolutionaries are materialistic, "serious" and of bad faith, since they evaluate the situation of man on the basis of a world to which they attribute more reality than to themselves. The principal figure of this bad faith is Marx, to whom Sartre opposes a Kierkegaard who for his part has properly grasped how play posits freedom and brings escape from *natura naturata*.

3. Every feeling of inferiority derives from a free choice. "It is up to us to choose ourselves as great or noble or as base and humiliated." Certainly it is not through free volition that one chooses to be or not to be a Michelangelo. But to choose inferiority is to choose an order of work, a domain of activity in which I will be the lowest. The inferiority Sartre is thinking of is that of the mediocre artist who has chosen to manifest himself in art *because* in it he is inferior, whereas in some other domain he would without difficulty have been able to "equal the norm": if I choose to be a modest artisan because in that domain my talents permit me to "equal the norm," this is not by a masochist choice of inferiority, but as a simple example of the choice of finitude (3). Inferiority is not thought in terms of the social hierarchy of tasks but in terms of the psychological perversion of the model of successful socio-professional career-choice — a model presupposing congenital aptitudes.

4. Frigid women suffer from pathological bad faith. They take pleasure in denying their pleasure. The proof is that their husbands (!) interrogated by the psychoanalyst (4) reveal that their wives have betrayed objective signs of pleasure. "And these are the signs which the woman, when questioned, insists on fiercely denying." It is they who have decided to be frigid, but they dissimulate the deliberate character of their attitude under the guise of facticity by declaring: "I am frigid," not "I have decided to mask my pleasure."

If the doctrine of authenticity leads to such a miscomprehension of every form of constraint, its having been used to describe the oppression of women must already seem paradoxical. But the most picturesque part is yet to come.

KNOWLEDGE-AS-RAPE AND ENVENOMED POSSESSIONS

Sexual metaphors (5) abound in the passage where Sartre explains in what sense knowledge is appropriation. "To see is to deflower." "Knowledge is at once a penetration and a superficial caress." The description of the appropriative delight (jouissance) in knowledge tends towards images which are indeed far from innocent: "the knower is the hunter who takes a blank nudity by surprise and violates it with his gaze." The reference, irritating enough in itself, to the "sleek, blank, polished, womanly body" on which possession leaves no traces, manifests a set of fantasies which even in 1943 had no claim to be taken seriously as epistemology, since by that date Bachelard's studies had demonstrated that in the course of every knowledge-process reason is transformed and must adapt itself to a particular form of rationality constructed by the conditions of a specific knowledge. This antiquated conception of "Knowledge," in which a mind obstinately endeavours to appropriate the object, can have no further basis except in a system of fantasies. It forms, moreover, one wing of a diptych whose pendant is located at the very end of the book, which closes with some considerations on the slimy and holes. The slimy reveals the possibility of an "envenomed possession," "there is the possibility that the in-itself may absorb the for-itself . . . the slimy is the revenge of the in-itself." Here again the sexual metaphors abound: the revenge is a "sickly-sweet feminine" one. Like "the honey which slides off my spoon on to the honey contained in the jar" this viscosity is a "collapse" "comparable to the flattening out of the overripe breasts of a woman lying on her back"; "it sucks at me. . . . It is a soft, yielding action, a moist and feminine sucking. . . . In one sense it is like the supreme docility of the possessed, the fidelity of a dog who *gives himself* even when one does not want him any longer, and in another sense there is underneath this docility a surreptitious appropriation of the possessor by the possessed," etc. Next the nightmare slides into the figure of the hole, of which the female sex is only a particular case. The hole "is originally presented as a nothingness to be filled with my own flesh"; "to plug up a hole means originally to make a sacrifice of my body in order that the plenitude of being may exist." "A good part of our life is passed in plugging up holes, in realising and symbolically establishing a plenitude." This "tendency to fill" is "one of the most fundamental tendencies of human reality." "It is only from this standpoint that we can pass on to sexuality. The obscenity of the feminine sex is that of everything which gapes open. . . . In herself woman appeals to a strange flesh which is to transform her into a fullness of being by penetration and dissolution . . . the experience of the hole envelops the ontological presentiment of sexual experience in general; it is with his flesh that the child stops up the hole."

Let us note that here, as usual, it is only masculine adult sexual experience that is in continuity with the child's "ontological presentiment of sexual experience in general." The female child will no doubt have to trade in her ontological presentiment and abandon the 'fundamental human tendency' which is to be fulfilled, in order to become instead that which is to be filled and identify herself with the hollowed, sucking in-itself. This phenomenology founds an ontological hierarchy, on the basis of which, for all eternity, woman can be posited as the in-itself and man as the for-itself. The masculine/feminine roles deduced from this phenomenology place woman outside the Subject. What place within the existentialist system are these pronouncements to be accorded? For my part I believe that they are more than a simple projection of the personal anguishes of Monsieur Sartre and that, far from being an accidental accretion, they form an indispensable part of the metaphysic of authenticity.

It was indeed necessary that, by some means or other, the for-itself should "find itself compromised" in such a way that "man-in-the-world" can succeed in realising only "a missing God." The conclusion of the book revolves around considerations on the perpetual failure of integration of the in-itself by the for-itself, "an ideal which one can term God." It is necessary for a counter-figure to undo the labour of integration, to regularly compromise the for-itself in such a fashion as to ensure the interminable character of the conquests pro-posed itself by the for-itself, and hence to guarantee that conservation of the very identity of the for-itself which is an absolute condition for the *reiteration* of the system.

Thus sexist reveries appear in the text in a contradictory manner: in the theory of knowledge, which marks the weak point in Sartre's megalomaniac ravings (6), as a means of re-assurance where it was, for historical reasons, somewhat shaky. And also, in conclusion, to endow that megalomania with a necessary weakness, an encounter with death, with woman as the "sugared death of the for-itself," which permits everything to begin over again — since a metaphysical system can proceed only through the reiteration of its beginning. Sexism takes charge of the inadmissable, unthinkable contention which is nevertheless necessary for the system to be able to stand up.

Even if it is not so much then a matter of Monsieur Sartre as of existentialism as such, it was certainly not enough for this theory to pass from a man's to a woman's hands to change from the phallocratic discourse it had hitherto been into the theoretical tool of a feminist investigation. Simone de Beauvoir operates a series of transformations on the existentialist problematic. The chief of these seems to me to be that of transposing this *Weltanschauung* from the status of *system* (necessarily returning back on itself) to that of a *point of view* oriented to a theoretical intent by being trained on *a* determinate and partial field of experience. Thus the necessity for the counter-figure of the sugared death of the for-itself comes here to be eliminated.

Moreover . . . there is this little sentence in the Introduction: "woman does not assert her demands as a subject because she lacks the concrete means." In Sartrianism it is above all a question of denying the effect of exteriority as an obstacle, constraint, adversity or alienating cause. Beauvoir here poses a displaced problem: it is not enough not to be persecuted by exteriority, it is also necessary for exteriority to furnish the means for one's self-affirmation as a subject. If she insists so heavily in the course of the book on feminine narcissism, this is directly in line with this initial observation. Woman is, first and foremost, deprived of exteriority; she cannot be "conquering," as the problematic of the for-itself demands. Being deprived, for example, of rights, what activity could she propose herself in the social world? Even her clothes "were primitively destined to vow her to impotence."

This situation itself still remains to be explained. This requirement, which assumes that the feminine condition is not a matter of course, could be posed by Simone de Beauvoir in its fully radical form only thanks to the ethic of authenticity which enabled her to sufficiently distance herself from the lot of women to be able to describe it as a shocking contingency, a strangeness, something non-natural to be transformed as rapidly as possible.

The Subject defined by its transcendence is neither a being nor a Nature. The existentialist ethic has the effect of expelling from the sphere of the person every possible determination, rejecting them on to the exterior plane of the situation that is to be transcended. In principle there can be no valid existentialist anthropology or psychology. Or rather, existentialist morality demands a non-psychology, a nihilation of every anthropological determinedness. For a break passes between the subject devoid of all density (a mere mathematical point, the site of a freedom and the origin of the vector of the "project," in the face of which all is alien), and everything else, which is thing, "in-itself," immanence, etc. This perspective enables Beauvoir to escape essentialism. Neither an eternal feminine nor a Dark soul—no human nature, diversified or otherwise.

Thus whatever is observed is only result: "one is not born a woman, one becomes a woman." Everything is contingent in the face of freedom: there is no longer any question of justifying such and such a state of things by reference to any nature or necessity whatever, but instead it is in a matter of setting-before-oneself every determination, referring it to an exterior situation ruled by the culturally arbitrary, and demonstrating its strangeness and its possibilities of variation: there is no destiny, everything can hence lend itself to an objectivising description—a description via which the subject (writer or reader) withdraws from implication in, and deprives of subjective sanction, that which is no more than a sign or an institution. Undoubtedly the liberating value of the book comes from this movement.

If the existentialist ethic demands a non-psychology, it thereby at the same time prohibits posing the question of happiness. The only value is "the freedom which must invent its ends unaided." Now the notion of happiness is one of the barriers to any investigation of domination and subjection. One can always declare a people whom one subjects to be happy. Moreover, the problematic of happiness inevitably reintroduces the idea of psychological tendencies (declared as being fulfilled by such and such a situation); it immediately reinstates the notion of a specified nature, a determinate "character," of assignable needs. Beauvoir rightly mistrusts the easy recourse to declaring happy a situation which one oneself imposes. But the radical quality of her rejection is underpinned, I think, by the neo-Kantianism of her ethic: it would be a lapse into the pathological determination of the will to pose the problem of choice on the terrain of pleasures and pains.

There remains the essential point. This world has always belonged to men. Even if women are—potentially at least—subjects, they do not contest the enfeoffment that men have imposed on them. What is the origin of such a situation? In the manner that Beauvoir treats this problem, it seems indeed as though the oppression of women is a scandal so unthinkable that she cannot arrive at assigning it to any origin or sufficient cause. Take the procedure of the first Part of the book: she examines in succession three possible types of explanation—and rejects them all. Perhaps some readers will recall Rousseau's procedure in the *Social Contract*. Whence comes the social order that sets man in chains? From nature? No. From the right of the stronger? The very phrase is a nonsense. By right of war? *Petitio principi!* Similarly, Simone de Beauvoir eliminates in turn biology (insufficient to found a hierarchy of the sexes), psychoanalysis ("the phallus assumes the value it does because it symbolises a sovereignty realised in other domains": *petitio principi*, then), historical materialism (manifest inadequacy); and, as each of these explanations proves inadequate, oppression comes to appear increasingly groundless and bizarre. In the end the text leaves us in the lurch. Because the "key to the mystery" (7) supplied in Part II is worth no more and no less than the explanations previously rejected. Moreover, Beauvoir founds nothing on this foundation, she does not put it to any use as the starting point for a deduction or a construction: ultimately, in order to retrace the history of the feminine condition she borrows much more from Engels than from this Hegelian "key."

One ends up then with the image of an oppression without a fundamental cause. Now this void has a very powerful, very dialectical effect. Everything happens as though, because this oppression is founded on nothing, it has consequently been necessary to set in place a host of apparatuses and institutional props to create and sustain it; lacking any basis on the side of the involuntary (nature, economy, the unconscious), the phallic order must secure itself against every circumstance with a forest of props—from the upbringing of little girls to the repressive legislation of "birth control," and from codes of dress to exclusion from politics. Certainly, I am interpreting here and describing above all an effect which the book has for me. But I would be prepared to wager that Simone de Beauvoir herself doesn't believe in her own "key," and this is what gives rise to her minute attentiveness to the polymorphous network of limitations imposed on women: daily life is all the more narrowly policed because the subjection of women has at each moment to be reinvented.

This depiction of an oppression ultimately without a cause is, in part, a corollary of the existentialist maxim already cited: "Constraint can have no possible hold on a freedom"; it was surely not any original relation of forces that enabled men to impose on women to the extent of making them renounce affirming themselves as Subjects. A truism, indeed: founding itself on the negation of determinism, the existentialist perspective has no means for thinking a causality. But in strict orthodoxy, it would then have been necessary to conclude that this oppression does not exist — unless in the bad faith of certain women, spiritual sisters of the revolutionaries sharing with them the error diagnosed by Sartre as "seriousness." Simone de Beauvoir does not draw this conclusion, and I see in this the proof of the primacy of involvement in the real over the reference-point in philosophy. Once applied to a field of conflicts, by one who is engaged in this field and who posits practical aims in relation to it, every philosophy undergoes remarkable modifications. In *The Second Sex* one finds none of the Sartrian incapacity to thematise oppression, apart from the bankruptcy of the speculations of the origins of that oppression. And at bottom what do these speculations (which are in any case always liable to be merely mythical) matter to us here when the very impossibility of accounting for the enfeoffment of women serves only the better to expose the aberrant character of this subjection?

For against the backcloth of the Hegelian-Sartrian problematic (every consciousness pursues the death of the Other, which opposes to it a reciprocal hostility), masculine/feminine relations appear as an incomprehensible exception. The philosophical referential which Beauvoir holds to be absolutely true is the one least adequate of all to explain the phenomenon and, for this very reason, the most suitable for its denunciation.

Should one then draw the conclusion of indifferentism (small matter whether you appeal to one philosophical position or another, once your practical aspirations are clearly defined; these aspirations will suffice to remodel your initial perspective), or that of the logic of "worse is better" — the inaptitude of such and such a philosophy for the requirements of a theory of female oppression serving as a kind of springboard for debanalising that oppression? Either way would be to close the issue a little too rapidly.

HUMANISM AS AN EPISTEMOLOGICAL OBSTACLE

Simone de Beauvoir made existentialism work "beyond its means" because she got more out of it than might have been expected. The fact remains that the choice of this referential was not without its drawbacks and that one must reflect on the type of miscomprehension which, in spite of everything, the limitations of this theoretical instrument brought about.

First of all one can see the *liberal* nature of Beauvoir's critique: "Woman has never been given her chance in any domain." This question of opportunities, announced in the introduction and reiterated right through the book, is readily identified: it is a matter, in a quite strict sense, of the problematic of liberalism which demanded that the distribution of roles should not be pre-established by law (written or unwritten), since every artificial regulation of the destiny of individuals impedes the free play of competition; and we know that thanks to this free play of competition, individuals tend to occupy the social place which corresponds to their capacities. Simone de Beauvoir pays a number of tributes to John Stuart Mill, and indeed the political tenor of her discourse is very close to that of *The Subjection of Women*. Here is one stumbling-block—politically this time—for me. Here is another: "On the whole, we have won out." Who is "we"? And when is this supposed to have happened, what is the historic mutation that has been brought about? I do not seek to denounce this optimism as an illusion but to mark it as the symptom of a gap in the analysis, a historical and sociological gap: this "we" is quickly replaced by "many among us"; but which ones? And are there really any? Certain of us may indeed have the impression of "personally escaping," as they say, from such and such an aspect of alienation. But these partial liberations are scarcely effective—even at the level of the individuals who appear to benefit from them. The free disposal of one's salary, for instance, does not *ipso facto* cause the attitude of submission towards parents or husband to crumble, even if it affords the means for doing so. Correlatively, we are beginning today to recognise that—once again, only as an example—the fact that a high percentage of women stay "in the home" is not without its effects on those who do not. The class/sex of women is not as dispersed as it seems, and there is a globality or a globalisation which needs to be thought: the common lot falls to each woman via a causality which passes through global society.

A classic schema, then: existentialism, focussed on the question of the individual, cannot get to posing all the problems, even on the individual level. In *The Second Sex*, everything happens as though, from the moment a minute gap is opened in the cage, it becomes the duty of the woman who benefits from it to utilise it to the maximum extent in order to posit herself as a subject condemned to be free. Every time Beauvoir speaks of a woman who has had some means of affirming herself, of creating, and has not been fully capable of exploiting her opportunity, down at once comes the moral reprobation, and such themes as those of complaisance, auto-complaisance, narcissism and the easy way out (etc.) are invoked. The analogy drawn between oppression and moral error has a boomerang effect. It supports a miscomprehension of the same type as that of the teachers in the universal, free, lay schools of yesteryear who erected failure in school into a moral infraction, unconscious of the socio-cultural mechanisms which produced that failure.

In order to think these problems one needs another problematic than that of the subject, and another perspective than that of morality. It is permissible moreover to think that this other philosophy begins to show its traces in Simone de Beauvoir's more localised interventions over the past few years.

Notes

1. This study was undertaken a year ago at the request of a research group on women and philosophy at the École Normale Supérieure de Fontenay-aux-Roses.

2. It should be made clear that *Being and Nothingness* is the only Sartrian text referred to here. When I speak of the existentialist system, this signifies only Sartre's systematic version of 1943.

3. And so: why not opt to become a "modest housewife, gifted for motherhood to an average extent"?

4. This is based on Stekel. Did Sartre and Simone de Beauvoir read the same book?

5. Margery Collins and Christine Pierce, in their contribution to the collective volume *Women and Philosophy: Towards a Theory of Liberation* (ed. Carol C. Gould and Marx W. Wartofsky, 1976), point out that it is questionable whether one should *immediately* regard as sexist the Sartrian distinction between the in-itself and the for-itself. Some commentators have indeed contended that the duality between a "being-in-itself" which has the massive passivity of a nature, and a "being-for-itself" defined through its project and its freedom, implicitly evokes the masculine/feminine opposition. This kind of interpretation, they argue, presupposes an interpreter already convinced that "passivity" implies "femininity," etc., which is as much as to say that the interpretation is itself sexist. I accept the point of view of Margery Collins and Christine Pierce, and for this reason I have chosen to study Sartre's *imagery*, in which his sexism is clearly expressed. But of course this imagery is not unrelated to the abstract ontology of the system.

6. Megalomaniac in its effort to repudiate the clutches of exteriority.

7. Women (in the epoch of the primal horde) were excluded from warlike expeditions; and "It is not in giving life but in risking it that man raises himself above the animal; this is why humanity accords superiority not to the sex which gives birth but to the sex which kills."

Women and History   Gerda Lerner*

The modern women's liberation movement has brought the political and economic demands of women into the forefront of social struggle and into general awareness. This has led to attempts at explaining the causes of the millenia of female subordination to men and the reasons for the multitude of discriminatory practices to which women are subject in virtually every known society. Explanations have been generally unsatisfactory. All traditional systems of thought, from natural rights philosophy and egalitarianism to Marxism and Freudianism have been applied. Nothing quite fits. Woman's "oppression" has been explained by comparisons to class and race oppression, thereby making of women a species of "minority." But women are not a minority; they are half of humankind. And the traditional systems of thought, which have been used to explain

*©Gerda Lerner 1979. This article was presented as a paper at the conference "The Second Sex—Thirty Years Later," held in New York City at New York University, Sept. 27–29, 1979. In a revised version, parts of the paper appear in Gerda Lerner, *The Creation of Patriarchy* (New York: Oxford University Press, 1986).

the situation of women, are neither value-free nor universal. They are patriarchal — that is, they assume that "man is the measure of that which is human." They assume that man is the norm, woman the deviant. All theories, even those which address themselves to human inequality as a problem to be resolved, tacitly assume the marginality of women to that which they are explaining. As a result they cannot adequately explain woman's subordination nor provide remedies for it.

General feminist theory has been hampered by the same difficulties. Focusing mostly on the denial to women of "rights" and on discrimination against them, feminist theories have expanded the concept of human rights to include the right to control one's body and to express one's sexuality. Feminist theorists have alerted us to the multiple ways by which the subordination of women is structured into civilization and its institutions, and they have sensitized us to "sexual politics," the ways in which the relations between the sexes reflect and express power relations.[1] But so far, feminist theory has been ahistorical, assuming as a given that, due to their having been oppressed, women have been marginal to history. The most influential exponent of this view has been Simone de Beauvoir, who, in her powerful work, has shown how patriarchal thought has defined woman as "the Other" of man and how patriarchal dominance has institutionalized her subordination.[2] Observing correctly that women have "never constituted a separate caste," she contrasts them, to women's disadvantage, with other historically subject groups, such as Russian peasants, Haitian Negroes, and colonials. "Women's effort," she states flatly,

> has never been anything more than a symbolic agitation. They have gained only what men have been willing to grant; they have taken nothing, they have only received.
>
>   The reason for this is that women lack concrete means for organizing themselves into a unit which can stand face to face with the correlative unit. They have no past, no history, no religion of their own. . . .[3]

This staggering conclusion is repeated elsewhere in the book. See for example:

> Most female heroines are oddities; adventuresses and originals notable less for the importance of their acts than for the singularity of their fates. . . . They are exemplary figures rather than historical agents. . . . Women are on the margin of history. . . .
>
>   It is not the inferiority of women that has caused their historical insignificance; it is rather their historical insignificance that has doomed them to inferiority.[4]

Historians working in Women's History research have been slow to challenge this ahistorical fallacy, although they have disproven it over and over again in their monographic studies.

Simone de Beauvoir correctly analyzed the condition and state of women under patriarchy, *as seen through the eyes of men*. She exposed, with more depth and range than anyone had before her, the process by which culture creates the female into "woman, man's 'Other.' " That is, de Beauvoir peeled away the layers of myth and mystification and enabled us to see the process by which "gender" is created—a cultural construct assigning sex-specific roles to men and women. She also revealed the overwhelming weight of cultural production and product which reinforces this gender assignment in the minds and psyche of both men and women. One may well quarrel with her biological determinism as well as with the negative weight she places on female biological function. She was a pioneer; much of the feminist scholarship refuting such deterministic assumptions was not yet available to her. Her solid contribution was to tear the veil of objectivity from all cultural production and reveal its androcentric core. In view of this feat, her willingness to accept the findings of this man-made, man-centered system of knowledge uncritically and to accept as absolute truths the cultural myths about the past of women is highly significant. It reveals the very process by which the continued subordination of even the most brilliant and emancipated women continues.

My thesis is that it is the relationship of women to history which explains the nature of female subordination, the causes for women's collusion with the process of their own subordination, and the conditions for their opposition to it, that is, the rise of feminist consciousness.

History is not a set of absolute truths, exact data, and eternally valid interpretations. History is not the record of all past events. We must distinguish history—lived past reality—and History as recorded in books, which is the record of past events as selected and interpreted by succeeding generations of historians.[5] History-making, the process by which this culturally constructed History is created, is an ongoing endeavor by which society expresses its values and beliefs. It is through the selection process of History-making that we assign significance to events. If we single out as significant events of the past the battles, coronations, and activities of kings, we assign value to such events in the present. If we single out as significant the activities of ordinary men—farmers, workers, businessmen—we implicitly assign cultural value to their activities in the present. It is in this selection process of History-making that women have been shortchanged. Thus, the marginalization of women of the past, the absence of women from written History, is not a manifestation of the actual experience of women of the past but a manifestation of patriarchal bias in the creation of a cultural construct.

"Men created values, mores, religions; never have women disputed this empire with them,"[6] de Beauvoir observed correctly. She might have added: "Men created History." Women, half of humankind, have always been active and essential in the creation of community, of culture, and of civilization. But History, as recorded and interpreted by historians has been, in fact, the history of the activities of men ordered by male values. We might properly call it "men's History"; women have barely figured in it. The few who did were exceptional women who performed roles usually reserved for men. The vast mass of women of the past has remained anonymous and invisible.

The basic contradiction which underlies the historical experience of women is this: women have always been central to historical process; yet they have been marginal to culturally created History. Women have always been active in building society; yet they were kept from creating the symbol system by which society is ordered and governed. Until the recent past, women have been excluded from creating the meaning systems of society. Women have not named themselves, they have not named gods or shaped them in their image. They have not created systems of thought or ideologies. They have not held power over symbols or over men. It is in this that their subordination is grounded.

Thus, women have participated in civilization building *in their own terms* in a world dominated and defined by men. The way in which women have functioned represents a separate culture *within* the culture women share with men. It is as though men had lived in one culture, women in two; the women's culture remaining largely invisible because it was unrecorded. This duality in women's historical experience is highly significant and uniquely different from the historical experience of other subordinate groups.

What are the universal features of women's situation? Over historical time, women have been subordinate to men economically and politically; they have consistently been educationally deprived; they have been subordinate in those elements of culture any particular society considers valuable and significant. Women have also been hemmed in by taboos and rules which have placed the mark of inferiority upon them and have thereby reinforced their subordination. They have, in short, suffered discrimination and exploitation. In this they resemble other oppressed groups.

What is unique to the subordination of women is that throughout historical time their reproductive function and with it their sexuality have been controlled by individual men or by church and state. What is unique to women is that in all periods of history they have not only been educationally disadvantaged, but they have been systematically and consistently denied the power to name, the power to think abstractly, and, thereby, the power to define and generalize.

Women have led lives suspended between defining bodies, which they did not control and which they have been taught to despise, and untrained minds, which functioned in terms defined and limited by men. It is these deprivations which have most profoundly affected the psychology of women by making them accept and internalize the idea of their own inferiority. Because of them, women have for centuries accepted the myth that they have no history. It is this myth which has made women cooperate in their own subordination and train their children in the values which sustain male dominance.

Women have had a historical experience significantly different from that of men. Women have moved through the stages of history at a different pace and in a mode different from men. For women, all history up to the twentieth century has truly been pre-History.

The subordination of woman antedates civilization. This insight was first enunciated by Simone de Beauvoir:

> Little by little man has acted upon his experience, and in his symbolic representations, as in his practical life, it is the male principle that has triumphed. Spirit has prevailed over Life, transcendence over immanence, technique over magic, and reason over superstition. The devaluation of woman represents a necessary stage in the history of humanity, for it is not upon her positive value but upon man's weakness that her prestige is founded. In woman are incarnated the disturbing mysteries of nature, and man escapes her hold when he frees himself from nature.
>
> Man learns his power. . . . He could achieve his destiny only as he began by dethroning her. From then on, it was to be the male principle of creative force, of light, of intelligence, of order, that he would recognize as sovereign. . . .[7]

> From humanity's beginnings, their biological advantage has enabled the males to affirm their status as sole and sovereign subjects; they have never abdicated this position. . . . The fact that woman is weak and of inferior productive capacity does not explain this exclusion; it is because she did not share his way of working and thinking, because she remained in bondage to life's mysterious processes, that the male did not recognize in her a being like himself. Since he did not accept her, since she seemed in his eyes to have the aspect of the *other*, man could not be otherwise than her oppressor. The male will to power and expansion made of woman's incapacity a curse.[8]

De Beauvoir identifies the "male principle" with creative force, transcendence, order, reason, technique, and physical strength. The "female principle," on the other hand, represents "nature," immanence, instinct, magic, and physical weakness. The important sentence, which de Beauvoir omitted, but which feminist scholars read into this text as they explicate it, is: "in the patriarchal world view." De Beauvoir assumes the patriarchal world view and thinks from within it; thus, she never sharply distinguishes between patriarchal myth about women and the actuality of women's lives. Feminist scholars, basing themselves upon her work, have elucidated this point and have shown how patriarchal myth created an ideology which reinforced, as it "explained," male dominance.[9] Other scholars have disproven or questioned her assumption of feminine biological "weakness," a point which seems to have been satisfactorily disproven by biologists, geneticists, and demographic historians.[10] What has remained unchallenged and has, in fact, been highly influential in shaping current feminist thought is the ahistoricity of de Beauvoir's theory. She repeatedly affirms this as in this sentence: "Throughout history they [women] have always been subordinated to men, and hence their dependency is not the result of an historical event or a social change—it was not something that *occurred*."[11] This statement seems to be in contradiction to her other statement that "the devaluation of woman represents a necessary stage in the history of humanity." The contradiction dissolves when we put these statements next to her observation that it is through his "symbolic representation . . . that the male principle has triumphed." Her argument can then be read as follows: The subordination of woman is older than civilization, hence outside of History, the cultural construct. Woman was subordinated in the very process of the creation of human civilization in her relationship to the symbol system of culture. Since the making of symbols gives humans power and the symbol system is an essential aspect of the making of civilization (and History), it is accurate to say that patriarchal civilization is based on the subordination of women. I would argue that this subordination of the female therefore represents not, as de Beauvoir puts it, a "necessary stage in the history of humanity," but that it represents a *historical stage*. The difference is important, for a *necessary stage* precludes alternatives; a *historical stage* signifies simply that a stage occurred historically and that we must explain why it occurred as it did. There is no implication that it might not have occurred differently.

Other authors have confirmed this thought. Erich Fromm writes: "Human beings are half-animal and half-symbolic."[12] Ernest Becker explains:

> Man has a symbolic identity that brings him sharply out of nature. He is a symbolic self, a creature with a name, a life history. He is a creator with a mind that soars out to speculate about atoms and infinity, who can place himself imaginatively at a point in space and contemplate bemusedly his own planet. . . . Yet, at the same time . . . man is a worm and food for worms. . . . His body is material . . . that is alien to him in many ways—the strangest and most repugnant being that it aches and bleeds and will decay and die. Man is literally split in two.[13]

Becker comments that by this split "man seeks to control the mysterious processes of nature as they manifest themselves within his own body. The body cannot be allowed to have ascendancy over him."[14]

If one takes Fromm's formulation—"Human beings are half-animal and half-symbolic"—as a point of departure, one needs to add: civilization has been founded on a sex-based division of labor, the animal (natural) assigned to women, the symbol-making assigned to men. While it is true that the first level of symbol-making—the creation of language, ritual images, and artistic metaphors—has been the joint product of human beings, both male and female, the creation of advanced symbol systems, such as philosophies and science, has been the work of men. Educated women have learned to "master" — not "mistress," mastery being male — these male-created systems in which they themselves appear as marginal, if they appear at all. Women have been forced into marginality by abstract thought.

How is it possible to have kept half of humanity from thinking? Obviously thought is not based on sex or race; the capacity for thought is inherent in humanity; it can be fostered or discouraged, but it cannot ultimately be restrained. This is certainly true for thought generated by and concerned with daily living, the level of thought at which most men and women operate all their lives. But it is abstract thought, the level of mental activity at which new concepts are formed and at which theories and systems are generated, which here concerns us. It is this level of mental activity which has ordered the world and laid the basis for most of the decisive advances of civilization. And it is from this level of mental activity that women have been notably absent until the past 100 years. The development of science, of academic knowledge, of institutionalized learning, have all taken place without the participation of women and have indeed been based on the exclusion of women as subjects and objects worthy of thought.

Abstract analytical thought, which defines "truths" and builds them into a coherent, closed system, does not, of course, encompass the totality of knowledge. The knowledge of particulars, of practice, of the significance of events and human actions, is not confined to the educated and those schooled in philosophies. In this kind of knowledge women have excelled; in fact, their assigned role in the history of civilization has been to mediate between the abstract generalizations of institutionalized knowledge and the daily reality of the actual world. Without this role of women, not only would educated thinkers not have the conditions out of which their thought arises, but their abstract creations would remain untested and devoid of meaning. This function of mediation and reality-testing women share with males of oppressed classes or races, but with a difference which will be discussed in more detail later. What concerns us here is the historicity of the sexual division of labor in regard to thought and its impact and long-range effect on women.

The historical break occurs at the dawn of civilization at the moment when knowledge becomes systematized and institutionalized. When the accumulated knowledge of past generations is no longer preserved in the oral tradition of a self-selected group of shamans and elders, but when it becomes codified in written documents, produced and watched over by a small group of educated scribes, priests, and teachers, the sexual division of mental labor becomes a reality. The time when learning becomes a tool for maintaining the power of ruling elites coincides with the historical moment when women are literally confined behind the walls of harems, women's quarters, or family enclaves. Elise Boulding has offered a persuasive description of the gradual process by which the enclosure of women and their separation from the administration and definition of power are accomplished in the urban centers such as Sumer and Ur.[15] While this is not the place to offer a detailed historical study of an immensely complex process by which women's status deteriorated in a period probably extending over several millenia, there is sufficient evidence to document the assertion that the exclusion of women from institutionalized knowledge is a historic event or, rather, a series of historic events.[16] As civilization develops, the institutionalization of knowledge becomes more formal, as in the establishment of universities. In turn, the body of knowledge transmitted to the educated becomes ever larger and more difficult to acquire for the uninitiated. Thus, the relative disadvantaging of women through their separation from the institutions which control and create abstract thought *increases* over historical time.

The educational disadvantaging of women by institutional exclusion and discrimination is only part of the story. Women, with very few exceptions, have also been excluded from those conditions which make abstract thought and the creation of theories possible. Such achievement depends on education in the best of existing traditions and on the acceptance by a peer group of educated persons who, by criticism and interaction, provide "cultural prodding." It depends on having private time. Finally, it depends on the individual thinker being capable of absorbing such knowledge and then making a creative leap into a new ordering. As discussed earlier, educational discrimination has disadvantaged women in access to knowledge. "Cultural prodding," which is institutionalized in the upper reaches of religious and academic establishments, has been unavailable to them. The kind of character development which makes for a mind capable of seeing new connections and fashioning a new order of abstractions has been exactly the opposite of that required of women trained to accept their subordinate, service-oriented position in society. Universally, women of all classes have had less leisure time than men, and, due to their child-rearing and family-service function, what "free time" they have had was generally not their own. The time of men, their work, study, and thinking time, is respected as private. Women have had to deal with the immediate, the material, the practical. We experience reality daily, hourly, in our service function, in our constantly available and interruptible time, our splintered attention, our lives mired in "dailiness." Can one generalize while the particular tugs at one's sleeve? Women have mediated between men and the world, affording men the time and space necessary for reflection and abstraction. This privilege, precisely, men have always denied women. He, who makes symbol systems, and she, who takes care of his bodily, psychic, and generative needs—the gulf between them is enormous. It is for these reasons women have never written History, created philosophies or systems of thought appropriate to their own needs and emancipation. The systematic and persistent educational deprivation of women has most profoundly affected their psychology and has made them internalize the idea of their own inferiority and of their historical insignificance.

It may be objected that large numbers of men — slaves, serfs, colonials, proletarians — have also for centuries been kept from creating symbol systems and controlling education, both of which have been privileges monopolized by elite males. But there is, for women, little comfort in this observation, for *no* man was excluded because of his sex, yet *all* women were and are. And sex, unlike race and caste, is not a condition subject to change through upward mobility or revolution. Each subordinate or oppressed group of men has been sustained by a tradition, a belief system that confirmed their equality as humans in some past age. Slaves were once free; serfs see before and behind them models of men like themselves functioning in freedom; Jews survived millenia of diaspora and persecution in the knowledge of a golden past in which they were the chosen people. Only women "know" that they have never been equal anywhere since the dawn of civilization. And women of oppressed classes and races have experienced the complex oppression of sex, class, and race in a manner which has as yet not found an adequate system of expression. All the terms of discourse commonly used to describe the males of their groups are singularly inept and inadequate to describe their own experience.

One aspect of the way in which class and race privilege manifests itself for women is that, throughout historical time, small numbers of women members of the elite group have had greater educational privileges than other women. Yet, even in the most recent past, when larger numbers of women have had access to equal education and to the preconditions for abstract thought and system-making, there is still no equality. For the mode in which abstract thought is cast also tends to perpetuate women's marginality.

Women have had to express ourselves through patriarchal thought as reflected in the very language we have to use. It is a language in which we are subsumed under the male pronoun and in which the generic term for human is male. Women have had to use "dirty words" or "hidden words" to describe their own body experiences. The vilest insults in every language refer to parts of the female body or to female sexuality. Women's identity — their very name — is in most cultures defined in relationship to a man: daughter, wife, widow. Thinking women have had to think in systems of thought in which the question-setting is androcentric. This limits woman's ability to think in a mode appropriate to herself.[17]

The way to think abstractly is to define precisely, to order ideas coherently and consistently, to create models in the mind, and to generalize into systems. Such thought, men have taught us, must exclude feeling. Women, like other marginals, have closer knowledge of ambiguity, of feelings mixed with thought, of value judgements coloring abstractions. Women experience much of our own body and life rhythms not in sharply divided segments, but in an ebb and flow, in wavelike motion, in interaction. We know a body which can be whole and divided at the same time, a self which can be at once whole and shared (mother and infant *in utero*). Women find some of the male-defined abstractions inapplicable to ourselves, if not wholly untrue. But in order to be trained in — and having certified as having achieved — the higher reaches of learning, each educated woman has had to suppress such notions and learn "to think like a man."

In order to "think like men" women have had to learn to mistrust their own experience and to devalue it as the foundation for abstraction. Living in a world in which women are devalued, their experience bears the stigma of insignificance, which androcentric education reinforces. Educated women have been turned into "men's understudies," as Mary Beard observed. Women are those humans who can only think abstractly in terms which affirm their marginality to civilization and which reinforce the idea of their own inferiority.

Today, thinking women have access to the best education and to all the tools necessary for creating our own systems of ideas, yet we are still held back by unacknowleged restraints imbedded deeply within our psyches. Emergent woman faces a challenge to her very definition of self: how can her daring thought coexist with her life as a woman, as a sexual being? The very venture threatens her with loss of approval by and love from the man or the men in her life. Does she not, by stepping outside of the construct of patriarchal thought, step outside of the social compact into "existential nothingness"?[18] Wanting the power that comes with naming, definition, and abstraction, emergent woman has to argue with — has possibly to conquer — the great male mind in her head. Each emergent woman has been schooled in patriarchal thought which she is now, bit by bit, discarding. Yet there is nothing to put in its place. No woman name-giver, system-builder, whose work is true to her own experience and not just expressive of what she has been taught, has ever existed, nor could she have by the terms of her own condition. So, thinking women refurbish the idea systems created by men, redecorating "his" house so as to make a little more space for themselves. Their work often begins with and sometimes stays limited to a dialogue with the great male minds in their head. Elizabeth Cady Stanton took on the Bible, the Church fathers, the fathers of the American republic. Simone de Beauvoir argued with Sartre, Marx, Camus; Kate Millett argued with Freud, Norman Mailer, and the liberal literary establishment; Juliet Mitchell, Sheila Rowbotham, and most Marxist-Feminists are in dialogue with Marx, Engels, and Freud. In this dialogue woman intends merely to accept whatever she finds useful in the great man's system. But in these systems woman — as a concept, an entity, even as an individual — is marginal or subsumed under the male term. In accepting such dialogue, thinking woman stays for far longer than is useful within the boundaries of the question-setting defined by great men. And just so long as she does, the source of new insights is closed to her.

The move of women from marginality to the center shatters the system. That is too dangerous a thought for most women to contemplate. We have not been prepared psychologically and spiritually for such a leap into the great unknown. And so we check our first thought before it is fully born. We abort our thought in order not to lose the spiritual safety provided for us within the patriarchy. We have long known how to do that to our bodies; now we know we have been doing it to our minds as well. Women have internalized the ideology of the patriarchy to such an extent that it is we who are training our children in its rule. Without our cooperation it could not exist.

Revolutionary thought has always been based on upgrading the experience of the oppressed. The peasant had to learn to trust in the significance of his life experience before he could dare to challenge the feudal lords. The industrial worker had to become "class conscious," the Black "race conscious," before liberating thought could develop into revolutionary theory. The oppressed have acted and learned simultaneously — the process of becoming the newly-conscious person is in itself liberating. So with women.

Against the enormous weight of patriarchal thought, valuations, and the thousands of years of institutionalized disadvantaging of women, there stands only the reality of the female experience of self and community, the *actuality* of women's historical past. Simone de Beauvoir, who was so marvelously right in showing us woman's immanence — her absence from the making of the meaning systems of civilization — erred in thinking that therefore women had no history. It is *not* "the historical insignificance of women which has doomed them to inferiority." Quite the contrary, it is the relegating of women's past to insignificance by patriarchal thought which has oppressed women and forced them to devalue themselves. Thus, a shift in women's consciousness about their past is essential to a transformation of woman's consciousness of self.

The shift in consciousness occurs in two steps: 1) women must, as far as possible, leave patriarchal thought, and 2) women must move from the margin to the center. We must become woman-centered in our inquiry.

1) *To step outside of patriarchal thought means:*

Being skeptical toward every known system of thought; being critical of all assumptions, ordering, values, and definitions. It means examining terminology and language to see if they apply to women, which more often than not they do not.

Testing one's statement by trusting in our own, the female experience. Since such experience has usually been ignored or trivialized, it means overcoming the deep-seated resistance within ourselves toward accepting our knowledge as valid.

Being critical toward our own thought, which, after all, is thought trained in the patriarchal tradition. It means tracing the steps of our rising consciousness historically so as to rid ourselves of the many errors based on patriarchal assumptions in our thought.

It means developing intellectual courage—the courage to stand alone, the courage to reach farther than our grasp, the courage to risk failure. Surely, the courage to withstand disapproval, attack, and ridicule.

2) *To be woman-centered means*:

Asking: If women were central to this argument, how would it be defined? If women's experience were considered coequal in importance with that of men, how would this statement be made?

It means ignoring all evidence of women's marginality because, even where women *appear* to be marginal, this is the result of patriarchal intervention; also, frequently it is merely an appearance. The basic assumption should be that it is inconceivable for anything ever to have taken place in the world in which women were not involved except if they were prevented from participation through coercion and repression.

When using methods and concepts from traditional systems of thought, it means using them from a different vantage point. That vantage point is the centrality of women. Women cannot be put into the empty spaces of patriarchal thought and systems—in moving to the center, they *transform* the system.

To be woman-centered we must expand Simone de Beauvoir's analysis and go to the next step: Women are not men's "other." Women are nobody's "other." Women are IT, just as men are IT. The difference between them is that they have a different historical past.

To understand the differences between men's and women's historical past, we must analyze woman's place in history *in its own terms*. Women have lived in a separate culture within and in addition to the dominant patriarchal culture in which they have participated and to which they have contributed essentially. The mode of their participation, which combines resistance and acceptance, is one of the major features of women's culture.

The sex-gender system, which has defined men and women and has been internalized by them, is a product of history.[19] I understand by it the system whereby a culture defines the role and behavior it considers appropriate to the sexes (gender) and whereby it allots property and privileges accordingly. It has developed over time. At times it has served useful societal functions; at other times it has been merely oppressive. The subordination of women has taken place within the framework of this system and must be considered part of it. The subordination of women has benefited, to some degree, *all* men, but it has benefited men of different classes differently. It has benefited some women at certain times; it has negatively affected both men and women through much of historical time. Implicit in the fact of its historicity is the fact that the sex-gender system is subject to change or abolition.

It is obvious from all that has been said that women's history is more than adding the story of women's collective past to the empty spaces in traditional (men's) History. Bringing women into the center of historical process — where they have always been, only unrecognized — means a transformation of History as we know it. Joan Kelly has spoken of the "doubled vision" of Women's History.[20] I believe, to refine her insightful phrase further, we should think of it metaphorically, as though traditional history, written and interpreted up to now, represented the vision of one eye. Adding the other eye to it, the eye of women, does not simply add another perspective, although it does that, but it transforms vision into three-dimensional vision, giving it a new range and depth. The transformation of History will demand new differentiation as to periodization, new values for ordering, new questions, applied to both men and women. It will demand the extinction of the artificial barriers between the public and private lives of persons, and the equally false hierarchy between those who move events "importantly" and those who simply keep life going. Much of this process of transformation has been going on for some years — now we need to be conscious of it and define it.

The rise of feminist consciousness is itself a historical phenomenon. It is now possible because historical forces have, for the first time, created the necessary conditions by which large groups of women, finally *all* women, can emancipate themselves from subordination. Some of these conditions are: greater longevity, falling birth rates, the ability of women to control their fertility and the modes of their sexuality, the participation of increasing numbers of women in the economy, the attainment of educational equality with men of sizeable groups of women. Feminist consciousness arises when women begin to be conscious of themselves as a separate and deprived group. It is reinforced when women join together, experiencing communality; so strengthened, they define their own goals and move to implement them. Testing their goals and methods in practical politics, women can begin to generalize in the light of their past and present experience. It is at this point that feminist consciousness can be transformed into a full-fledged feminist world view.

Humans have always used History in order to find their direction toward the future: to repeat the past or to depart from it. But women, until recently deprived of their past, did not have the self-knowledge from which to project a desired future. Thus, women have not been able to create a social theory appropriate to their needs. As long as both men and women regard the subordination of women as "natural," it is impossible to conceptualize a society in which differences do not connote either dominance or subordination. Feminist consciousness is a prerequisite for the formulation of the kind of abstract thought — feminism as a world view — which may liberate both sexes from the compulsion of dominance.

What is needed is for thinking women to reclaim their freedom of mind from patriarchal thought as they reclaim their past. The millenia of women's pre-History are at an end. Women's History holds the key to women's emancipation and to the creation of a new epoch in history, one in which women *and* men will stand at the center of the human enterprise.

Notes

1. Eighteenth- and nineteenth-century feminist theories were based largely on arguments derived from natural rights philosophy. Yet, the "right to control one's body" was demanded by such early feminists as Frances Wright and Elizabeth Cady Stanton.

The concept of "sexual politics" was first developed theoretically as a theme by Kate Millett in her *Sexual Politics* (Garden City: Doubleday, 1970). See also "Notes from the First Year," *Journal of New York Radical Women*, June 1968.

2. Simone de Beauvoir, *The Second Sex*, trans. and ed. H. M. Parshley (1952; New York: Bantam, 1970), 119.

3. De Beauvoir, xix.

4. De Beauvoir, 122.

5. In order to distinguish the two concepts more clearly, I have decided to spell with lowercase "history" (past lived reality) and uppercase "History" (the cultural construct).

6. De Beauvoir, 118.

7. De Beauvoir, 69–70.

8. De Beauvoir, 71–72.

9. Sherry B. Ortner, "Is Female to Male as Nature Is to Culture?" *Woman, Culture and Society*, eds. Michelle Zimbalist Rosaldo and Louise Lamphere (Stanford: Stanford UP, 1974), 67–88.

10. Cf. E. E. Maccoby and C. N. Jacklin, *The Psychology of Sex Differences* (Stanford: Stanford UP, 1974); Julia Sherman, *On the Psychology of Women: A Survey of Empirical Studies* (Springfield, IL: Charles C. Thomas, 1971).

11. De Beauvoir, xviii.

12. Erich Fromm, *The Heart of Man: Its Genius for Good and Evil* (New York: Harper, 1964), 116–17.

13. Ernst Becker, *The Denial of Death* (New York: Free, 1973), 26.

14. Becker, 32.

15. The process by which learning becomes transformed into a tool for maintaining the power of ruling elites and the impact this development has on women is well described in Dorothy Smith, "A Sociology for Women," *The Prism of Sex: Essays in the Sociology of Knowledge*, eds. Julia Sherman and Evelyn Beck (Madison: U of Wisconsin P, 1977), 135–88.

Elise Boulding, *The Underside of History* (Boulder: Westview, 1976), chaps. 5 and 6.

16. Robert M. Adams, *The Evolution of Urban Society: Early Mesopotamia and Prehispanic Mexico* (Chicago: Aldine, 1966); Samuel N. Kramer, *The Sumerians: Their History, Culture and Character* (Chicago: U of Chicago P, 1963).

17. Cf. Robin Lakoff, *Language and Woman's Place* (New York: Harper, 1975); C. Miller and K. Swift, *Words and Women: New Language in New Times* (New York: Doubleday, 1975).

18. Mary Daly, *Beyond God the Father* (Boston: Beacon, 1973), 23.

19. The anthropologist Gayle Rubin first introduced the term "sex-gender system" which has found wide currency among feminists. She defined it as "the set of arrangements by which a society transforms biological sexuality into products of human activity, and in which these transformed sexual needs are satisfied." Gayle Rubin in Rayna Reiter, ed., *Toward an Anthropology of Women* (New York: Monthly Review, 1975), 159. She suggested the term as a preferred substitute for "patriarchy."

20. Joan Kelly, "The Doubled Vision of Feminist Theory: A Postscript to the 'Women and Power' Conference," *Feminist Studies* 1 (1979): 216–27.

Peelings of the Real   Catherine Clément*

In her essay on old age, as in the wonderful account of her mother's death in *A Very Easy Death,* Simone de Beauvoir displays the admirable wisdom of those itinerant Indian women storytellers and an attention to the real sufficiently precise so that she can peel off the skins one by one without ever bruising the real.

What strikes me above all is the constant alliance that is never broken between a certain dryness in the writing and a latent tenderness. There is no overflowing, there is little sentimentalism, in comparison to the sentimentalism that poisons almost all our novelistic production: no big words, few exclamations; a quality of reserve that only reveals itself in secret. The word "reserve" suits her: it describes the behavior, which has never been completely lost, of the former dutiful daughter; it situates the enormous amount of work accomplished over the years outside the world of marketing in the publishing trade, outside the university imprimatur, work that is both solitary and public. But with this word "reserve" there appears, in a back corner of my mind, the enclosed space in which the white men keep their Indians. Simone de Beauvoir is, to a certain extent, our Indian; for long periods of time she was forgotten on that reservation where her life continued, coming out briefly for each book and taking again her own path. Today, it's the moment of one of her comings out, and we watch with astonishment this Indian whose eyelids are a bit heavy, her beautiful face, on which age has only inscribed what are called "expressive wrinkles," those which underline the smile, the high cheek bones, the crinkling of the eyes, and the life of a woman who looks at you directly. In the same manner as the Indian woman, Simone de Beauvoir possesses the acquired wisdom and the serenity of a mode of thinking that is true to itself; but that is the result of a long story.

Indian women have an understanding of storytelling; they keep

*Translated by Elaine Marks for this volume from *Magazine Littéraire*, no. 145 (February 1979):25–27. © 1979 by *Magazine Littéraire*. Reprinted by permission.

secrets that are transmitted orally in order to perpetuate, in spite of all attacks, a culture without writing. Simone de Beauvoir has an understanding of storytelling; and her writing rejoins miraculously, in a space without affectation and without makeup, the word that unwinds, for those of the same culture, the thread of an essential spool, the thread of her life and, therefore, also, of ours. In certain cases, for lack of a better word, we try the term "witness"; when we have nothing else to say, we write that such a chronicler was the "witness" of her time. This may be acceptable, if we keep the judicial roots of the word "witness," because it is true that she continues to follow the trial of her time. But something else is going on, something that is related to a femininity that is written and understood. A witness (un témoin) is not a woman; and the word "témoine" fortunately does not exist. What Simone de Beauvoir brings us, as a supplement, is a bare story in which we find the meaning of the tempo of life, with its stages, the initiation rites which she depicts with a new innocence, and women's questions; and all of her work follows what happened to her and, therefore, to others.

The wisdom of a simple woman: yes, and we should be grateful. The wisdom of a simple woman, the inheritor of the prodigious and misunderstood wisdom of the witches who Michelet so correctly said were, during the period of medieval obscurantism, the first doctors. Helpful to everyone, attentive to the Other whatever the Other's forms of distress may be, simple women, cronies, witches heal the wounds of the soul and of the body. They are referred to as talkative because they transmit the life of the community; they are referred to as carriers of disorder, and that is true because they sow trouble in the little masculine machines, and among themselves they reassure each other and back each other up. With her eternal turban wound tightly around her head, and her manner, without manners, of "chatting" about life, Simone de Beauvoir could be mistaken for a kind of witch; and that is the most beautiful homage—since the word "femmage" does not exist either, and so much the better—that we can pay her.

In 1964, she published *A Very Easy Death*. In 1963, her mother died following the fracture of a thigh bone which hid an intestinal cancer. She transformed that experience into a story. No, it's not a novel; other men or women would have written a fiction about the death of the mother; it has been done and it will be done again. A story is something else. It is the detailed description of events that took place in the real, and it is the real that she is looking for with all her concentrated energy. A story (récit) is also, in musical terms, that part which is played by a solitary instrument that narrates a melody without any other harmonic support. In order to write a story one must have both a sense of decorum and a good memory, and truthfulness is not a simple thing. *A Very Easy Death* could not have sustained the novel form; it may be that the author would not have allowed a fiction, with its weight of narcissism, to impede the work of mourning that is written into this book.

The facts are stubborn and naked. "On Thursday, the 24th of October, 1963, at four o'clock in the afternoon, I was in Rome, in my room at the Hotel Minerva; I was supposed to return to Paris the following day by plane, and I was organizing my papers when the telephone rang. Bost was calling me from Paris: 'Your mother has had an accident,' he said. I thought: a car ran her over." A simple account. These are the facts. It is she, but it is you, it is me. The facts are naked; naked too, for the first time, is the body of the old woman who is very ill and who does not want to know it to the very end, at which Simone de Beauvoir was not present. The body is first of all the face with its circled eyes; soon after, it is the belly "bruised, creased with small wrinkles, and her bald pubis." It is the belly that contains all the sickness, and death that is so near, but we will only know that later, when the author discovers it as she unwinds the thread of her memory. And this nakedness is the first sign of mourning; when the dutiful daughter can see the genitals of her mother, when the taboo is broken, this means that the event is threatening. "For the first time, I see her as a corpse under suspended sentence." Little by little, but also very quickly, with little bits of information that are held back and then released, the story gets worse. An operation is necessary; is it really, is it worth it? They open her, they use clamps, it was not worth it. The belly is all rotten inside. They set up those instruments that in our world accompany a hospital death: the intravenous needles in the arm, the tubes in the nose, immobility, bed sores, impotence, and the indifference of the world of doctors and nurses for whom this death, as horrible as it is for those who are close to the dying person, is "a very easy death." And, obliging herself to think, this daughter in mourning understands in what way this death was a privileged death: without a screen put in front of the bed in a public ward, which tells the dying person that her turn has come, and without interminable suffering. Always with the same stubborn reserve, the words tell of the remorse that is part of every mourning; the guilt that sets itself up and then effaces itself, while the peaceful portrait of the dead woman is constructed bit by bit, and then the definitive image.

But, some years later, in 1970, Simone de Beauvoir published an essay on old age. When the mother dies, an age begins when one is no longer the child of someone; and this book produces, like all the books by Simone de Beauvoir, a reflection on a topic that is contemporaneous with her own life. Like all of her essays, like *The Second Sex* whose historical importance continues to grow as the history of women's liberation develops, *Old Age* is made of multiple stories. Stories by ethnographers, by historians, by philosophers: stories in any case, stories intertwined, marvelously told, small works of art in detailed writing. For example, the epic of the Narte, taken from the Ossets of the North, in which there is a quarrel between the little old man and the little old woman to determine which of the two should die first, and the teeth of the old woman have not fallen out as yet, and "they carried off the grumbling old man, they obliged him to drink some beer and they threw him into the valley." The licentious and healthy old age of Victor Hugo, and the strange death of Chateaubriand, attended by Juliette Récamier, and he was deaf and she was blind, and they were holding hands. . . . The story of the old man called Durand, like so many others, who dreamed only of his bowel movements; a young woman companion, Mademoiselle G., spent a great deal of time with him and helped him to masturbate. When he died, she remained for twenty-four hours on his tomb. The great, the small, the famous, the obscure, all come together in her memory which tells and tells again; small epic dramas are put into place, tiny dreams create strange spaces where the ultimate madness takes the form of sacred inspiration, where the little known and repressed world of the old discovers its grandeur, its secret explosions, its fury, and its bliss. Where, in terms of the simple morality of a woman whose ethical concern has never wavered, is spoken the injustice of a monstrous gagging, as deep as that of the gagging of women, but more serious, much further from its liberation. Such is also the story: at the end, like the fable, it furnishes a moral and gives food for thought.

There are few women philosophers. In the past this made me angry, but I am beginning to wonder if we should not, on the contrary, rejoice. And make our way, as she has done, toward that narrative path which, when recounting the real, tells more than the novel, more than the reflexive construction. But, if I had to define the philosophy of Simone de Beauvoir, I would say that it is the philosophy of a peeler. She peels, quietly, the onion skins of the world, one after the other; with this kitchen knife that we call in our kitchens the "(s)paring" knife because it peels very thin skins. Have you ever seen a man peeling potatoes? He makes enormous and ridiculous peelings where the skin and the flesh mingle, and he ruins the vegetable; he will have no sense of the skin, of its delicacy, and of the precision required to bring about the dividing line between the peeling and the rest. Simone de Beauvoir has, to the highest degree, the sense of the multiple skins that constitute us; but when she detaches them, for herself and for others, it is with tenderness and precision. It is with the immemorial talent of all the peelers who, working until now in the shadows, have accomplished material kitchen work. She does the same thing in culture, but, in place of the servant or the mother of the family, let us see in her the woman writer, the woman philosopher, the woman storyteller who cooks culture for women and for men and who will not draw back before the sight of any skin, whether it be that of a dying mother or an old man.

Views of Women and Men in the Work of Simone de Beauvoir

Mary Evans*

Simone de Beauvoir occupies, and deservedly so, a central place in the history of feminism. *The Second Sex*, published in 1949, is a classic study of the status of women and the causes of their subordination in all aspects of social life.† Her other works, which include novels, essays on existential philosophy, a four-volume autobiography and a lengthy study of old age, demonstrate a capacity for intellectual breadth (and, one must add a quite monumental talent for documentation) which is comparable to that of her life long companion, Jean-Paul Sartre. Yet whilst any essay on de Beauvoir must note her considerable intellectual power and range, it is also important to examine her work more critically than has generally been the case. Accolades, particularly from feminists, have been so generously heaped on her work that some of its shortcomings have been obscured. I would like to suggest here that whilst de Beauvoir claims that much of her work is concerned with the overall condition of women, she turns away from many of the issues which are central to women's lives and in particular accords very little place in her epistemology to areas of human experience which are not immediately amenable to rational understanding. Thus in this paper I shall argue that a major weakness in de Beauvoir's work is a rejection of many of the problems which women (and indeed men) face and a failure to acknowledge that the actions of both sexes are often motivated by needs and desires which, although frequently explained and rationalized from the conscious mind, do not always derive from it.

In a relatively short space it is impossible to do more than summarize and indicate the work of a prolific writer whose career has now spanned almost 40 years. De Beauvoir was born in 1908, the elder daughter of a lawyer, whose fortunes became progressively worse during his daughter's childhood and adolescence. A limited secondary education at a Catholic girls' school was followed by the study of philosophy at the Sorbonne, where at the age of 21 she received her degree and almost immediately afterwards the *agrégation*, the coveted qualification allowing her to teach in lycées and universities. De Beauvoir's earliest published works did not, however, follow rapidly upon her brilliant academic career: she graduated from the Sorbonne in 1929, but her first novel (*She Came to Stay*) did not appear until 1943. It was rapidly followed by other works: two more novels (*The Blood of Others*, published in 1945 and *All Men are Mortal*, published in 1947) and two essays on existential philosophy (*Pyrrhus et Cinéas* and *Pour Une Morale de "l'Ambiguité"*). But the two works which

*Reprinted with permission from *Women's Studies International Quarterly* 3, no. 4 (1980):395–404. © 1980, Pergamon Press, Ltd.

†I would like to thank David Morgan for his comments on an earlier draft of this paper.

brought her lasting, and international, fame were *The Second Sex* and *The Mandarins* (the latter published in 1954 and for which she won the Prix Goncourt). In the 1950s and 1960s she wrote further novels, but increasingly she turned away from fiction to non-fiction: four volumes of autobiography (*Memoirs of a Dutiful Daughter*, *The Prime of Life*, *Force of Circumstance* and *All Said and Done*), a short, very powerful account of the death of her mother (*A Very Easy Death*), descriptions of her various travels (*The Long March* and *America Day by Day*) social and political commentaries (*Brigitte Bardot and the Lolita Syndrome*, *Djamila Boupacha* and *Must we Burn De Sade?*) and a study of the process and effects of ageing (*Old Age*) all appeared during this period.[1]

De Beauvoir's personal history has, since 1929, been intimately linked with that of Jean-Paul Sartre. Their relationship has been one of the better documented aspects of French intellectual life in the twentieth century and although the couple's emotional equanimity has occasionally been upset by what de Beauvoir and Sartre describe as "contingent" love affairs, the association has clearly remained central to both their lives. Information about the history of the relationship has been provided for the public exclusively by de Beauvoir; Sartre has remained, at least in print, quite silent on the subject and the only emotional relationship of his life which he has exposed to the public view is that with his mother, which is discussed, albeit briefly, in *Les Mots*.

The relationship between de Beauvoir and Sartre was, from its outset guided by the principle of what might be described in another context as over-determination. They agreed not to marry and that both of them would be free to engage in affairs with others. "Sartre," de Beauvoir wrote, "was not inclined to be monogamous by nature: he took pleasure in the company of women, finding them less comic than men. He had no intention, at the age of 23, of renouncing their tempting variety."[2] Yet this decision, taken in the cold light of day and mutually agreed and accepted, was to provide numerous subsequent problems. For example, de Beauvoir was to admit in the second volume of her autobiography that her first novel (*She Came to Stay*) was written in an attempt to clarify and exorcise what she saw as a major crisis in her life with Sartre: the intrusion of a third party, a woman who threatened to replace her in Sartre's affections. This first (or at any rate the first fully documented) instance of the problems jealousy, emotional ties and constraints raised for the couple was to be repeated on subsequent occasions: de Beauvoir's own affair with the American writer Nelson Algren forced her to face the same problem, whilst Sartre's affair with a woman identified as "M." threatened once again the stability of her emotional world. In this last instance, the uncertainty of her own position eventually forced her to ask Sartre, in an uncharacteristically direct way, "Who means most to you, M. or me?"[3] The answer is somewhat ambiguous, but eventually the situation was resolved by a quarrel, and the subsesquent parting, between Sartre and M.

After the difficulties encountered with Algren (and M.) neither de Beauvoir, nor Sartre, entered again into a relationship likely to threaten their own. De Beauvoir's friendship with Claude Lanzmann, and Sartre's with a woman named Michelle were in no sense challenging or disruptive.

The accounts given by de Beauvoir of these instances of personal anguish and misery reveal, I would argue, one of the central weaknesses in de Beauvoir's view of the world: the supposition that personal, and highly charged emotional relationships are always amenable to rational control and organization and that human beings are capable of the rigid compartmentalization of their emotional and intellectual worlds. When faced with situations which are rationally comprehensible, and quite predictable, yet deeply disturbing, de Beauvoir is clearly appalled at her failure to subject such experiences to her conscious will. Both de Beauvoir and Sartre show a marked reluctance to acknowledge, or come to terms with, anything outside their rational beings and nowhere is this more marked than in the attitude of each of them to their physical selves. Although de Beauvoir writes that she is critical of Sartre for his refusal to countenance the demands of the body, she herself is far from innocent of exactly the same attitude. She observes of Sartre: "I criticized Sartre for regarding his body as a mere bundle of strained muscles, and for having cut it out of his emotional world. If you gave way to tears or nerves or seasickness, he said, you were simply being weak. I, on the other hand, claimed that stomach and tear ducts, indeed the head itself, were all subject to irresistible forces on occasions."[4] And it is clear that Sartre's views were practised as much as preached. On one occasion, de Beauvoir is overcome by terrible seasickness and unable to answer with any degree of coherence the questions about their itinerary that Sartre is asking. Unmoved by her pleas, Sartre remained persistent in his questioning and ascribed de Beauvoir's seasickness to "deliberate malice."[5]

Whilst de Beauvoir denies that she shares Sartre's views on the possibility of the absolute subordination of the body to the mind, her autobiography reveals numerous occasions when she expresses an exactly similar position. The ills and sorrows which flesh is heir to are, in practice, no more an acceptable part of her view of the world than they are in the case of Sartre. Moreover, de Beauvoir is loathe to consider that there might be a link between the physical and the emotional self. For example, during her twenties she and Sartre were involved in a complex tripartite friendship with a younger woman. When relations between the three reached a particularly difficult stage, de Beauvoir fell dangerously ill. The possible psychosomatic origins of this illness are never mentioned or entertained — de Beauvoir admits that she might have become physically tired at the time but the possibility of a relationship between emotional stress and tension and physical illness is not canvassed.

The denial of the force, and in particular the incapacitating force, of physical needs and desires, is part of de Beauvoir's general dismissal of significant areas of human existence, and relations between men and women, as irrational and unworthy of serious attention. Thus we find, in her account of the early years of her relationship with Sartre, that de Beauvoir describes sexual passion as a "poisoned shirt" and a "shameful disease." She writes: "I was forced to admit a truth that I had been doing my best to conceal ever since adolescence: my physical appetites were greater than I wanted them to be. . . . I said nothing (to Sartre). Now that I had embarked on our policy of absolute frankness, this reticence was, I felt, a kind of touchstone. If I dared not confess such things, it was because they were by definition unavowable. By driving me to such secrecy my body became a stumbling block rather than a bond of union between us, and I felt a burning resentment against it."[6] The reader is left with the distinct impression that the physical self, and particularly so in the case of women, is liable to lead only to uncontrollable, threatening passions and the destruction of all peace of mind. But no clues are provided as to how sexual relationships are to be conducted or physical affection is to be incorporated into personal life. Whilst we are told, quite explicitly, that Sartre and de Beauvoir were initially lovers, we are not told (although it is easy to make certain guesses on this point) why and when their relationship lost its sexual element and became an association in which the expression of physical affection no longer played a part. All we learn is that separation from Sartre (they took jobs hundreds of miles apart) allowed de Beauvoir, as she describes it, to "subdue my restless body."[7] The transformation of the nature of the association is of interest which goes beyond biographical or voyeuristic concerns, namely that in it two problems are posed. In the first place one must ask how de Beauvoir both allows, and yet attempts to minimize, physical desire and secondly, how she conceptualizes relationships between the sexes.

In admitting the existence of physical desire, de Beauvoir also observed some of its problems and difficulties. She accepts, indeed condones, the physical expression of love, although she is critical of sexual promiscuity, especially in women. But she has no deeply ingrained fear of sexual activity *per se*, what is detectable is a concern, indeed almost a fear, of its possible results. For women, the integration of their sexuality into their personalities as a whole appears to be an impossible task. A constant threat seems to hang over all those women who, in either her novels or her non-fiction, indulge in the pleasures of the flesh: the threat of being hurtled down some slippery slope to moral and intellectual ruin. The majority of love affairs described in her novels do not bring happiness ever after to all those concerned, on the contrary, they tend to bring, and particularly so to the women, destruction and humiliation. Portrayed with some considerable perception in de Beauvoir's novels are women who are fighting desperately to maintain relationships with men who are long tired of them. Women, in most cases, who have staked all on another human being and found that such complete dependence has left them with no alternative resources. One of the central characters in *The Mandarins*, a woman named Paule, goes almost mad with grief when her lover rejects her, *She Came to Stay* involves not just passion, but *crime passionel*, as a result of the conflict between old and new affections and *The Woman Destroyed* is a vivid account of a woman tortured by her husband's infidelity.

The path of true heterosexual love (homosexuality does not appear as a central theme in the fiction of either Sartre or de Beauvoir) clearly does not run smoothly in de Beauvoir's life or work. And it is difficult to see exactly where the path might run. One direction in which it does not lead is towards the establishment of domestic and family life. Both the characters in her novels and the friends and acquaintances she describes in her autobiography are nearly always both unmarried and childless. Women, in both de Beauvoir's fiction and non-fiction, do not express any desire for children, neither do they demonstrate any interest in their existence. The Parisian café society which de Beauvoir, and her created characters, inhabit is thus quite atypical of the world at large in that it is composed more or less entirely of adults, many of whom have no personal committments or responsibilities. From the volumes of her autobiography it is clear that de Beauvoir knew few families; when family life is mentioned it is generally in negative terms.

Sexual relations between men and women do not, therefore, in de Beauvoir's world lead to the establishment of family and domestic life. She quite rightly defends the right of women not to bear children and is deeply critical of the more repressive aspects of family life. Yet this attitude is hardly sufficient as an analysis of domestic and family life. Whilst the account, given in *The Second Sex*, of the social construction of false maternal desires is both relevant and laudable, there is also the possibility to consider — and in both its material and psychological aspects — that a desire to bear children does exist in women and is independent of all social and environmental pressures and expectations. The intellectual and social problems thus posed are considerable, in that it may be possible that the sexes have quite different, and perhaps irreconcilable, sexual needs and expectations.

But de Beauvoir is much concerned, as Margaret Walters has pointed out, to minimize the differences between the sexes and to show that feminine behaviour (and femininity) is a social construct. In short, she is sometimes very close to asking, Why can't a woman be more like a man? This is not to deny that de Beauvoir is absolutely correct to attack the more absurd and exaggerated notions of appropriate female demeanor but that her attack is sometimes so massive that the female baby is thrown out with the feminine bathwater. Both in *The Second Sex* and in the autobiographical works there are few positive statements about the female condition and many suggest that the physical world of women is in some sense beset with more problems and difficulties than that of men. In particular, she stresses that woman's physical nature makes her essentially and inevitably dependent. Thus in the section on "The Mother" in *The Second Sex* Simone de Beauvoir writes, of childbirth: "It is significant that woman . . . requires help in performing the function assigned to her by nature. . . . At just the time when woman attains the realization of her feminine destiny, she is still dependent. . . ."[8] Women, it would seem, are naturally dependent and helpless creatures: the very essence of femininity is that of dependence, a state which above all others is to be avoided.

De Beauvoir, having argued that maternity is the basis of woman's dependence is much concerned to demonstrate that no "natural" desire for motherhood exists. If women would refuse to be duped by the social construction of false maternal instincts, they would no longer be mothers and hence no longer dependent. In short, they would be able to act in all respects as men act, free from social and sexual constraints and, in a quite literal sense, masters of their own fate. Yet such a possibility, and the argument on which it rests, takes for granted two premises which, I would argue, are incorrect. The first is that there is a rigid distinction to be made between a "natural" and a "social" instinct and secondly, that men's behaviour, and their attitude to sexuality and reproduction, is as homogeneous and free from constraint and dependence as de Beauvoir suggests.

As we have seen, and as is amply illustrated by *The Second Sex*, de Beauvoir distinguishes very sharply between behaviour which is "natural" and that which is "social." But she does not reject the possible existence of such a thing as "nature": in a quotation earlier in this paper we have seen that she speaks of Sartre as "not being monogamous by nature." And her work is littered with references to such attributes as "natural" grace and a "natural" liking and aptitude for philosophy. So it is admitted that people can be borne with certain characteristics, be they views on monogamy or intellectual ability. Yet throughout *The Second Sex* she attacks the very possibility of instinctive or "natural" predilections and desires. In making a perfectly justifiable attack on a society and a set of social conventions which regard women's sole role as that of wife and mother she ignores, and dismisses out of hand, the very complex sets of social relationships which can either exaggerate or suppress "natural" behaviour. If she had dismissed altogether the idea that people are born with any innate characteristics, her argument would have been both more powerful, and a great deal more consistent. As it stands, she can be said to use "nature" in two contradictory ways: as a taken for granted concept, uncritically accepted and integrated into her main argument or as an impossibility, a concept with no real intellectual basis. It is not suggested here that "nature" has to be defended against its detractors, merely that it is perfectly viable to argue that innate abilities and characters do exist, be they differences in intelligence or inclinations towards maternity and that what constitutes the real issue for anyone interested in differences between the sexes is to try and determine the extent to which such differences are socially or naturally produced.

In *The Second Sex*, de Beauvoir argues with some insistence, that much of woman's psychological self is socially constructed. She illustrates her argument by referring to the passivity which is often encouraged by girls, by documenting the narcissism which is frequently regarded as a natural female trait and by showing how the education of girls, both moral and intellectual, is at best limited and constraining, rather than liberating. Very few critics would be able to question her attack on the socialization of girls: the argument has been too well substantiated for it to deserve or demand rational opposition. However, what is questionable in de Beauvoir's discussion is the way in which she sets the education of girls against the education of boys, and then suggests that men represent some sort of standard of self-hood and behaviour which women are prevented from emulating by the collusion of their fathers, mothers, and husbands.

Men emerge from *The Second Sex* as an extremely undifferentiated category. They constitute, in the existential terminology in which at least part of the book's argument is couched, the "other." Thus an opposition between the sexes is introduced in which few individual, let alone social, differences are allowed to emerge. Such an opposition—which must at least in part be derived from de Beauvoir—has become a characteristic of much feminist writing of recent years, two notable examples being Susan Brownmiller's *Against Our Will* (in which all women are constantly threatened by the superior physical force of men) and Germaine Greer's *The Female Eunuch* (in which women are exhorted to take on "male" psychological characteristics). But such an opposition is too simplistic for it to be analytically useful (whatever its rhetorical uses) since it obscures—most obviously—the differences between men, and—what is more complex—the way in which women's subordinate status is used by women as a weapon against men and is hence often fiercely defended by women themselves. It might be the case that the social elaboration of differentiation between the sexes, is the result not of a male conspiracy to suppress the interests of women but of the development by women of forms of social and sexual relationships which are best suited to allow the establishment of a female world which is independent of male interests. There is no doubt, of course, that such a world is a sub-world, or an under-world, but it is nevertheless a world which is able to manipulate certain processes in its own interests, precisely through those habits and patterns of behaviour which de Beauvoir regards, somewhat dismissively, and perhaps naively, as absurd and ridiculous. Just as Western feminists are appalled by some Islamic customs and conventions about women and fail to comprehend the totality of social relationships in which such practices are to be found, so de Beauvoir sees in the development of feminine characteristics behaviour which is, compared to that of men, merely childish and irrational.

The view of men which emerges from *The Second Sex* is that of human beings who are, compared with women, rational, independent and able to transcend their sexuality in a way which is unknown to women. Men are able to integrate their sexuality into their lives with little ado, not for them the tortured concerns about the proper conduct of sexual relationships, or the inevitable horrors of guilt or frigidity which are pictured as accompanying the sexual life of women. Men's sexual life is apparently one of blissful enjoyment and the fulfillment of all erotic desires: the only stumbling block being that at some point such pleasures generally demand the presence of women. Unfortunately, as de Beauvoir points out, women cannot be relied upon to be sensible and rational about sexual relations. She writes: "Feminine sexual excitement can reach an intensity unknown to man. Male sex excitement is keen but localized and it leaves the man quite in possession of himself; woman, on the contrary, really loses her mind."[9] Again, we are confronted with the idea that for women, sensual life, pleasure and activity is beset with the threat of the loss of her rational and conscious self. It is not so much that love constitutes woman's very existence, rather than physical affection, and its expression, threatens women by forcing them to lose all control over the direction of their lives.

In many ways, *The Second Sex* can be seen as a reaction against a highly particularistic set of social expectations. The prohibitions and conventions that surrounded de Beauvoir in her childhood and adolescence were part of a bourgeois world whose outward appearance changed rapidly after the Second World War. But it would be incorrect simply to assume that the book is no longer relevant and that the contemporary world no longer forces the sexes into rigid and artificial stereotypes. In one important respect, however, the world has changed, in that women are now much better able than they were at the time when *The Second Sex* was written, to control their own fertility. The fears and tensions which de Beauvoir describes between the sexes have, perhaps, been much lessened by reliable methods of contraception and by a much greater public understanding of elementary physiology. Yet despite these changes, many feminists would argue that the inherent differences between the sexes, and their needs and desires, are so great as to be insuperable by mere improvements in social organization or technology. Thus we are still confronted, nearly thirty years after the publication of *The Second Sex*, by arguments that suggest that men and women are irreconcilably different. They are no longer to be reconciled (*à la* de Beauvoir) by the assumption of more masculine behaviour by women; it is now supposed, often with a ferocity to match that of John Knox, that not only do men not know what women want, it is no business of either sex to inquire into the wishes and desires of the other. And it is invariably the existence of the possibility of sexual relations between men and women which is held accountable for the fundamental irreconcilability between the sexes.

Such an argument, I would suggest, is implicitly contained in de Beauvoir's work, although never clearly stated and never allowed to question the ideal which she advances of rational, independent and freely chosen sexual relationships. The argument can be most clearly deduced from de Beauvoir's autobiographical works, in which she speaks with a ruthless, but somewhat incomplete, honesty of her relations with others. Of those who inhabited her adult world by far the most significant is, of course, Sartre, and it is Sartre who is her most constant companion. At the beginning of their association he explained to her (the sex of the subject and the object of the sentence, is not, perhaps, without significance) that their relationship was one of "essential" love. It was to be interrupted, as mentioned earlier, by contingent love affairs, but nothing was to be allowed to question or alter this fundamental love. The relationship did survive various interruptions and difficulties but not without the growing realization by both the central characters that a primary committment could not allow a secondary committment of any real substance or importance. However, whilst it survived, the relationship also changed, and in particular the sexual relationship between Sartre and de Beauvoir was abandoned. This fundamental change in the nature of the relationship clearly allowed de Beauvoir to develop a greater personal freedom and autonomy. What is being suggested therefore, is that whilst de Beauvoir does not reject heterosexual relationships she does, implicitly, argue that sexual relations in long standing relationship between men and women can only lead to the loss of the woman's happiness and independence. The happy and successful relationship between Sartre and de Beauvoir is mirrored in de Beauvoir's fiction in the marriage of the Dubreuilhs in *The Mandarins*: a relationship which seems to function very well and in which the two characters concerned live virtually separate lives.

Throughout de Beauvoir's fiction and volumes and autobiography relations between the sexes tend to fall into two categories: they are either relationships in which sexual relations have been abandoned (as in the case of Anne Dubreuilh and her husband or of Sartre and de Beauvoir herself) or they are relationships in which sexual attraction and passion are of fundamental, if not single, importance. The conflict between the demands of the body, and the needs of the mind are apparently irreconcilable: sexual relations between men and women are admissable but they are, ideally, transcended. And it is to the advantage of women if this is the case, for they are much less able than men to maintain some distance from their physical selves and are, as we have seen, likely to lose their heads in moments of passion or to become pregnant and hence finally, and irrevocably dependent.

The view of men, and women, in *The Second Sex* (and elsewhere in de Beauvoir's work) does not offer a great deal of hope to those who would advocate the integration of the sexes nor to those who have any interest in the possible maintenance of social life and human society. A perceptive critic has pointed out that de Beauvoir's vision of the ideal woman is somewhat bleak, and writes: "de Beauvoir's emancipated woman sounds just like that familiar nineteenth century character, the self made man. . . . Early capitalist man, dominating and exploiting the natural world, living to produce, viewing his own life as a product shaped by will, and suppressing those elements in himself — irrationality, sexuality — that might reduce his moral and economic efficiency."[10] And association with others, particularly in emotional relationships, is one of those situations that reduce most rapidly women's efficiency.

Explanations of de Beauvoir's view of the world, and in particular her view of sexual relations, must inevitably involve some reference to her own childhood and to her parents. Whatever other significance is attached to the relations between parents and children, few would deny that parents are very powerful models for their children, although not always ones that are necessarily accepted. De Beauvoir's father seems to have been proud of his elder daughter's intelligence; it was an attribute which he valued and praised. He had much less praise for his daughter's appearance and particularly during her adolescence was ruthless in his criticism. But criticism, however pointed, must have been limited, since much of his time was spent in cafés and theatres and with little reference to his wife and daughters. The world of men was outside the home, full of fascinating, and quite forbidden, exploits and activities. The world of women was, at least as far as de Beauvoir knew it as a child entirely domestic. Her mother had no training for a job or a profession, but this was hardly exceptional at the time and neither did any of the female cousins and aunts whom de Beauvoir knew in her childhood. Bourgeois women did not work outside the home and were well employed managing their large households and supervising their children and servants.

So the association of women with the domestic world which de Beauvoir acquired from her childhood must have been very strong. And there was another association which was just as powerful, namely that between women and religion. De Beauvoir's father was an agnostic, but his wife was a convinced and practising Catholic who was determined that her daughters should remain within the influence of the Church and never be exposed to the rigours of secular education. To this end, both daughters were sent to an appalling (although utterly respectable and socially well regarded) Catholic school for girls, an institution whose shortcomings were made all too painfully clear as soon as Simone faced competition from those boys and girls who had been educated at the state *lycées*. Despite the pleadings and pleas of her mother, de Beauvoir's loyalty to the Catholic church was as shortlived as her confidence in its secondary education and she abandoned all religious faith at the age of 15. It produced a breach between mother and daughter which would seem never to have healed.

In reading de Beauvoir's account of her childhood and her adolescence in *Memoirs of a Dutiful Daughter* it is striking how strongly there emerges an association of women with all that is superstitious, petty, narrow minded, domestic, trivial, uneducated and ignorant. The concerns of de Beauvoir's mother and her other female relatives never extended much beyond their households. In contrast to this, the world of men must have seemed an alluring and exciting prospect, all the more so since the rigid demarcation between the worlds of the sexes inevitably enhanced the magic and glamour of the unknown, masculine world. The most positive character that emerges in *Memoirs of a Dutiful Daughter* is de Beauvoir's cousin Jacques, by all accounts a very ordinary bourgeois youth and yet the first person to whom she was able to talk on subjects outside the supposed interests of young girls. Even de Beauvoir's much loved friend Zaza could not match Jacques in the scope and range of her interests. Moreover, Zaza was to remain utterly loyal to Catholicism and obedient to the demands which her mother made upon her. She, unlike Simone, did not question the endless succession of domestic tasks that were required of her or challenge the complete authority of her mother to organize and control every aspect of her social life. Zaza's eventual fate is tragic for forbidden to see the man whom she wishes to marry she develops meningitis and dies. Women, it would seem, cannot allow dissension in their children but neither can their female children oppose them without grave risks to themselves.

Psychoanalytic explanations of de Beauvoir's view of men and women would no doubt claim that in Sartre she found a man who fulfilled for her all the disappointed expectations which she had of her father and that her rejection of a traditional female role (and in particular of maternity) is derived from a hatred of all that her mother was and represented. Such an explanation is discounted by de Beauvoir herself, as indeed she rejects psychoanalysis in general. The work of Freud, and others, holds little interest for her since it relies upon the belief that an unconscious exists in the human mind and that it is not susceptible to conscious, rational control. The patterns of human relationships so dear to the heart of psychoanalysts are dismissed as "quasi-mechanical rationalizations"[11] and although Freud is later accorded some more serious attention it remains limited.

Yet such a form of analysis might help to explain the intense grief that de Beauvoir describes in her book about the death of her mother, *A Very Easy Death*. Of all her books it is the most economical, the most terse and in some ways the most engaging. The relationship between mother and daughter had never been very close or sympathetic but they had managed to evolve some kind of *modus vivendi* since the time when Simone left home and established a way of life quite foreign to all her parents' wishes and expectations. But confronted by the possibility of her mother's death de Beauvoir is shattered and helpess with misery and despair. Despite the fact that she still finds her mother irritating and, on a conscious and rational level, someone with whom she has little in common, she is nevertheless, as she admits, virtually prostrated with grief at her death. It would seem that an imperfectly understood relationship has finally been revealed to her and that at last she has had to confront the ties, albeit unchosen and unwilling, that have united her with this particular dying woman. Precisely because de Beauvoir has always refused the possibility of maternity herself so perhaps the acknowledgement of her own relationship to her mother is the more surprising and disturbing to her. The conscious rejection that de Beauvoir had to make, at the age of 15, of her mother and all that she stood for, could always be seen as a conscious, rational design as long as the rejected figure remained alive. But as soon as the rejected figure dies, so the rejection becomes traumatic and much less easy to rationalize, since the threat of an emotional loss — and not just a conscious disagreement — now becomes present. There is no rational reason for de Beauvoir to mourn the loss of a woman whose opinions she finds childish and incoherent and yet mourn her she does, and with an intensity which she has not shown on the deaths of those who had been intellectually and politically much closer to her.

Simone de Beauvoir's work has provided, for many women, by far the most systematic and coherent account of the subordination of women. Yet precisely because of the influence that her work has had, it is necessary to consider the shortcomings and limitations of her understanding of the female, and to a certain extent, the male condition. Without wishing to elevate "nature" or the irrational to romantic levels of importance and explanation I would suggest that certain aspects of human life and experience, whilst entirely amenable to rational understanding and analysis, are not always derived from it. The real possibilities for the emancipation of women lie not in the denial of the "feminine" or the supposedly irrational needs and desires of women, but in their acceptance and integration within a totality of human experience. To deny women the possibility of bearing children and expressing maternal affection and commitment cannot be an aim of feminism. On the contrary, feminists should assert that women have the right to express all aspects of their creative potential and should not be asked to reject or suppress their emotional needs and desires for reasons of social and/or male convenience. Undeniably, the social construction and elaboration of motherhood and sexual relations between the sexes has often been to the disadvantage of women but the assumption by women of male patterns of behaviour can only increase, rather than lessen, the oppression of both sexes. The opposition suggested throughout de Beauvoir's work between the rational male and the irrational female reflects, all too uncritically, one of the more irrational elements in Western thought, and one which has long been used to distort the behaviour of both men and women.

Notes

1. Also published during this period were the fictional works, *The Woman Destroyed* and *Les Belles Images*.

2. de Beauvoir, Simone. 1965. *The Prime of Life*, p. 22. Penguin, Harmondsworth.

3. de Beauvoir, Simone. 1965. *Force of Circumstance*, p. 69. Andre Deutsch and Weidenfeld and Nicholson, London.

4. de Beauvoir, *The Prime of Life*, *op. cit.* p. 129.

5. de Beauvoir, *The Prime of Life*, *op. cit.* p. 306.

6. de Beauvoir, *The Prime of Life*, *op. cit.* p. 63.

7. de Beauvoir, *The Prime of Life*, *op. cit.* p. 100.

8. de Beauvoir, Simone. 1964. *The Second Sex*, p. 477.

9. de Beauvoir, *The Second Sex*, p. 367.

10. Walters, Margaret. The rights and wrongs of women. In Oakley, A. and Mitchell, J., eds. *The Rights and Wrongs of Women*, p. 357. Penguin, Harmondsworth.

11. de Beauvoir, *The Prime of Life*, p. 127.

On "Clearing the Air": My Letter to Simone de Beauvoir
Carol Ascher*

In June 1980, while writing *Simone de Beauvoir: A Life of Freedom*, I stopped to compose an imaginary letter, which I then somewhat brazenly included as a chapter, "Clearing the Air—A Personal Word."[1] The following is a slightly shortened version.

Dear Simone de Beauvoir,

I am in the midst of writing my book about your ideas, and I have been badly troubled by you—by my book on you—over the past weeks. Often in the morning as I go to my desk, I feel resentful, begrudging, sick of the lack of reciprocity between us. I know that if I am to convey to others what is admirable about you, I must do more than mechanically edit out my off-balance sentences. Besides, continuing on mechanically seems to me a kind of "bad faith." So I shall sit here until I have put down on paper what has happened to me in relation to you over the past years, but particularly over the last months of intensive reading and writing about your work.

I first heard of you when I was twenty years old and, ignoring my immigrant parents' hopes that Vassar College would turn me into a dignified and socially prominent young woman, had just transferred to

*Reprinted from Carol Ascher, Louise DeSalvo, and Sara Ruddick, eds., *Between Women* (Boston: Beacon Press, 1984), 85–103. © 1984 by Carol Ascher, Louise DeSalvo, and Sara Ruddick. Reprinted by permission of Beacon Press.

Barnard College in New York City. In the deteriorated rooming house where I settled, one of several students in my suite was a dark-haired Brooklyn girl with hazel eyes. In my first memory of her, she is standing against my doorway in jeans and a black turtleneck, holding a ragged paperback with a naked lady draped across its cover. I look at the book fearfully: it reads *The Second Sex* by Simone de Beauvoir. This was 1961. Somehow this new sophisticated roommate must have told me what the book was about. I know she remarked, in the offhand way she assumed at the time, that she was a feminist, as was her mother. I had never even heard the word before. I certainly did not want to read the book.

My other early memory of the woman, who would become one of my dearest friends, is of her going everywhere for an entire semester carrying a canary yellow-jacketed book with *Being and Nothingness* striped boldly in black. A high-strung person, she nervously tore off the corner of each page and twisted it into a ball as she read; and I recall *Being and Nothingness* growing as ragged over the months as *The Second Sex* had been.

It amazes me to imagine how rapidly I must have changed, at least in my grasp of the world around me. In my late teens, I had loved the Beatnik writers but must have sensed that I could not travel alone like Jack Kerouac. After graduation, I married a young man, who "was going to be a writer" and went to live in Spain and Morocco with him. For the first time in my life, I smoked kif and glimpsed the lonely world of expatriates. Back in New York a year later, I found myself ill with a serious case of hepatitis. While I was in the indigent ward of the hospital, my Barnard friend brought me *The Mandarins*. That was the first book by you I actually ever read. Rereading it recently, I was astounded at how little of the political discussions which form the core of the book I could have understood then. Raised in the Midwest by refugee parents whose fears were aggravated by the cold war, my one childhood moment of political daring occurred when I told my schoolmates that my parents were voting for the Democratic candidate; and just as they had warned me, the schoolchildren taunted me for it. In college I read Marx's *Communist Manifesto* as part of a nineteenth-century philosophy course; but if there was any discussion of its political power or role, I don't remember it. Certainly, the discussions in *The Mandarins* about whether to expose Stalin's slave labor camps to a European public must have passed me completely by. What I do remember clearly from my first encounter with the novel, as I lay flat on my back in the hospital, is my erotic pleasure at the sections on Anne and Lewis in Chicago and my discomfort and fear at the idea of Anne's husband waiting for her to return home to Paris. In a Spanish seaside village, I had watched American and French writers and painters in their own little society of "free love," but had found it too disturbing to enter.

My marriage ended in the roughhousing, careless optimism of 1968.

Although I didn't like the idea, I believed monogamy and the family were clearly dead; and being the obedient, serious woman I still was, I set out to adapt to the new sexual festival. If I had been told to live out my days strapped in a roller coaster I couldn't have been more baffled and unhappy. I sincerely thought I wanted to change, I worked hard at it, but I also knew that deep inside me lay a spiteful resistance and a longing for the old conservative ways.

In 1972, in a women's consciousness-raising group, I read *The Second Sex* for the first time. The flowering women's movement had already created enough of a new demand for the book that the paperback now sported a snappy white cover with sharp black and gold lettering. This copy, marked up then, as again over the years, stands in my bookshelf at my side as I write. There are pen notes indicating identification — "Yes," "Me too" — but also irritation — "Bah!" from this early reading. And on the empty back page are two old notes: "This is a very unsexy world," and a longer one expressing my annoyance that, given your relentless analysis of patriarchy throughout history, your final offer of socialism and a changed consciousness about women seemed unconvincing. Even at this early reading, a combination of recognition, fear, and anger characterized my responses to what you had written.

These days when I read *The Second Sex*, I feel the same frustration, though in different terms. It seems to me now that you depict a world where radical feminism is the only solution: a world where there really is no possible accord between women and men. At the same time, you clearly have little patience with what biology and society have made of women. In your despairing view, all those qualities that make women differ from men lead only to our demise. And so, while your picture of the world of patriarchy would lead women readers to feel that we must band together and go off on our own, your dislike of women (perhaps a kind of self-hatred) makes this completely unpalatable. It's a cul-de-sac that many women, including myself at times, have felt. But it makes your bid for men to take a different attitude toward women appear dubious and your proposal of socialism seem extraneous.

I understand your urge to offer a solution, even when none must have seemed clear. But there is an unhappy space I sense in general between the complexity of your description of the way things are and have been and the alternative visions you propose. I find this equally a problem in *The Coming of Age*, where your proposals for ending the plight of the aged seem unconvincing and almost silly given what has come before.

Perhaps the trouble lies at a deeper level. Even in your memoirs, you have a way of brushing aside the pain and ambiguity with which you have described an event or period and asserting the thing a success. I feel this, for example, when you assert that in your entire relationship with Sartre the two of you have "only once gone to sleep at night disunited."[2] Can the reader really be expected to believe this, after all your descriptions of bewildering, lost, or angry days? It is as if you must put a stamp of approval on your memories in order to go on. But the stamp simplifies the honest profusion of your life, and draws me to focus on your apparent dishonesty rather than on the brutal and wonderful honesty of the remaining passages. At times, writing this book, I have taken out such summary sentences, feeling a generosity toward you. For instance, when I quoted a section from *All Said and Done*, in which you spoke of not wanting to marry because Sartre did not — "I never should have been capable, even in thought, of forcing his hand in any serious matter" — I ended the matter there, since even that seemed to stretch your honesty. Yet there is an additional sentence that concludes the paragraph: "Supposing that for reasons I can scarcely imagine we had been obliged to marry," you say, "I know we should have managed to live our marriage in freedom."[3] Really! After what you've said about marriage in *The Second Sex* and elsewhere, how can one believe that you take that sentence seriously? Or do you see yourself so above all the traps life sets for others?

Perhaps a person as easily made testy about a writer should not write a book on her work. Certainly, I myself have often wondered about that over the past year or more. Yet there is another side to my reactions to you that comes out mainly in my sleep. About three or four years ago when I was deciding to leave the university and devote myself solely to my writing, you appeared in a dream to warmly wish me well. The dream was very important to me, the sternness with which I sense you in the day (so like my mother's) turning to kindness and support. And a few months ago, just after Sartre's death, when I was already deep in the writing of this book, I dreamed I had come to Paris to interview you. In the dream, you seemed so much softer than I had imagined you would be; and I made a note to myself to be sure to write this in the book. But I was also unsure about what to ask you. I seemed to have forgotten my notes, or else I had neglected to prepare. The house began to fill with other women. You went out and returned with a black tiara to indicate your mourning, and I thought I should offer my condolences. But then I let myself sit quietly in the room with the other women, feeling I was learning more about you by watching than if I had forced my way with a prepared interview. Waking from the dream, I felt peaceful and lighthearted. As in the earlier dream, my meeting with you had left me refreshed.

You must know that women my age and younger look to those of your generation as models, since our sense of what women can be has been so cramped by history (or its lack). Of course, this puts a pressure on your life and work which you only partially have asked for. At a deeper level, at least in my case, there is also the wish to repair the way we have been mothered by creating other relationships, even if only literary, intellectual, or in dreams, with other women. Unfortunately, you aren't that "good mother" I long for in my weakest moments. Although you have always taken young women under your wing, I sense your aloofness. Because of its echo in your memoirs, I take seriously the words you put into Anne's mouth in respect to her daughter, Nadine, in *The Mandarins*.[4] You have Anne say she feels "remorse because I didn't know how to make her obey me and because I didn't love her enough. It would have been more kind of me not to smother her with kindness. Perhaps I might have been able to comfort her if I simply took her in my arms and said, 'My poor little daughter, forgive me for not loving you more.' "[5] Of course, Anne doesn't take Nadine in her arms, partly because Nadine has become a bristly young woman who couldn't bear it; just as my mother, too, long ago gave up trying to embrace me, because it seemed I couldn't bear it. You are brave for saying fictionally that Nadine's resistance to Anne's signs of affection is her knowledge of her mother's lack of deep acceptance. My mother has never been able to admit this in reality and is no writer of fiction. And who knows, in my case, where the first causes lie. I do know that in my waking life I am irritated by this and other traits that resemble my mother's, although in my dreams I have thankfully become able to give myself the warmth for which I long.

Why do I make you the mother in these fictional moments when your experience may as likely come from the side of the daughter? I wonder if you also tensed under your mother's embraces, feeling that she loved you insufficiently. Particularly after your loss of faith, you may have felt estranged. Or maybe, like me, you were tense because you knew you wished her harm in your competition for your father. And the images of Anne and Robert, or you and Sartre, as a unit alone are only resolutions of that wish to be a third no longer—to get rid of the third. But then why always crowd your life with him with "contingent" lovers? I can answer my own question: The symptom is an expression of, and a defense against, the unacceptable wish.

I don't believe in objectivity and I cannot pretend my attitude is neutral.

This June, it is exactly fifteen years since I first read *The Mandarins* and eight years since I first read *The Second Sex*. From time to time I have gone on to read your other books and now have read, I think, all of the books you have written and a number of Sartre's as well. I often do this, particularly with a woman writer: it is a way of getting beyond the work to the person. And just as I tend toward long friendships, I find myself drawing out my relationships with writers who interest me by returning again and again to the library for more of their books. With you, the relationship has always been ambivalent; perhaps that is its power. Certainly, it has never been strongly negative enough to push me away altogether. Yet, as with my mother, the anger seems ready, as if lying in wait for the least crime against me. And less accessible, but also there, is the longing for a deep warmth and acceptance.

It seems strange to me now that we know so little about how most biographers or writers of literary or philosophical criticism feel about the writers whose lives and works they are describing. I'm not talking just about whether the biographer liked or admired the person, although that interests me too. Over the past months, I, for example, have worried far less about whether my imperfect knowledge of French and France detract from my right to write about you than about whether my complicated feelings and needs take away this right. But I am also talking now about how the daily intense concern with another person — perhaps most similar to the attitude one takes when hovering over the sick — made the writer feel. Perhaps admissions on this score are too dangerous, given our prevailing demands for an objectivity born of distance. If a writer confessed to editing out angry, ironic, or pleading sentences, what would happen to the reader's trust in those nicely balanced, Olympian sentences left standing?

I know that, since one of the themes I find over and over in your writing is that of tension and confusion between the "I" and the "we," I can easily be accused of projecting my own difficulties in the world, in general, and in writing about you, in particular, onto you and your work. It's almost a joke, isn't it — too close for comfort — that we might share some of the same weaknesses? Possibly also some of the same strengths. My own sense of being an intellectual has certainly gotten stronger as I have studied your writings and experienced your own solidity in the area. But I am still talking of a "we" between us, where the boundary is unclear.

My first sense of distance slipping was, in fact, an eerie and continuing recognition of our similarities. I note that in early April I wrote in my journal, "These days as I read de Beauvoir I find myself less able to assert, 'I'm not like her.' I recognize the aloofness combined with the hysteria — and then wonder if I am distorting my own image of myself in order to be like her. In short, I'm losing the distance I had a year ago: liking her more, feeling more like her for better or worse." I was reading *The Mandarins* at the time.

A few days later, having just finished *A Woman Destroyed* [a slim volume containing three stories about older women], I noted, "Feel like de Beauvoir is making me experience death and aging as I've never experienced them — even though I've written about both for years." Both parts of the sentence are utterly true: You had just made me feel I had never before *really* experienced death and, in fact, most of my fiction is about death — including a novel on which I had worked for three years and had only recently completed. It seems, as I look at these notes, that a kind of annihilation of myself by you was threatening to occur.

Then, on April 16, while I was looking at early book reviews of your works, a young woman I didn't know glanced over my shoulder. "You know, Sartre just died," she said, concernedly. "It was in this morning's paper." Tears came to my eyes; I felt confused: a friend, a husband, a father? What was/is he? My own father had died fifteen years ago, and all deaths call up that time. Then, over the next days, I began to worry about what it meant to write about a woman who is part of a duo and then, suddenly, midstream, whose companion is dead. All my sentences about you and Sartre, once in a continuing present tense, had to be changed. Going over the text to make those changes made the death real to me. More important, his death seemed to bring a sacredness to your relationship; a superstition cautioned me: You can't attack anything connected to the dead.

When my father died, it seemed at first an enormous tension had drained away between my mother and me. I identified with her suffering. In my arrogance, I felt at times that I suffered more than she. Yet soon I began to focus with her on the ways in which she was better off without the domination and demands of my father.

But you see, for me the gestalt has a terrible way of reversing itself. These days, when I am with my mother I find myself ruthlessly attacking my father. My mother, who is protective toward him but also knows how I once loved him, is astonished — and so am I! Because when I am in New York and she is back in her city, I, in fact think longingly of my father and often wish he were alive — at the same time as the slightest provocation, whether through memory or a letter from her, sends me directly to irritation and anger at my mother.

It is no wonder then that I feel anxious about my changing reactions to you, and particularly about my attitudes toward your relationship with Sartre. Whenever you write that Sartre's ideas had changed, and yours with his, I hear a scream rising inside me. Even now, my mother maintains that she always felt in complete harmony with my father, who made several dramatic changes during their time together. I don't want to stretch the parallels. Yet your decision to remain with Sartre, to make him the center of your life, seems to have entailed a heavy sacrifice of body, emotions, and, yes, sometimes even mind. "I should never have been capable, even in thought. . . ." Surely, he did nourish you intellectually; but to my generation, the emotions and the body are terribly important, offering truths and pleasures, a path to the self, which cannot be arrived at by a highly trained rational mind alone. At times, I have felt that she sacrificed some inner core in order to be a witness. Here is Anne in *The Mandarins* speaking: "I've always been able to avoid being caught by the snare of mirrors. But the glances, the looks, the stares of other people, who can resist that dizzying pit? I dress in black, speak little, write not at all; together, all these things form a certain picture which others see. I'm no one. It's easy of course to say 'I am I.' But who am I? Where to find myself?"[6] I know that Anne is not you. Yet you speak similarly of Françoise in *She Came to Stay* and of yourself at times in your memoirs — who were you in relation to Zaza, you wondered. Writing itself does not seem to solve the problem of identity for you. Since at times I doubt your separateness from Sartre, or that of your female characters from their mates, the witness who is "no one" slides into being a surrogate witness for

Sartre, Dubreuil, Pierre. I must say, I am suspicious of Sartre as well as you, when he also says that the two of you, in understanding each other perfectly, could evaluate each other's work "objectively," as if from the point of view of a witness who was "no one."[7]

I think that I must be terribly threatened by and weary of this level of merging, having fought so hard for separateness and still so often tempted to let my boundaries dissolve. It seems clear that my main difficulty in working on your writings is my fear or wish that the boundaries between us will simply disappear. That I will become a witness to you, who is "no one." I note a May entry: "Afraid of being swallowed up by her — afraid of losing the separateness I've struggled so hard for."

On the other side, just as I love my mother when she assumes her independence, I love your urge toward freedom, your sense of yourself continually creating your life through courage and imagination. Particularly the first two books of your memoirs are filled with this power. And while you are critical of the individualism of your early years, I find a tone of joyous exuberance that I miss in much of the descriptions of an older you who had become politically responsible and respectable. Perhaps that is the influence the 1960s still holds on me: I want a joyous political movement, one with fun and humor, no matter how grim our situation or how powerful our enemy.

Yet how grateful I was when, some years ago, I began to read Jean-François Steiner's *Treblinka*, the story of the daring rebellion by starving and exhausted Jewish inmates inside one of Hitler's extermination camps, and found that *you* had written the introduction. I had been among the millions of Jews who had been led to believe our relatives had "gone like sheep to slaughter." Treblinka had a more daring, hopeful message — which included the possibility for freedom inside the worst hell. As you say about the incredible rising of resistance at Treblinka, "If it takes only a few cowards to make the entire series become cowardly, it takes only a few heroes to make people recover confidence in each other and begin to dare."[8] Steiner had tried to re-create this shift from fear and deathly resignation to incredible courage; and you understood how crucial this message of freedom would be, perhaps particularly to Jews.

Oh, I sometimes find myself griping about your notion of freedom. Although you increasingly grounded it in the social world — to the point where in *A Woman Destroyed* or *The Coming of Age* one loses the sense of individual freedom and responsibility — I don't think you ever grasped sufficiently the way the unconscious can hold one back from grasping a freedom consciously chosen. Too often I see your sense of freedom being based on a rationalism that denies that murky inner world over which we have as little, or much, control as the world outside us. And, in fact, control would be your word, not mine. For I've come to believe that we have to love this deep inner self and try to be in harmony with it. We can't make our life a "continuous flight from the past," to paraphrase Sartre;[9] it often backfires when we try. I understand that your rationalism is a reaction to the Catholicism of your childhood and to the enormous leap you had to make to step out of the life that had been planned for you. It was a step into freedom, but it must have meant denying old longings for comforts you knew were poison. Music, even more than fiction (which you approach somewhat rationally), seems to be the one area where you allow that nonrational self to play in pleasure; and you have said that listening to music has become increasingly important to you in later years.[10] I think, though, that my generation, which didn't have to fight the irrational domination of religion, may be able to feel out some of the nonrational areas, including that of spirituality, which you so understandably shun, without losing our freedom, allowing us to become more whole.

Sometimes I fear that my arguments with you, however right they may be in content, are also a way of showing myself that we are separate. I hear in myself a tone that indicates a pulling away, an assertion of my own individuality. But, as my parents used to take pleasure in reminding me, I was always a rebellious child. Perhaps my temperament, in this sense reminiscent of your own, is not the best suited to that of a biographer or critic. Perhaps one needs either to be certain at all times of being separate, or to be comfortable with stretches of merging, to be able to offer the gift of empathy.

My trouble with working on my book about you reached a crisis about a month ago: it centered around a kind of mothering. Or around my unwillingness to mother. Like you, I am childless. Generous to my friends, I actually often feel stingy in my own eyes. And also easily drained. For years, I thought I wasn't having a child because I needed first to give to myself. Once, when unintentionally pregnant, I dreamed of being gnawed at by the fetus, as by a crow inside me. Later, when I began to give myself more of what I needed, that very self-feeding, since it came in the form of writing, seemed to take up all my time. I feel sad that I won't have a child: giving birth is an act of optimism about oneself and the world.

At moments, I have felt a rancor whose expression is: Why should I be devoting myself to you when you never did anything for me? Now, I know that through your books, you have done a lot for me. And the writing of this one is doing still more. But when I feel deprived and unacknowledged, I resent your righteous success and feel stingy about contributing toward the attention you already receive. Perhaps this resentment adds to my wish to be critical. In any case, one day I heard about a woman who wanted to give her pubescent children away; and, without understanding why, I felt compelled to turn her story into fiction. Putting aside your books, I stuck a new white sheet in the typewriter, wrote "Nothing for Nothing" as its title, and a short story poured out of me. For several days, I alternated between working on "your book" and writing my story. I find a note in my journal: "A feeling of congestion from working on de Beauvoir, as if I had a child who was home all the time and left me no space. No wonder I'm writing 'Nothing for Nothing.' "

I can assure you that this period, although highly productive, was quite miserable. By writing the story, I let my stinginess come out in full force. I contacted the feeling in me that I had nothing left to give another person, that I was fragmented, exhausted, worn to shreds by caring. For a few days, no one could give to me: all interaction was negative, stripping my depleted self further and further, until I felt the only rest was to lie on my bed quietly, out of reach of sound and light.

It seems to me now that this division into give and take, like the absolute division of subject and object, was at least part of the problem. I was "giving" by poring over your works, but I was holding myself back and trying desperately to keep you an object so that I would not be submerged. At a purely physical level, this posture can engender a severe backache — and it did. Is it possible that, if I could have let myself become more a part of you, at least temporarily, without the fear of losing myself, I could also have felt the rush of your giving, and mine wouldn't have seemed such an extraction?

This period is over, its culmination, at least in part, this letter to you. I wonder what other stages I will go through in the next months before I am done with my project. Yes, a lot of my anger has been relieved, some of my confusion and discomfort lessened. Certainly I can more easily send you affectionate respect now than three days ago when I began this letter; and I do send that to you. But I also know that I will remain me, and I suspect we may have some trouble again before the end of our mutual road.

June 4–7, 1980

Placed in the middle of my book, this letter tended to draw readers to it as immediately as a sexy centerfold and to create a stir with both its critics and its admirers. Including it within the pages of a book that, traditionally speaking, should have been about Simone de Beauvoir, *not* Carol Ascher (one in which Carol Ascher should have been invisible), was an act of bravery that warmed up the work to those who liked it and was both intrusive and proof that the rest of the book could be little more than projections and confusions of identity to those who didn't. Though one reviewer, expressing the positive end of the spectrum of reactions wrote that this "interesting interlude . . . does, in fact, clear the air and bring the reader, writer and subject closer together," the negative end was expressed most dramatically in an exceptionally large review headline: "de Beauvoir Biography Overshadowed by Its Author."

Granted that it was useful for me personally to "clear the air," why did I insert the chapter, in the center no less? At the time, what struck me as I looked through biographies and literary criticism was *exactly* the absence of such confessionals within their pages. Women and men had spent years — far more than I — thinking and writing about the lives and works of others. They must have come to impasses such as I was experiencing; I'm not that odd. Yet they had covered their tracks. *I*, I thought to myself, would leave for others a record of what might be entailed in a long, intense involvement with another woman on whom one was writing. The letter not only would describe the acts of regaining balance or objectivity and convey the quality of my experience, but it would also offer readers a clue about the perspective from which the remainder of the book was written.

What interests me now, nearly three years later, and with the insights engendered by the book's reception, are two issues. Put bluntly, they are *truth:* in what ways did my epistemological exercise help me regain my balance and aid my readers in gaining theirs? And *beauty:* what kind of an aesthetic experience was I offering?

To speak first to the issue of truth — as it concerns myself: I believe that, insofar as one sees things with any "objectivity," one does so only by clearing out those ignored and unresolved emotions that function like brambles, stinging one's eyes and blocking one's vision when one tries to look outward. Obviously, this "clearing out" is an ideal. Most of us know of that disinterested but ecstatic emptiness from which the world is seen "as it really is" only from tales of yogic and other mystic states. The more usual, "impartial" perspective of, say, scholarship or journalism is produced by a combination of psychological muffling and the obscuring (to the authors themselves, much of the time) of vested interest. Humbly acknowledging my incapacity for the former and my disaste for the latter, my supposition was still that, once I had "cleared the air," the remainder of the book would proceed with the same measure of evenhandedness which until then had satisfied me.

Emotionally, the letter was effective. Once I had written it, I continued working on the book with more fluidity and joy and an easier, warmer feeling toward Simone de Beauvoir. In a friendship, when one finally stops the flow of daily life to say exactly what has been driving one crazy, there is invariably an enormous relief and freeing up afterward. Just so with this book. Though a letter clearly couldn't resolve the deep issues that years of introspection still had left tangled, I *felt* back in balance. I had the distance I needed, I could see what was really there. At one level, I had simply given my "I" enough run to rectify the rested imbalance of attention.

Does all this mean that I judge truth by the way I feel? Partly. But not completely or necessarily. It seems an important aspect but one that demands constant tempering by self-reflection. Clearing the air may leave one even blinder, if one has gotten rid of discomforting emotions that act as warnings signs. Moreover, two people's blind spots—the author's and her subject's mutually (but blindly) corroborated—don't create a reliable vision.

As I look back on my time studying Simone de Beauvoir's life and work, I am able to categorize my responses into several attitudes or kinds of feelings: (1) Coldness, utter disinterest, a sense that she was wrong, but I was insufficiently interested to sift through details and arguments. An endless volume on China, which she wrote rapidly after a visit in the 1950s and which quickly proved naive, didn't seem even worth treating in my book. (2) Neutrality, brief or minor flares into negative or positive responses, but in areas that were clearly central to de Beauvoir's life and thought, so that I felt obliged to give them play. Her ideas on aging and death are a good example: Where Elaine Marks's work on de Beauvoir focused entirely on de Beauvoir's vision of aging and death, I devoted merely a chapter to the subject (3) Appreciation of an area of de Beauvoir's life or work where, although I might disagree or disapprove of points, it seemed easy to separate my own point of view and where I never felt caught. Her ideas of freedom and choice are good examples—perhaps the content itself helped here. Finally, (4) irritation, conflict! Areas where my own personal conflicts seemed to both contaminate and illuminate what I was seeing in her. Interestingly, the areas that provoked me most were those showing the underside of freedom and choice: In my book, I dealt with them in the two chapters of which I wrote in my letter that my conflicts overlapped with hers. In one I traced de Beauvoir's life according to the concepts of the "I" and the "we"; in the other, I followed her early novels as they worked out a similar struggle between what I called "the self and other."

As I read and reread Simone de Beauvoir's memoirs, I found myself wincing at the failures in freedom she herself so often noted: She's not separate in her relations with a friend! She wants to merge with Sartre! She is trying to dissolve her personal identity and problems in the world's atrocities! (This last, in reaction to a passage in which she slipped back and forth between rage at the torture of an Algerian boy and at her own aging.) The question that her life and work continually raised, but did not solve, was for me: How can one be an "I" at the same time as one is part of a "we"? How can one retain one's separate identity when one is a devoted lover, a loyal friend, a committed activist—or, for that matter, an engaged biographer?

A major category in Simone de Beauvoir's writings is that of "the Other." It is handled overtly in *The Second Sex* and in *The Coming of Age* to describe women and the aged, respectively. And, though more covert, it is key to understanding most of her novels, from *She Came to Stay* to *The Blood of Others*, *All Men Are Mortal*, and even *The Mandarins*. A Hegelian category that Sartre transformed for his own philosophical purposes, the notion of the Other was seen by both de Beauvoir and Sartre as directing attention to the most primitive aspect of human beings: our refusal (in their view) to accept finiteness and our wish to obliterate the frailty of our finite selves through either dominating or being dominated by others, thus creating illusions of infiniteness. Many of Sartre's plays explore the sadomasochism of human relationships as his characters seek omnipotence. With a slightly different emphasis, de Beauvoir stresses the wish to merge, and in a sense to accept domination, in her female characters. Moreover, in *The Second Sex* de Beauvoir uses the same concept for historical explanation, arguing that the oppression of women could not have occurred (neither social class nor penis envy nor biology is sufficient to explain it) "if the human consciousness had not included the original category of the Other and an original aspiration to dominate the Other."[11] That is, in men's domination of women throughout history, a psychological necessity has been played out in which both women and men give up their freedom through women's becoming the Other, the Object, of men's domination.

But all philosophies, as I asserted in my book and still believe, are both personal philosophies and systems intended to be universal. The desire to dominate or be dominated—to merge—that both de Beauvoir and Sartre saw as the failure of our mortality was also a failure that they themselves were aware of in their relationship. One might say, in fact, that their own conflicts illuminated this area of existence. Though existentialism both evolved out of de Beauvoir's and Sartre's difficulties and gave them a tool with which to see their problems with "the Other" in both life and art, it only partially helped them resolve or overcome these problems. That they gave to the problem of "the Other" an existential, necessary character may also be one reason it had such a continuing hold on them. Living without God meant for them an irrepressible wish to *be* a god, to be infinite by obliterating those awesome distinctions between oneself and another that are essential to our mortality.

It seems to me now that de Beauvoir's very preoccupation with the self's tendency to merge with the other was partly responsible for my increasing discomfort as the months progressed. That is, not only was I not projecting my problems onto her (as I feared in my letter) but her problems in this area—the very painful way they appeared in her novels and memoirs—evoked the same uncertainties in me. As a good writer is able to do, she made me feel what she had experienced as well as stirring up my own unresolved difficulties.

My invention of the "I" and the "we" was an attempt to incorporate but also transcend her terms and conflicts, which seemed to offer no resolution as stated. Philosophically, I simply did not accept the primal place of the Other. To me, the idea of the Other, as worked out in de Beauvoir's memoirs, sociology, and fiction, seemed, at best, a powerful image or insight and, at worst, a rather pompous inflation of jealousy or hatred to a world view. Whereas philosophically and personally the "we" for de Beauvoir was always either unstable or a merged unity that threatened the existence of one "I," I had a vision of a "we" that was both ongoing and made up of simultaneously autonomous "I"'s. Reaching toward this ideal in my own life, I also used my belief in its possibility to cut through the scenes of de Beauvoir with Sartre, the fictional characters she created, and her basic term, the Other.

Did I achieve truth? About myself or Simone de Beauvoir? To avoid endless regression, I will answer the question as it relates to de Beauvoir. Certainly I did not re-create her "as she really is." Since I was writing, not creating clones, this couldn't even have been my goal. The portrait I painted, at best, would have related to the richness and complexity of her being as a good gesture drawing relates to a live person standing before the painter. This is particularly so in my case, since I had no intention of covering every aspect of de Beauvoir's life and character. The arms or the feet of my drawing, say, were deliberately only sketched in.

With or without the letter, was there a truth in my gesture drawing? And having written the letter, did I have a special line on truth? By whose judgment? I was thrilled when Simone de Beauvoir, upon seeing the completed manuscript, was satisfied by its truth and penetration. (It was a moment that gave me a much needed mothering.) Yet approval from the source, however comforting, might mean only that my distortions coincided with hers! Others—friends, even critics—thought they saw de Beauvoir in my drawing. Shall I then trust in the corroboration of numbers? How would Sartre, or someone who knew her intimately, have judged it? Did Lanzmann, the man with whom she lived for seven years while retaining her relationship with Sartre, see her in the same way as Sartre did? What if one of them had seen a side of de Beauvoir that was nowhere else revealed? Would it throw off the outlines of my drawing or simply fill in a hazy area with delicate detail? I imagine Simone de Beauvoir sitting in the live-model drawing class I once took. People sit or stand on all sides of her. Some see her from the right, others from the left. One drawing focuses on a bent elbow; another captures the edge of a cheek. All the drawings are of Simone de Beauvoir, but only the teacher, who moves godlike about the room and rests momentarily beside each student, can begin to perceive the whole. And even then. . . .

The drawing class has brought me to the epistemological and aesthetic question of including the letter in the book. In an interesting portrait, the painter Velázquez inserted himself at the edge of the painting. Some find that this oddity enhances the painting. Others think it an annoying intrusion: His other portraits, filled solely by their subjects, are so much more powerful! Because it is a painting, a form that has been accepted as subjective, and not a biography or a work of litrary criticism, the issue of truth is of little concern to most viewers. Yet by putting himself in the painting Velázquez tells his audience, "Here are some characteristics of the man who created the picture. You may be able to judge something about the accuracy of the portrait by seeing my face and the similarities and differences I have chosen to portray between myself and my subject." This act of rectification and warning may well help attentive viewers gain their "balance" or sighting in judging the painting.

Through my verbal self-portrait, I hoped I was giving readers information about myself that would help their capacity to judge my portrait of Simone de Beauvoir. My letter made clear, for example, that I was someone who valued personal honesty and attention to one's feelings and who would therefore be more critical than most of de Beauvoir in these areas. On the other hand, while another writer might one day devote herself to an analysis of the shifts in de Beauvoir's political positions and their relation to her activism, this was only of peripheral interest to me.

The question of inserting oneself in the portrait is also an aesthetic one. I imagine a different history of painting in which all pictures show the eye of the artist within the frame. In fact, the last five hundred years of painting offer us something like this, although we have come to read it so easily that we scarcely take notice. Until the Renaissance, paintings were executed as if from a universal point of view ("the eye of God"), which is not so different from our current objective voice in prose. However, starting in the fourteenth or fifteenth century, the institution of perspective in painting created for the first time a reference to the specific point from which the painter eyed the scene. Thus, houses receding in one way indicated that the painter had stood a little to the right, mountains falling away in another implied that the eye of the painter had been on a hill behind the viewer, looking down on the scene.

I suspect that those early painters who inserted perspective into their paintings worried that they were diminishing the grandeur and beauty of the art to insist on the truth of the specific human point of view. Certainly, they must have understood that they had given up representing the universal, God-like stance. On the other side, their new style also asserted the centrality of the "I" and its very specific perspective. It raised the eye of the individual creator to new importance.

The courageous step these painters took nearly five hundred years ago reminds me, in fact, of de Beauvoir's and Sartre's break with the world view of Catholicism to create a philosophical view, existentialism, in which human beings alone and together are the moral judge, the measure of all things. And the awkwardnesses and ugly moments in de Beauvoir's writings are the combined result of her being new at the enterprise and our being unused to seeing its expression.

Perhaps the insurgents of each generation must in their own way fight once again to "clear the air" of the conventions of the powerful solidified into universal truths. Increasingly during our century, the universal God-given standards have been replaced by those of science. And as God as judge and mediator had his prose style, so science has its. Yet the human interests that these truths protect remain the same: the interests of ruling white, Western men. As Simone de Beauvoir herself remarked in the opening pages of *The Second Sex*:

> But if I wish to define myself, I must first of all say: "I am a woman"; on this truth must be based all further discussion. A man never begins by presenting himself as an individual of a certain sex; it goes without saying that he is a man. The terms *masculine* and *feminine* are used symmetrically only as a matter of form, as on legal papers. In actuality the relation of the two sexes is not quite like that of two electrical poles, for man represents both the positive and the neutral, as is indicated by the common use of *man* to designate human beings in general; whereas *woman* represents only the negative, defined by limiting criteria, without reciprocity.[12]

And if one must strike out again and again to assert the *humanness* of one's perspective, its specificity, then that movement into what seems uncharted space must necessarily seem awkward. Cranky. Even grandiose. Until it becomes a new convention, viewed as aesthetically satisfying by the current standards, and must again be broken down.

Days when I look at "Clearing the Air—A Personal Word" nestled as it is in the midst of a book dotted with "I"s, I wince at whatever aesthetic judgment allowed me to place it there, whatever I thought of its value as truth. Why couldn't I have written a book whose clean, sleek surface lay unbroken, invulnerable, unruffled by the squirms of a conflicted "I"? The "I" of a woman still seems so much more naked on the page than that of a man. The aesthetic almost has a moral component: A good girl wouldn't expose herself that way, and in public! But then I imagine a new aesthetic (and a new morality) in which people, including myself, are more at ease with closeness, with uncertainty about truth, and with the confusing mix of subject and object that constitutes what is finally there to be seen—and what the reader's eye and mind take in with her or his own predispositions. I suspect that if such an aesthetic were to develop it would be accompanied by an easing of the stranglehold of fact and science, which in our day so often makes us fear a world beyond our control. It would likely be a nicer, more egalitarian, safer world all around—perhaps more beautiful as well.

Notes

1. Carol Ascher, *Simone de Beauvoir: A Life of Freedom* (Boston: Beacon Press, 1981), 107–22.

2. Simone de Beauvoir, *Force of Circumstance*, trans. Richard Howard (Harmondsworth, Eng.: Penguin, 1968), 569.

3. Simone de Beauvoir, *All Said and Done*, trans. Patrick O'Brien (New York: Warner, 1975), 28.

4. This is Anne speaking of Nadine:

I hadn't wanted her; it was Robert who wanted to have a child right away. I've always held it against Nadine that she upset my life alone with Robert. I loved Robert too much and I wasn't interested enough in myself to be moved by the discovery of his features or mine on the face of that little intruder. Without feeling any particular affection, I took notice of her blue eyes, her hair, her nose.

And you in *The Prime of Life*:

A child would not have strengthened the bonds that united Sartre and me; nor did I want Sartre's existence reflected and extended in some other being. He was sufficient both for himself and for me. I too was self-sufficient: I never once dreamed of rediscovering myself in the child I might bear. In any case, I felt such absence of affinity with my own parents that any sons or daughters I might have I regarded in advance as strangers.

Simone de Beauvoir, *The Mandarins*, trans. Leonard M. Friedman (Glasgow: Fontana, 1960), 81; and Simone de Beauvoir, *The Prime of Life*, trans. Peter Green (Harmondsworth, Eng.: Penguin, 1965), 77.

5. de Beauvoir, *Mandarins*, 78.

6. de Beauvoir, *Mandarins*, 48.

7. Michel Sicard, "*Interférences: Entretien avec Simone de Beauvoir et Jean-Paul Sartre*," *Obliques, Numero Spécial sur Sartre, dirigé par Michel Sicard* 18–19 (1979), 325–39.

8. Simone de Beauvoir, preface to *Treblinka*, by Jean-François Steiner, trans. Helen Weaver (New York: Simon & Schuster, 1967), 10.

9. See Hazel E. Barnes, *Sartre* (Philadelphia: Lippincott, 1973), 22.

10. de Beauvoir, *All Said and Done*, 210.

11. Simone de Beauvoir, *The Second Sex*, trans. and ed. H. M. Parshley (New York: Vintage, 1974), 64.

12. de Beauvoir, *Second Sex*, xvii–xviii.

Simone de Beauvoir . . . Autobiographer

Kate Millett*

It is in this century that autobiography has come into its own as a genre. Occupying, sometimes even displacing the novel in narrative interest, in the development of character, in the portrait of an age — things we have loved and cherished in the novel. But the novel was always "made up," a "fiction," "invented": autobiography, on the other hand, has the virtue of appearing "real," "true," "fact" — or at least accountable. And perhaps that's the difference; for however an event is narrated in autobiography, it not only partakes of the conventions of fiction — character, dialogue, scene, commentary — it partakes ultimately of the same "arrangement" of reality which we expect in fiction. But autobiography has

*An earlier draft of this essay was presented as a paper at the Colloquium on Simone de Beauvoir held 4–6 April 1985 at Columbia University. It is included by permission of the French House of Columbia University and the author. © 1985 by Kate Millett.

the added element of accountability. The author is involved in the first person. Doris Lessing once teased me about this difference. She had just read the first draft of *Flying* at the dining room table at the farm and then came upstairs to my bedroom where I was dying of a fine combination of editorial indifference and disapproval which had produced jaundice and a gall bladder condition that in another week would verge on peritonitis. "You really have guts if you print this stuff; it's wonderfully brave," she said. "Ah, but all the Martha Quest books," I countered, knowing them as autobiography. "Who is Martha Quest?" she answered. "You know I always have that out—I can go blank and say innocently, 'But who is Martha Quest?' You can't."

In the same way de Beauvoir, who has written of a love triangle in fiction—*She Came to Stay*—has a certain safety there which she surrenders in autobiography, *The Prime of Life*. There when Simone de Beauvoir pulls every string to get behind German lines and visit Sartre who is a lowly soldier in a country town, spends days on trains and talking her way past officers—and is finally sent away after only one night with him—there is a special pathos and vulnerability. Because it is the first person, the actual person. And, being that model of integrity which she is, the accountability of this narrator is something we believe, give allegiance to, learn from, identify with. Experience is perceived and understood through a narrator. Because of the first person, because of the actual self, the public made private and then public again. The risk taken.

If autobiography comes into its own in our time—for men as well as women writers: Henry Miller, for example, or Jean Genet—it is, par excellence, the medium of modern women writers, whether oblique as Lessing or direct as Anaïs Nin, Violette Leduc, or de Beauvoir. And because this conference will, for obvious reasons, concentrate upon de Beauvoir's *The Second Sex*, I would like to reach out to another form which she has mastered and wherein she has had as profound, if not so well recognized, effect on the women of her time—that exploration of the self and the analysis of experience which we call autobiography. (One could also make a case here for de Beauvoir as a writer of fiction—*A Woman Destroyed*, for example, is my idea of the perfect text, the quintessential document of feminist protest: richly ironic, funny, experimental, beautifully observed—the destruction of the dependent being already destroyed by the dependence which has been built into that being. Or we could very profitably use *The Coming of Age* as the achievement of the great essay, much as is *The Second Sex*. We are, after all, dealing with a giant here, a series of achievements in one lifetime which we are accustomed to see in many.)

All these books affect us. But autobiography affects us where we live. De Beauvoir is like some magical elder sister/aunt who did everything we dreamt of in graduate school—really did it. Lived it, didn't just think about it. Knew everyone, endured the war and the occupation. Fought and won her freedom as a woman, found in Sartre the ideal companion, measured that relationship out in decades without ever giving into marriage, cohabitation, family life, respectability; a lifelong liaison that was open and admitted other amorous adventure, never smothered and yet was constant. De Beauvoir's biography is in itself an edification, a life plan, an admonishment to our own sloppy, illogical arrangements, our failures, our great romances that endured but a time or even too long a time. It is a life lived by logic and one which practiced its own ideals—a paralyzing thought.

And yet the narrative of it—the autobiography: *Dutiful Daughter* and *Prime of Life* are adventure stories of one very uncertain woman, extremely vulnerable, hardly ever doctrinaire, frequently poor and confused, a long time producing work, a long time tied to dreadful teaching duties, cheap hotels, travel by bicycle, crummy food, constant terror of German soldiery or the principal who might not hire her back or would fail to grant the transfer that would put her within long tedious hikes or cycle tours to the one she loved. Who was not all that attentive at times, didn't share her every interest, was absorbed in his own projects and, though encouraging as guys go, still not that fervent a supporter always and she had to struggle with him constantly and just as constantly with herself so that she would give in neither to him nor to the world. If she had other lovers or were to have them later, he had them right now and pretty often right in her face, she had to endure the companionship of these ladies and be their friend as well—inasmuch as she could force herself to do that until she had her revenge in print and they were long gone by then—or there'd be another and she had to live with that too . . . all in the service of ideals they had arrived at together, at least in theory, whose practice would be the achievement of their lives. And others to follow. But at the moment all this free love and free enquiry business was first thought up and she tried to live it, she was utterly alone with a pack of crazy notions no one shared: she loved and felt a fool, her friends were not that supportive, her family was continually shocked. She was an exile. From the bourgeoisie. From family life. From the teaching profession which was always tossing her out. She could go on forever being a nobody living in cheap hotels.

In the midst of that life it was quite possible to write a book like *The Second Sex*. Why not, she was sufficiently removed from success, literary good manners, accepted notions, hopes of recognition or advancement along the usual lines? Cheap Paris hotels are full of strange women with strange ideas; but no one else ever came up with *The Second Sex*. Once it was written, it was a scandal from which de Beauvoir never recovered. I mean it guaranteed she would go on doing outrageous things. Her autobiography is one of them. I emphasize this because if autobiography is par excellence a woman's form in our time, it is the form of a woman who will take enormous risks. Reveal herself. For a subject class taught to hide, to be ashamed even of our thoughts—autobiography is a terrifying, exhilarating vertigo to women. O sex, of course. There isn't a great deal of sex in Anaïs Nin—much eroticism, little sex. She is pregnant at one point and never divulges the name of the father of the child—she is still discreet at fifty hiding material and deleting things so as not to offend her husband, a husband acquired much after the facts. Violette Leduc is never discreet at all—it is her strong point. Her lovable honor, her magnificent lesbian eroticism, her sad funny attempts with younger men in later life. De Beauvoir's autobiography is without torrid passages, but her fiction is as well.

That is not what interests her. What interests her is the play of personality, the tug between her ego and Sartre's. It is what interests us as well, everyone who has tried to convert whatever well meaning male consort into the peer of a lifetime companionship: friends forever, lovers here and there and forever, comrades in ideas and courage and principle. And not the mundane couple of ordinary life. Try creating that. We have tried. We have all tried. We have all searched for and thought we found our Sartres. And failed and gave it up; but while it succeeded, it succeeded largely because there was such a model. For—and this is an idea the French perceive at once and we only grope for in order to name it—one of de Beauvoir's chief accomplishments is to create and even to live out the ideal of a peer relationship between a man and a woman. Dimly perceived in the Brownings and elsewhere, but not lived with the freedom and insistence on freedom—the fact of never being married, never even living together—which accounts probably for the fact that the woman is not, as elsewhere now and in the past, swallowed up in the man and in being the function of that service to him which is a wife. Leonard and Virginia Woolf are a fine example of companion mates perhaps, but it is the luminosity of both intellects in the Sartre–de Beauvoir liaison—and the fact that it is conducted as a liaison with entirely separate selves and abodes which accounts for its parity in each party, its romantic endurance, its eternal autonomy, the courage never to marry, never to move in with each other, nail each other down—that could keep it going.

That is how to live, we thought. My generation. Trying out our ideas. Looking around for how to practice them. We never did it as well. But we did have in de Beauvoir always the spectacle of conscience in action, consciousness in action. She taught us how to live. Not only how to think—The Second Sex, the theory of feminism in that book and in her wonderful constancy within the feminist movement in France and in the world when it emerged some twenty years after she had announced it in The Second Sex—but she also taught us more than that. In her autobiography as well as in all those countless petitions and manifestos and declarations—against the war in Algiers, against Apartheid, for abortion, for a free press, against capital punishment, for the foreign workers, against torture, for political prisoners—because she and Sartre have been the conscience of

France and even of Europe for decades now — de Beauvoir by the very conduct of her life has been our model. Something we have needed particularly in America where there is no equivalent female — or male either — public figure of comparable stature, here where intellectuals exist peripherally and have miniscule value or effect in public life.

She has been wisdom to us. Conscience. A moral understanding to aspire to, learn from. A teacher in the greatest sense. Also someone young and unsure, struggling and nervous, trying over and over to dare to write a book, to dare to finish it. Here is the moment and the manner in which *She Came to Stay* was conceived:

> We were done with the provinces at last. Now we both lived in Paris: no more train journeys, no more hanging about on station platforms. We moved into a hotel that Sartre had discovered while I was convalescing in Provence, and which was a great improvement on the Royal Bretagne. It stood between the Avenue du Maine and the Montparnasse cemetery. I had a divan, and bookshelves, and a really comfortable working desk. I also got into a new daily routine: every morning I had coffee and *croissants* standing at the counter of a bright, noisy brasserie called Les Trois Mousquetaires. Also I often now worked at home. Sartre lived on the floor above me; thus we had all the advantages of a shared life, without any of its inconveniences.
>
> What was I to write, now that my stories were finished? Certain themes had been going around in my head for a long time now, but I had no idea how to tackle them. One evening, shortly after the beginning of the school term, Sartre and I were sitting inside the Dôme, discussing my work, and he criticized me for my timidity. In my last book, he said, I had dealt with questions that concerned me, but through the medium of persons for whom I felt either active distaste or else a qualified sympathy only: it was, for instance, a pity that I had observed Anne through Chantal's eyes. "Look," he said, with sudden vehemence, "why don't you put *yourself* into your writing? You're more interesting than all these Renées and Lisas." The blood flushed up in my cheeks; it was a hot day, and as usual the place was full of smoke and noise. I felt as though someone had banged me hard on the head. "I'd never dare to do that," I said. To put my raw, undigested self into a book, to lose perspective, compromise myself — no, I couldn't do it, I found the whole idea terrifying. "Screw up your courage," Sartre told me, and kept pressing the point. I had my own individual emotions and reactions; it was these that I ought to express in my writings. As happened whenever he put himself behind a plan, his words conjured up a host of possibilities and hopes; but I was still afraid. What in fact was I afraid of? It seemed to me that from the moment I began to nourish literature with the stuff of my own personality, it would become something as serious as happiness or death.[1]

The brave Simone who gave herself adventures by climbing mountains near her provincial school teaching posts, hitching rides with strangers, hanging out in cafés full of whores when she came to Paris, a nighttime Paris full of underworld clubs with blacks and artists—still when it comes to writing—afraid at first. Then brave, daring to do it. This book the first of many risks. We know them. We are the inheritors.

I want to close with a passage of life, not literature, for the passage itself creates life, abundantly. Paris under the German occupation, Nazi strictures . . . and in the midst of it a perfectly silly little play by Picasso is staged by a bunch of friends clandestinely in an apartment where you don't dare dance and can't have many lights and there is a shortage of most foods and only a miracle can provide you enough to drink—but you manage. Because you are joy against terror, amusement against tedium, liveliness against death. There is something about the passage that marks the golden age—a life lived in that milieu:

> A little later we took part in another literary occasion. Picasso had just written a play, *Le Désir attrapé par la queue (Desire Caught by the Tail)*, reminiscent of avant-garde writing in the twenties: a distant and belated imitation of *Les Mamelles de Tirésias*. Leiris proposed the idea of a public reading, and we fell in with his suggestion. Camus undertook to compère the proceedings. He had a big walking stick in one hand, with which he rapped on the floor to indicate a change of scene; he described the setting and introduced the characters; he also rehearsed the actors—though Leiris was responsible for the casting—during several afternoons beforehand. Leiris had the lead, and delivered the long speeches of Big Foot with enthusiastic fervor. Sartre was Round End, Dora Marr, Fat Misery, and the poet Hugnet's wife, Thin Misery. Zanie Campan, an extremely pretty girl who was married to Jean Aubier the publisher and had ambitions to go on the stage, played The Tart, and I was The Cousin.
>
> The reading took place about seven o'clock at night in the Leirises' drawing room. They had set out a few rows of chairs, but so many people turned up that a large proportion of the audience remained standing at the back, or in the anteroom. We stood in a group with our backs to the window, facing the spectators, who paid great attention to our performance and applauded it with positively religious zeal. For Sartre and Camus and me the whole thing was a great lark; but in these circles, or so it seemed, Picasso's least word and gesture were taken seriously. He was present in person, everyone congratulated him. I recognized Barrault, and someone pointed out Braque to me: he was very good-looking. Part of the audience left, and the rest of us then went through to the dining room, where Zette's ingenuity and some generous contributions had combined to produce a real prewar atmosphere. An Argentine millionaire and his wife, who had had their flat decorated by the finest artists in Paris—Picasso had painted them a door—brought along an enormous chocolate cake. It was on this occasion, I think, that I first met Lucienne and Armand Salacrou, Georges Bataille, Georges Limbour, Sylvia Bataille, and Lacan: comedies, books, a beautiful doll-like screen personality—all these now became real flesh-and-blood people, and I began to exist a little for them, too. How much bigger and

richer the world had become, all in a few short months! And how wonderful it felt to be alive! I had gone to considerable trouble to dress up for the occasion: Olga lent me a beautiful red angora sweater, and Wanda contributed a necklace of big blue pearls: Picasso delighted me by commenting favourably on this combination. I smiled at people, and they smiled back at me. I was pleased with myself, and with them too: my vanity gave itself an enjoyable airing, and the atmosphere of amiability went straight to my head. All these polite remarks and effusive greetings and pleasantries and small talk had some special quality that saved them from being the usual insipid commonplaces; they left a sharp yet unacknowledged aftertaste. A year before we would never have dreamed of gathering together like this and having a noisy, frivolous party that went on for hours. Prematurely, and despite all the threats that still hung over so many of us, we were celebrating victory.

About eleven o'clock most of the guests took their leave. The Leirises made the performers and a few close friends stay on: why not keep the party going till five in the morning? We assented, and found the irremediable nature of our decision rather amusing. The moment midnight had struck, choice also became necessity: of our own free will, yet willy-nilly, too, we were shut up in this apartment till dawn, with a forbidden city all around us. We had lost the habit of sitting up late, but luckily there was enough wine left to dispel our drowsiness. We didn't dance, for fear of annoying the tenants on the floor below, but Leiris played some jazz records, very softly. Mouloudji sang "Les Petits Pavés" in a pleasant, still childish voice; Sartre, in response to popular request, gave us "Les Papillons de nuit" and "J'ai vendu mon âme au diable"; Leiris and Camus read a scene from one of their favorite melodramas; while the others all cheerfully produced something or other, though I forgot the individual items. From time to time a wave of sleepiness would come over me, and it was then that I relished this unusual night most keenly. Outside, except for the Occupation forces and their protégés, the streets were thoroughfares no longer but barriers, which instead of linking up the blocks of houses, isolated them, and revealed them for what they really were: rows of prisoners' barracks. Paris had become one vast Stalag. We had defied the inevitable moment of dispersal, and though we might not technically have infringed the curfew order, at least we had frustrated its intentions. To drink and talk together thus in the heart of darkness was so stealthy a pleasure that it seemed illicit to us, and partook of that special delight to be had from forbidden joys alone.[2]

Notes

1. Simone de Beauvoir, *The Prime of Life*, trans. Peter Green (originally published in French, 1960; Cleveland: World, 1962), 251–52.

2. De Beauvoir, 449–51.

Death Sentences: Writing Couples and Ideology

Alice Jardine*

"To write is to embalm the past . . . , it leaves it a bit congealed — like a mummy." Simone de Beauvoir

"Mummy — from Low Latin: a dead body preserved in a dry state from putrefication; . . . or, figuratively, a dark, thin person."
— Webster's Dictionary

As my reader may or may not have had time to remark, there is a moment of modest ambiguity in my title — if only in terms of the signified.[1] At the first level, there is the question of writing couples, of what it means to "write couples," to write-in-couples with/as/through ideology. At the second level, there is the perhaps — but only perhaps — more referential question of the "Writing Couple," couples who write, and their shared ideology.

In order to open the way for and approach the first sense in which I evoke "Writing Couples" quickly, let me briefly invoke the other, larger title which brings this text here (today), our entitlement-so-to-write: *Poetics Today*. Let me infuse "poetics" into the title and re-mark it "Writing Couples and The Ideology of Poetics." And let me concentrate on today.

Today, then, "The Ideology of Poetics." By "ideology," I do not mean here the everyday sense of the term — one ideology as opposed to another; capitalist versus communist ideology, etc.; nor even — although this definition might be closer to our concerns here — Paolo Valesio's definition of ideology as decayed, dead rhetoric (Valesio 1980). I will remain in fact hopelessly Althusserian on just this one point and invoke his now infamous definition of ideology as "the 'representation' of the Imaginary relationship of individuals to the Real conditions of existence" (Althusser 1971:162). Through this definition, I would insist upon ideology as the conceptual glue of culture, that which makes culture seem natural, that which holds any cultural system together, that which, in fact, makes any system of relationships appear natural.

By "poetics," I mean something relatively straightforward: that theoretical discourse which would desire to account for what may certainly be called here, after Jakobson, "the poetic function" (Jakobson 1960) — as well as that discipline concerned with theories of literature.

My concern, under the title of "The Ideology of Poetics," is with that conceptual, culture glue which insists upon naturalizing, holding together,

*Reprinted by permission of the publishers from *The Female Body in Western Culture*, edited by Susan Suleiman. Cambridge, Mass: Harvard University Press. © 1986 by the President and Fellows of Harvard College.

indeed *reifying* any poetics grounded in and dependent upon binary opposition, whether those oppositions are static — structural — or put into movement — dialectical. As Hélène Cixous has put it:

> Always the same metaphor: we follow it, it transports us, thru all of its figures, everywhere discourse organizes itself. The same thread, or *tresse double*, leads us, if we read or speak, across literature, philosophy, criticism, centuries of representation, of reflection
>
> [Western] thought has always worked by opposition . . . the law organizes the thinkable thru oppositions (whether as irreconcilable dualities or incorporative, uplifting dialectics). And all of these couples of oppositions are *couples*. Might that not mean something? That logocentrism forces all thought — all concepts, all codes, all values to submit to a system of 2 terms, might that not be in relationship to "the" couple: man/woman? (Cixous 1975:116)

The question of "the couple" has become the object of contemporary philosophical fascination, where *all* metaphysical couples are in the process of being discoupled, recoupled differently and urgently: active/passive, form/matter, speech/writing, conscious/unconscious. This work has been pursued by some of us because these couples, intrinsic to the ensemble of symbolic systems in the West (cf. Cixous 1976: esp. p. 7), would indeed appear to be modeled on *the couple:* Man/Woman, Masculine/Feminine.

Since Lacan at the very least, it has been made quite clear, particularly in France, that One never writes without the Other, One never writes Alone; One is always at least two, usually more: One is always coupled with Others. My hand is moving across the page according to different scripts, different readings, with different names, different faces, on ready or distant call. The lone *cogito*, fully in control of a message, even if in anguish while finding it, has been thrown on the philosophical junkheap; the lonely image of the lone author, always male, remains alive only for die-hard romantics. The couple, therefore, has not only become the privileged *object* of contemporary interpretive fascination, but has become its doubled *subject* as well.

Couples. We tend to think in couples even when we try very hard not to; we revise the concept of the couple, we re-write it, we mediate it in new ways, but couples are very hard to get away from. It's just the way we think in the West, have been trained to think — based on the force of the *copula*, of copulation (cf. Derrida 1972).

The question of copulation brings us to the second not unrelated level of what I mean by "Writing Couples," the "Writing Couple": here and now, the historically heterosexual, famous, totally necessary to each other, oh too human, writing couple.[2] For there would appear to exist a seeming historical necessity for the heterosexual woman who wants to create, to write — and be read — to couple herself, in fact or fantasy, albeit if only temporarily, with a man who also writes or wrote, a famous man in her life or in her writing—if not the *necessity*, then the *desire* to do so, under the illusion that it will be easier that way. . . . Anyone who has tried to write "on" or with women who write has undoubtedly run across this problem at some point. My own most intimate textual encounters have been with Virginia and Leonard, Lou Andreas and Friedrich, Julia and Philippe, Simone and Jean-Paul.

How this second way of reading the words "writing couples" is linked to the first, should become clear in what follows. And while I will be insisting upon this second more biographemic sense of the term "Writing Couple," the first, more philosophical sense should not and, indeed, cannot be forgotten. Nor can we forget the *very* famous couple, "literature and philosophy." For what Plato called "the ancient quarrel between poetry and philosophy" is being acted out once again at the end of the twentieth century—with the stakes involved in whether this couple stays together or separates getting higher by the day. What follows is, then, a first gesture towards exploring the various possible ideologies and logics of "writing couples," towards establishing a typology of coupling, especially in relationship to the maternal body. Here I will be able to look only at a first kind of possible configuration for male and female, a first kind of occidental glue. I will be exploring very explicitly the poetics of an ideology that insists upon killing the mother and therefore, although more implicitly, will be exploring the ideology of the poetics responsible for that murder.

For many reasons, not the least important of which is the current hysteria surrounding the couple "literature and philosophy," it was the writing couple Simone de Beauvoir and Jean-Paul Sartre that came to occupy the center of my attention as I began to think about writing couples at the intersections of literature and philosophy, poetics and ideology, modernity and feminist theory. The decision made me very nervous.

First, because Sartre and Beauvoir do, of course, represent for many *the couple*, not only in a general "People Magazine" kind of way, but also, I think, within a certain feminist fantasy: Beauvoir is the woman who managed to find a man with whom to share her intellectual passion without sacrificing either "intimacy" or "independence," as she herself might put it. Because of the strong grip this feminist fantasy holds on a certain heterosexual imaginary, especially here in the United States, I hesitated to continue the tradition.

Second, Sartre and Beauvoir do incarnate, in an embarrassingly old-fashioned way, the philosophy/literature split and its most idealistic kind of synthesis: "they each do a little of both," but Sartre is the philosopher and Beauvoir is the novelist, they say. As Nancy Miller has reminded me, the way in which Beauvoir has positioned her texts to deal only with that which Sartre's undeniably classical philosophical discourse cannot deal with is a problem in itself.

Third, Beauvoir and Sartre, as a couple, provide perhaps too easy a symbol of the old *versus* all that is new in the realm of poetics and literary theory. Sartre did not want to represent any formal, theorized poetics; he proposed, nonetheless, a theory of language and literature that is no longer acceptable to many theorists and writers of modernity, for example Roland Barthes, who highlighted his differences with Sartre early and irrevocably (Barthes 1953). In fact, in one of Sartre's last interviews, when pressed by Beauvoir to be more precise about what he meant when he qualified *Les Mots* as "literary," he replied simply, "It was full of clever tricks, artful writings, word-plays almost."[3]

Finally, and most importantly perhaps, Beauvoir and Sartre are no longer a couple. There have been so many deaths of the Fathers in France over the past few years: Lacan, Barthes, Sartre, Foucault. Talking about any one of these four Dead Fathers can be painful—what one has to say becomes so quickly elegiac or vulturesque . . . and Sartre was of course, *The Father* for intellectual France.

Beauvoir has been left alone, at home, but as a Widow for France, not as France's Mother. By what authorization may I write of "them" now?

But I will, because one of the things the thousands of people (including myself) who walked behind Sartre's coffin in Montparnasse were saying was that we both can and cannot continue, now, without the couple, Beauvoir and Sartre; that, in any case, no one can continue to think/write in the ways that it is urgent for us to think/write in the West without first having written and thought with Sartre the philosopher. Phenomenology, empiricism, metaphysics, the *ego cogito*, the Imaginary, the Other, dialectics, even "ideology," or "poetics," become just so many contemporary buzz words unless one has recognized that 25 years of French thought have been transcribing those words through Sartre, *against* Sartre—killing the Father. Foucault was one of the very few to recognize that fact. And what of our still-alive-feminist-mother? My thoughts of her are haunted by this death of a monolithic couple and its discourse.

Thinking in a soundly referential, biographical way, there is not much new to say about this somewhat mysteriously, perhaps only superficially heterosexual couple. But the insistent questions keep repeating themselves. How was it that they actually managed to remain a couple? They were always sleeping in separate beds—next door, down the street, in the other room, in different cities. And then there were all of Sartre's "contingent women"—so lovingly and openly laid before our eyes in so many places—Melina, Camille, *la fiancée*, Mme Morel, M, Olga, *la femme lunaire*. As Sartre himself put it, "I was more a masturbator than an 'intercourser' of women" (CA, p. 385).

Many people have remarked upon this strange set of affairs, especially feminists: "except for Sartre, Beauvoir is wonderful." That is, the feminist response to this couple is usually divided, ambivalent, an ambivalent reaction most recently evoked by Carol Ascher's very moving imaginary letter to Beauvoir in her book, *A Life of Freedom*. Ascher questions Beauvoir's way of: "capping a description of pain and ambiguity with the assertion that the period or relationship was a success. It's a little like the *deus ex machina* of Socialism or genderless roles—the seal of the present or future riding in on a white horse to blot out historical suffering. . . . It is as if you must put a stamp or seal on your memories in order to go on" (Ascher 1981:111).

It is always these last capping sentences that are cited as tokens of Beauvoir's courage and wisdom by her feminist admirers, never their discursive placement or the blackest pages of passion, despair, and rage they negate.

As *feminist fantasy*, the Beauvoir-Sartre phenomenon has never been described so succinctly as by Beauvoir herself:

> . . . we might almost be said to think in common. We have a common store of memories, knowledge and images behind us; our attempts to grasp the world are undertaken with the same tools, set within the same framework, guided by the same touchstones. Very often one of us begins a sentence and the other finishes it; if someone asks us a question, we have been known to produce identical answers. The stimulus of a word, a sensation, a shadow, sends us both traveling along the same inner path, and we arrive simultaneously at a conclusion—a memory, an association—completely inexplicable to a third person. . . . Our temperaments, our directions, our previous decisions, remain different, and our writings are on the whole almost totally dissimilar. But they have sprung from the same plot of ground (Beauvoir 1965a:643).

I read and reread the passages of her memoirs and interviews where Beauvoir continually speaks (of) this strange, disembodied "we"—and into this dark continent of pure, clear, platonic couplehood, I began to imagine, between the lines, a make-believe letter from Beauvoir to Sartre containing the following words: "You put yourself in my mouth, and I suffocate. . . . Continue to be also outside. Keep yourself/me also outside. Don't be engulfed, don't engulf me, in what passes from you to me. I would so much like that we both be here. That the one does not disappear into the other or the other into the one" (Irigaray 1979:9–10).[4]

These lines are from Luce Irigaray's *Et l'une ne bouge pas sans l'autre*. I evoke them here so as to provide a space of slippage in my own discourse—and eventually, I hope, in Beauvoir's—from writing in this comfortable descriptive tone towards writing more uncomfortably about the most intimate Other possible for any writer and, most especially, for any woman writer: *the mother*.

The issue of how to think about the relationships among women/ writing/maternity is among the most important in feminist thinking today, especially in France. It is important to recall here that when Hélène Cixous states in her seminars that the vast majority of women writers to date have written within a masculine economy, one of her first and most often repeated examples is Beauvoir. The classical writing economy, the one that belongs to a *masculine* economy, according to Cixous, requires two conditions: for anyone to write, they need (1) maternal love and support, and (2) paternal identification. How this is true for men writing in a patriarchal culture is fairly clear. Male writers have needed the loving support of their muses, mistresses, or mothers in order then to put them aside, deny them, reject them, idealize them or kill them in their writing, but, in any case, to *ingest* them so as better to evacuate them, purify themselves, and identify with the Father—if only then to kill him like the good sons they are.[5] According to Cixous, in a patriarchal culture, a woman's writing depends in great part upon her relationship with her imaginary father. For her, Beauvoir provides the classic case of a woman writer who has "chosen" to write within the masculine economy just described: she identified with the Father and rejected the Mother. It is, in fact, Beauvoir who has come to represent, for a number of contemporary French women theorists, the proto-typical father-identified-feminist: *Athena*—the one who has no need of a mother.

Most obviously, and still at the most referential level, Beauvoir provided what has remained, in spite of everything, *the* feminist myth: the baby *versus* the book. When she says, "I have never regretted not having children insofar as what I wanted to do was to write" (Beauvoir 1965b:36), she means it and feminists have believed in her sincerity. In the classical feminist economy, you cannot have them both; you cannot have it all.

Over the past few years this mutual exclusivity has been seriously questioned—more referentially in this country, more theoretically in France (see Suleiman 1985). To concentrate here on the latter, for women theorists like Cixous, Luce Irigaray, or Julia Kirsteva, Beauvoir's decision not to have children in the world might be seen as but an acting out of her complete denial of the maternal, of her refusal of the maternal body within a classical male economy—a refusal of the maternal body's most intimate influences upon her own body and body of work. For these women, Beauvoir's work represents an exemplary denial of woman, of the mother, and it is against the Beauvoirian myth of Anti-Maternity that they set out 10 years ago to *revalorize the maternal* for women: in and through women's writing for Cixous; before and on the other side of our writing for Irigaray; because of marginal men's and women's writing for Kristeva.

Our monolithic heterosexual couple has been decidedly displaced, but it has not disappeared. In order to think about what for me has turned out to be a battle between the old and new mothers — a battle in which my desire not to deny any of them has proven somewhat futile — and in order not to lose sight of *the couple* as our subject, I turned to Beauvoir's last published book: *La Cérémonie des adieux*.[6] I took with me to that text two questions: (1) what *did* Beauvoir do with the jealousy, anger and rage at Sartre that I evoked earlier and (2) *what about* mothers? What about Beauvoir's mother? What I found was most troubling — more than troubling, frightening. How to talk about it without denying my own first feminist mother? I am really not sure I can move without her.[7]

La Cérémonie des adieux is a very strange book; first of all, in its form. It is a ceremony — a sacred rite — in two parts: the first part is written by Beauvoir as an account of Sartre's last ten years — as a narrative, it moves forward most methodically; the second part of the book, twice as long as the first, is the transcription of an oral, taped interview between Sartre and Beauvoir done entirely in the summer of 1974. There is no visible link between the two parts. Neither novel, memoirs, nor biography, the *Cérémonie* is an ambitious project of writing-*qua*-oral-history that, even while a monument to Sartre, is a kind of strange simulacrum of Sartre's own last uncompleted project: a book he wanted to be written truly by two people — not by Sartre and Beauvoir, but by Sartre and his intellectual son Victor (Benni Levi) where, as he puts it, ". . . a thought could exist really formed by you and me at the same time," exactly what Beauvoir had always described as Sartre's and her own economy (CA, p. 126).

This book is, however, remarkable as other than simply monument or simulacrum. The first part of the book is the first thing Beauvoir has ever written and published unseen by Sartre; the second part is completely different — familiar, already said and published to the point of explicit repetition. This book is cut up, cut down the middle, not a simulacrum of and monument to Sartre, but to his death. It is the particularly intense quality of the first part of the book that solicits attention: a flood of words to embalm the past; a compulsion, seeming obligation, *to say everything* about another cut-up-body-to-be-"entombed" — that of Sartre: a corpus in decomposition.

What is so disturbing about this discourse is not that Sartre's referential, historical body is somehow rendered more mortal, less deified — that would be laudible; but rather that this body named Sartre is cut up by the violence of (Beauvoir's) discourse — an explosion of words with razor edges.

A few pages of politics and then the body-talk begins — with the mouth of course: an abscess in the mouth, a threat of the flu (CA, p. 22). But then the well-recognized "capping sentences" appear: "In spite of these health worries, Sartre continued his political activities" (CA, p. 23).

More pages of referential recounting, ticking off the days. But then there were his teeth, he had to get false teeth: he was afraid — "for obvious symbolic reasons," she says (CA, p. 24).

Politics, politics. His eating habits. Ingestion: "a bit of sausage, some chocolate." He begins to tremble, sputter, jabber — "his mouth was a bit twisted" (CA, p. 31).

After the mouth come the hands that can no longer grip, perform, act upon the material world — that function Sartre valued the most (CA, pp. 32–33).

1972 — more politics, more voyages, until Sartre finally begins to wet his pants and leave brown stains where he was sitting; ruining his clothes; acting like a child, just before he's off on more trips, seeing more people until finally he begins to lose — his arteries, his veins, his nose, his skin, his head. He forgets. He can't get it right, and finally, he loses his eyes. While "eating messily" — "his mouth soiled with food" (CA, p. 75) — Sartre goes blind. "And my eyes. What about my eyes?" he asks (CA, p. 88). And his bladder and intestines completely out of control.

The unrelenting stream of words occasionally betrays an almost comic relief: he still shaved himself, "very well in fact thanks to a [new] electric razor . . ." (CA, p. 97). And he is, after all, still seeing such a lot of women: Sylvie on Sunday, Liliane on Thursday; Michèle on Monday and Friday — and the other days it is Arlette (CA, p. 117). But Sartre's kidneys and intestines only get worse with all this feeding. The doctor talks about cutting off his toes, his feet, his legs: "He seemed more and more tired, he was beginning to get open wounds and scabs and his bladder was not working — it became necessary to do bypass surgery and when he got up, now very rarely, he trailed behind him a little plastic bag full of urine . . ." (CA, p. 154).

I do not cite these sentences to provoke disgust (or sadness), but to try and evoke the horror of this discourse without reprieve, where there is no *arrêt de mort* — no one death sentence and/or reprieve but *only death*. I felt that I had finally discovered what Beauvoir had done with her anger and rage.

Why would Beauvoir do this? How could she so coldly dissect, for the entire world, this supposedly beloved body with, at times, the edges of Sartre's own words?

In Paris, it has been suggested by critics and reviewers across the political spectrum, that this book is Beauvoir's revenge on Sartre. But revenge for what? For his love affairs with all those contingent women? For writing with his pseudo-son Victor his last book, the ideal book, the one she had always wanted to write with him?

No, I do not think things are that clear cut *or* that banal.

Julia Kristeva (among others) has defined *le récit*, narrative, in the following way: "Narrative is, in sum, the most elaborative kind of attempt on the part of the speaking subject, after syntactic competence, to situate his or her self among his or her desires and their taboos; that is, at the interior of the Oedipal Triangle" (Kristeva 1980:165). These days, in the wake of deconstruction, schizoanalysis, and feminist post-Freudianism, it is difficult to feel comfortable speaking of Oedipus. But I do think this book may be an instance of one last way for the feminist, in this case Beauvoir, to act out the Oedipal Triangle. Might this not be Beauvoir's last attempt at writing her truest family romance? After all, she wrote so many in the past, both in her memoirs and her novels. One thing is certain. In this narrative, Beauvoir is placing herself in relation to only one privileged body, the female body, the one that has been designated as female by Western, and more importantly and most paradigmatically by Sartre's own philosophical discourse. It is the body that Sartre hated: his own, of course, but more relevantly, the one that smells, bleeds, and falls apart; the one that is sometimes too large, sometimes too small — *the Maternal Body*. Sartre became "too female"; his body must be desexed, evacuated, the narrative body must be purified of what Kristeva has called the abject, of its abjection, that which the discourse of mastery cannot tolerate. This is the ceremony we read. *Eschatologies*. This book is a Tomb, its cadaver purified by the logos with ultimate lucidity.

Sartre has been seen as filling many roles in Beauvoir's Family Romance — her father, her son, her brother. But never her mother — the one *with* the phallus.

And what of Beauvoir's other mother? The weak one, *without* the phallus?[8]

I returned with some trembling to that other Tomb-Book, *Une Mort Très Douce* (*A Very Easy Death* — Beauvoir 1964) and read it simultaneously with this second Tomb. Another tomb, where Beauvoir's other mother is also buried in and by narrative. I read as her (dark, thin?) mother's body "decomposed" in the same way as Sartre's; with amazement, I listened to the same rush of words. Is that because all bodies disintegrate in the same way? No, I do not think so. These two bodies are too linked by their classical sameness and difference: "His open wounds were terrifying to look at (but happily they were hidden from him, covered up): large purplish red patches . . . gangrene was attacking his flesh . . ." (CA, p. 155).

The decomposing body named Sartre is never sexed; the sexual organs, the wounds of this (textual) body are hidden, covered up.

Not those of that other "reprieved cadaver" (1964:28) — Beauvoir's "biological" mother whose rotting flesh and scars are described uncovered in the full light of the daughter's vision. Here I invoke the full Greek/Indo-European force of the word "ideology": the *eidos*, the logos of the image, visible idea, vision.[9] The mother's revealed sex and uncovered sex organs force Beauvoir the daughter to turn her gaze away, towards the window — out into the garden, so as to avoid seeing: "her strained belly, creased in

minuscule wrinkles, shriveled, and her shaved pubis . . . Seeing my
mother's sex organs (*voir le sexe de ma mère*): that gave me quite a shock.
No body existed less for me—nor existed more" (1964:27). The scars of this
maternal body are not covered, but exposed in words—an open body, its
belly the object of devouring cancer. Dead-alive, "she's rotting alive," as
Beauvoir's sister put it (1964:118).

With or without the phallus, good or bad, both versions of this body-
of/in-writing must be subjected to catharsis, must be purified by the *Logos*
(cf. Kristeva 1980). Beauvoir purifies and exorcizes it—like all writers who
fear that which would threaten the integrity of their discourse. She must
evacuate the dangerous body, the poisoned body, so that she may continue
to write.

Just after Sartre's death, Beauvoir wants to lie down, stretch out,
against his body—close and alone—under the sheets.[10] She cannot, of
course, because of the poisonous gangrene that has taken over this textual
cadaver. Incest is denied because of the poisoned body—she does lie down
next to Sartre, but separated from him by the thin white sheet between
them. She sleeps.

But she does not dream, as she once did at the side of that other
deathbed, of her other mother's bed, while she was grieving the death of
her mother: "I spent the night by her side; forgetting my distaste for this
nuptial bed where I was born, where my father died, I watched her sleep
. . . Usually, I thought of her with indifference. In my sleep, however—
where my father appeared very rarely and then only in a dull way—[my
mother] often played *the essential role:* she became confused with Sartre,
and we lived happily together . . ." (1964:146–147) (My emphasis).

Turning to a man for nurturance in this culture is one thing; but when
doing so involved revalorizing the fantasy of the all-powerful phallic
mother, the difficult exploration of sexual difference may become impossible.

Is there a way to move out of the Family Romance without a certain
existential feminism turning men into our mothers?; without revalorizing
the phallic mother?; without reinforcing an ideology that requires this
particular kind of coupling; or a poetics that must ultimately silence the
mother's tongue? Is there a way to write without embalming the past?;
without writing tombs? Without dismembering the female body; without
killing other women in the name of epistemological purity; without killing
our mothers, the mother in us?

At the end of *L'Invitée* (*She Came to Stay*), leaving Xavière to die in
her bed, Françoise reflects "It was she or I, It shall be I'" (Beauvoir
1975:405–407).

Our mothers and grandmothers have done, without a doubt, what it
was they had to do. But it is, at least for this daughter, that sentence "It
shall be I," *the* patriarchal sentence increasingly turned feminist—that

new kinds of feminist subjects need to begin uncoupling and rewriting, without repeating the death sentences of the past.

Notes

1. Earlier versions of this paper were presented both at a special session of the 1982 MLA organized by Naomi Schor, entitled "Intimate Influences: The Writing Couple," and at the Seventh Columbia University Colloquium on Poetics (November 1983) organized by Michael Riffaterre, entitled "The Poetics of Ideology." I am grateful to Nancy Miller for her careful readings and suggestions at each rewriting. Translations in text are my own unless otherwise indicated.

2. "Historically heterosexual" for two reasons: first, because I am using the word "heterosexual" in its everyday sense. That is, we are concerned here primarily with the couple consisting of a man and a woman as historically defined — although such dominant forms of heterosexual logic can of course appear in the most unlikely places. But, secondly, I also want to underline the potential for, the possibility of, new logics for radical heterosexualities, beyond the hetero/homo dualism, and especially beyond the common and conservative notion of heterosexuality which, as Jane Gallop has put it, "has always been a veiled homosexuality, one modality of desire, one libidinal economy" (Gallop 1982:127).

3. My translations. Simone de Beauvoir, "Entretiens avec Jean-Paul Sartre" in *La Cérémonie des adieux* (CA) (1981:276). All further page references in text.

4. I adopt here Jane Gallop's translation of this passage (Gallop 1982:114).

5. Barthes put it more mildly, but never flinched faced with his recognition that "L'écrivain est quelqu'un qui joue avec le corps de sa mère." Cited by Susan Suleiman (1977).

6. It is difficult to call *Lettres au Castor* (1983) *Beauvoir's* most recent book to date, as some have, since it includes only Sartre's letters.

7. The often painful question of how to explore more freely the political and intellectual differences between feminist mothers and daughters without repeating Oedipal, biological, history-patterns, is being increasingly asked today. In a sense, that question serves as palimpsest to Luce Irigaray's *Et l'une ne bouge pas sans l'autre.* My generation's search for new ways to explore new conceptual territories *with* our mother(s) and grandmother(s), with respect and without denying their experience, is what is at stake. For one of my own first, shaky attempts, cf. my "Interview with Simone de Beauvoir" (1979).

8. On the phallic mother as organizing fantasy for the denial of sexual difference, see esp. Kristeva (1974 and 1980).

9. On how the relationships among the Idea, the Image, and Vision are valorized within the traditional male libidinal economy, see Irigaray (1974).

10. I cannot here explore this complex desire and its implications with(in) the state of mourning; but this is the place to reveal one of my important intertexts here: the work of Melanie Klein. Cf., esp., her "Mourning and its Relation to Manic-Depressive States" (1940).

References

Althusser, Louis, 1971. *Lenin and Philosophy* (New York: Monthly Review).

Ascher, Carol, 1981. *Simone de Beauvoir: A Life of Freedom* (Boston: Beacon Press).

Barthes, Roland, 1953. *Le Degré zéro de l'ecriture* (Paris: Seuil).

Beauvoir, Simone de, 1964. *Une mort très douce* (Paris: Gallimard Folio).

1965a *Force of Circumstance*, trans. Richard Howard (New York: G.P. Putnam's Sons).

1965b "Interview," *Paris Review* 9:34 (Spring–Summer), 23–40.

1971 *She Came to Stay*, trans. Y. Moyse and R. Senhouse (Glasgow: Fontana Books).

1981 *La Cérémonie des adieux* (Paris: Gallimard).

Cixous, Hélène, 1975. "Sorties," in: *La Jeune née* (Paris: 10/18).

1976 "Le sexe ou la tête," *Les Cahiers du GRIF* 13 (October), 5–20.

Derrida, Jacques, 1972. "Le supplément de copule," in: *Marges* (Paris: Minuit).

Gallop, Jane, 1982. *The Daughter's Seduction* (Ithaca: Cornell UP).

Irigaray, Luce, 1974. *Speculum de l'autre femme* (Paris: Minuit).

1979 *Et l'une ne bouge pas sans l'autre* (Paris: Minuit).

Jakobson, Roman, 1960. "Linguistics and Poetics," in: Thomas Sebeok, ed., *Style in Language* (Cambridge, Mass.: MIT Press), 350–377.

Jardine, Alice, 1979. "Interview with Simone de Beauvoir," *Signs* 5:2, 224–236.

Klein, Melanie, 1975(1940). "Mourning and Its Relation to Manic-Depressive States," in: *Love, Guilt and Reparation* (London: Hogarth Press).

Kristeva, Julia, 1974. *La Révolution du language poétique* (Paris: Seuil).

1980 *Pouvoirs de l'horreur* (Paris: Seuil).

Sartre, Jean-Paul, 1983. *Lettres au Castor* (Paris: Gallimard).

Suleiman, Susan, 1977. "Reading Robbe-Grillet: Sadism and Text in *Projet pour une révolution à New York*," *Romanic Review* (January), 43–62.

1985 "Writing and Motherhood," in: S. Garner, C. Kahane, M. Sprenghether, eds. *The M(other) Tongue: Essays in Feminist and Psychoanalytic Interpretation* (Ithaca: Cornell UP).

Valesio, Paolo, 1980. *Novantiqua: Rhetorics as a Contemporary Theory* (Bloomington: Indiana UP).

Simone de Beauvoir: Feminine Sexuality and Liberation
Béatrice Slama*

In proposing this subject for discussion at this colloquium, I realize that I come up against two difficulties. These difficulties are linked — very differently — to a problem of "time."

The first difficulty: how can I reread with you in a half hour the discourses of Simone de Beauvoir on feminine sexuality, on sexuality and liberation? We could have to be able to examine *The Second Sex* but also her autobiography, her novels, especially *The Mandarins*, her interviews, and why not her own life? . . . Not only because her texts invite us to do so but because the myth which has formed itself around Beauvoir and Sartre, around their relationship, founded on a reciprocal "authenticity" and sexual freedom, on a "necessary love" and "contingent loves," has

*Translated by Amy Scarr for this volume. An earlier draft of this essay was presented as a paper at the Colloquium on Simone de Beauvoir held 4–6 April 1985 at Columbia University. It is included by permission of the French House of Columbia University, the author, and Editions Tierce (France).

functioned, for certain generations of women—including mine—as a kind of "new model" of a "liberated" couple. And we know how much this "new" kind of relationship can appear problematic, notably such as it has been experienced-fantasized in autobiography and fiction or such as we ourselves can fantasize it through, for example, the reading of *Letters to Castor*.

The second difficulty: 35 years have passed since *The Second Sex*, 30 years since *The Mandarins*. From an academic perspective, this is very recent. I am not speaking of Louise Labé nor even of the "New Woman" of the 1920s. But these 35 years, these 30 years, represent a very full period of time. Full of inquiries, reports, studies on feminine sexuality. What doctor, what psychoanalyst—man and woman—does not think he or she has something to say to us about it? The flow of the women's movement has swept away many taboos. Women have spoken about their bodies, their sexuality, their sensual pleasure. As Simone de Beauvoir has written,

ed her in boldness. Sexual
is spoken in a society which,
Beauvoir began to write, has
or all women, of course, still
:om two proscriptions which
of pregnancy and the fear of
1 *The Second Sex* a striking
ontrol in the very intimacy of
him" (the male partner).
the fight for abortion, the
g of numerous prohibitions
younger generation—and the
olex (and it is to the credit of
e relations between feminine
'e also functioned elsewhere.
this problem bear witness to
example, the colloquium held
or not—traversed the Atlan-

auvoir today? I am going to
me, to question her texts in
their singularity, their boldness, in their limits, their contradictions, which are those of her epoch but also her own when they stem from her personal experience.

To try to read the discourses of Simone de Beauvoir on feminine sexuality, on sexuality and liberation, is to be confronted with what was for her the profound ambiguity of this problem. I would like, through this reading, to acknowledge as well our own ambiguity, mine, yours. We, women, who ask questions and question ourselves. With our differences—between generations, between countries.

Simone de Beauvoir has shown in *The Second Sex* that what is at stake in sexuality is not only a relationship to the body, to desire, to pleasure, to identity, a relationship to oneself, to the other, but also a *relationship to power*, a *relationship of power*.

Simone de Beauvoir's entire analysis aims to elucidate the mechanisms of the imposition of man's domination over woman and the internalization by women of this domination, of their dependence.

She concentrates on the stages and forms of what was—what still is in many places and in many societies—the "training" of women: an education which devalued her own body and imposed taboos; sexual initiation linked to ignorance and often violence, to the dissymmetry of masculine and feminine eroticisms which, according to Simone de Beauvoir, rarely permits women to attain pleasure at the beginning of their sexual relations and makes of the first penetration a breaking in, a rape (even if, in other respects, Simone de Beauvoir evokes the sensual curiosity of the young woman, the indeterminate appeal to the body of the other); the distribution of roles—active/passive—and of places—the woman lying under the man, penetrated by him—in the sexual scenario over which man has every intention of remaining the master. Man takes, woman gives herself, is taken. Taken also by the look of the other who gauges her, judges her. Taken, had, lost: it is a paradigm in *The Second Sex* as well as in so many novels by women through the centuries.

Given over to man, to the masculine initiative, to conjugal service, to the reproduction of the species, woman is reduced to the state of sexual object-for-others or exalted and justified in her function as mother, as mother of others. Her pleasure? Simone de Beauvoir reproduces citations and references which demonstrate that, over the centuries, men have rarely been preoccupied with the sexual pleasure of their companions and they have at times deliberately refused to acknowledge it in order not to awaken potential "uterine fury."

Raised as she is in the devaluation of her sex, in the shame of sexuality, woman *accepts herself* as a passive sexual object. She is passive, writes Simone de Beauvoir, because she *thinks (of) herself (as)* passive. She internalizes the desires to be dominated by a superior being, to consecrate herself to him, to be indispensable to him. Through pleasure in a happy sexual relationship she becomes attached and this reinforces her dependence. Reduced to the state of being-for-others, she overvalues the "altruism" which justifies her existence. Love is her supreme legitimation: "for woman, love," writes Simone de Beauvoir, "is a supreme attempt to overcome, while assuming it, the dependence to which she is condemned" (*SS*, II, 506).[1]

In sexual relations, amorous relations, these most intimate of relations which can also be the most distant, Simone de Beauvoir points out that which is unique, with respect to other oppressions, to the oppression of one sex by another, of one individual by another individual: the consent to dependence.

All this is well-known. And if many women today do not recognize themselves in this picture, it is because a profound mutation in women's relation to sexuality and in women's raised consciousness began during these last twenty years.

But in 1949, in this analysis as in others, Simone de Beauvoir brought "to maturation in the order of language" what was then only the "possible consciousness" of a large number of women. Whence comes the extraordinary impact of *The Second Sex* which has helped women to elucidate their situation, their reactions, their contradictions, their fantasies. This pioneer text placed the accent — and I suspect that on this point we still have a lot to learn from *The Second Sex* — on the mechanisms of internalization and self-justification. Simone de Beauvoir sees the traditional woman as "a mystified and mystifying consciousness." Today there are other ways, always renewed, of mystifying oneself and of mystifying others.

Sexuality as a relationship to power, women as mystified consciousness: we are in the logic of the culturalistic thesis which underlies the entire *Second Sex*.

In this logic of "one is not born a woman, one becomes a woman," this sexuality which Simone de Beauvoir describes — passivity, fear of man, frigidity as a refusal and a defense, masochism, amorous demands, need for appropriation, duration, and attachment — this sexuality lived out by women could only be an effect of the "situation" of women, a product of history — in sum, feminine sexuality is what it has "become" and what has to be surpassed in this perspective of assimilation and liberation which Simone de Beauvoir sketches at the end of *The Second Sex*. "The free woman has not yet been born," says Simone de Beauvoir. In other words, the sexuality of the liberated woman does not yet exist.

Now, when it comes to sexuality, it seems that Simone de Beauvoir's position is much more ambiguous. This domain is without a doubt the one in which the thesis of *The Second Sex* at one and the same time finds its illustration and comes up against a kind of wall — as if one were confronted there by the singularity of woman and by the irreducible difference between the sexes: "woman is other than man and this otherness is experienced concretely in desire, in the embrace, love" (SS, II, 383). "The conditions in which the sexual life of woman unfolds depend," among others, writes Simone de Beauvoir, "on the whole picture of her social and economic situation." But "erotic experience is one of those which expose human beings in the most poignant way to the ambiguity of their condition; they experience themselves as body and as mind, as other and as subject"; "it is for woman that this conflict assumes the most dramatic character because she perceives herself at first as object, because she does not immediately find a sure autonomy in pleasure; she must reconquer her dignity as a free and transcendent subject while assuming her carnal condition" (SS, II, 168).

Throughout *The Second Sex* Simone de Beauvoir affirms the singularity of feminine eroticism, the dissymmetry of eroticisms, the enmity between the sexes and the differences between them.

She articulates feminine pleasure, its dispersed sensuality, its desire for fusion and duration. She links vaginal pleasure to a consent of the whole being and defends the clitoral orgasm against Freud. She evokes the different rhythms of masculine and feminine eroticisms, the difficulty of reconciling the progressive gliding of woman toward pleasure with the manner in which man means to direct the sexual scenario, the nonconformity between woman, bound by pleasure, and man, driven to rapid satiation.

It was necessary to abridge, to simplify, but how can one, in so few minutes, not betray a text of several hundred pages? But it is particularly necessary to keep oneself from hearing as banalities, as rehashed ideas, that which appeared to Simone de Beauvoir's contemporaries as a subversive or scandalous discourse.

As early as pages 90–91 of the first volume, Simone de Beauvoir underlines "the poverty of descriptions of the feminine libido" in Freud and in the different texts which she examined. If one can regret that, without critically distancing herself very much, Simone de Beauvoir has nevertheless used existing discourses, those of Krafft-Ebbing, Havelock Ellis, Stekel, Helen Deutsch, those discourses which Foucault has shown to contribute to the medicalization and "hystericization" of the representation of feminine sexuality, it still remains — and *The Second Sex* is still in this area a forerunner among texts — that Simone de Beauvoir tried to say about feminine sexuality things that had not yet been said or to say things differently, from another point of view. And without a doubt the most beautiful pages of *The Second Sex* are those in which she attempts to write feminine eroticism.

For Simone de Beauvoir, feminine eroticism is passivity and activity at the same time. Eroticism of passivity: desire; waiting; opening; letting oneself glide; plunging into the night, into the indistinct; the effacement of limits; the loss of identity in fusion, the fusion of bodies, cosmic fusion, dizziness. Active eroticism would be the need to take, to make of the other a "prey." "It is not the organ of possession which she envies in man," writes Simone de Beauvoir against Freud, "it is his prey."

This need to touch, to caress, this need for contact — but it is the same Simone de Beauvoir who writes, in the manner of Sartre, in the same *Second Sex*: "Nothing so suspicious as a touch" — confounds itself for her with this attraction of women for what is smooth, soft, velvety, this nostalgia for the lost contact with the warm body of the mother. Which means that for every woman, woman is, as for man, an object of desire. "It is a curious paradox," writes Simone de Beauvoir, "that man lives in a sensual world of sweetness, of tenderness, of softness, a feminine world, while woman moves in the male universe which is hard and severe; her hands keep the desire to embrace smooth flesh, melting pulp: adolescent, woman, flowers, furs, baby; a whole part of herself remains unattached and desires the possession of a treasure analogous to that which she gives to the male." This explains for Simone de Beauvoir that in "many women there is, in a more or less latent manner, a tendency toward homosexuality" (SS, II, 169): "if one invokes nature, one can say that every woman is naturally homosexual" (SS, II, 173). An ambiguous discourse in which the echoes of older discourses on sexuality are mingled with a new voice which speaks as if from the interior. A discourse in which the profound ambiguity of Simone de Beauvoir also reveals itself. Two examples seem to me illuminating.

Simone de Beauvoir refuses the equivalence man = active/woman = passive. Man is also passive, she says; he is also "the toy of his hormones and of the species" (SS, II, 573). Woman is also active, "in her carnal fever." *To play* the passive role, says Simone de Beauvoir, is not *to be* passive. However, the "carnal passivity" of woman is constantly evoked in *The Second Sex*. Thus, homosexuality is presented as "one attempt among others to reconcile her autonomy and the passivity of her flesh" (SS, II, 173). And, evoking the difference in eroticisms, Simone de Beauvoir takes up once again the opposition masculine activity/feminine passivity which she previously seemed to put in question: "the tension and the activity are in keeping," she says, with the eroticism of man, "while woman, in refusing passivity, destroys the magic which leads her to sensual pleasure" (SS, II, 533). Such is the difficulty of extricating oneself from the dichotomies anchored in language and mentalities at the very moment when one wants to liberate oneself from them.

The second example concerns the relation to the other. Simone de Beauvoir dreams of a recognition, of a reciprocal acceptance by *the other* as subject, and of an erotic relation which would be exchange, friendship. But, when she evokes the ambivalence of the sensual attraction of man for woman, comprised of attraction and repulsion, of the appeal to and the refusal of the male, of desire and fear of penetration, Simone de Beauvoir speaks of the roughness, the hairiness, the odor of man as if it were a universe profoundly foreign to woman. One thinks of Alexandra David Neel who had the window opened after a man passed through her office. "It smells like a deer," she said. While Lou Salomé saw in the sexual relation the discovery, the appropriation through the other, by the other, of this other part of oneself — masculine or feminine — that had been repressed, Simone de Beauvoir believes she discovers in it, at the end of *The Second Sex*, a struggle against oneself "where each projects onto the other that part of the self which has been repudiated" (SS, II, 573). Complicity, reciprocity? It is very often a reciprocal repulsion of two foreign bodies which Simone de Beauvoir conjures up. Thus, lovers after coitus: "when the lovers have disunited their flesh, they become strangers again; and the masculine body even seems repulsive to the woman; and the man sometimes experiences a sort of insipid disgust before that of his companion" (SS, II, 188).

It is in the relation to the "same," in female homosexuality — what the medical texts often cited in *The Second Sex* presented as a pathological anomaly — that Simone de Beauvoir seems to find the model of a "liberated" relationship — in the reciprocity, the tenderness, and the equality. Between women, "the caresses" are "destined less to appropriate the other than to slowly re-create oneself through her; the separation is abolished, there is neither struggle nor victory nor defeat; in an exact reciprocity, each is at once subject and object, sovereign and slave, the duality is complicity" (SS, II, 184). She cites Colette: "the resemblance reassures sensual pleasure. The friend takes pleasure in the certitude of caressing a body whose secrets she knows and whose preferences her own body indicates to her" (SS, II, 184). This similarity, Simone de Beauvoir believes, "engenders the most total intimacy" (SS, II, 188). Outside of institutions, outside of conventions. "They can love each other in equality. Due to the fact that the partners are homologous, all combinations, transpositions, exchanges, acts are possible" (SS, II, 187).

In this incessantly reaffirmed thesis which is summarized in the density of the famous formula, "one is not born a woman, one becomes a woman," in this long demonstration of what we analyze today as the social construction of "gender," "the original structure" of feminine sexuality (SS, II, 172), such as Simone de Beauvoir analyzes it, can appear as a crack in the foundation.

Thus, we could read the need which Simone de Beauvoir had to return to this analysis in her last chapter, "Toward Liberation," as if tomorrow the last obstacle, the most obstinate, the most archaic in the consciousness — or the unconscious — of women could perhaps find itself there with a solution — the assimilation, the nondifferentiation of the sexes.

It is truly paradoxical that, in the conclusion of this book which offers as a necessary path toward liberation the assimilation of women to men ("it is in assimilating herself to them that she will free herself," SS, II, 559), Simone de Beauvoir dedicates the last lines to affirming again, as an irreducible difference, the dissymmetry of eroticisms, the singularity of feminine sexuality, of the relation of women to their own bodies, to the body of man and of the child. And this text which delineates a future in which woman will be the equal, the counterpart, the same as man, in which differences and otherness lives as a reduction to the state of object, of second, will be eliminated, this text finds, in order to speak of the "miracles" of this division of humanity into two separate categories — desire, possession, love, dreams, adventure — the accents which will be those of Duras in *Atlantic Man* when she evokes "the miracle of this difference which separates us." The prospect of a *reciprocity* between equal *and* different beings, of a friendship, an exchange which will replace the struggle in what Simone de Beauvoir calls "the erotic drama" — the perspective from which "liberation" is fantasized and on which *The Second Sex* ends.

Thus should female sexuality be understood in the "situation" which society has made for women. But *The Second Sex* also uncovers the play of obscure, archaic forces — the relation to the maternal body, the relation to the self, to the other, to life, to desire, to sensual pleasure, to death — which function in it. A situation and obscure force in which the relation to power does not cease operating.

Desire, power: one thinks of Foucault's analysis of the common representation of power which, according to how one uses it and the position one recognizes with regard to desire, has two opposing consequences. It leads either to the promise of liberation, if power has only an exterior hold on desire, or, if power is constitutive of desire itself, to affirm that: you are always already trapped (*Volonté de savoir*, 109; *History of Sexuality*).

And it is indeed between these two positions that the ambiguity of *The Second Sex* and, more generally, of the texts of Simone de Beauvoir is located. There is at one and the same time — it is the final perspective of *The Second Sex* — a promise of liberation and a "you are always already swindled."

Like Georges Bataille, Simone de Beauvoir thinks that one begins to write when something goes wrong, when something questions you. At the beginning of *The Second Sex* (I, 13) she declares: "no woman can claim, without bad faith, to situate herself beyond her sex." This is what she discovers in those years. We find the echo of it in her autobiography. It is the new question which is put to her. Without a doubt, Simone de Beauvoir also touched upon what she called "the most serious of my problems": "to reconcile the concern that I have for my autonomy with the feelings which throw me impetuously toward the other." When she is divided against herself, she joins those women from whom she seems, by her position in the writing of *The Second Sex*, to put herself at a distance.

There is in Simone de Beauvoir a relationship to writing which goes beyond the need to express, to fix an experience with words, to save it from usury, from oblivion, to give it a form, to re-create it: to write is to engage in an adventure in which she has the feeling of risking herself, in which she tries to *uncover* with words, *in* words which she does not yet know very well, to indicate "the horizons which we do not touch, which we hardly perceive, although they are there" (*PL*, 622).

"Truth is ambiguity, abyss, mystery" (*SS*, II, 553). It is these "ambiguous, separate, contradictory truths" which fascinate Simone de Beauvoir, and she thinks that the novel — because it neither demonstrates nor proves — is best at making their "whirling meanings" (*FC*, 282–84) play.

Perhaps it is in *The Mandarins* even more than in *The Second Sex* — in these ambiguous truths which are also hers — that Simone de Beauvoir "risks herself" on feminine sexuality, on liberation, on this horizon "which we hardly perceive" and which she attempts to indicate.

There is no doubt that we have here two forms of writing, of enunciation. On one hand, the tone of the essayist, the distance of the enunciator facing her words, who describes, establishes, demonstrates: woman, women, never "we," the erudite apparatus of citations and references; on the other hand, a "story" of individuals in the process of living, the burning *I* of a female character.

A woman writer had never before laid bare, as Simone de Beauvoir does in the face of shame and taboos, sexual relations between a man and a woman, experienced in this manner from the inside, from the viewpoint of a woman.

I read *The Mandarins* in 1954. I read it as Simone de Beauvoir desired it to be read: I did not turn off the light until the last page of the novel late in the night. The female readers of 1985 are no longer those of 1954. This eroticism of waiting, of appealing, this burning fever, this body rediscovered in the taxi, this meeting at last on the rug before the flames — do they still appeal to women? Do women still feel challenged, threatened by this female body that climaxes, abandoned to the gaze, to the horror or the indifference of a man who no longer desires her?

I would like to be able to read certain scenes line by line, but I must move on. To do it quickly then, let's say that *The Mandarins* depicts the fundamental ambiguity of sexuality for a woman: the overwhelming revelation of pleasure, fusion, the "coming" of the body, of the *I* finally recognized by the other, indescribable pleasure but also the profound narcissistic wound, putting the self in question again, the feeling of being reduced to an object, a "pleasure machine."

In *The Prime of Life* Simone de Beauvoir writes: "When the heart, the head, and the flesh are in unison, the body lives in a great festival" (67). But for Simone de Beauvoir, when bodies alone respond to each other, each is returned to its difference and its solitude. "There is no sexual relation," Lacan said. The scene in which Anne, "caught up in a mirage of carnal well-being," spends the night with Scriassine is an admirable acting out of the analyses of *The Second Sex*: the singularity of feminine eroticism which is shattered under the words, the gestures of the man who wants to dominate the sexual scenario and arrange the sensual pleasure of the woman. "Extracted" pleasure is nothing more than a "remote, solitary" pleasure, a "cut, mutilated flower" which "exhales down there." Cut off from *I*: "and I was bored." Solitude and splitting. The bed becomes the arena, the field of struggle. Against the violence of the man, Anne "defends herself with her head" and refuses herself through frigidity. Pretense, failed act. The derision of the "I want you to climax at the same time I do," of Scriassine. "That's what they've found, synchronization! As if this could take the place of understanding. Even if we climaxed together, would we be less separate?" (*M*, 75). Climaxing? — "it is still necessary that the pleasure of the one have an echo in the heart of the other."

In *The Mandarins*, only this "echo" protects the woman in the sexual relationship. Through Paule and Henri then, at the moment of the decline of Lewis and Anne's relationship, Simone de Beauvoir shows from the inside, by the alternation of viewpoints which structure the text, the horror felt by the man who no longer desires the woman who climaxes, Paule "so totally given, so frightfully lost," the humiliation of Anne who feels rejected, frustrated by the indifference of Lewis, in a relationship that is then only "strange, frivolous, incongruous gymnastics" in which she feels reduced to being only a "pleasure machine."

We find in *The Mandarins* the violence of social discourse on women. It is a drunken Volange who sneers: "the guys get on top of them, they open their legs and they want to be respected." It is Nadine who summarizes cynically: women, "they're made to be laid." It is Paule who, abandoned by Henri and passing from one adventure to another, is treated like an "overripe ogress," a "collector of asses."

Women see themselves from this perspective. They internalize the vulnerability of their bodies — age which renders it less desirable, time which extinguishes the desire of a man — as well as the dependence of this body itself and of its desire on the desire of a man. At the beginning of the text, Anne has been "chaste without regret" for five years; she has "forgotten" that she has a body. Deprived of Lewis's desire, her body dies once again. Man's desire marks the rhythm of the intermittences of woman's body.

Every sexual relationship is a relationship of power. Desire, love are always dependence. "When one loves, one is not free," Anne thinks. Only reciprocity makes this dependence happy, justifies it. It becomes interdependence: you are necessary to me, I am necessary to you. If Anne agrees to give herself, to abandon herself in the arms of Lewis — I have found "my true place: I am free of myself" — it is not simply resignation nor masochistic effacement. There is an act of assuming on Anne's part. She receives everything from Lewis: herself, her new body, her unique identity. She is transfigured, accepted, justified. She no longer asks herself questions. She is "delivered"; she is nothing more than this *I* who admires herself in the desiring gaze of the other, "a pure marvel." Not masochism but healing narcissism.

In her autobiography, Simone de Beauvoir evokes the women of her generation who have experienced sexual experiences as "relative beings" and expresses their ambivalence: they felt themselves "diminished and enriched."

But, at the very heart of resplendent reciprocity, the day after the long night of Anne and Lewis, one can read, strangely, something which undermines this beautiful certitude: some archaic resistances, an obscure fear. One should be attentive to the words, to the metaphors which tell the fear of what appears as the "debauchery" of happiness, the fear of being enclosed in a bed denoted as a "dungeon," a "prison," the fear of losing oneself in giving oneself, of no longer being this chaste, inaccessible woman whom Lewis had loved, for whom he had written a sonnet. One should reread the scene in which Lewis slips a ring on Anne's finger, as if it were necessary to go through this marriage ritual to reassure sensual pleasure, to sanctify carnal fever.

In *The Second Sex*, Simone de Beauvoir calls to mind the need of the woman who works and has responsibilities — in short, like men — to find "joy, relaxation, diversion in happy sexual relations" — precisely as men enjoy them. Does sexual freedom bring to Anne what Simone de Beauvoir recognizes in the modern woman: autonomy in pleasure? Cut off from her own body, absent from this pleasure which the caress of this casual encounter with Scriassine "extracts" from her, Anne finds again with Lewis her body and sexual joy in reciprocity. But in the intimacy of this "free" relationship in which Anne took the initiative because, in her American solitude, she suddenly burned with desire for a body and for a presence, the old fantasies surface, and in delight, fear, and guilt, the mechanisms of love-dependence emerge again.

Ambiguous, contradictory truths of fiction. But also in the essay, memoirs, life. Ambiguity due to cultural and social conditions, whose decisive effects Simone de Beauvoir illustrates in *The Second Sex*, due to the necessity of thinking about sexuality in existing discourses — even if it be against them — due to the personal experience of Simone de Beauvoir.

The difficulty of totally liberating herself from a puritan education, from the influence of Sartre, from the profound ambiguity of her relation to sexuality: Simone de Beauvoir, like her heroine, knew this dazzling revelation, this discovery of her own body, this feeling of fusion which the embrace and pleasure bring, "these pleasures which one lightly calls physical," Colette had already said. Like Anne in America, she experienced desire as an exultant but guilt-ridden alienation. She recounts in *The Prime of Life* how, when Sartre is absent, she experiences with disarray, even horror, this indeterminate call, these "solitary languors" which "solicit anyone," this desire, this physiological "need," "like thirst or hunger," that an anonymous hand on the train is sufficient to awaken, this too physical desire which gives her the intolerable feeling of a "freedom engulfed in her flesh." One thinks of the "fall into complicity with the body" which Sartre evokes in *Being and Nothingness*. Simone de Beauvoir speaks about the feeling of a "downfall," of "guilt," of "shameful evil." This body "hungry, begging, plaintive" "repulses" her (*PL*, 67–68).

This woman who finds the words and the rhythm which express the joyous fever of united bodies, the nostalgia for the death of desire, the desert of "never more" is also the one who, interpreting the symbol of fire in the denouement of Faulkner's *Sanctuary*, evokes "those intimate and shameful flames of desire which in secret devour male and female stomachs" (*PL*, 193). "We detested the notion of eroticism," she says, speaking of Sartre and herself, "because it inflicts a specialization which at the same time exaggeratedly exalts and degrades sex" (*PL*, 144).

Her ideal is the lovers of Hemingway who "loved each other body and soul at every instant: sexuality penetrated their acts, their emotions, their words, and when it was unleashed in desire, in pleasure, it united them in their totality" — A total eroticism — feminine? — for Simone de Beauvoir. Let's listen to her evoke this "game of morals which encouraged me to assume sexuality blithely: my experience contradicted them, for me the mind did not isolate itself from the body, and my body compromised me entirely" (*PL*. 68–69).

How, from that time onward, could she live the "freedom" of the "pact" proposed-imposed by Sartre, if not against herself?

In *The Second Sex*, Simone de Beauvoir insisted on the difference in eroticisms. In *The Mandarins*, from time to time Robert needs to pick up some young flesh in a bar, but Anne finds her body again with Lewis only "to compromise herself entirely." In *She Came to Stay* the sexual relation that Pierre ends up having with Xavière is only one fragment of a strategy of conquest, of appropriation of the other, a power relation, the need of reassurance of this power. The relationship with Gerbert is experienced by Françoise as physical warmth, tenderness, friendship.

Sexuality occupies a very important place in *The Second Sex* and in *The Mandarins*. But it is not what is essential. "We have lost almost nothing," Anne says to herself, evoking her relations with Robert, when desire has died between them. Denial? One thinks of Hemingway's lovers. The reality of an exceptional intellectual and emotional understanding? Sensual pleasure occupies only a small place in the desert of love, Colette said in *The Vagabond*. So ablaze that one sees nothing but that. But when lovers recover from their embrace, they then have to live together.

It is in the living together, in the complicity, the esteem, the intellectual sharing, the total openness, the common project, that Simone de Beauvoir grounds her union with Sartre, and she projects it through Pierre and Françoise in *She Came to Stay*, through Robert and Anne in *The Mandarins*. But *She Came to Stay*, like *The Prime of Life*, tells how misleading is the phrase "we are one and the same," and Anne suddenly realizes that she is perhaps not indispensable to Robert.

In the lucid enterprise which she wanted her life to be, which her memoirs have tried to be, the ambiguity of Simone de Beauvoir's relationship with Sartre did not cease to be a problem. We no longer know in what is said, in what is suppressed, in what is denied, the part of occultation, of blindness, of mystification — of "bad faith"? — of repressed suffering and/or reasoned acceptance, of trust in what appears to her the essential — in this story, from the viewpoint of Simone de Beauvoir, of this couple who, in the eyes of the postwar generation, incarnated sexual freedom, reciprocal transparence, "liberation."

What we have read between the lines in Simone de Beauvoir's fiction and autobiography is brutally illuminated by Sartre's *War Diaries* and *Letters to Castor*. And this new light has the violence of "lived experience" in the process of living and telling itself.

In her autobiography, Beauvoir recognized that the "pact" had not taken into account the suffering of the third parties, who had ultimately paid the cost of the privileged Sartre-Beauvoir relationship. But in the *Letters to Castor*, in this "game of three," in the silence of the absent but present voice of the addressee, we no longer know who burns, who the third party is. In this game of truth worthy of Laclos, based on lying to another, we no longer know what is truth and what is falsehood and if truth, so-called, is not more deceitful than falsehood.

Moreover, Simone de Beauvoir is too lucid not to have divulged — it is true that she does not speak of Sartre and herself as a couple — any trickery in the practice of a sincerity which can furnish a "tranquil alibi" to the one who confides his or her infidelities, while "in fact it inflicts a double violence on the partner" (*PL*, 28–29).

Simone de Beauvoir's wager was no doubt to confront the obstacles of a "freedom" more difficult to face or evade than she had thought, a union which, for her, as for him, should only end in death.

For the young adolescent who dreamed of a destiny in the image of Hellé's, the heroine of Marcelle Tinayre — "made for being the companion of a hero" — (*MD*, 182–83), meeting Sartre took on the character of a dazzling Necessity, the "realization of the wish" of her "fifteen years." This man by whom, "for the first time in her life," she felt "intellectually dominated" was the dreamed of "double," the one with whom she could "always share everything" (*MD*, 342–44) — the one who was going to help her to free herself from the dutiful young woman whom she could have become, to liberate the woman writer she wanted to be.

The ambiguity of Simone de Beauvoir, protected by the feeling of having an exceptional destiny, is to have shared the dreams, the concessions, the dependence, the contradictions of many women of her generation while still believing herself, like Mme de Clèves, "different from other women." And without a doubt she strove, faithful to her "ideal self," not to resemble those "relative beings" whom she describes in *The Second Sex*. Pioneer of new couple relations, leading figure of "liberated women," the difficult conciliation between her "concern for autonomy" and the feelings which "threw her impetuously toward the other" remains, however, her "problem."

In her first novel, *She Came to Stay*, the path of liberation involves the murder of the other woman.

When she begins *The Second Sex*, on the advice of Sartre as she insists (on this fact), no doubt she searches confusedly for answers to questions which she does not know very well. She will understand later that, in speaking of the feminine condition, she also speaks of herself. Posing the problems of sexuality, love, dependence, liberation, she undoubtedly feels that to be the equal of man, recognized by the most intelligent among them, does not, however, suppress the "erotic drama," the power relations at stake in the carnal and amorous relationship, the difference in eroticisms, the decline of desire and the need for duration, the concern for autonomy and the need for the other.

Don't we hear the echo of this ambiguity in our own ambiguities?

It is still not easy in 1985 to put this problem of feminine sexuality and liberation—which sexuality? which liberation?—without our being personally involved in this "division" which Simone de Beauvoir analyzes and which is still in us.

Today women live in a period of mutation, of new experiences, of experiments in a society traversed by other discourses: the right to pleasure, to orgasm, to the blooming of the libido and to all the potentialities of the body. The 1970s were years of a sense of liberation, of a march toward "another economy of bodies and pleasures," perhaps the one which Hélène Cixous calls "the feminine libidinal economy"? But today's doubt gnaws at yesterday's exaltation. Have women ceased being sexual objects or are they—as a perverse effect of sexual freedom—even more than yesterday, bodies offered to the free disposition of men? From *The Small Difference and its Big Consequences* to a recent issue of the Belgian journal *Cahiers du GRIF*, "On Love and Reason," the question is raised. Just as in the debate on advertising or pornography. Has the sexual freedom of women—of certain women—accelerated the transformation of the "erotic drama" in the way Simone de Beauvoir wanted it, or does it lead, as a French woman novelist humorously titles it, to the "rout" of men or to a new servitude of women, summoned to be "active" and to "climax." Women were saying: there are no frigid women, there are only impotent men. Today men say: there aren't any impotent men, there are lazy women; and they reproach women for this "passivity" which yesterday comprised their essence.

The joy of bodies, the search for renewed sensations in the multiplication of meetings—do they satisfy women? Does the female Don Juan of *The House of Desire* make many women enthusiastic? Is this the new eroticism whose arrival we've been waiting for? Doesn't the dissociation of eroticism and love lead to a return of the repressed yearning for love? And, at the very moment I ask these questions, what is the role of the old representations in these questions themselves?

Are we advancing? Are we marking time? Where are we going? Are we playing with reversed scenarios whose metonymic representation we can "read on the screen": are women more liberated because the "missionary" position, to which Simone de Beauvoir attaches such a symbolic value—man lying on top of woman—is deliberately replaced by the image of a woman riding, in her turn, the man's body? The new advertising for Buffalo jeans plays on a woman's body sprawled lasciviously on an enormous serpent. Are we repeating the same scenes—sadomasochistic, for example—which would become "revolutionary" because we would appropriate them for ourselves and resell them? Or, because experienced between women, they would be "subversive perversion" between "equals"? Is there a feminine sexuality? Constructed? "Natural"? A "feminine libidinal economy"? What do we do with the categories of "masculine" and "feminine" which Simone de Beauvoir reproaches psychoanalysis for having reproduced directly from traditional discourses and which she still has not been able to rid herself of?

"To denounce dependence," wrote Simone de Beauvoir, "that is already a liberation." It is this liberation which *The Second Sex* wants to inaugurate. "We must dispel the mirages; it is from this that everything begins." And she adds: "We must not stop at the threshold of reality" (*SS*, II, 553).

Simone de Beauvoir has "named" this reality. The women's movement has tried while advancing to transform it. But mirages spring up again, and we must never stop at the threshold of reality. A complex reality: yesterday's reality which still sticks to our skin, today's reality which offers itself to us and slips away in its very newness which we grasp with difficulty, and without a doubt already tomorrow's reality which we hardly perceive.

We sense that "liberation" does not only function in sexual freedom, that it is not only liberation of desire and of pleasure, that the relation to power entangled in liberation must be profoundly modified and not inverted.

What operates in "liberation" is a change in relations between the sexes, in all social relations—from the most intimate relation to the relation to power and to freedom.

And we are taken, taken by new (how new?) "phantasmatics" which bring us back to contradiction, to ambiguity, to the difficulty of going beyond a reality, of going toward the unknown.

I would like to speak about this by evoking two very different domains.

The first one, decisive when one speaks of feminine sexuality and liberation, touches the dissociation of eroticism and reproduction. We should not speak only of the pill and the freedom in relations which it makes possible. But we must also remember current genetic manipulations. A new freedom for women or a step toward the loss of their most ancient power: the giving of life? Liberation from old servitudes or a symbolic aggravation of women's service to the species, women's reduction to the status of taxed "belly bearers"?

The second domain is science fiction, where the fantasies and utopias of our epoch are projected. Of the many possibilities, we'll look at three visions.

A society of women-insects organized around a "queen" — a huge, monstrous, shapeless mass of rose-colored, sticky flesh, shaking with slow convulsive movements — a nightmare sprung from a Fellinian imaginary; men reduced to the status of reproducing drones condemned to a sacrificial death. Penis-body entirely plunged in a devouring vagina. André Dorémieux in *Prisoner of the Women-Insects* imagines the end of men's power while pushing to the limits of his logic the old masculine fantasy, the fear of woman's genitals, the phobic fascination for the all powerful and terrifying Mother.

The other two are visions by women.

The phantasmatic meeting of two societies irrevocably separated by a long war and condemned to sterility. We know only at the end of Tanit Lee's novel, *The Truce*, that one society is only men, the other only women. Then comes the impossible meeting of two representatives delegated by their camps to attempt a reconciliation. But man and woman no longer know each other, and the man's attempt at penetration is experienced by the woman as an act of war, a treason which will be punished by death. The societies are condemned to sterility and disappearance forever. A parable of the biblical phrase: the sexes will die one without the other, but also the representation of the primordial rape, the return of the Amazons, the utopia of a society of sister-lovers like that dreamed of by a part of the women's movement.

Further still: the utopian representation of a humanity without a rift, in which masculine and feminine circulate in everyone in a fundamental androgyny. This is the universe of Ursula LeGuin. Phantasm of fusion, of reunion, modern realization of the mythic hermaphrodite in which we can read the aspiration of many women — of Simone de Beauvoir, without a doubt, at the end of *The Second Sex* (but the "miracles" of the division of humanity into two separate categories?) — the aspiration for the end of the division of "genders," for the possibility for every person to be man and woman successively, man and woman at the same time. It is, however, a problem of "gender" which the critics have put to Ursula LeGuin. Should this new human be written "he" or "she"?

In science fiction, we can read exemplarily how the differences between the sexes, the women's movement, the problems of reproduction and power nourish the imaginary and the relations between the sexes. Old phantasms, new utopias.

One last word, one last doubt.

Speaking about sexuality as we do, we think, like Simone de Beauvoir, that what is needed is a work of necessary elucidation. But what if Foucault were right when he wondered about the deployments which have led, in the West, to this "general reduction to an economy of desire" and which have permitted the endless extortion of these discourses of confession, whose aim is to track down that "part of night which is in us," to obtain by force and without respite that which is hidden in the depths of each of us?

Listen to the last sentence of *History of Sexuality*: "The irony of this deployment is that we are made to believe that the very possibility of our 'liberation' is involved."

Notes

1. Translator's note: All page references are from the French texts. Following is a list of abbreviations used in this essay: *FC, Force of Circumstance*; *M, The Mandarins*; *MD, Memoirs of a Dutiful Daughter*; *PL, The Prime of Life*; *SS, The Second Sex*.

Hats and Cocktails: Simone de Beauvoir's Heady Texts
Mary Lydon*

"Sartre's mouth positively watered [Sartre fut vivement alléché] at what he had heard rumoured about German phenomenology," Simone de Beauvoir records in the second volume of her autobiography, *La force de l'âge (The Prime of Life)*, published in 1960.[1] "Raymond Aron was spending the year at the Institut Français in Berlin," she continues, and

> He told Sartre about it when he came to Paris. We spent an evening together at the *Bec de Gaz* on the rue Montparnasse drinking apricot cocktails, the house specialty. Aron pointed to his glass: "You see *mon petit camarade*, if you were a phenomenologist, you could talk about this cocktail and it would be philosophy. Sartre virtually blanched with emotion. Here was exactly what he had been wishing for for years: to talk about things just the way they *felt* to him, and for that to be philosophy. (*FA*, 141; my italics)

In the text of the sound track of *Sartre*, a film made by Alexandre Astruc and Michel Contat in 1972 and released in 1976, we find the following exchange:

SARTRE: There was realism. The idea of doing realist philosophy. And realist would be neither materialist nor idealist.

POUILLON: That was already Husserl. "The things themselves. . . ."

SARTRE: You're right, it was Husserl. That's why, when Aron said to me "But you can reason about this glass of beer. . . ."

SIMONE DE BEAUVOIR: No, it wasn't a glass of beer. It was an apricot cocktail (Laughter).[2]

*This essay was written specifically for this volume and is published here by permission of the author.

The incident referred to in both these accounts took place, by my calculation, early in 1933. Simone de Beauvoir, who officially recorded it for the first time in 1960, twenty-seven years later, is still bent on keeping the record straight in 1972, thirty-nine years after the original event. She was sixty-four (the climacteric made famous by the Beatles) at the time the Sartre film was made, and he sixty-eight. When they were discussing (in the fullest sense of that word, which may also mean "to consume with zest") those philosophical cocktails ("discuss" derives furthermore, from *discutere*, to shake) at the Bec de Gaz, they would thus have been twenty-four and twenty-eight respectively. A little young, hindsight allows us to conclude, to have yet reached their prime, Beauvoir's title, *The Prime of Life*, notwithstanding. But the word apricot, as it happens, means literally "the early-ripe," from the Latin *praecox*, which also gives precocious. And because the evening at the Bec de Gaz is a text, and because words count in unpredictable and uncanny ways, one must applaud Simone de Beauvoir's insistence on the record. The fact that it was a cocktail they were discussing, and an apricot cocktail at that, ought not to be dismissed as small beer.

It will be clear by now that I wish to claim for the apricot cocktail episode an interest beyond the anecdotal, but before going any further, the word "anecdotal" itself, which carries a generally pejorative connotation, bears scrutiny. For one might legitimately question whether the anecdotal as such (from the Greek *anecdota*, literally "unpublished") has any proper application to lives so elaborately documented as are those of Sartre and Simone de Beauvoir. The sheer weight of the published material undermines the very notion of the anecdote properly so-called, and this all the more thoroughly because the joint Sartre/Simone de Beauvoir archive is so heavily reliant on the anecdotal in the popular sense of the word. There precisely lies its power to *fascinate*: to charm but also to transfix, to arrest movement, and ultimately to kill inquiry, to foreclose interrogation.

It is not insignificant that this weighty archive was initiated by Simone de Beauvoir herself, on whose monumental autobiography the spate of secondary material that continues unabated is inevitably parasitic. It might indeed be argued that Beauvoir's entire opus has the character of autobiography, and this circumstance, together with the fascinating power of the anecdotal, produces a curious impasse for the critic. On the one hand, few oeuvres lend themselves more appropriately than Beauvoir's to an interrogation of that dynamic border that separates life from work, or as French allows us to say: *corps* from *corpus*, body from body of work. On the other hand, the undecidability of this boundary mark, an undecidability that the anecdotal precisely renders more acute, has the effect of blurring the distinction between *autos* (self) and *bios* (life). This is indeed the reef on which most readings of Beauvoir's oeuvre perish. The siren song of the biological, historical Simone de Beauvoir constantly threatens to lure us off course, away from the only Simone de Beauvoir who is actually accessible: she who is generated by the texts she signs, hence always a "Simone de Beauvoir" in quotation marks.

In Derrida's account, the border between *autos* and *bios* may not be located either outside or inside either the body or the work.[3] Neither active nor passive, a line that is neither invisible nor indivisible, it cuts across *both corps* and *corpus* indiscriminately, according to as yet uncodified laws. This border, I venture to suggest in the present context, is none other than writing itself, *graphein*, the third term in the autobiographical composite, and it is precisely writing, I would argue, that gets lost in the critical evaluation of the Beauvoir oeuvre, which invites as few others do a fatal slippage from *corpus* to *corps*.

One might say that the anecdote is paradoxically antithetical to writing, to the degree that the latter is on the side not of *signification*, which according to Barthes "belongs to the plane of the product, of the enounced," but of *signifying (signifiance)* which, as process, is irreducible to "communication, representation, expression."[4] In the measure that Simone de Beauvoir is regarded as a reliable witness, a chronicler nonpareil, a purveyor of anecdote, she is eclipsed as a *writer*, in a movement parallel to that by which the life masks the work and the biological the textual body.

"Je suis moi-même la matière de mon livre," Montaigne's device ("I am myself the matter of my book") is singularly and poignantly applicable to Simone de Beauvoir's writing project. Poignantly because of that fatal belatedness that makes every book a tomb, and more acutely, every diarist, every autobiographer a memorialist. For the book at once brings into being the self that provides its matter and sounds the knell of that very self. It is not for nothing that "corpse" is the English cognate of *corpus*. Death's trace persists like a watermark, *en filigrane*, as the lovely French phrase expresses it, in every "Life." Memoirs then, even those of a dutiful daughter (especially perhaps those of a dutiful daughter), are all *Mémoires d'outre tombe*.[5] They issue from beyond the grave. The first movement of the autobiographical impulse, as Simone de Beauvoir records it in *La force de l'âge*, is exemplary of this complex temporality.

While on a solitary walking-tour in the Auvergne (it is the summer of 1938) she calls her childhood to mind. "Je me remémorai mon enfance," the verb has a resonance that the more commonplace "se souvenir" or "se rappeler" lacks (*FA*, 353). One of her earliest memories surfaces, of "the flower I was accused of picking in Aunt Alice's garden." "I said to myself," she continues, "that I would like to restore that distant little girl to life in a book." "Ressusciter," literally to resurrect, is her choice of verb, underlining the death that the projected book will mourn, even as it memorializes a life. And consider that when Simone de Beauvoir was writing those words at the end of the fifties, not only the little girl, but the young woman of thirty who thought wistfully of resurrecting her was no more.

But Montaigne's motto seems to me poignantly à propos in the case of Simone de Beauvoir's corpus for reasons specific to her, having to do with her historical situation and her role as a public figure. To put it as succinctly as possible: readers of Beauvoir and feminist readers in particular, receive her texts for the most part primarily on what Barthes, in his essay "The Third Meaning," calls the "informational level."[6] This is the level of the message, to which even the symbolic level of her texts (the term is again Barthes's), if or when it is perceived, is inevitably reduced. Thus the relations between men and women as Beauvoir represents them, for example, are inevitably boiled down to an evaluation of her "real-life" association with Sartre, or the treatment of maternity is judged as a refusal on her part of the positive aspects of femininity, and the historical Simone de Beauvoir becomes an "image" whose inspirational value for today's women is dubious, at best.[7]

I have already indicated that Beauvoir's corpus invites, perhaps even compels, this response, but might it not be more interesting and ultimately more rewarding, to pursue another reading across that overexposed body? To trace the (from an analytic point of view) slightly ridiculous, "carnivalesque" progress of Barthes's third meaning, in order to produce neither *corps* nor corpse, but rather something akin to the surrealists' *cadavre exquis.*

Hence my title, "Hats and Cocktails," both of which figure prominently in the Beauvoir legend, though they are not usually remarked, and which, I would argue, function as purveyors of that third meaning that promises "an authentic mutation of reading and its object" (*TM*, 62), in this instance "Simone de Beauvoir."

In contrast to the informational level, which is that of communication, and the symbolic level, which is that of signification, the third meaning (which Barthes associates with hearing, the third of the five senses in the classical paradigm) is the level of signifying, *signifiance.* "Erratic yet evident and persistent," the third meaning consists of "signifying accidents" whose signified one cannot name (*TM*, 42). "I am not certain whether my reading of this third meaning is justified," Barthes writes, "but its signifier possesses a theoretical individuality. . . . [Exceeding] the copy of the referential motif, it compels an interrogative reading . . . bearing precisely on the signifier, not on the signified, on the reading, not on intellection . . . a 'poetic' apprehension. On the other hand it cannot be identified with the episode's dramatic meaning" (*TM*, 43).

Barthes's insight would seem highly suggestive for a reading of Simone de Beauvoir's corpus. Let us then interrogate the apricot cocktail, the precocious beverage with which this essay began and which I take to be the locus of a third meaning in excess of (1) communication, which might be rendered in shorthand as "Rumors about German Phenomenology confirmed for Sartre, 1933, Le Bec de Gaz," and (2) the more elaborate signification: "German Phenomenology good enough to eat (or drink). Sartre, anticipating psycho-sexual impulse well documented in later oeuvre, prepares to ingest, digest and eventually excrete new philosophy. German Phenomenology goes to the head."

Beyond this symbolic meaning, which Barthes designates as "obvious" because intended by the author and drawn from a general lexicon of symbols, it "seeks me out" (*TM*, 44); beyond the obvious meaning, the "obtuse," scandalous, supplementary third meaning (represented here by the apricot cocktail) lingers, "like a guest who persists in staying at the party without saying a word, even when we [imagine] we have no need of him" (*TM*, 48). Barthes's image immediately puts one in mind of Beauvoir's first novel, *L'Invitée* (*She Came to Stay*) and her remarking of the apricot cocktail with which I began (evidence of Beauvoir's own exceptional staying power) might consequently be susceptible to a different reading. One might interrogate, in her insistence on the record, the presence of a certain "mechanical beaver-intellect," to quote Carlyle. (He was referring to the intellect of the nineteenth century, it is true, but he adds elsewhere that "All intellect will tend to become beaverish.")[8] The laughter that greeted Beauvoir's remark—"It wasn't a glass of beer. It was an apricot cocktail"—is also a locus of the third meaning.

But to return to what it is tempting to call the primal scene (the more so since it is the origin of *L'être et le néant*, *Being and Nothingness*), let us note that it *is* a scene, presented dramatically, and that the apricot cocktail is an image that may appear to be trivial, supplementary, even stupid, but which the *metteur-en-scène*, Simone de Beauvoir, insists upon. To follow the itinerary of the cocktail rather than the more clearly sign-posted routes of Sartre's initial encounter with German phenomenology, say, or the body-language of his philosophy, opens the possibility of a counternarrative that would not destroy the anecdote, but would subvert and transcend it. The story would then no longer be merely "a powerful system," but as Barthes has it, would be "a simple space . . . the field of displacement" of the signifier (*TM*, 58).

What *does* the apricot cocktail mean? The third meaning, says Barthes, is a signifier without a signified, or at least one whose signified I cannot name. The word "cocktail," which passes "untranslated" into French (it was "des *cocktails* à l'abricot" they were discussing that evening at Le Bec de Gaz), has an undecidable etymological origin. No one (on either side of the Atlantic) seems to know where it comes from, although the French *coquetier* (egg cup), the English *cocked tail* (indicating a nonthoroughbred horse), and the Aztec *Xochitl* (an Aztec noble's daughter and purveyor of cactus juice) have all been proposed. The cocktail is recognized, however, as an American invention, and first appeared in literature in Washington Irving's *Knickerbocker History*, published in 1809.[9] Defined in the Hudson, New York, *Balance* on 13 May 1806 as "a stimulating liquor, composed of spirits of any kind, *sugar*, *water* and *bitters*," it was bitters that were "the differential ingredient," in the words of one expert, that created the cocktail, distinguishing it from the existing "sling." Bitters were also the source of the cocktail's reputation as a stomachic, or remedy for stomach disorders, so that a Martini or a Manhattan had from the outset the character of a pharmakon.[10]

Lowell Edmunds, in *The Silver Bullet: The Martini in American Civilization*, claims that the first reference to the gin cocktail occurred on the occasion of a mock battle between two French warships, *L'Hercule* and *La Favourite*, off Newport, Rhode Island. "The boat was to start at 9," wrote the author of an unsigned eyewitness account in the *Boston Morning Post*. "We had about ten minutes grace, and went down to the forward cabin where the Drab Beaver and the younger imbibed a gin cocktail each." "Drab Beaver" and "the younger," Lowell informs us, were the writer's traveling companions. The apparition of Sartre's nickname for Beauvoir at the origin of the gin cocktail is uncanny, to say the least, although "drab" would hardly be the epithet one would choose for her, given the constant concern she expresses for her toilette throughout the memoirs. Her taste for cocktails equals that of her random namesake, however, and its origin and development in her writing bears tracing.

"What intoxicated me ["ce qui me grisa"] when I returned to Paris in September 1929 was first and foremost my freedom." So runs the opening sentence of *La force de l'âge*, and an important ingredient in that freedom, she specifies, were the evenings spent at the Falstaff and the College Inn with Sartre, when "we drank, indiscriminately, Bronx cocktails, side-cars, alexanders, martinis; I had a weakness for the mead cocktails at the Vikings, [and] for the apricot cocktails which were the specialty of Le Bec de Gaz on the rue Montparnasse . . ." (*FA*, 21).

Montparnasse is indeed an appropriate location for the nectar of the gods, and one wonders which was more intoxicating: the cocktails themselves, or their heady names, but in any case, cocktails are inseparably linked, for Simone de Beauvoir, with liberation from the deadly routine of the dutiful daughter, whose conformity is, in her words, "the reflection of [the mother's] timidity."[11] Cocktails furthermore have a powerful erotic connotation for Beauvoir. She was introduced to them by her first love, her cousin Jacques, and her description of this rite of passage deserves to be quoted in full.

> We didn't go to the cinema. Jacques took me to the Stryx, on the rue Huyghens, where he was a regular and I perched on a stool between himself and Riquet. He was on first-name terms with the barman, Michel, and ordered a dry Martini for me. Here I was, who had never even set foot in a café, at night, in a bar, with two young men. For me it was quite extraordinary. The pale or violently coloured bottles, the bowls of olives and salted almonds, the little tables, everything as-

tounded me; and the most surprising thing of all was that for Jacques this decor was old hat. I knocked back my cocktail quickly and since I had never swallowed a drop of alcohol before, not even wine, which I disliked, I was high almost immediately.[12]

Given that experience, Simone de Beauvoir's insistence on its having been an apricot cocktail seems hardly surprising. The scene I have just quoted (which could be the pendant to the scene at the Bec de Gaz) is at the origin of the litany of cocktails that punctuates her memoirs, including *A Very Easy Death* and *Adieux: A Farewell to Sartre*, and I wonder indeed what erstwhile dutiful daughter (of a certain generation at least) can read unmoved that description of the first encounter (not, significantly, with German phenomenology) with the culture of the bar.

According to Barthes, it is in fact another important characteristic of the third meaning that "It carries a certain *emotion* . . . which simply designates what is loved, what is to be defended; it is an emotion-as-value, an evaluation" (*TM*, 51). Contemplating the people in the stills from Eisenstein's movies that are the occasion for his essay, Barthes remarks that "they are essentially lovable"; "We enter into a complicity, an *intelligence* with them," he claims. Not many of her critics, even among those who admire her, have found Simone de Beauvoir lovable. A consequence of the apprehension of the third meaning in her texts is that one may find her so.

A first possible locus of this third, obtuse meaning in the bar initiation scene is the name of the bar itself. The Stryx was subsequently to become the scene of Beauvoir's solitary cocktail-drinking escapades, her touchingly halfhearted attempts at looking for Mr. Goodbar: what she calls her *frasques* (a word for which Collins-Robert gives the quaint but appropriate "high jinks"). But that is at the informational, anecdotal, communicational level. What holds my gaze is rather the word itself, with its apparently supplementary *r*, blurring the immediate reference to the mythological river, boundary between the land of the living and the land of the dead. This heavily overdetermined meaning is subverted, transcended, without however being destroyed, by that *r* which deflects our attention from ancient Greece and rites of passage toward nocturnal predators, for there is an actual word *strix* in French that is applied to such *rapaces nocturnes* as owls, for example. It is related to *strige*, from the Latin *striga*, vampire, "tenant de la femme et de la chienne," associated with *woman* and *bitch*, as *Le Petit Robert* tersely notes.

It seems not inappropriate that the Stryx should figure so prominently at the origin of Simone de Beauvoir's independent life, the life she set out to create as a "beautiful story" that would gradually come true while she was telling it to herself (*MJ*, 237). Schematically put, the vampirish relation between life and work that I initially presented in slightly different terms seems curiously prefigured in the Stryx.

In addition to its curious name, however, the bar's decor, or more accurately Jacques's familiarity with it, is a further locus of the third meaning. This familiarity, which contrasts so sharply with the exoticism of the very same scene for Beauvoir, I have chosen to render by the slightly old-fashioned English idiom "old hat."

The counternarrative of *La force de l'âge*, if the itinerary of the cocktail be traced, emerges as the account of Simone de Beauvoir's appropriation of a new terrain, one to which as a dutiful daughter she would have normally had no claim: the space of the bar, the latter-day agora, where the citizen-philosophers meet. Thus when she insists on the apricot cocktail as the object of phenomenological description, the remark uncannily exemplifies the de-familiarization, the bracketing-off of experience characteristic of that philosophic stance. Beauvoir's gaze has the naive penetration of Montesquieu's Persian visitors. Whereas the attitude of the blasé Sartre and Aron might be rendered as "A glass of beer, an apricot cocktail, what's the difference?" Beauvoir, like Edith Bunker, insists on taking things at their word, and like the turbanned tourists of *Les lettres persanes* she sends despatches that reveal the Paris of the last sixty years in the light that only the eye of the outsider (or of the avid little girl) can reflect.

But the dutiful daughter, as she herself makes clear, is the precise counterpart of the at once timid and tyrannical mother, repressed and repressive at the same time. Still in pursuit of the cocktail, let us consider the following scene from *A Very Easy Death*, Beauvoir's account of her mother's last illness.

Mademoiselle Leblon, her nurse, is braiding Madame de Beauvoir's hair, when the old lady, irritated, demands that she cut it off. "She insisted, curiously headstrong" ("avec un bizarre entêtement"), Simone de Beauvoir recounts, but when the nurse gently winds the silver braid round her head, the old face assumes the serenity of a Leonardo drawing in the daughter's eyes. "I wasn't bad-looking in my day," is the mother's response to this comparison, and she confides in a slightly mysterious tone to the nurse that she had had lovely hair which she wore, as a young woman, in bandeaux round her head. She then goes on to talk about the librarian's diploma she had earned later in life, and of her love of books, while the nurse is preparing a flask of serum for the intravenous feeding. The clear liquid contains glucose and salts, Mademoiselle Leblon tells Simone de Beauvoir, who replies instantly: "A positive cocktail."[13]

When she returns the next day, Beauvoir finds her mother much worse and lamenting her own lack of lucidity. She had had a waking dream the night before, she tells her daughter, in which her room was invaded by wicked men in blue overalls who wanted to take her away with them to drink cocktails. Poupette, Simone's sister, had sent them away. Beauvoir hastens to provide a rational interpretation of this dream for her own benefit. She had uttered the word cocktail in her mother's hearing the day before, she tells herself. Mademoiselle Leblon had been wearing a blue nurse's veil. The men in question had wheeled Madame de Beauvoir into surgery. But the fact remains (the reader must insist) that Madame de Beauvoir had never drunk a cocktail in her life, that her librarian's diploma is a pathetic shadow of her daughter's literary career, and that the cocktails Simone drank in Montparnasse were (and were so perceived by her mother) in direct defiance of maternal authority: at once a headstrong refusal of the life the mother represented and the emblem of her own liberation, sexual and intellectual. On the threshold of death (one recalls the Stryx), the mother's unconscious, seizing on the word "cocktail," uncannily reproduces the drama of her relationship with her first-born.

The episode has a sequel. A few days later, when Poupette is too exhausted to spend another night at her mother's bedside, Simone offers to take her place. The mother reacts to the suggestion with some anxiety. " 'Will you know how to put your hand on my forehead when I have nightmares?' 'Yes of course I will.' She thought for a bit, then looked at me searchingly, saying, '*You* frighten me, you do' " (*MD*, 94).

Reflecting on this exchange beside her sleeping, moribund mother, Simone de Beauvoir recapitulates their troubled relationship. Poupette, she concludes, less respected and less influenced by their mother, had not inherited her rigidity ("raideur") and hence was on easier terms with her. As far as she herself was concerned, on the other hand, even Madame de Beauvoir's maladroit efforts to be friendly produced the opposite effect. "She would say," her elder daughter recounts, " 'I know you don't think I'm intelligent, but in any case you get your vitality from me and that pleases me' " (*MD*, 98). Prepared to agree wholeheartedly with the second half of this statement, Beauvoir is nonetheless so repelled by the beginning that she rejects the whole thing. Thus they paralyzed each other ("Ainsi nous paralysions-nous mutuellement"), and it is this painful situation that leads her mother to say, on her deathbed, "You frighten me."

The accuracy of this analysis, its pathos, the complexity of Beauvoir's relationship with her mother: all the "obvious" meanings of this scene will not be my direct concern here. Pursuing rather the "obtuse" meaning "which my intellection cannot quite absorb," a meaning both "persistent and fugitive" (*TM*, 44), I am led to interrogate the word *entêtement* that I have rendered as "headstrong."

Considerations of space dictate that one instance must serve to exemplify the adventures of the word *entêtement* and its cognates, *tête*, *tête-à-tête*, etc., in Beauvoir's texts. In *La force des choses* (*Force of Circumstance*), Beauvoir specifically refuses to be identified in any simplistic way with Anne, the heroine of her novel, *Les Mandarins*, by declaring that she had lent her pen ("J'ai confié mon stylo") not to Anne, but to her writer-husband, Henri. She had done so, she says, because although she and Anne share certain feelings, reactions, memories, and tastes, Anne signally lacks her appetites and her capacity to be headstrong: "elle n'a ni mes appétits, ni mes entêtements."[14] (The apricot cocktail demonstrates amply how important both of these are to Beauvoir.) Above all, Anne lacks "the autonomy that I owe to a trade (*métier*) I love," Beauvoir declares, adding: "For want of goals and projects of her own, [Anne] leads the 'relative' life of a 'secondary' being. It is primarily the negative aspects of my experience that she embodies: the fear of death and the vertigo of nothingness, the vanity of worldly distraction, the shame of forgetting, the scandal of living. *Joie de vivre*, the gaiety of beginnings, the pleasure of writing, these I attributed to Henri" (*FC*, 367).

"The autonomy I owe to a trade I love": Simone de Beauvoir's entire oeuvre may indeed be viewed as a continuing declaration of independence, about which we might ask, echoing Derrida on the American document of that name, whether it is a constative or a performative, producing the independence it declares by declaring it. This is to restate the opposition I began with, the opposition between the historical, biological Simone de Beauvoir and "Simone de Beauvoir." Gertrude Stein "had not yet covered her name with a name," William Gass has presciently and economically remarked of the unpublished young Gertrude, still dominated by her younger brother Leo.[15] To cover one's name with a name is another way of putting the complex spatiotemporal relationship between *corps* and corpus and it is miraculously (Barthes's epithet for the functioning of the obtuse meaning) illustrated in Simone de Beauvoir's case by the image that more than any other figures as her signature: the turban.

Barthes's intuition about the third, obtuse meaning was inspired by his contemplation of a series of stills from Eisenstein movies: visual images that function for him like quotations and that have the effect, under interrogation, of subverting and transcending the film's plot, the diegetic, anecdotal horizon against which they appear. The images I have dealt with so far have been verbal, albeit characterized by a certain dramatic intensity, but Simone de Beauvoir's autobiography, her corpus, is not represented exclusively by the written word. Hundreds of photographs of herself and Sartre haunt the imaginations of a whole generation of readers, photographs to which her texts serve as diegetic horizon. Indeed a more productive way of viewing the Sartre/Beauvoir romance (in the fullest sense of that word) might be to see it as the archetypal photo-novel of the century, and I would refer the reader to Barthes's essay on the comic-book version of *The Story of O* by Guido Crepax, in this regard, but that discussion cannot be undertaken here.[16]

Looking at the photographs of Simone de Beauvoir, I have never been able to detach my gaze from the turban, which now seems to me to be the very embodiment of Barthes's third meaning; the more especially because the latter is associated for him with the top of the head, most notably with the "absurdly low" fold of an old woman's kerchief in one of the Eisenstein stills (*TM*, 48).

"Turban," which like "cocktail" passes untranslated into French, is a Persian word whose first definition according to *Le Petit Robert* is a man's headdress (remember that Henri gets Simone's pen) and secondarily means a woman's headdress designed to evoke the oriental turban fashionable during the First Empire and again in the years between 1941 and 1945. Following his customary practice, Robert provides a quotation to illustrate this usage, as follows: "Getting one's hair done was becoming quite a production, hence turbans were in fashion (in 1941); they served at once as hat and hair-do. Simone de Beauvoir."

This is the informational, anecdotal, rational account of the turban, but photographs of Beauvoir taken several years before 1941 show her wearing one, and I prefer to see this characteristic headgear as emblematic, not so much of her hardheadedness, her practical good sense, as of her *writing*, her *entêtement* (the verb *entêter* is related to *coiffer*) and of a certain eroticism: *coiffer* may mean to seduce, and the reflexive form, *se coiffer de*, means to become infatuated with.

The line of the turban, which follows the line of the hair so closely as almost to be indistinguishable from it, recalls to me the duplicity of writing, the dynamic line that traverses *corps* and corpus and that takes the form, in Derrida's phrase, of "un paraphe biographique," a biographical flourish, or signature.[17]

A paraph denotes the stroke or strokes added to a signature in order to make it distinctive; or the initials appended to a document to authenticate revisions, etc. In its supplementarity, the paraph also has something of the third meaning's capacity to *accent*, to add what Barthes calls "an elliptical emphasis" (*TM*, 48). One might say, elliptically, that Simone de Beauvoir writes, covering her name with a name, and signs with a turban. (Castor, her nickname, also means a man's hat, both in English and French, incidentally.)

At once hat and hair-do, the turban reveals and conceals femininity: eroticizing the head, like the drape clinging to the legs of the Venus Anadyomene, which enhances her naked beauty but can remain unnoticed unless it is pointed out. The turban poses the question of Beauvoir's femininity (a question raised with increasing frequency by feminist critics) in terms that uncannily reproduce the gnomic verse quoted by Freud to accent the heads that have knocked themselves out against femininity's riddle:

> Heads in hieroglyphic bonnets
> Heads in turbans and black birettas
> Heads in wigs and thousand others
> Wretched sweating heads of humans.[18]

Hats and cocktails, heads and tails: Simone de Beauvoir's seduction (objective and subjective genitive) must await another occasion. Let me suspend the present discussion by quoting one of the most moving portraits of Beauvoir that we have, provided by her friend Colette Audry, who describes the transformation wrought by the arrival of Beauvoir's first published novel in the mail from Gallimard: "We found her just as we knew her, and yet different (*autre*), other. And from that moment on, while continuing to be herself, she would not cease to be henceforth for us that part of herself which had been transfused into printed lines, that superimposition of herself upon herself which was undistinguishable from her yet nonetheless never to be confused with her."[19]

There it is, beautifully stated: the line (*dynamis* is Derrida's term) between *corps* and *corpus*, the writing-effect that is emblematized in Simone de Beauvoir's case by the turban, a superimposition if ever there was one. It is the fascination with the turban that brings *significance*, the "erratic yet evident and persistent" third meaning in Simone de Beauvoir's texts to light, revealing that writing (*la plume*) is the feather in her cap, the cocktail that goes to her head.

Notes

1. *La force de l'âge*, Paris: Gallimard, 1960); hereafter cited as *FA* in the text. All translations of this and other works cited are mine, unless indicated otherwise.

2. Alexandre Astruc and Michel Contat, *Sartre* (Paris: Gallimard, 1977), 39.

3. See Jacques Derrida, *Otobiographies: L'enseignement de Nietzsche et le nom propre* (Paris: Galilée, 1984), 40.

4. Quoted in *Image, Music, Text: Roland Barthes, Essays*, Selected and trans. Stephen Heath (New York: Hill & Wang, 1977), 10.

5. Chateaubriand's autobiography, written during the period 1830–1841.

6. Roland Barthes, "The Third Meaning," in *The Responsibility of Forms: Critical Essays on Music, Art and Representation*, trans. Richard Howard (New York: Hill & Wang, 1985), 41; hereafter cited as *TM* in the text.

7. See, for example, Mary Evans, *Simone de Beauvoir: a Feminist Mandarin* (London: Tavistock, 1985).

8. Thomas Carlyle, *Latter-Day Pamphlets*, 4. 2–3, quoted in the *O.E.D.*

9. See Wilfred Funk, *Word Origins and Their Romantic Stories* (New York: Bell Publishing Co., 1950), 162.

10. Washington Irving, *Knickerbocker History* (Westport, Conn., 1981), 68. I am grateful to professors Anne Callahan and Walter D. Gray of the University of Loyola, Chicago, for this and the preceding reference.

11. *Memoirs of a Dutiful Daughter*, trans. James Kirkup (New York: Harper & Row, 1974), 114. The French text reads, "mon conformisme traduisit sa timidité," literally, "my conformity *translated* her timidity" — an interesting formulation.

12. *Mémoires d'une jeune fille rangée* (Paris: Gallimard, 1958), 379; hereafter cited as *MJ* in the text.

13. *Une mort très douce* (Paris: Gallimard, 1964), 69; hereafter cited as *MD* in the text.

14. *La force des choses* (Paris: Gallimard, 1963), 367; hereafter cited as *FC* in the text.

15. William H. Gass, "Gertrude Stein and the Geography of the Sentence," in *The World Within the Word* (Boston: David R. Godine, 1979), 68.

16. Roland Barthes, "I Hear and I Obey. . . ," in *On Signs*, ed. Marshall Blonsky (Baltimore: Johns Hopkins University Press, 1985), 54–55.

17. Derrida, *Otobiographies*, 40.

18. Freud, "Femininity," in *New Introductory Lectures on Psycho-Analysis* (London: The Hogarth Press, 1981), 22:113.

19. Colette Audry, "Portrait de l'écrivain jeune femme," in *Simone de Beauvoir*, by Serge Julienne-Caffié (Paris: Gallimard, 1966), 37.

Simone de Beauvoir and "The Woman Question": *Les Bouches inutiles*

Virginia M. Fichera*

Simone de Beauvoir's only play, *Les Bouches inutiles*, was first produced on the Paris stage in November 1945.[1] Although it is a major work exploring the relationship between gender and power predating *The Second Sex* by about four years, it has been unfortunately almost completely neglected by critics and scholars of her work. However, in 1945, critic Marc Beigbeder wrote of *Les Bouches inutiles* that "It has been a long time since we have seen a play of as great scope as that of Simone de Beauvoir; alongside it even *Caligula* and *The Flies* appear to be bourgeois psychological dramas."[2] Simone de Beauvoir herself recalls the play in several brief passages of her memoirs in which she gives it short shrift, depreciating the play's originality and ground-breaking themes. She records in *Force of Circumstance* that Genet sat next to her for one of the performances and kept whispering, "This isn't what the theater's about! This isn't theater at all. . . ."[3] In the end, she dismissed the play (though not, she added, without reservation), saying, "My mistake was to pose a political problem in terms of abstract morality."[4] In spite of this early and seemingly categoric dismissal, a reading of *Les Bouches inutiles* today raises serious philosophical and political issues which are of growing concern in our nuclear age. The themes of war, gender, and society are conjoined in a situation far more poignant and realistic than the legendary *Lysistrata*. Beauvoir's play poses the following questions: In a world of scarce resources, in a crisis of political legitimation where the stakes appear to be life or death, how shall people govern themselves? How is power defined and established? How is power shared? How are societal values determined? Are some persons seen as having more intrinsic worth than others? On what basis? What does it mean to be useful or useless to society? How do the governed consent to their rulers? Can they participate in their fate to ameliorate it? Or is it only possible to perpetuate a democracy at the intervention and the decision of the governing?

Inspired by the Italian chronicles of Sismondi, the play presents the

*Reprinted by permission from *Yale French Studies* 71 (Spring 1987).

town of Vaucelles in Flanders as having freed itself from the rule of the tyrannical Duke of Burgundy and established a form of representative government. As the play opens, the Burgundians have Vaucelles under heavy siege in the winter and the town is running out of rations. The King of France promises to aid them but only in the spring. The soldiers are constructing a belfry to symbolize their achievement and to pass the time until the king's arrival. Everyone is slowly starving: spring is three months away and the town has rations for only six weeks. The all-male Town Council and magistrates decide that the survival of the town depends upon sacrificing "the useless mouths": the women, children, the old and the infirm. The play is a dramatization and analysis of the effects of such a decision.

The play centers around the reactions of the family of the chief magistrate, Louis d'Avesnes. Catherine, his wife, and his daughter Clarice confront not only the betrayal of the Town Council but also of their son and brother, Georges, who reveals a penchant for incest and political opportunism. The Council will not be swayed from this path, however, until Jean-Pierre and Louis reveal Georges' and another magistrate's murder and plot to take over the town. The Council then votes to share the remaining food with all of the town's inhabitants, to burn the town, and attack the Burgundian camp together. With the townspeople prepared for the counter-attack, the gates of the town open as the play ends.

Les Bouches inutiles owes much of its cool critical reception to the conditions and time of its composition and performance. Indeed these contextual factors are the key to its cool reception by the public. Just as the French were trying to put the Vichy government behind them, Simone de Beauvoir's play posed the question "has one the right to sacrifice individuals for the general future good?"[5] Although the play is set in fourteenth century Flanders, the plot revolves around a town under siege and the compromises among which the government must choose in order to survive despite the scarcity of food. The author and her audience knew those conditions only too well. She wrote in *Force of Circumstance* that even after the war, in 1945, "It was still difficult to find food and lodging. . . ."[6] Her play would thus have very likely been perceived, consciously and unconsciously, as an allegory for Paris and France, only here, the role of the Jews was played by women, children, and old people. The title, "the useless mouths," would have rung in everyone's ears as the translation of the infamous Himmler slogan, "nutzlose Esser."[7]

The play could not have been without resonance for the French who had collaborated with the invading Nazis in the establishment of the Vichy government, and its many parallels with the events of World War II explain the discomfort with which it was first received. Although there was a Resistance movement in France, recent work has shown that the Paris intellectual was not very vocal in protesting the collaboration government.[8] Simone de Beauvoir's play presents several slippery "we's," collectives with allegorical implications. Sacrificing French Jews to the Nazis as though they were not French was not a democratic solution to France's state of siege. If you were French, during the war itself, were you really other than a supporter of Vichy? After the war, could you be other than a supporter of the Resistance movement? The "we" of collective "reality" thus shifted. *Les Bouches inutiles* is, in a sense, a critique of the French who did not really resist the Nazis or the Vichy government (and was perhaps, for Simone de Beauvoir, a self-critique). It is also, by extension, an ironic critique of the so-called liberated France which never, until recently, considered the real liberation of women from their subordinated position. The plight of the women of Vaucelles is potentially the plight of all women, the play seems to say. And a proper solution of "the woman question" will determine whether a society is truly just and democratic.

Les Bouches inutiles may thus be read as a play about women and power: it addresses issues directly related to the role of women in society, women's expectations of society, and society's debt to women. The play underscores the clear sex division in society between the governed and the governing. Women (and those who share woman-like qualities by association with them, i.e., children and the aged) are the governed, "les bouches inutiles." Men, the warriors and builders, govern. But while the play thematically concerns women, depicting women as the major interest group, it nevertheless sees its audience as imbued with male values. It pleads the cause of women, in a real sense explains and defends women's perspective, yet does not address women collectively. The play almost seems to be in search of enlightened men, men who are sensitive to women, who appreciate women, men who have a sense of honor which includes women. It is conscious of power in society, of who has it and who does not, and it seems to be asking those who have it not to abuse it.

Les Bouches inutiles was an early exploration in the then relatively uncharted territory of modern feminism, and as such it contains the seeds of many of the most challenging and important debates of our modern and post-modern culture. Beauvoir's play presents a society not unlike our own in that male experience is publicly valorized, taken by the men and often by the women to be the norm of personhood and even of humanity or humanness. Men are the public actors with many women in the wings, to be sure, but not at the sites of social and political organized power: the Council is male; the magistrates are male; and power is male. It is therefore a disturbingly logical extension of this monopoly for the male identity to consider itself the essential identity, supported by replaceable, interchangeable beings whose primary duty is to ensure its survival and well-being. Simone de Beauvoir's play, therefore, only concretizes the societal, psychological, and even linguistic dominance of the male by giving it its most absolute possible form: the power of life or death over the "other," the non-male, in the name of the survival of the city and the state.

Les Bouches inutiles rises from the ashes of World War II to protest that a democratic collective can not legitimately be formed by the mechanism of opposition to and destruction of an "other." The play's underlying objectives are to present, to critique, and ultimately to change relationships which are based on dominance rather than interdependence.

The male characters of the play are a mixed group, and function much like an emblematic sampling of the men of a society. There are common workmen and noble magistrates, a good father but an incestuous brother, loyal citizens and traitors. What they have very obviously in common is a sense of their importance to their city, their absolute, unquestioned usefulness. Lest even the lowliest mason question his ultimate usefulness, the Council has mandated the construction of a belfry to make all of the men useful. Of course, even setting aside all possible Freudian implications of the construction of a tower, in the context of a limited food supply, of limited resources, the construction of a celebratory (and therefore ultimately *useless*) tower is an obvious case of conspicuous consumption and an effectively ironic symbol of the subjective nature of male self-perception in the play.[9] Last but not least, the play presents Jean-Pierre, an existentialist intellectual, who hopes to lose all responsibility by refusing to claim any, but who eventually assumes the role of a magistrate.

The women of the play are equally emblematic. Catherine is the good mother, the noblewoman, first lady of the city who is there to support the men, to help guide the women and children, and who, despite her lack of any real political power, is truly convinced of her equality with the men. Clarice is the sceptic or, rather, the realist. When condemned to die against her will, she decides in a somewhat existentialist manner that freedom lies in choosing one's own death. Nevertheless she is often quite properly scornful of male-defined goals, authority, and protocol. She has fallen in love with Jean-Pierre and is carrying a child by him, but she is unwilling to accept his view that life is without commitment or responsibility. Neither she nor Catherine feels there are options for resisting the male survival plan. When women of the town join together to ask Catherine to intercede for them, she does not attempt to organize a revolt or some other form of collective action. Both Catherine and Clarice respond individually rather than collectively to the command to die. Clarice contemplates suicide; Catherine decides to try to kill Louis so that they can be together in death. At this point the women are locked into the classical position of believing they are powerless against a male-defined government and accepting its terms.

Catherine very poignantly spells out the injustice of the men's position, attacking the sleight of hand which renders the women invisible, makes them victims and robs them of whatever freedom they may have had:

> Come closer. Look carefully at these men. They assembled with thirty other men, and they made a declaration: we, MEN, are the Present and

the Future, we are the whole town, we alone exist. We declare that the women, the old men and the children of Vaucelles are now nothing more than useless mouths to feed. Tomorrow they will all be led through the city gates and condemned to perish of hunger and cold in the ditch at the foot of the fortifications.[10]

There is more at stake here than a question of justice in this particular instance of the exercise of the male power prerogative. First of all, what Simone de Beauvoir has isolated is a fundamental problem of the establishment of identity. Catherine states that the men have defined all political and social reality from the starting point of the male sex. Men alone are subject; all other beings in the social and physical order are objects to be acted upon. The entire plot of the play is contrived to illustrate this one basic observation concerning male subjectivity.

To many contemporaries, the plot must have seemed a sweeping generalization, a *reductio ad absurdum*, an oversimplification. At the time of the play's production, Simone de Beauvoir had not yet written *Le Deuxième sexe* and, although the French public was doubtless aware of suffrage movements, it was in no way seriously acquainted with the basic tenets of feminism.[11] Yet it is just such generalized observations which have become the point of departure for many serious philosophical, sociological, and psychological studies of gender roles in society. Four years later in *The Second Sex*, Simone de Beauvoir wrote, echoing her Catherine: "But women do not say 'We,' except at some congress of feminists or similar formal demonstration; men say 'women,' and women use the same word in referring to themselves. They do not authentically assume a subjective attitude."[12] It is interesting to note that in both passages it is the collective subjectivity, not an individual man's or woman's ability to say "I," which determines identity. The degree and nature of participation in a "we" appears to play the decisive role.

Since drama is the art form which most completely embodies the major components of human communication (precisely because it literally embodies language), a communications approach provides useful concepts for an analysis of the paradoxes and binds of the play's global structure. The late Gregory Bateson, perhaps the best-known proponent of communication theory, developed a basic classification model describing human interaction patterns as symmetrical or complementary relationships. A simple summary of the behavior patterns the model describes can be found in his article, "The Cybernetics of 'Self' ":

> If, in a binary relationship, the behaviors of A and B are regarded (by A and by B) as *similar*, and are linked so that more of the given behavior by A stimulates more of it in B, and vice versa, then the relationship is "symmetrical" in regard to these behaviors.
>
> If, conversely, the behaviors of A and B are *dissimilar* but mutually fit together (as, for example, spectatorship fits exhibitionism), and the behaviors are linked so that more of A's behavior stimulates more of B's

fitting behavior, then the relationship is "complementary" in regard to these behaviors.[13]

If this communications model is used to examine the relationships in this play, several interesting observations result. First of all, it would seem accurate to say that the women of the play basically view their relationship to the men as complementary. They perceive themselves as acting in a manner quite different from the men, as having unique and important roles to fulfill in the town. But they also believe that their behavior complements that of the men and furthers the common good of the town. For example, in the first act, Catherine explains this to Jean-Pierre: "It was I who laid the first stone of this Belfry. The banner that floats above City Hall was embroidered by these hands. Will you ever know the joy of looking around and saying to yourself: This I have achieved?" (281). The men, on the other hand, do not seem to see themselves as engaged in complementary but rather in a more symmetrical mode of behavior. They view their role not simply as dissimilar from the role of the women, but as more important, more essential, in fact, essential to the town's existence. The women are clearly subordinated in the political sphere: the town is governed by thirty artisans and three magistrates, all men.

A major consideration in the plot is the fact that the inhabitants of Vaucelles have overthrown a tyrannical duke and have instituted a new, model democratic government. Obviously, all of the inhabitants of the town found the old regime, which denied them participation in their destiny, oppressive and unjust. In defending this new government against attack, the inhabitants are confronted with the harsh reality of finite resources. In this crisis situation, the new form of government finds itself under intense scrutiny. If it can equitably deal with the pressures in a manner qualitatively different from the old regime, if the democracy can, in short, survive, then it will have proven itself a model town.

But in order to survive, given its situation, the town must first establish its priorities, which, in a manner of speaking, entails a form of self-definition. The reality of political power, however, ensures that the definition or perception of the definition held by the powerful will become apparent and crystallize since those perceptions will guide decision-making. Thus, the men of the town consciously or unconsciously perceive themselves as the town. The less powerful find that such times of crisis rob them of their illusions concerning their perception of self-definition inasmuch as their perceptions do not coincide with those of the powerful.[14] For example, Catherine, who considered herself equal but complementary to the men, discovers that she is not equal in political power where she does not find herself really represented as a woman. Equality based on complementarity is found to be a male fiction which, from the male make-up of the Council, could have been foretold.

The men, on the other hand, continue to propagate the fiction of complementary equality, while reserving and exercising the power to define equality. The women are thus told that since they are the equal partners of the men in the establishment of the town, they cannot object to being condemned to die for the survival of the town. One learns from the title, *Les Bouches inutiles*, that the basic perception of the men is that the women, by eating, use up the finite amount of food which the men want for themselves. Thus, upon hearing the Council's decision, Clarice remarks, "So this is what you have come up with? You are going to murder us in order to gorge yourselves with food!" (39). Since, in a zero-sum game (i.e., where there are a finite number of elements), competition for resources is evidence of a symmetrical relationship, it is clear that the men do not view the women as complementary partners. Their elaborate justification of their competitive, symmetrical behavior, however, assumes the disguise of a complementary partner.[15]

In his article on "The Cybernetics of 'Self,' " Bateson also notes that "Various sorts of 'double binds' are generated when A and B perceive the premises of their relationship in different terms — A may regard B's behavior as competitive when B thought he was helping A, and so on."[16] According to Bateson, a double bind is said to occur when, in the context of an intense, important relationship between two or more persons, a message is communicated which both asserts something and denies its assertion, while forbidding meta-communication and escape from the situation.[17] The basic communicational structure of *Les Bouches inutiles* can be described as a double bind in which the men of Vaucelles assert the equality of all the town's inhabitants then deny it by condemning to death all the women, aged and children as useless and inessential to the town's survival. The men refuse to see that simultaneously to categorize the women (and those non-males associated with the women) as their equals yet to keep the power to treat them as subordinates or even, in this case, as non-persons, is to establish a paradox which generates a schizophrenogenic state. Although meta-communication is not totally blocked in that the women attempt to discuss the situation, it is effectively blocked since, with the exception of Jean-Pierre and eventually Louis, their complaints are completely ignored by the men. The women cannot escape the situation since the men intend to force them out of the gates of the town.

Viewers and readers of the play are perhaps quite tempted to consider the basic situation contrived and unrealistic, assuming that no men would really be foolish or egocentric enough to equate their survival alone with that of their town, government or civilization. Yet events of relatively recent history confirm Simone de Beauvoir's dramatic imagination. A 1982 article in *The Washingtonian*, discussing evacuation plans of the United States government in the event of nuclear attack, reported: "Just who is on the lists to be saved is among the most closely held of government secrets. The First Lady has a pass, but other spouses do not. When the late Chief Justice Earl Warren learned his wife was not included, he is supposed to have said: 'If she's not important enough to save, neither am I.' And he gave up his pass."[18] As the fear of a nuclear holocaust spreads, the question of survival, the issues of government and women's role and participation become ever more timely. Simone de Beauvoir's play openly and directly questions the survival strategy of men. The men of Vaucelles appropriate women's reproductive labor. But the women are replaceable; only male survival and possession of the town matter. For the women, on the other hand, all of the townspeople physically embody the continuity of the town. Male detachment from the physical reproductive survival process prompts the men to eliminate their children, too, from the Vaucelles to-be-saved list. Women, children, and the aged are replaceable commodities. The men would appropriate (make into property) other women and have other children. Moreover, the only significant property for the men is material property (the town), and only such property is equated with power. Such egocentric callousness has been seen to have its roots in the male lived experience of alienation from reproduction. As Mary O'Brien argues in her book, *The Politics of Reproduction*, "The fact is that men make principles of continuity because they are separated from genetic continuity with the alienation of the male seed."[19] Simone de Beauvoir understood this basic *lived* difference and set up, in her play, a political confrontation of the female and male *lived* perspectives on reproduction and the survival of society.

"Les bouches inutiles" are, in addition, the organs of language, and the play possesses an equally paradoxical linguistic component which both summarizes and embodies these issues of identity, power, and survival in its concern with the semantic and political rules for the interpretation of the phrase, "we, the town." The dissimilar use of personal pronouns cited earlier effectively polarizes the disjunctive concepts of identity. The women, in using the first person plural pronoun "we," assume or presume a cooperative complementarity with the men. Their use of "we" before the Council's decision is inclusive of all the inhabitants of the town, i.e., not referring to themselves as women collectively and as distinct from the men. The Council's decision destroys this inclusiveness and establishes a total exclusiveness based on the already established absence of the women from the official modes of government. "We, Vaucelles" shifts ground and the men declare that "we" is male and Vaucelles is male. The women are then trapped in the men's language game, for as they refer to the town as "other" in discussing or debating the decision, they are granting the men their premise. Louis composes the formula thus, addressing Catherine: "This community was built by you as much as it was built by us, and you want its final triumph as much as we do. We have the right to ask you to give up your life for Vaucelles" (38).

The plight of the women is, of course, highly ironic. They have worked side by side with the men to build a new existence, believing they were important and essential, only to discover that their subordination in government undermines their participation in all other aspects of the town's life. The play presents this double bind as the touchstone, the crucial test of democracy. The play's argument is, in a sense, a meta-communication concerning this issue, a search for a viable solution. But breaking a double bind is never easy. If the survival strategy applied to all, and if the persons deciding truly represented the persons bound by the decision, that is, if all of the collective uses of "we" had the same inclusive reference or subject, then the double bind would not exist.

But the play's greatest irony lies in the fact that it "solves" the problem without really breaking the double bind. And of course, any solution which does not alter the double bind leaves the system basically unchanged, and therefore offers no lasting solution. First of all, the new decision is reached without the women's participation; their distress is real and their expression of distress is heard, but ignored. Jean-Pierre is very clearly upset with the Council's decision even before hearing any of the women's objections. He is, in many ways, the single deciding factor in the reversal. Louis does change sides on the issue, ostensibly after confronting Catherine's extreme passion and emotion. But the context of his decision is not the isolation of one man against the multitude. He is aware of Jean-Pierre's support and thus finds himself more easily able to change his mind. One may speculate as to whether he would have even considered an alternative without the leadership of another man or at least a sense of male bonding.

Secondly, even when presented with strong arguments from Louis and Jean-Pierre, the Council does not immediately abandon its project. It is only with the revelation of François' treason that the Council is put in the position to change its vote. The men are not swayed so much by the moral arguments of their chief magistrate as by the fact that their original plan must have been flawed if another magistrate could so quickly take advantage of the situation. The realization that the equality of all the men was jeopardized by the decision, making them vulnerable to the possible despotic rule of François, turns the tide.

Third, when confronted with the fact that their system of self-governing is not perfect, since the reason would not have been easily found out, the men do not question the form of government but only the individual in power. Ironically, the treason is discovered by a woman, Jeanne, but it is her brother Jean-Pierre who bears the messenge since she is murdered by the traitors because of her fidelity to the town. The men do not hold a memorial for her, nor does she really receive full credit for her information and her sacrifice. Instead of learning from this episode that women deserve to participate in the exercise of power, the men simply continue to perpetuate their familiar structure. Jean-Pierre becomes the third magistrate and the Council does business as usual.

Lastly, the decision to share the food and plan a counter-attack by all of the inhabitants appears to include the women, aged, and children, but in reality it simply repeats the structure of the earlier decision. An exclusive group, "we, the men," has decided the fate of the inclusive group, "we, the townspeople." One might object that it is not obvious that the women, if given political power, would have decided otherwise. Although it appears that reversing the decision was the primary concern of the women, the female characters' preoccupation with their equal status implies that their value in society and the form and process of government are indeed the central issues. At one point, Clarice, when addressing Jacques van der Welde, clearly states, "If I were in your position or in my father's position, I would not let thirty workmen rule the town" (19). Catherine also protests: "You have made your decision without me, and all the words that I could pronounce would only be the words of a slave. I am your victim, you are my executioner" (53).

In a very real sense, a male democratic government can only legitimately impose obligations upon the male population. The male ordering of women's lives is illegitimate and achieves its ends only through the creation of double binds like those we have been examining. Simone de Beauvoir's play, by recreating the situation of the Vichy government's participation in the Holocaust using women in the place of Jews, adds a new dimension to an analysis of legitimation and government. The characters of the play do not spend very much time debating the fairness of an all-male council; only the morality of an order which does not include the men is questioned. In fact, the legitimacy of the order is not disputed at any length. It is as if the play did not dare to attack seriously the fact of men's governing provided they ultimately treat men and women equally. The inhabitants of Vaucelles recognize, on the one hand, that the situation is hardly democratic if laws do not apply to all. On the other hand, the situation is not democratic if the governed do not participate in the making of the law. There is no true democracy unless both conditions obtain. In short, although the women have won this battle, they have lost the war.

In the final scene, Catherine is obviously disturbed by the entire outcome, but seems unable to identify her malaise. Jean-Pierre credits her with saving the town, saying, "Vaucelles owes you its salvation" (64). But the town and we, the readers-spectators, know that officially the town's fate has been decided by Jean-Pierre and Louis. Catherine reveals her confusion, replying: "Maybe I should have let them throw me in the ditch. Have I saved these children and these women? Have I condemned these men to die?" (64). In fact she has done neither, since she has never been allowed to claim full responsibility for any of her thoughts or actions. The play ends with Jean-Pierre and Louis summing up the situation, giving the orders. But there is nowhere any other evidence that something is amiss, that democracy has not really had a victory at all. Perhaps the enemy, stunned by the town's desperate yet open willingness to annihilate itself rather than surrender, will retreat.[20] More likely, as most of them fear, the inhabitants will be killed. The uncertainty of the ending is most appropriate. Simone de Beauvoir was grappling with the evolution of individual and collective feminist consciousness. A positive solution would have ratified the decision of the Council, crowned the outcome with a certain victory, and denied the dilemma.

About four years after the play's first production, in *Le Deuxième sexe*, Simone de Beauvoir abstracted the action of her play into a theoretical discussion of the dialectical structures involved. She describes male subjectivity as resulting from an Hegelian master-slave dialectic, but with the added twist that there are two types of "other": the slave and the woman.[21] As O'Brien points out, in *The Second Sex* "[i]t is only women, she [Beauvoir] argues, who take no risks and gain no recognition. She does not consider the risk inherent in childbirth, for women do not choose (or did not choose) to take these risks. She also implies that no known society grants recognition to women as the reproducers of the people who must be born before history or value can have any meaning at all."[22] Interestingly enough, objections to *The Second Sex* on these grounds do not apply as directly to *Les Bouches inutiles*; Simone de Beauvoir appears to have been more radical in her play than in her theoretical work. For the women of Vaucelles do indeed argue that their work, though different, is of comparable worth and they imply that their reproductive labor has value for the town. Indeed, the lesson of the play is that human inter-relationships form society. In part, the men of Vaucelles confront their alienation from reproduction and achieve an understanding of the value of women, children, and the aged. If the play's ending does not completely satisfy Catherine, Simone de Beauvoir, or today's reader, it is because it fails in the end to address the issue of women's need for a collective consciousness and collective action. Although Clarice questions the legitimacy of the male government, the women of Vaucelles do not demand to determine their own fate. However, Simone de Beauvoir consciously understood and acted upon this issue in the 1970s and 1980s.[23]

Les Bouches inutiles is remarkable in that it was and is a very contemporary play. Feminists of the eighties find dramatized the issues of comparable worth and the continuing struggle for democratic justice. But we also find a parable of the betrayal we experience if we accept to be governed by the principles of the New Right. If we trust that men will recognize our worth and grant us equality, we will be disappointed, for recognition will be achieved only with our collective struggle. A few enlightened men under certain conditions may be reasoned with, but government is illegitimate if women cannot participate. Projected into the past rather than the future, the play does not present radical solutions because it fails to present new, collective action by women. Its unsettled ending is, however, conscious of these flaws. Simone de Beauvoir's theoretical achievement here is nonetheless significant. She sensed that male alienation from reproduction affects political decision-making and is thus a crucial issue for feminism to address. Attempting to present the dilemma and choices of an entire town, she used the theater as a medium for exploring gender relations in society rather than the plight of a single "hero." Beauvoir thus began a critique of subjectivity and legitimacy in government which is continued in her later work. In so establishing the terms of "the woman question," *Les Bouches inutiles* is a powerful forerunner to *Le Deuxième sexe*.

Notes

1. Simone de Beauvoir, *Les Bouches inutiles* (Paris: Gallimard, 1945).

2. Marc Beigbeder, "Le Petit et le grand," *Les Etoiles*, 27 November 1945, No. 29, 6 (translation mine).

3. Simone de Beauvoir, *Force of Circumstance*, trans. Richard Howard (New York: Putnam, 1965), 51.

4. Beauvoir, *The Prime of Life*, trans. Peter Green (Cleveland: The World Publishing Co., 1962), 465.

5. Simone de Beauvoir, *The Prime of Life*, 465.

6. Beauvoir, *Force of Circumstance*, 35.

7. Hannah Arendt, *Eichmann in Jerusalem: A Report on the Banality of Evil* (New York: Viking Press, 1964), 105. I am grateful to Jeffrey Larson for identifying the slogan and bringing it to my attention.

8. Cf. Herbert R. Lottman, *The Left Bank: Writers, Artists and Politics from the Popular Front to the Cold War* (Boston: Houghton Mifflin Co., 1982).

9. Cf. Thorstein Veblen, *The Theory of the Leisure Class* (New York: Modern Library, 1934), esp. Chapter 4: "Conspicuous Consumption."

10. Simone de Beauvoir, *Who Shall Die?*, trans. and intro. Claude Francis and Fernande Gontier (Florissant, Mo: River Press, 1983), 39. One regrets that the translators did not retain Simone de Beauvoir's title. The force of the Himmler reference is diminished for the English-speaking reader. (Hereafter, page references will be given in the text.)

11. Women voted in France for the first time only a month before the play's opening on the Paris stage.

12. Simone de Beauvoir, *The Second Sex* (New York: Knopf, 1952), xix.

13. Gregory Bateson, "The Cybernetics of 'Self': A Theory of Alcoholism," in *Steps to an Ecology of Mind* (New York: Ballantine, 1972), 323.

14. Cf. Elizabeth Janeway, *Powers of the Weak* (New York: Knopf, 1980).

15. Of course, in some cultures and sub-cultures, there is no effort at disguise in the competition for food. Cf. for example, Maxine Hong Kingston, *The Woman Warrior: Memoirs of a Girlhood Among Ghosts* (New York: Vintage Books, 1977), 54, in which she recounts the Chinese adages which haunted her American childhood: "Feeding girls is feeding cowbirds" and "There's no profit in raising girls. Better to raise geese than girls."

16. Bateson, "The Cybernetics of 'Self': A Theory of Alcoholism," 323–324.

17. Gregory Bateson, Don D. Jackson, Jay Haley, and John H. Weakland, "Toward a Theory of Schizophrenia," in Gregory Bateson, *Steps to an Ecology of Mind*, 208.

18. Howard L. Rosenberg, "Who Gets Saved?," *The Washingtonian*, November 1982, 110.

19. Mary O'Brien, *The Politics of Reproduction* (Boston: Routledge & Kegan Paul, 1981), 33.

20. In a similar, but historical situation, the Duchess of Tyrol abandoned her siege of

Hochosterwitz in 1334, Cf. Paul Watzlawick, John Weakland, and Richard Fisch, *Change: Principles of Problem Formation and Problem Resolution* (New York: W. W. Norton & Co., Inc., 1974), xi.

21. Cf. *The Second Sex*, 66–81.

22. O'Brien, *The Politics of Reproduction*, 70.

23. Cf. especially the interviews entitled "I am a feminist" (1972) and "A vote against this world" (1980) in Alice Schwarzer, *After the Second Sex: Conversations with Simone de Beauvoir*, trans. Marianne Howarth (New York: Pantheon, 1984).

INDEX